D0076443

IMPORTANT:

HERE IS YOUR REGISTRATION CODE TO ACCESS
YOUR PREMIUM McGRAW-HILL ONLINE RESOURCES.

For key premium online resources you need THIS CODE to gain access. Once the code is entered, you will be able to use the Web resources for the length of your course.

If your course is using **WebCT** or **Blackboard**, you'll be able to use this code to access the McGraw-Hill content within your instructor's online course.

Access is provided if you have purchased a new book. If the registration code is missing from this book, the registration screen on our Website, and within your WebCT or Blackboard course, will tell you how to obtain your new code.

Registering for McGraw-Hill Online Resources

TO gain access to your McGraw-Hill web
resources simply follow the steps below:

1. USE YOUR WEB BROWSER TO GO TO: **www.mhhe.com/tuggle2**

2. CLICK ON **FIRST TIME USER**.

3. ENTER THE REGISTRATION CODE* PRINTED ON THE TEAR-OFF BOOKMARK ON THE RIGHT.

4. AFTER YOU HAVE ENTERED YOUR REGISTRATION CODE, CLICK **REGISTER**.

5. FOLLOW THE INSTRUCTIONS TO SET-UP YOUR PERSONAL UserID AND PASSWORD.

6. WRITE YOUR UserID AND PASSWORD DOWN FOR FUTURE REFERENCE.
   KEEP IT IN A SAFE PLACE.

TO GAIN ACCESS to the McGraw-Hill content in your instructor's **WebCT** or **Blackboard** course simply log in to the course with the UserID and Password provided by your instructor. Enter the registration code exactly as it appears in the box to the right when prompted by the system. You will only need to use the code the first time you click on McGraw-Hill content.

Thank you, and welcome
to your McGraw-Hill
online Resources!

0-07-292377-6 T/A TUGGLE: BROADCAST NEWS HANDBOOK: WRITING, REPORTING, AND PRODUCING IN A CONVERGING MEDIA WORLD

REGISTRATION CODE

IL3K-9ZTL-8T29-NHDQ-55W8

BROADCAST NEWS HANDBOOK

WRITING, REPORTING, AND PRODUCING IN A CONVERGING MEDIA WORLD

Second Edition

C. A. Tuggle

*University of North Carolina
at Chapel Hill*

Forrest Carr

WFLA-TV

Suzanne Huffman

Texas Christian University

Boston   Burr Ridge, IL   Dubuque, IA   Madison, WI   New York
San Francisco   St. Louis   Bangkok   Bogotá   Caracas   Kuala Lumpur
Lisbon   London   Madrid   Mexico City   Milan   Montreal   New Delhi
Santiago   Seoul   Singapore   Sydney   Taipei   Toronto

Higher Education

BROADCAST NEWS HANDBOOK: WRITING, REPORTING, AND PRODUCING IN A CONVERGING MEDIA WORLD
Published by McGraw-Hill, a business of The McGraw-Hill Companies, Inc., 1221 Avenue of the Americas, New York, NY, 10020. Copyright © 2004, 2001, by The McGraw-Hill Companies, Inc. All rights reserved. No part of this publication may be reproduced or distributed in any form or by any means, or stored in a database or retrieval system, without the prior written consent of The McGraw-Hill Companies, Inc., including, but not limited to, in any network or other electronic storage or transmission, or broadcast for distance learning. Some ancillaries, including electronic and print components, may not be available to customers outside the United States.

This book is printed on acid-free paper.

4 5 6 7 8 9 0 DOC/DOC 0 9 8 7 6 5 4

ISBN 0-07-285351-4

Publisher: *Phillip A. Butcher*
Developmental editor: *Laura Lynch*
Editorial assistant: *Christine Fowler*
Senior marketing manager: *Sally Constable*
Lead media producer: *Erin Marean/Jessica Bodie*
Project manager: *Jean R. Starr*
Production supervisor: *Carol A. Bielski*
Designer: *Sharon C. Spurlock*
Supplemental associate: *Kathleen Boylan*
Permissions: *Marty Granahan*
Cover design: *Amy Evans McClure*
Typeface: *10/12 Palatino*
Compositor: *Lachina Publishing Services*
Printer: *R. R. Donnelley and Sons Inc.*

Library of Congress Cataloging-in-Publication Data

Tuggle, C. A.
    Broadcast news handbook : writing, reporting, and producing in a converging media world / C.A. Tuggle, Forrest Carr, Suzanne Huffman.—2nd ed.
        p. cm.
    Includes index.
    ISBN 0-07-285351-4 (spiral bound : alk. paper)
    1. Television broadcasting of news—Handbooks, manuals, etc. I. Carr, Forrest II. Huffman, Suzanne. III. Title.
PN4784.T4T76 2004
070.1'95—dc21

2003046338

www.mhhe.com

DEDICATIONS

From C. A. Tuggle
To my wife Tracey and children Brynne, Bethany, and Jenny, and to the memory of my father, T. B. Tuggle, my inspiration to always do my best.

From Forrest Carr
To the memory of Bruce Breslow, a good friend and the finest photojournalist I have ever known.

From Suzanne Huffman
To my husband August F. Schilling III and to my parents, Carrol Statton Huffman and Margaret Anne Byrd Huffman.

ABOUT THE AUTHORS

Dr. C. A. Tuggle began teaching at the university level in 1994 after a 16-year broadcasting career in local television news and media relations. He spent the majority of his career at WFLA-TV, the NBC affiliate in Tampa. He has held numerous newsroom positions, but spent the bulk of his career reporting and producing. He covered both news and sports, including six Super Bowls. Tuggle earned undergraduate and master's degrees from the University of Florida in Gainesville, and his Ph.D. from the University of Alabama in Tuscaloosa. He is currently teaching electronic communication at the University of North Carolina at Chapel Hill. His research has appeared in nearly a dozen scholarly journals and trade publications, and centers on television news practices and procedures. He regularly conducts writing workshops for local stations, professional and academic groups, and high school journalists. He has overseen student newscasts at three universities and his students have won numerous regional and national awards. In addition, he helped to develop more than 50 interns during his professional career.

Forrest Carr began his broadcast news career in 1980 as a radio reporter but quickly switched to television, starting as a copywriter and fill-in reporter before working his way into newscast producing and eventually into management. After working in the Memphis, San Antonio, and Tampa markets, in 1997 his travels took him to KGUN9-TV in Tucson, Arizona, for his first news director's job. During his tenure there, KGUN9 made waves locally and nationally with innovations in viewer service and community-responsive journalism, including a statement of news coverage principles known as the "Viewers' Bill of Rights." Carr returned to Media General's widely known converged Tampa news operation in 2001 as news director for WFLA-TV. In 2002, the News Center partners launched what is believed to be journalism's first converged statement of news coverage principles, "The News Center Pledge." Carr has contributed to numerous scholarly and trade publications, and has won or shared credit in four dozen professional awards, including a regional Emmy for investigative reporting. He is a 1980 graduate of the University of Memphis.

Dr. Suzanne Huffman is an associate professor of journalism and broadcast journalism sequence head at Texas Christian University in Fort Worth, Texas. She earned her B.A. at TCU, her M.A. from the University of Iowa, and her Ph.D. from the University of Missouri at Columbia. She has reported, anchored, and produced news at commercial television stations in Tampa, Florida; Santa Maria, California; and Cedar Rapids, Iowa. Dr. Huffman taught at three other universities before joining the TCU faculty, and her former students occupy newsroom positions throughout the South and Southwest. Her academic research centers on the practice of broadcast journalism and her research articles have been published in *Journal of Broadcasting & Electronic Media* and other academic journals. Dr. Huffman is co-author with Dr. Judith Sylvester at Louisiana State University of *Women Journalists at Ground Zero: Covering Crisis,* published by Rowman & Littlefield in 2002, about the experiences of women journalists who covered the 9/11 terrorist attacks on the United States. She is a contributing author to *Indelible Images: Women of Local Television,* published by Iowa State University Press in 2001.

FOREWORD

Bob Dotson

Senior Correspondent
"NBC Nightly News" with Tom Brokaw

My grandmother always worried about my life's work. The first time she got a chance to see one of my stories on "NBC Nightly News," I called to see what she thought.

"Did you like my story on Tom's show tonight?" I asked.

There was a long pause on the other end of the line. Then she said, "Bobby, I think you should learn a trade."

"A trade?"

"Yes, they're not going to keep paying you for two minutes of work a day."

Well, they have. For 37 years I've been traveling the world on someone else's nickel. I've been in more motel rooms than the Gideon Bible.

And it's been a wonderful life.

The ticket to that life begins on the pages that follow. They contain the nuts and bolts of our business—the basics that hold us all together. This book will help you master our complex and challenging profession. It will also refresh your memory in the years ahead, so keep it handy.

I went to college back when the earth was cooling. Every technical thing I learned about is now in a museum. But the things you'll find on these pages are timeless. They're lessons that will last a lifetime.

So, read on. Have a good life. Call your grandmother.

PREFACE

Dana Rosengard

University of Memphis

Broadcast news was born in the 20th century as radio and television developed in the United States. Radio was something of a "gadget" at first. Radio, or wireless telegraphy, was a technological improvement compared to the wired telegraph that was widespread in the mid-1800s. Telegraph lines were vulnerable because they could be cut, but that wasn't a problem with "wireless." Guglielmo Marconi's experiments with a wireless telegraph in 1890s Europe led to the invention of radio. Early wireless equipment was installed on ships at sea so that they could stay in touch with each other and with the shore—a better system than flashing lights and flags. The sinking of the White Star Line luxury liner *Titanic* in 1912 drew attention to the new invention and led to more widespread use of it.

By the 1920s, individuals were "tinkering" with radio at home and experimenting with what we know today as broadcast programming. In those days, the programs were broadcast live and might consist of sermons, musical performances, news headlines, election returns, or play-by-play of sporting events. Filling hours of time every day with live programming was problematic and station owners began to work out ways to share programs with each other. Early "networks" of radio stations began to form. Station owners were often individuals who were exposed to radio at schools or newspapers or department stores who decided to start tinkering with radio in their spare time. Visionaries such as David Sarnoff at RCA/NBC predicted that radio would become a "household utility" and he was right. Radio quickly became a popular mass medium, and millions of individuals bought sets for their homes. Radio was both an entertainment and a comfort to Americans in the years of the Great Depression and the First and Second World Wars. Listeners grew to recognize and trust the voices of reporters such as Edward R. Murrow at CBS.

Television was already in development in the 1920s when radio became popular in the U.S., but the economic depression and the wars overseas delayed its introduction. By the late 1940s and early 1950s, television stations were going on the air, Americans were beginning to buy television sets for their homes, and programs that had been popular on the radio moved to television. So did the network programming system. Early television programs were broadcast live and might consist of cooking shows, comedy acts, news headlines, election campaigns, and sporting events.

Talk about television was everywhere in the early 1950s, and the emergence of the medium was one of the defining elements of the decade. The actual invention and mechanical processes that would become the television known to the post–World War II generation go back to 1884 and German inventor Paul Nipkow, but it was not until 1923 that a man named Vladmir Zworykin, who started at Westinghouse and then switched over to RCA, developed the iconoscope (from the Greek words eikon [image] and skopein [to view]). This device aimed a beam of electrons across a target that had been charged by light imprinting on it. What he had developed was, in effect, a camera tube. He also developed the kinescope—the TV picture tube. It gave off a phosphorous glow with the electron stream. Together, his inventions became the television we watch today.

But because of the initial production costs and the interruption of World War II, it took a few decades (until the 1950s) for television to truly arrive and begin sweeping the nation. Television set ownership grew nearly 700 percent between 1950 and 1955, from 4.6 million to 32 million receivers.

Television news programming in the early 1950s came in the form of sponsored 15-minute evening broadcasts. NBC's John Cameron Swayze's "Camel News Caravan" and CBS's "Television News with Douglas Edwards" fought the technological demands of the new and growing medium and fought one another. Edwards led in the ratings until NBC introduced "The Huntley-Brinkley Report" in 1956. In 1963, CBS punched back, expanding its nightly network newscast to 30 minutes, incorporating longer reports and more film, and featuring an interview with President John F. Kennedy on the premiere expanded version of the broadcast.

Less than three months later, November 22, 1963, is the day most believe television news came of age, and the new CBS news star, Walter Cronkite, bore the burden of being under the bright lights on that dark day. People sat glued to their television sets through days of national mourning as Cronkite reported the assassination of President Kennedy. As news came in from Dallas by telegraph and telephone, Cronkite brought the scenes from Texas as well as the procession in Washington to the American public hour after hour after hour, almost four nonstop days of coverage. Cronkite's broadcast of the Kennedy funeral and events surrounding it signified the growing power of television news and helped propel Cronkite to his "most trusted man in America" title.

A big part of the power of the new medium was its ability to bring word of events from across the world and country as well as from across the town and region right into the American living room. In many ways, local television news is the most visible element of the local station in U.S. broadcasting. The news at the local level developed partly in response to the dictum of the Communications Act of 1934 to operate in the "public interest, convenience, and necessity." And so, the local newscast was born as a way for stations to demonstrate responsiveness to the local community and to ensure their license renewal: 30 minutes of sights and sounds to keep cities and towns and neighborhoods abreast of events in their areas, regions, and nation.

But news was almost always one of the programs; and the voices, faces, and images in the news became part of the public consciousness. Americans alive in the 1930s remembered the voice of President Franklin Roosevelt in his first inaugural address saying, "The only thing we have to fear is fear itself," in response to the economic depression then sweeping across America. That generation remembered radio reports about the explosion of the dirigible *Hindenburg* as it approached its mooring base in Lakehurst, New Jersey, in 1937. Americans in the 1940s remembered newsreel footage and still photographs of the Japanese aerial attack on the U.S. naval fleet at Pearl Harbor, Hawaii. In the 1960s, Americans remembered the televised images of the assassination and state funeral of President John Kennedy. Later in the decade, they remembered grainy video images of U.S. astronaut Neil Armstrong stepping out onto the surface of the moon. And in the 1980s, they remembered the explosion at launch of the Space Shuttle *Challenger* in Florida with Teacher-in-Space Christa McAuliffe on board. Those twentieth-century sounds and images have been joined in the twenty-first with the terrorist attacks against the World Trade Center in New York City. News coverage of the two hijacked passenger planes crashing into the two buildings, the explosions and fires that followed, and the debris cloud that formed as the Twin Towers collapsed have become part of the public memory of the generation that heard it on radio and saw it on television.

It's the job of reporters to observe and record such events. And it's the job of reporters and news writers to put them into words. Reporters and writers and producers need to be concise, correct, and clear in their observations and explanations—so that the listening or viewing audience can understand and comprehend those events.

PREFACE TO THE FIRST EDITION

A university professor once noted that a student told him she decided to study broadcast journalism rather than print journalism because she didn't like to write that much. It is, of course, a misconception that there isn't much writing in broadcast journalism. Anchors and reporters don't just stand (or sit) in front of a camera or microphone and pour forth interesting information. To understand the real world of broadcast journalism is to learn the step-by-step process involved. Good writing is the heart of that process.

Pioneer stations put news on the air to inform their viewers, to build their audiences, and to sell radio and television sets. Decades later, changes in corporate ownership, the unrelenting need for corporations to generate profits for their shareholders, and a series of corporate mergers have led some news managers to talk about "convergence" in their newsrooms. What this means can vary, but it broadly suggests that reporters in the 21st century would be wise to prepare themselves to write not only for broadcast, but for the Web and newspapers as well.

Our Approach

With *Broadcast News Handbook,* our goal is to teach aspiring broadcast or cross-platform journalists how to write, how to craft the language, and how to be effective storytellers using all the technology available to them without letting technology drive the process. Together, we have more than 50 years of broadcast journalism experience. In the final two decades of the 20th century, we saw many technological advancements that affected how news is covered: videotape, microwave and satellite technology, digital editing, and the list could go on. Technology has changed and will continue to change. But the need to be an effective storyteller hasn't changed, and won't. Regardless of what the tools are, those who can use those tools well to impart interesting information will always have a place in journalism. Foremost among those tools is the language itself. We don't buy into Marshall McLuhan's contention that "the medium is the message." We think the message is the message and the medium is simply a means to get that message to an audience. Technology and journalism are intimately connected in radio, television, and online applications, but content must always drive which stories are selected for coverage and how they're covered.

Who Will Benefit from the Book

We've tried to construct a text that will be useful to beginning broadcast journalism students as well as to those who have advanced in their college training and education and even to those who have entered the workforce. We believe the practical "how-to" sections of this text and the real-world advice will serve students and early career professionals well. We hope the book becomes a resource for students as they progress through their studies and for working journalists as they further their careers in the information business. We believe this book could also be a valuable resource for news workers and managers in traditional print and broadcast newsrooms as they face convergence and the need to cross-train.

Special Features of the Book

The book is written by three people with decades of broadcast news experience. Between us, we've held every newsroom position there is. We approach this book from the perspective of what worked for us, as reporters, producers, and managers, and what we know will work for others. We believe the practical tips and guidelines we've included will not only help you break into the highly competitive world of broadcast news, but will also help you advance while remaining true to the ideals that led you to pursue a journalism career.

Although the book is written using three different "voices," and although each author approaches the material from his or her unique perspective, we are frankly somewhat surprised at the cohesion that has emerged during the process of writing this book. There might be minor differences in our approaches, but there is unanimity about how the product of broadcast journalists should look and the steps necessary to get to that point.

- To help readers understand and remember those steps, we've included a DOs and DON'Ts box at the end of each chapter as a quick study guide and desk reference.
- Words in **bold** are defined in the glossary.
- Producing and writing are so closely tied together in broadcast news that a writing book would be incomplete without a thorough look at producing. The chapter about producing was written by the member of the team who is a working news director. As with other chapters in the book, the producing chapter is filled with practical tips—both about how to become an effective producer and how to make yourself stand out in the producer ranks.
- Broadcast writers write stories that are intended to be heard, not read. Therefore, we place emphasis on the performance aspect of radio and TV reporting.
- Although the book contains a wealth of information about how we do certain things, we have also included a chapter titled "Why We Fight"—a close look at the ethical component of the

broadcast news business. We believe strongly in the power of the media, but with power comes responsibility. We work in and teach about one of the most important aspects of a democracy—media that are free from government control. Protecting rights as we deal with the public's right to know is a vital part of journalism.

- The book ends with a very important appendix. The appendix is a look at some problem words that good writers must master. Language is our foremost tool, and we need to know how to use that tool extremely well. Material used in the grammar and word precision quizzes that accompany this text comes from the appendix.

In general, the book advances from the characteristics of broadcast writing to the story selection process and writing tips that apply to all broadcast story forms. Interviewing and writing for radio chapters introduce us to the vital role of sound bites and natural sound. The book then presents three distinct television story forms: VOs, VO/SOTs, and packages. Chapter 13 is new to this edition and addresses media convergence and how writers on various platforms should approach it. We use what is arguably the world's most widely known converged operation—Tampa's News Center—as our model. The chapter is written by the news director of WFLA-TV, one of the three media companies that are part of the News Center.

Supplements for the Second Edition

A brand-new CD-Rom is now included in the Second Edition. On it are included numerous semi-raw video clips—both b-roll and sound bites. We also provide story notes that, along with the video, give students the material they need to write VOs, VO/SOTs, and packages. On the Instructor's Resource CD (also new to this edition), we provide finished scripts that were generated by professionals. That way, students can compare what they did to what working broadcast journalists did with the same material. The same is true of a producing exercise, which appears on the Student CD. Students can put together a show rundown, then compare how they structured the show to how the show actually aired on a network affiliate in a Top-20 market (with the professional producer's rundown available on the Instructor's CD). Both CDs also contain links to numerous examples of award-winning broadcast journalism from student news competitions. The Instructor CD features a brand-new Test Bank, with a mix of essay, multiple choice, and true/false questions for each chapter, as well as grammar and broadcast style/word precision quizzes, complete with answer keys. Please contact your McGraw-Hill sales representative for further information to obtain a copy of the Instructor's Resource CD.

Both CDs and the book's expanded website, www.mhhe.com/tuggle2, also contain:

- A brand-new chapter, "What Television Producers Want: A Quick-Reference Convergence Guide for Print or Web Journalists 'Just Visiting' a Broadcast News Platform."
- Two updated chapters included in the first edition:
  - "Writing Sports Copy"—about reporting sports for the electronic media.
  - "The 21st Century"—what broadcast journalists can expect in the years ahead.
- Tips about how to prepare your résumé and résumé tape from someone who has reviewed hundreds of each.
- The News Center Pledge, referenced in Chapter 13 about convergence issues.
- Suggested test questions and the answers to those questions.

Again, please contact your McGraw-Hill sales representative for the access password for the Instructor's materials available online.

Final Thoughts

Throughout, we acknowledge that radio and TV news is a business, but also stress that it's more than that. It's a calling, both work and passion, and a means to document and be a part of history as it's made. We hope that we've imparted some of our passion for the craft of broadcast writing through this text.

ACKNOWLEDGMENTS

The authors thank a number of people for their assistance in bringing this project into being. First we'd like to thank the following institutions, employers, friends, and former colleagues who supplied script samples:

At WFLA-TV in Tampa, Florida:
General Manager Eric Land and Media General Director of News Dan Bradley, for permission to use station scripts, and Assistant News Director Kathryn Bonfield and Sports Producer Dave Cook for their assistance in selecting them.

At KGUN9-TV in Tucson, Arizona:
Former General Manager Karen Rice, for permission to use station scripts.

At KRLD News Radio in Dallas, Texas:
Mike Rogers, B. J. Austin, and Jack Hines, for providing radio script examples.

At the *Tampa Tribune* in Tampa, Florida:
Senior Vice President and Executive Editor Gil Thelen, for permission to use story excerpts.

At TBO.com in Tampa, Florida:
General Manager Kirk Read, for permission to use copy excerpts.

At KERA Radio in Dallas, Texas:
Sam Baker for providing radio script examples.

At KFWB Radio and California State University in Los Angeles, California:
Tony Cox for providing radio script examples.

At WNYC Radio in New York City, New York:
Beth Fertig and Marianne McCune, for providing radio script examples.

At KUAF Radio at the University of Arkansas in Fayetteville, Arkansas:
Rick Stockdell and Kyle Kellams, for providing radio script examples.

Photographer Cliff McBride

Numerous industry professionals provided stories and insights that added breadth, scope, and a personal touch to the work:
Melissa Antoccia of KLAS-TV in Las Vegas, Nevada

Chandra Clark of WVTM-TV in Birmingham, Alabama

Kelli Durand of WLIO-TV in Lima, Ohio

Dan Hicken of WTLV-TV in Jacksonville, Florida

Greg Kelfgun of KABB-TV in San Antonio, Texas

Joe Kovacs of WAMI-TV in Miami, Florida

Robyn Kinsey-Mooring, formerly of WTVD-TV in Durham, North Carolina

Tom Loveless of WFAA-TV in Dallas, Texas

Terry Meyers of WCBS-TV in New York City

John Miller of KTVT-TV in Fort Worth/Dallas, Texas

Glenn Mitchell of KERA Radio in Dallas, Texas

Matt Morin of WPTZ-TV in Plattsburgh, New York

Diane Pertmer of WFLA-TV in Tampa, Florida

Jill Rackmill of ABC News in New York City

Several colleagues at universities throughout the nation offered very helpful suggestions and insights that helped make the book useful and relevant in a new millennium:

Dale Cressman at Utah State University

Pam Doyle at the University of Alabama

Sonya Forte Duhe at the University of South Carolina

Bill Knowles at the University of Montana

the late Travis Linn at the University of Nevada–Reno

Jim Upshaw at the University of Oregon

At McGraw-Hill, Developmental Editor Laura Lynch, Project Manager Jean Starr, and Media Producer Erin Marean have been exceedingly helpful in getting the second edition and all of the elements associated with it ready for publication and distribution. We look forward to working with them on subsequent editions. Thanks also to publisher Phil Butcher, his assistant Christine Fowler, Supplements Editor Kathleen Boylan, Marketing Manager Sally Constable, Production Supervisor Carol Bielski, and Designer Sharon Spurlock.

Additionally, Forrest Carr would like to thank:

Bob Steele of the Poynter Institute for Media Studies, for invaluable guidance in the preparation of the ethics portion of this book.

Al Tompkins, Jill Geisler, and Lillian Dunlap, also of the Poynter, for their assistance, leadership and inspiration on the subject of ethics.

The 2002 Poynter Ethics Fellows and participants of the "Doing Ethics 99" Poynter workshop, for their advice and support.

The RTNDA's *Communicator* magazine, in which earlier versions of some of this material first appeared.

The many readers of *Communicator* and *Shoptalk* who have shown steadfast support and encouragement through the years.

KGUN9-TV General Manager Ray Depa, for being one of the world's great bosses.

Lee Enterprises, Inc., the former owners of KGUN9-TV, whose corporate mission and vision created an environment in which viewer-oriented journalism could thrive.

Media General, Inc., for its strong and unwavering faith and support for the ideals of quality journalism, community service, and public accountability.

At the *Tampa Tribune:* Donna Reed, Morris Kennedy, Pat Minarcin, and Malanda Saxton; and at TBO.com: Jim Riley, Peter Howard, Clarisa Gerlach, and Adrian Phillips, for their invaluable assistance in the preparation of this manuscript.

At WFLA-TV: General Manager Eric Land, for his steadfast enthusiastic support; Dana Tomlins for her great graphics work and support over the years; Julie Cowan, for additional graphics help; Investigative Reporter Steve Andrews, for his example and inspiration on the subject of journalism, writing, editing, and ethics and, above all, for showing that it is possible to be an aggressive reporter and still treat people with professionalism and respect.

And, finally, his wife Deborah, who has allowed him to disappear into his study for long periods. Whether she has found this to be a burden or a blessing, she's graciously kept to herself.

CONTENTS

CHARACTERISTICS OF BROADCAST NEWS WRITING

Writing is easy. After all, most of us learned to do it by the time we graduated from kindergarten. However, *good* writing is difficult. Sometimes it's very difficult. If it weren't, most of us would be novelists. So what is it that distinguishes writers from good writers? In very simple terms, it's the ability to craft the language, not just use it. In this book we'll help you learn how to craft the language for a broadcast audience—to tell stories in ways that will grab attention, impart information, and leave television news viewers or radio news listeners with the impression of having been at the event themselves. But before we can get to that, we need to lay some groundwork. First, let's point out some of the differences between broadcast writing and most of the writing you've done during your formal education and look at some general characteristics of broadcast style.

1

We Get Only One Opportunity to Make Ourselves Understood

Chances are you've written a number of essays in your time; you might have even written for the school newspaper. In both cases, you were writing for the eye. In broadcast, you'll write for the ear. When your English teacher read through one of your essays, the teacher had the opportunity to go back and reread sections that weren't immediately clear. Readers of newspapers, magazines, and other printed material have the same opportunity. Broadcast audiences don't. (Most people, we assume, don't tape the evening news to go back and look at it later unless they or family members or friends were part of the news that day.) So, we have to make every sentence we write very clear so that audience members understand what we're talking about after having heard it only once.

Additionally, even if something looks good on the page, we don't know how it will sound until we read it out loud. Every broadcast script should be read aloud so that the writer can hear how it will sound when the words are spoken. Writing for the ear is one of the biggest differences between print and broadcast writing, but there are others.

Story Structure Is Different

Although print writers seem to be moving away from rigid adherence to the inverted pyramid style, it remains the basis of many newspaper stories, especially hard news stories. With inverted pyramid style, stories begin with the most important facts and continue with facts of lesser and lesser importance. This is done primarily to make it possible for editors to shorten stories without affecting the most important information. You might have noticed that some newspaper stories you've read seem to end rather abruptly. Most likely, that was the work of an editor trying to fit a 450-word story into a 400-word space.

In broadcast writing, we don't use the inverted pyramid style. On the contrary, television and radio news stories are written in such a way that the viewers would definitely notice something was missing if we "trimmed from the bottom" because we don't build stories in descending order of the facts. Also, the end of longer broadcast news stories either should contain a summary statement or should leave the viewers something to think about and that might be lost if the viewers started to tune out toward the end. So we need to hold their attention throughout the story. Note that a summary statement isn't necessarily intended to indicate that we know all we're going to know about that story. Often, the resolution of stories isn't known for days or even months after the event occurs. Frequently, the summary statement is to let the viewers or listeners know that the story is a continuing one and that we'll follow it to its conclusion.

Broadcast Writers Use Conversational Tone

This doesn't mean speak as you would on the basketball court or at a club with your friends, but broadcast writing is a bit less formal than print writing is. You might have already noticed that this book is written using contractions. That's one of the main things that separate broadcast and print writing. More about contractions in a bit. When you write for television or radio news, the goal is to tell a story to someone who knows less about what happened than you do. You want to impress this person, but you don't want to make that desire obvious. The way to impress without appearing that you're trying to impress is to use common words but use them very well. Many of us have used some words incorrectly for so long that they sound wrong when we use them the right way. Sound confusing? Just think what the viewers and listeners might be going through. Some of them know when you use a word incorrectly or try to talk above their heads; others just have a feeling that something is amiss. In either case, you, the writer, have distracted the audience members momentarily. One of the things to avoid in broadcast is anything that distracts the viewers or listeners. There are already too many things fighting against us for their attention for us to be fighting against ourselves.

We mentioned that broadcast writing is less formal than print writing is, but it's more formal than how we speak to one another. When we talk, we don't often think about rules of grammar, sentence construction, and the like. But when we write, we have to think about those things. Why? Because for now, television and radio news flows one way only with no immediate interaction between audience members and reporters or anchors. Just as viewers and listeners have nothing they can reread to make sure they understand it, likewise, they're unable to ask the person speaking what he or she meant by what was just said.

Writing for Broadcast Includes Using Contractions

You don't want the anchor (one day it could be you) to sound stiff or as though she's talking down to the audience. One way to avoid this is to use contractions, because contractions are a big part of sounding conversational. But, as with most "rules" in broadcast writing, there are exceptions and you shouldn't use contractions in every instance.

For example, if you want to place emphasis on something, a contraction is *not* as strong as using both words. Additionally, some contractions don't roll off the tongue very smoothly and should be avoided. Some examples are "that'll" for that will, "it'll" for it will, and "there're" for there are. Avoid those three and any others that just don't sound right to you when you read the script out loud. You should also be careful with contractions that sound like plurals. If you say, "The plan's giving her reason for hope," it's unclear at first whether you're talking about one plan or more than one. Television and radio audiences know only what they hear; they can't see the apostrophe. But for the most part, write with contractions.

In Broadcast Writing, We Use Short, Declarative Sentences

This is closely related to using conversational tone. This doesn't mean that all sentences should be simple sentences along the lines of "See Dick run," but we should stick to sentence construction that makes it very evident who and what we're writing about. Hence, we rarely use complex sentences because it's very easy for our meaning to get lost in the shuffle. Broadcast writers also keep the subject and the verb as close to each other as possible. For example, "This morning, police arrested a suspect" is easier to follow and sounds better than "Police this morning arrested a suspect." We also don't often deal with complex stories as part of everyday coverage. They're difficult to tell and difficult to follow. Even in fairly straightforward stories, it's better to present a few well-developed facts than lots of little bits of information. The viewers are apt to get lost (in more ways than one) if you hit them with too much information in a short amount of time.

Active Voice Is the Choice of Broadcasters

Simply put, active voice is someone doing something and passive voice is something being done to someone or some thing. Here are examples of both:

Active. The governor gave a speech.

Passive. A speech was given by the governor.

There are occasions in which passive voice actually sounds better, but they're fairly rare. Write in active voice unless the sentence sounds strange when you read it aloud. If that's the case, try it in passive voice to see if it sounds better. But you'll rarely go wrong using active voice. The key to constructing sentences in active voice is to make sure the action is preceded by the actor, and that there *is* an actor mentioned. In the active voice example above, the actor is the governor; his action was giving a speech. Broadcast writing is full of passive voice because writers don't follow this simple rule. "The gunman was arrested" is the worst kind of passive-voice construction because not only did the writer fail to put the actor first, *there is no actor mentioned.* Active voice helps us with another broadcast writing guideline: keeping the subject and verb together. We'll look more closely at active voice and its importance in Chapter 3.

Broadcast Writers Use Present or Future Tense When Appropriate

Some writing coaches and textbook writers advise the use of present tense at all times, but that just doesn't make sense. If there's a reference to World War II in your story, you certainly wouldn't write about that as if it were currently taking place. However, you should use present tense as often as you can. Remember, we want to give today's news, not yesterday's news. Also, don't use more than one tense in the same sentence; for example, you wouldn't write "Police arrest a Carrville man and charged him with arson." You could place both verbs in the past tense, but your best bet is to use the present tense with both words (unless the arrest happened some time ago and we're updating the story). There will be more about tense in Chapter 3.

Broadcast Stories Are Written in Today Language

The word "yesterday" isn't allowed in the lead sentence of broadcast news stories. If something happened yesterday (or last week) and nothing new has developed, why would we include that story on the evening news? But using today language doesn't necessarily mean using the word "today." For example, "Police are continuing to investigate" indicates that something is going on today without us having to use the word "today." Further, today language doesn't mean that we can't update something that happened yesterday. It might even be necessary to use the word "yesterday" somewhere in the story. After all, if that's when the event occurred, we can't change that. Just don't use "yesterday" in the opening sentence.

Also, keep in mind the news program on which your story will appear. Starting a story that's part of the 9 P.M. update or the 11 P.M. newscast with "this morning" indicates that either nothing has happened since this morning or we aren't out there digging for the latest information. In a world of round-the-clock news channels and program interruptions to bring viewers and listeners the latest news live from the scene, failing to "freshen" stories for subsequent newscasts is a major failing indeed.

How to Deal with Dates and Days of the Week

Although we don't want to use the word "yesterday" in the lead sentences of our stories, if something happened yesterday, you'll have to use the word at some point in the piece. *When* something happened is important, and we can't say it happened today if it didn't. If you make time references in a story, use these guidelines: Use the words "yesterday" and "tomorrow" if the event in question is only one day in the past or one day in the future. If it's more than one day distant, give the day of the week. Dates aren't necessary unless the event happened more than a week ago or will happen more than a week from now. For example: The bill became law yesterday. The trial begins tomorrow. The concert will be Sunday. (Note: If you write *next* Sunday, you leave a question as to whether you mean a few days from now or a week and a few days from now. Delete the word "next" if you mean the Sunday to follow, and put the date if it's a Sunday that's more than a week away.) If you use a date, it's acceptable to write it in shorthand form rather that fully written out, such as 2nd, 4th, 21st, and so on.

Some news operations use the day of the week rather than the words "yesterday," "today," or "tomorrow." CNN does this frequently because a piece might run on Wednesday evening and again on Thursday morning, or it might already be Thursday somewhere in the world. If you refer to today and the piece runs again on Thursday, it's now a different day. So, keep in mind when your story will run when deciding how to refer to the day that something happened. Wednesday could be yesterday, today, or tomorrow, depending on what you're talking about. But it will always be Wednesday. So, although the words "yesterday," "today," and "tomorrow" are preferred, there are cases in which you'd use the day of the week instead.

Broadcast Writers Use Last Names and Put Titles First

Except on first reference or when more than one person with the same name is part of the story, use the last name only. Hence, the first reference to a person in the story would be to Bill Smith, but use Smith in all subsequent references to that person. If Bill's brother Tom is also part of the story, it might be necessary to use the full names of both men on all references to avoid confusion. Some writers like to use the first name only, but the only time you can get away with that is when the person you're talking about is a child. It would sound strange to refer to six-year-old Tommy Jones as Jones. So when you're referring to children, it's okay to use the first name alone on subsequent references.

When you use a title, place it in front of the name. Again, this is to avoid confusion and keep the sentence flowing smoothly. It sounds better to say "Former Midville Mayor Jane Brown says . . ." than to say "Jane Brown, former mayor of Midville, says. . . ." But please, if some government official you talk to has a title like "Texas Railroad Commission Pipeline Regulatory Division Engineer," shorten the title to something the viewers or listeners can digest. For TV, you're going to have to do that to get it to fit on the screen for a **super** (graphics information superimposed over the video) anyway.

There's some disagreement among television news writers about the need to verbally identify the people whose on-camera quotes we use because their names and titles will be shown in a super on the lower-third of the screen. However, a number of studies have shown that many people don't watch the news closely from beginning to end.[1] Often, people are preparing dinner, dealing with the kids, getting ready for bed, or talking about work that day as they watch or listen to a news program. The viewer might even be in another room during parts of the newscast. So it isn't advisable to depend on a super as the only means of identifying a speaker.

Additionally, even with those viewers who watch the news program intently, supers don't always suffice. Any producer or show director who has been involved with television news for any length of time will tell you that when mayhem reigns in the control room (and that isn't uncommon), getting supers on the air falls far down the list of priorities. Therefore, we suggest verbally identifying each on-camera source the first time he or she is about to appear. We'll have more about introducing sound bites in Chapter 8 on **voice-over/sound on tape (VO/SOTs).**

In Broadcast Writing We Use Phonetic Spelling and Avoid Foreign Names When Possible

Although broadcast writers are supposed to spell correctly under most circumstances, there are times when spelling a word correctly might result in its being pronounced incorrectly on the air. Therefore, any

---

1. See, for example, *Study of Media and Markets: Television Attentiveness & Special Events* (1994), Simmons Market Research Bureau; R. Neuman (1991), *The Future of the Mass Audience,* Cambridge, United Kingdom: Cambridge University Press.

uncommon word should be spelled the way it sounds. This presents some special problems for closed-captioned television, but most newsroom computer systems make it possible to deal with those concerns. Viewers tend to phone the station en masse when an anchor or reporter mispronounces the name of a person or place, especially if most of them know the correct pronunciation. One of the goals of writers is to keep this from happening by spelling those names phonetically. "Davis" doesn't need to be spelled phonetically, nor does "Miami." But there's no predicting how "Sarmiento" or "Kazakhstan" will come out of someone's mouth unless you indicate that those names should be pronounced Sahr-me-in-toe and Kahz-ahk-stan.

Some fairly common words should also be spelled phonetically because they have two pronunciations. On more than one occasion, an anchor or field reporter has been known to pronounce "bass" the way it should be pronounced in reference to a fish when the word was used in reference to a low tone on the musical scale. When that happens, it's embarrassing for the person whose face is on-screen and for the news operation as a whole. In such an instance, write "base drum." Although the word isn't spelled correctly, the overwhelming majority of viewers don't see the words but hear them only, and it's certainly not good for the news operation's credibility for one of its anchors or reporters to say "bass drum" (as in a drum that holds fish). Several other words are spelled the same but pronounced differently. Watch out for them. One note of warning: if seeing a misspelled word distracts your anchor, you might want to spell the word correctly, review the script with the anchor, and hope that he or she pronounces the word the way it's supposed to be pronounced. Audience members always seem to notice even the slightest double-take by someone on-camera.

In reference to hard-to-pronounce names, sometimes we can do without using a foreign name at all. It might be important to mention the name of the French president, but if we're referring to the French undersecretary of defense, using the title might be enough for the viewers to understand that person's role in the story without having to deal with a difficult foreign name. However, when the name is important to the story, if you think there's a chance it will be mispronounced, spell it phonetically whether it's a foreign name or not.

When you're not concerned about a chance that a word will be mispronounced, spell it correctly. Also, don't count on a spell-check program to catch your mistakes. The computer doesn't know whether you were writing "tired" or "tried" and will accept "tired" when you meant "tried" because, to the computer, you spelled the word correctly. It's just not the word you intended to use. Computers are great tools, but they can't match the human mind on some things, such as editing copy. At least not yet.

Broadcast Writers Avoid Abbreviations and Are Careful with Acronyms

In broadcast writing, avoid almost all abbreviations. The fairly common abbreviation "St." can mean either street or saint. News anchors have plenty to think about without having to figure out which one it's supposed to be. Some abbreviations aren't used simply because they aren't needed. This is the case with courtesy titles such as Mr., Ms., and Mrs. Generally, a person's marital status isn't important to the story. One exception to the no-courtesy-title rule is with heads of state and their spouses. It's appropriate to refer to President Bush or Mr. Bush, or Mr. Blair or Prime Minister Blair. Likewise, the spouses of those particular heads of state would be Mrs. Bush or Mrs. Blair.

It might be important to identify someone as doctor, but when it is, spell the word out rather than use the abbreviation. "Dr." is short for both doctor and drive. The same is the case with president (you wouldn't want an anchor to say pres, so don't write it that way), senator, or representative. (Note: Such titles aren't courtesy titles. They're earned titles. There's a difference between the two.)

Some agencies and entities are better known by the acronyms that identify them than by their full names, and the acronyms are easier to say. For example, F-B-I is more widely used than is Federal Bureau of Investigation. But notice how we write F-B-I. When you want the anchor to pronounce each letter, place hyphens between them. This is also true with A-M and P-M in references to time.

Other acronyms that are acceptable on first reference are C-I-A, N-C-A-A (but if you want the anchor to say N-C-double-A, write it that way), N-B-C, C-B-S, A-B-C, C-N-N, and so on. Let your guide be the way you're accustomed to hearing it. Almost no one says American Broadcasting Companies in conversation, and most probably don't even know what E-S-P-N stands for. For local or regional groups that might not be familiar to all the viewers, give the entire name on first reference, then go to the acronym. For example, the group Save Our Cumberland Mountains might be called SOCUM on second reference.

In Broadcast Writing, Keep Hyphenated Words on the Same Line

Any words that are meant to be read together should be hyphenated to alert the anchor as to how they should be read. In addition, all parts of the hyphenation should appear on the same line. There could be a brief delay as the words are rolling up on an electronic prompter. It looks silly when an anchor gets out half a hyphenation but has to wait for the other half to appear. For the same reason, a sentence shouldn't carry from one page to another.

Hyphenation is called for when two or more words are used as a unit to describe something. "A long-running trial" could come out sounding as if we're talking about a lengthy trial about running (a long running trial) without the hyphenation.

Broadcast Writers Use No Symbols

Unlike print writers, we don't use any symbols in broadcast. All references to dollars, cents, percent, and other such words should be spelled out. We also don't use the number sign, the "at" sign, the ampersand (symbol for the word "and") or any other symbol you can come up with. Even the point in one-point-two million dollars should be spelled out. If symbols were included in scripts, it could cause the news reader to pause momentarily trying to figure out exactly what has been written. That, of course, would break the flow of the story and might even make the anchor look or sound foolish.

In Broadcast Writing, There Are Different Guidelines for Dealing with Numbers

Quite often, the precise amount or number of something is unimportant in broadcast. Certainly, if 163 people are killed in an airplane crash, the number is important. But it's better to say a budget of nearly two million dollars than to say a budget of one million—865 thousand dollars. Additionally, filling a story with too many figures and statistics brings the flow of the story to a screeching halt and sends the viewers scrambling for their remotes. Most of the time, round off numbers.

When you write numbers in broadcast, it's important to make them easy to read. Here are some simple guidelines.

Numbers 1 through 9—write out the word (some news operations prefer that you write out the words through eleven)

Numbers 10 through 999—use numerals

Numbers higher than 999—use a combination of words and numerals. For example: 37,915,776 should be written 37 million—915 thousand—776.

Write phone numbers and years using all numbers because that's how we're accustomed to seeing them. For example: 610-555-0201, 1776, 1492.

Often, Addresses and Ages Aren't Important in Broadcast Writing

Chances are that most of the viewers in a given market wouldn't know where 1600 Eagle Street is, but they might be familiar with a certain section of town. Hence, referring to an area or pointing out landmarks close to the place where an event occurred is preferred instead of giving a street address. Likewise, a person's age usually isn't important unless we're talking about a 10-year-old college graduate or a 73-year-old snow-skiing champion. However, there are exceptions. When a local person has been killed, it might be necessary to give the age and an address so relatives of other people with the same name as the dead person aren't alarmed for no reason. Also, when someone meets an untimely death, the age adds some context, as when a 28-year-old dies of a heart attack. Remember, in broadcast writing there are few rules that came down from the mountain on stone tablets—only guidelines.

Making Corrections to Copy

The standard markings used by print writers and editors to indicate changes in a script can be very confusing to an anchor trying to read a story on the air. The final version of the script should contain no such markings. Also, even if something is corrected on the hard copy of the script, it still has to be corrected in the computer. Most newsroom systems send the script directly to the prompter, and if you don't make the corrections electronically, the anchor will be seeing an uncorrected version of the script. Producers should make any corrections that are necessary on the computer, send the revised story to the prompter, and print out another copy for distribution to the anchors and all other news personnel who get copies.

Broadcast Writing Is Punctuated Differently

The most common forms of punctuation in broadcast writing are the comma and the ellipsis. The comma indicates a standard pause, the ellipsis indicates a slightly longer pause. The ellipsis is often used for effect. Additionally, words that the anchor should emphasize are underlined on hard copy. Hence, this short sentence could be read three different ways:

<u>Sue</u> loves you.

Sue <u>loves</u> you.

Sue loves <u>you</u>.

The way you write the sentence is the way it's going to be said.

Other than the comma, the ellipsis, question marks, and periods, we use few punctuation marks in broadcast. Remember, broadcast writing is meant to be heard, not read. You should write copy to make it as easy to read as possible. The easier it is for an anchor to read, the easier it will be for audience members to listen to the copy.

Quotations Are Handled Differently in Broadcast

In broadcast writing, we rarely use direct quotations in the script, but normally paraphrase instead. Most people don't speak as succinctly as we're supposed to write, so we paraphrase what they've said in as few words as possible, being careful, of course, not to change the meaning. In those few instances when a writer feels compelled to use a direct quotation, it's important to make the sentence flow as smoothly as possible, as is always the case in broadcast writing. For example:

THE PRESIDENT SAID . . . I WON'T SIGN THE BILL UNLESS IT'S AMENDED TO
INCLUDE PROVISIONS FOR LOWERING THE DEFICIT . . . MISTER CLINTON ADDED
THAT HE DOESN'T EXPECT THE REPUBLICAN MAJORITY IN THE HOUSE TO ADD
THOSE PROVISIONS.

Setting the direct quote off with an ellipsis tells the anchor (and the listener or viewer) that what is about to be said stands apart from what has been said up to this point and from what will be said afterward. However, if you sense that the audience members might be confused, set off the quote by adding "in his words" after "the president said." However, definitely avoid these pitfalls: "The president said, quote," and "end quote" at the conclusion of the sentence.

Again, however, we rarely quote in text. If what someone has to say is important enough for us to quote that person, we'll get a taped comment. In a visual medium such as television it's better to see and hear the person who makes the comment rather than quote the person in the script. The same is true for radio, except, of course, the visual part.

Broadcast Writers Are Careful with Pronouns

Pronouns are acceptable in broadcast writing, but only if there's no question about to whom the pronoun refers. Clarity is vitally important to broadcast news, and pronouns can create a problem in that regard. For example: "The police officer tackled the fleeing robber. He's a former football player." In this sentence, it's unclear whom the pronoun refers to, the officer or the robber. It's likely that the writer used "he" to refer to the officer, the person who did the tackling. However, there's room for doubt, and that's something that broadcasters can't afford to raise in viewers' minds. In this example, it's best to delete "he" and restate the noun.

Broadcast Writers Use Attribution before Statements

If we don't tell the viewers or listeners beforehand who made a particular comment, stated a fact, or offered an opinion, it sounds as though those things are coming from our anchor. For example, "Sally Johnson extorted thousands of dollars from X-Y-Z Bank during a three-year period, according to bank officials" sounds as though we're making an accusation until the viewer hears the end of the sentence. Inverting the sentence takes care of that. "According to bank officials, Sally Johnson extorted thousands of dollars from X-Y-Z Bank during a three-year period" lets the viewers or listeners know right away that bank officials are making the charge, not the members of the news team.

Almost everything we know about a particular story comes from someone else and should be attributed. Exceptions would be that an event is taking place somewhere, at a certain time, costing a certain amount. There's no need to attribute common facts, but most other information can't stand without the writer needing to tell the audience its origin. Words and phrases such as "accused of," "convicted of," or "charged with" help us in this regard. If we say someone is a convicted murderer, it's obvious the person was convicted by a jury, but even in that circumstance, we don't know for sure that the person did the crime. Plenty of people have been on Death Row for years and were later found to be innocent. Hence, we advise against saying someone did something unless a television news crew captured the event on videotape and there's no doubt that the person we're talking about is the person we see on the tape.

Conclusion

Former network anchor David Brinkley was once asked if he considered himself a journalist or a broadcaster. Brinkley replied that there's no difference because good writing is good writing. In a sense, that's true. If you can write good print copy, you can easily make the transition to broadcast writing. But, as you've seen, there are some differences between the two media in how we arrive at good writing. The guidelines listed above don't change the language, but do slightly alter how we use it. All the guidelines are designed to make the copy easier to read and, therefore, easier to listen to. Remember, the key in broadcast writing is *don't make viewers or listeners work to get their information*. As a writer, you should do all the work so that the audience members don't have to do any. Otherwise, they'll turn to a newscast (or other programming) that requires less effort.

 General DOs and DON'Ts

Do
- Be clear and concise.
- Make life easy for the anchor.
- Write like people talk (to a degree).
- Be careful with pronouns.
- Attribute.

Don't
- Forget that you know more about stories than audience members do.
- Depend on the computer to catch mistakes.
- Fail to make corrections on the prompter as well as on hard copy.

SELECTING STORIES AND STARTING TO WRITE

In radio and television newsrooms across the country, some of the youngest people in the operation are writing stories and making decisions about which stories should be included in the newscast and in what form. It isn't uncommon for associate producers and assignments desk personnel to start right out of college, even in some of the largest markets in the country. So you could be helping to make major decisions sooner than you think.

Chandra Clark knows all about that. Because she got a lot of experience by interning and working part-time during her college days, she was able to land a job as a producer in the Tuscaloosa market right after graduating from the University of Alabama. Eight months later, she was the executive producer at the other station in town. That station merged its news operation with two other central Alabama stations nine months after that, and Chandra was tapped to produce the new operation's first newscast in what was now the 39th largest market in the country. She was 23.

She skipped the midnight sign-on party so she'd be well rested for the big day. She arrived at 7 A.M. to prepare for the 5 P.M. (Central Time) newscast. The network was airing a golf tournament that afternoon and, of course, it went to a play-off. The delay in getting the newscast on the air added to an already intense environment. As the minutes dragged on, the people in the control room were getting more and more anxious. The news director, the executive producer, the station vice president, the general manager, and the president of the parent company were in the cramped room, standing behind Chandra. The golf tournament was *still* on. Chandra got on the **IFB** communication system (which she had used only during rehearsals) with one of her field reporters to ask about the **outcue** to his live shot **package** insert. He told her the outcue was "Trust in God and everything will be OK." Everyone in the control room burst out laughing, easing the tension, at least momentarily. The show finally went on, nearly 27 minutes later than scheduled. Chandra says producing hasn't gotten a whole lot easier since then.

Terry Meyers is another young person who rose through the ranks quickly. At 21 and fresh out of college, Terry landed a job as an assignments editor in the 35th market and says it was "sink or swim." She had to make dozens of decisions a day and had a nervous feeling in her stomach when the news began each afternoon, hoping she didn't miss any big stories that the other stations got. She moved into producing and worked in the 24th market, the sixth market, and is now an executive producer in the nation's largest media market, New York City. She got that job a mere seven years after graduating from college.

The experience she got on the assignments desk laid the groundwork for successively bigger jobs in bigger markets, and decision making has become increasingly more difficult with each move. There are so many stories to cover, you can't possibly get to them all. Terry says it's critical to look at all aspects of a story, especially what's in it for the viewers. Because she's young, that can be difficult. Sometimes she's not that interested in stories that people older than she is might find interesting, and she may not be as knowledgeable about some things as they are. Also, she works with people who have been in the business a lot longer than she has, and through the years some of them have thought she was too young or didn't have enough experience to make the right decisions.

Sometimes she can get input from others in the newsroom about whether to air a particular piece of graphic video, or whether a story warrants a package or not, but other decisions have to be made in seconds and she has only her instinct to go on. She reads a lot (at least five newspapers every morning) and she watches and listens to news veterans, and that certainly helps, but she continues to fight the "age battle" and has to prove herself again and again. You might have to prove yourself as well, but if you have the talent, the determination, the drive, and the people skills needed to be a news decision maker, even hardened news veterans will come to appreciate you, despite that baby face of yours.

Chandra and Terry are examples of where you might be in this business in a few short years. Neither works in front of the camera, but each is a critical cog in the news machine at her station. If you like being involved in the big picture and don't mind being "on the hot seat," think about pursuing producing or assignments desk work. You could find yourself in a big market before long and making important decisions about what is and isn't news.

In this chapter, we'll look at the factors assignments managers and producers consider when deciding which stories are worthy of inclusion in radio and television news programs, and we'll start to get down to the nitty-gritty of writing for broadcast news. We'll look more at the joys of producing live news in a later chapter.

A highly respected network news anchor once noted that the script for a half-hour news program wouldn't fill the front page of a major newspaper. Most television and radio stations air more than 30 minutes of news a day, but the point remains the same. Newspapers have a lot more room for stories than broadcast news operations have time for stories. Hence, there are fewer stories on television and radio news programs than in newspapers, and most broadcast stories are shorter than most newspaper stories are.

WFLA-TV producers and assignment editors discuss breaking news.

Television news stories might last for only 10 or 15 seconds and rarely run longer than a minute-and-a-half to two minutes. Radio newscasters face similar time constraints. So, broadcasters have to be very choosy when it comes to deciding which stories make it on the news. There are several factors that influence what's been called the **"gatekeeping** process"—deciding which stories are selected from the hundreds or even thousands that are possible on a given day.

Newsworthiness

Newsworthiness is a highly subjective matter, but people in the news business must decide every day which stories are the most deserving of coverage. Excluding weather and sports, only 15 to 20 stories are reported in a 30-minute television newscast. Even 24-hour radio news programs are limited regarding the number of stories that can be broadcast. The decision regarding which stories are included and which are rejected is based on what those in the newsroom think those in their living rooms or cars are most likely to watch or listen to. Attracting viewers is undeniably part of the equation. Because of that, those involved in the news business strive to present what's been called **infotainment**—information presented in an entertaining way.

Some critics have charged that television news is too entertainment-oriented—stressing flash and trash over substance—and some of the criticism is warranted. But news programs must compete for attention with other television programs, the Internet, movie rentals, and a myriad of other choices. Hence, the finest information in the world is of little value if no one is watching or listening. If broadcast news is guilty of turning the equation around and producing **entermation**—entertainment with only a dash of information—then all the criticism we could heap on those who think entertainment is the first mission of news is deserved. But presenting information in a way that will make your station stand out (while maintaining fairness and accuracy) is simply good business. We think well-told stories are informative, interesting, and entertaining, and hope that you'll embrace higher ideals while recognizing that we work in the information *business*.

Before writers, editors, videographers, and others involved in news gathering can begin the process of telling stories in compelling ways, someone has to decide which stories will be covered. The assignments manager, show producers, the executive producer, and other newsroom managers are often the ones who make these coverage decisions, with input from reporters and other personnel. The decisions are based on a nebulous concept called "news judgment," but there are ways to make the process more objective than relying on a "gut feeling." Many of the factors television and radio news workers take into account when selecting stories are the same criteria used by newspaper editors, but others are different.

Proximity

Where an event occurs is important. If a six-car pileup delays traffic on a major local thoroughfare for hours, that's likely to make the news. If the same accident occurred elsewhere in the state, it's unlikely the story would air on your market's local news program. An old maxim in television news says that one local death is worth (in terms of news interest) five elsewhere in the state, twenty elsewhere in the country, and hundreds elsewhere in the world. It might sound cold, but it's assumed that what happens locally is more important to local viewers than what happens elsewhere is. Of course, there are many other factors that influence the decision to include those stories that happen in other places, such as how the deaths occurred, the prominence of the people involved, and other factors. But all other things being equal, local stories take precedence over stories from elsewhere.

In the earliest days of broadcast news, proximity was of paramount importance for a very practical reason. If something happened very far from the station, it was simply impossible to get to the scene and cover it, drive back, process film or edit audiotape, and get the story on the air. Therefore, news operations were geographically limited by the technology. That changed dramatically with the introduction of electronic news-gathering and satellite news-gathering technology. Now it's possible to get video and/or audio from almost anywhere in the world and to get it pretty quickly. What's been called "a river of video" is there for the picking from any number of organizations that supply video to local television stations for a fee, or from cooperating stations that might even be affiliated with different networks. Many cooperatives (called consortia, one would be a **consortium**) exist in both radio and TV, and some stations belong to four or five of them. So, proximity might not be as important as it once was because a local station's reach extends so much farther, but it's still pretty important.

Timeliness

Some news observers contend that timeliness is even more important on today's local news scene than it was in earlier days, because of the technology. Local stories can be covered live and with very little time needed to get a microwave truck operating once the news crew arrives on the scene. Local stations can arrange to get a live report from another part of the region or the world, and can get that on the air just as quickly as the local news operation in that area can. A story being reported live in Los Angeles can be on the air live in Miami (and plenty of other places) simultaneously and within minutes of news managers learning of it.

All this has led some news outfits to operate as if something that happened this morning is no longer news at 6 P.M. So local news has gone from not being able to get something on the air at 6 P.M. if it occurred after 4 P.M. to being able to get something on the air if it happens during the newscast. Many news workers across the country believe timeliness has taken on too much importance in television news. A nationwide survey of news directors and senior reporters conducted in the late 1990s indicated that many respondents in both groups think that plenty of local news operations give far too much attention to stories that happen to occur close to or during the news hour. Stories that might have been covered briefly (if at all) had they occurred earlier in the day are afforded live coverage early in the news programs (both "going live" and placing a story early in the newscast indicate the story is important) simply because they lend themselves to live coverage.[1] So timeliness is an important factor, but news managers have to guard against letting timeliness outweigh all other factors and their good news judgment. But even in the dark ages of television news, timeliness was important. No one wanted to present information that viewers had already read in the newspaper.

Impact

Clearly, one of the things that news managers consider when deciding which stories to cover is which ones will impact the greatest number of listeners or viewers, whether directly or indirectly. A cure for cancer, the abolition of the income tax, or the surprise resignation of the city's mayor would certainly affect almost everyone in the audience to one degree or another. But KABB Executive Producer Greg Kelfgun warns against reacting to breaking impact stories at the expense of everything else.

Greg says you have to go after the big stories, and go after them hard, because this is a competitive business and nobody wants to get beat on the big story of the day. Many producer job ads now ask for evidence of that producer's "owning" the top story. But Greg says the pursuit of the big story often leads producers and other managers to lose sight of the rest of the show. When the big story breaks, you have to immediately start thinking about not only how you'll cover it, but also how you'll shuffle everything else. Remember, you still have other stories that deserve quality treatment, and for some of your viewers,

---

1. C. A. Tuggle and S. Huffman (1999), "Live News Reporting: Professional Judgment or Technological Pressure? A National Survey of Television News Directors and Senior Reporters," *Journal of Broadcasting & Electronic Media*, 43(4), pp. 492–505.

one of those stories might be the most important one of the day. The story about a third grader using the Heimlich maneuver to save his teacher's life deserves a featured place in the newscast. Greg says station personnel go crazy trying to "own" the top story, but the idea is to put together a winning newscast, not just beat your competitors on the top story of the day.

Emotional stories can also affect large numbers of viewers. A story about a young child battling a life-threatening disease, a "good Samaritan" story in which a person does something good for another with no tangible reward, or the death of a celebrity who millions found interesting are all examples of emotional stories that attract attention and impact the audience.

The number of people involved in an event also affects whether it receives coverage. When a rock concert fills a large stadium, it's apparent that a lot of people are interested enough to pay good money to hear the musical group and gives an indication that many viewers might be interested in a story about the concert, even if they couldn't attend for some reason.

Prominence

One of the things that made the Princess Diana story of interest was her prominence. A person's standing in society or recognizability plays a role in making stories about that person newsworthy. For example, should your instructor be involved in a minor car accident, it's unlikely that story would make the evening news. However, should the governor be in town on the same day and be involved in the same fender bender, then we have a story. It's not that your instructor isn't an important person, but many more people know who the governor is, and something minor that happens to her is of more interest than something minor that happens to most of us "average" people. So, when the president of the United States gets a dog, we hear about it on network news.

The same is true with athletes, rock singers, movie stars, and other entertainers. They're among the country's most widely known residents, and even mundane things that happen to them are of interest to some people. If that weren't true, tabloid newspapers and television shows would quickly be replaced by something else. What producers and assignments editors have to do is avoid letting a person's celebrity be the *only* factor they consider when deciding if a story is newsworthy: the shows about what's happening in Hollywood come on *after* the news.

Conflict

Disagreement makes for good copy and even better video. Confrontations between protesters and police are interesting because the viewers don't know what might happen next. A shouting match at the city council meeting is likely to draw coverage, but the passage of uncontested ordinances probably wouldn't. Good broadcast writers know how to highlight conflict *without* embellishing it. However, showing conflict simply for the sake of showing it isn't good decision making. Unless we provide some context, we've done the viewers a disservice. As with all the other factors that go into deciding whether something is newsworthy, conflict shouldn't stand alone. Otherwise, we'd show 30 minutes of bar fights every night, and viewers might confuse the news with a national talk show known for violent outbursts from the guests.

Unusual or "Human Interest" Stories

Stories about "average" people are interesting if those people do unusual things. A story about a college student who collects the pictorial covers of a popular sports magazine becomes more interesting when the viewers learn that the student has nearly 1,000 magazine covers and that all are signed by the athletes pictured on the covers. If a local person has a few unpaid parking tickets, that might not be of interest, but if he had 200 unpaid tickets and was thrown into jail, that would probably attract some attention.

Also, many television news producers seek out interesting and unusual stories to place at the end of news blocks or at the end of the program. These stories are typically called **kickers** and involve something amusing or cute, such as a water-skiing squirrel or a ladder-climbing dog. Such stories aren't likely to impact anyone's life, but they do give the viewers a little bit of relief from what some complain is too often 30 minutes of death, destruction, and corruption.

Simplicity

Complex stories are often dismissed as "print stories" by news decision makers. It isn't because such stories are necessarily uninteresting, but it takes time to tell complex stories, and because they're complex, they're also difficult for the viewers or listeners to follow. A minor change in the tax law might affect a large number of viewers, but such a story would likely receive minimal attention on television or radio because the details would be difficult to present and absorb. It has been said that television news is little more than a headline service. In many ways, that's probably right. But other than occasional investigative pieces, local news isn't designed to offer a lot of detail on stories, and news workers might even alienate a portion of the audience if they tried to pack too much detail into short stories. However, complex (even seemingly nonvisual) stories can be told on TV news. So don't dismiss stories automatically if they don't seem simple: make them simple. Relate difficult concepts to common things, such as comparing information flowing through a computer chip with highway traffic.

This gives viewers a concrete representation of an abstract idea. Also, remember graphics. They help with pacing and are a very good way to relate information for which you have no video.

Can We Get Good Video and Natural Sound?

Television is a visual medium, so pictures (and the audio that goes with them) are worth thousands of words. To be sure, stories sometimes make the news when there's no video to accompany them, but such stories would be very short and would probably include a promise from the anchor to bring pictures to the viewers as soon as the video becomes available. But in many cases, a story for which video wasn't available wouldn't make the news. Frequently, a story is dropped when video is available but simply isn't very compelling. Maybe this shouldn't be a part of the equation, but it is. Again, however, we strongly suggest that decision makers consider all factors when deciding whether to air a story, and not drop it simply because of a lack of video. The most important question to ask is, "Is this story important to our viewers or listeners?" There is no quick and easy answer. It takes thought, research, and intuition. Consider carefully and decide wisely. What's selected for presentation and how it's presented are vitally important.

There's one other thing to consider related to visuals. Television news operations use file footage extensively. The station might not be able to get video of a famous entertainer being arrested for soliciting prostitution, but would probably have clips of his television show on hand to illustrate the story. The video that's used affects the way a story is written, of course. More about the importance of writing from available video and incorporating natural sound in Chapter 7.

What Else Is Happening?

One of the most difficult things to deal with in television and radio news is that producers have a set amount of time to fill, regardless of what's happening in the world. Of course, for a huge story news managers can choose to stay on the air beyond the normal end time of the news program, but in most circumstances, the news ends at an appointed time and certainly never before that time arrives. One television news operation used to end its program by having the anchor say, "And that's all the news we have time for."

So, in a typical 30-minute TV news program or 5-minute hourly radio update, there's room for only a certain number of stories. Whether a particular story is included in that mix sometimes depends on what else is being covered. Coverage of a plane crash might knock out other stories that on slower news days would be included. One day the news might be 90 percent local and only 70 percent local the next day because major stories are happening elsewhere and not much is happening locally. Holidays, which are often very slow news days because businesses and institutions are closed, bring out all the standard holiday stories because there's little or no breaking news to cover. With TV, on those days when a lot is happening, it's not unusual for the time allotted for weather and sports to be trimmed (rarely commercials, though) in order to free up more time for all the news. So the decision of whether a story makes it on the news can depend on other stories against which the story must "compete" for attention.

Such was the case for Robyn Kinsey-Mooring and her colleagues at the ABC affiliate in the Raleigh-Durham market when Hurricane Floyd hit the Carolina coast. In some ways, it was easy for producers and other decision makers to decide what to cover—power outages, rooftop rescues, cleanup efforts—all important and visual stories. But what do you do with non-hurricane-related stories that at other times would wind up in the A **block** or might even lead the show? Because of hurricane and hurricane aftermath coverage, Robyn and her cohorts were forced to give short shrift to the groundbreaking for a controversial mega-mall; a plea agreement for a man accused of kidnapping, raping, and beating a local principal; and an involuntary manslaughter trial in an outlying part of the coverage area.

The new mall had already been the subject of much debate because it was being built in an area where many residents thought development was already out of control. Because of the hurricane, the groundbreaking wasn't even mentioned until a week later, when, in a 15-second **voice-over (VO),** the viewers found out that construction was already under way. The rape and beating case ended quickly with the plea bargain, and a story that had been covered heavily because of concerns it raised about safety in area schools garnered 20 seconds of airtime with file video. The weeks of aftermath coverage meant that the news operation couldn't devote resources to the manslaughter trial on a daily basis (the case was the result of a hunting accident), so that trial was covered as a voice-over/sound on tape (VO/SOT) one day and the video was used as file for all subsequent stories.

Robyn says these were all important stories that should have received more attention, but they just didn't pull enough weight in the grand scheme of things to compete with 48 dead, thousands homeless, and the eastern portion of the state under water for weeks. Deciding how to allocate resources is never an easy process, and it's even more difficult when one major story dominates.

What Are the Viewers/Listeners Talking About?

If snow is predicted to fall later in an area that rarely receives snow, many viewers or listeners are likely to watch or listen to the news program to find out what the chances are. If a widely known celebrity is set to visit the area, members of the audience are likely to be curious about the appearance and plans being made to accommodate the person. News managers use focus groups and other research methods to try to figure out what the viewers are interested in and what they might want to know. Often, though, a good gauge of what the viewers are talking about is what everyone in the newsroom and in other departments are talking about.

The Role of News Philosophy in Story Selection

In some modern newsrooms, traditional news judgment values aren't the only factors at work in the story selection process. *News philosophy* might also play a role—sometimes, a huge one. What is news philosophy? Essentially it's a set of values the station uses to emphasize some types of stories over other types. The philosophy might be unwritten and informal. It might be written and quite formal. In some cases it may be not only unwritten, but also unspoken, simply a part of the newsroom management culture that causes decision makers to put their thumbs on the scale when weighing certain types of stories against others. If no station in a market has a unique news philosophy, then each station's coverage will look about the same. Each will cover car crashes, chases, murders, fires, city council meetings, civil rights disputes, consumer investigations, and so on, in about the same proportion, and will tend to choose similar leads for their newscasts every day. But in the modern competitive environment, it's not unusual at all for one or more stations to make a concerted effort to deviate from a traditional "middle of the road" news philosophy and stand out with a unique coverage profile. For instance, one station might fancy itself as the hard-nosed, investigative station. It tends to choose, lead with, and promote stories that are investigative in nature. Another station might portray itself as the consumer advocate station. It will choose, lead with, and market consumer stories. Another might be the "tabloid" station, choosing to emphasize chases, murders, and celebrity news. News producers and reporters working at a station with a unique news philosophy will be expected to know that philosophy and help execute it. (Hint: learn all you can about a station's news philosophy before taking a job there. Such advance knowledge might help you land the job—or lead you to turn it down if the station's approach to news conflicts with your personal values.)

A Final Note about Gatekeeping

There are many factors that play a role in the gatekeeping process in television and radio news. There's no way to say whether one is more important than another, because there are often several at work at the same time. Also, one of the factors listed above might sway news managers to include a certain story, but another factor might prove to be the most important in the decision behind whether or not to include a different story.

For television producers and assignments managers, paying close attention to which stories are included each evening is important for a number of reasons. Since 1964, Roper surveys have shown that most Americans have said they get most of their news from television and would believe the television version of a story if other media had different accounts of the same event. At the height of the Persian Gulf War, 81 percent of Roper poll respondents indicated that they got most of their news from television and 54 percent said they got *all* of their information about the world from television news.[2] Many others get at least some of their information from drive-time radio news. Some have questioned the accuracy of these polls and whether the way the questions are worded leads respondents to answer in certain ways. But if these polls are even close to being an accurate reflection of how Americans get their news, those of us in broadcast news have a big responsibility to include the most important stories in the limited time available.

Additionally, a long line of research has shown that the media (television in particular) often set the agenda for what's considered important. Researchers McCombs and Shaw noted that the media might not tell us what to think, but are remarkably successful at telling us what to think about.[3] The other side of that coin is that when stories aren't included, television news decision makers are saying, in essence, that those stories aren't as important as the ones that are included. People become interested in pursuing careers in television or radio news for a number of reasons. One can only hope that being part of one of the most important conduits of information in the information age is a major reason that young people become interested in the field.

The Page F Test

Deciding which stories to include in the newscast is only part of the battle. The next step is to present those stories in the most clear, concise way possible, and that goes back to writing. What we suggest is that you write a script, go ahead and get something on the page, and

---

2. "Poll: Most Got War News on TV" (1991), *Gainesville* (FL) *Sun*, May 2, p. A8.
3. M. McCombs and D. Shaw (1993), "The Evolution of Agenda Setting Research: Twenty-Five Years in the Marketplace of Ideas," *Journal of Communication*, 43(2), pp. 58–67.

then apply the Page F test to it. Then have someone else (usually a producer in TV) do the same thing. If it doesn't pass all five parts of the test, then it isn't written as well as it should be written. Even the best writers in history were rarely completely pleased with the first draft of their writing. The five parts of the Page F test are:

P—Are the words precise?

A—Is the story accurate?

G—Is every element germane?

E—Are all actors treated equitably?

F—Does the story flow?

Precise Words

We're sure that you've heard people who are struggling in their attempts to learn English say that it's not an easy language to pick up. There are a number of reasons for this. Those of us from the United States use a lot of slang and clichés, the language is full of words that sound alike but mean different things, and the language is full of words that we think mean the same thing when there are subtle and not-so-subtle differences between them. For example, do you know the difference between anxious and eager? If you ever come across two words that mean exactly the same thing, rid your vocabulary of one of them. Why would we need both?

Toward the end of this book you'll find an appendix containing words and phrases that are often misused. Sometimes, textbook readers tend to read only what they have to read and skip appendices. We strongly encourage you not to do that in this case. The section on word usage is very important because you'll never be a very good writer if you don't use words correctly. You might be able to fool most of the people most of the time, but it's likely that someone in the audience will catch every word usage mistake you make. How credible will you be as a purveyor of information in the minds of people who've caught you misusing words? You might even be surprised at how many words you think you know how to use correctly that you actually use incorrectly. So, the first part of the Page F test is to make sure that each word you use means exactly what you think it means.

Accuracy

Many people who teach or practice journalism will tell you that if what you write isn't accurate, your credibility and that of the news operation is sure to suffer sooner or later. Even if every word you use is precise, your story might not be true. All of us were kids at one time (believe it or not), and we know that there are shades of untruth. Often, you can get away with something really bad by admitting to something a bit less heinous. But that's not the way it is in journalism. We must tell the truth, the whole truth, and nothing but the truth. The viewers count on us to tell them what went on as best we can without letting our own biases interfere. They also count on us to do the legwork necessary to ensure that what we report is actually what happened.

Of course, very few newspaper writers or broadcast journalists set out to deceive the public. But if we pass on something as fact without doing any digging to find out if it's true, our laziness serves the same purpose. People want to trust what they hear on the news. Unfortunately, they've been given a lot of reasons in the past several years not to.

Germane Information

In addition to being accurate, what we write has to be germane; it must be relevant to the story. All broadcast writers have a common enemy: a lack of time. A rush to get things on the air can lead to factual errors, and because of the limited time we have to tell stories, the information we choose to include must be the most important information. Is the age, sex, marital status, or race of a person germane? Does the information add understanding, or does it just take up space? If a presidential candidate is caught in an affair, is that germane? It might be relevant in a story about the candidate's character and might not be in a story about the candidate's stance on a flat-rate income tax.

Part of the failure to include only relevant information comes from the writer's *inability to decide what the story is about.* Many broadcast news stories today are a little bit of this followed by a little bit of that, with no theme running through the story. Report about one thing. Is your story about the huge crowds at the auto show or the newest technology on display? We're not saying that you can't mention the technology, because that's probably one of the things that attracted the huge crowds. But decide what the theme of the piece is and *concentrate* on that. So, before you write a single word of copy, *make a one-sentence commitment to the story so you know what to write about.*

Are All Groups Treated Equitably?

Treating groups differently can take many different forms. Using sexist language is one of them. Not only might certain terms alienate members of the audience (and every news director will tell you we need all the viewers or listeners we can get), but they aren't very precise. Words such as fireman, policeman, and congressman are throwbacks to a time when women didn't occupy those roles. Many of us still tend to think of certain jobs as being filled by men (doctors, for example) and others by women (such as nurses). Of course, men and women fill roles today that were once the exclusive domain of the other sex. So don't let archaic thinking slip into your writing.

Now, don't get us wrong. We're not talking about being politically correct, which has come to mean "don't do or say anything that has the remotest chance of offending someone." Hence, old people are referred to as "chronologically challenged," short people are "vertically challenged" and corrupt people are "morally challenged." If someone is corrupt (and we have proof), then the person is corrupt. But a firefighter isn't necessarily a fire*man*.

Also, in terms of being equitable, there are almost always two sides (or more) to an issue. If you devote two-thirds of your story to one side of the issue and only a third to the other side, one group thinks you're siding with the other. It's especially important to make sure both sides are heard on issues that generate intense feelings, even if one side seems to be in the minority. It could be that most people agree with the second position but just aren't very vocal about it. Don't let the number of activists involved sway your thinking about which is the most widely held opinion about an issue.

Does the Story Flow?

Even if your words are precise, your story is accurate, the information is germane, and everyone has been treated as equitably as possible, you still might not have a very good piece if it doesn't flow. Each thought must flow logically into another. If you don't work to make the sentences flow, the viewers can be caught off guard when you introduce new information without showing its relationship to the information that's already been presented.

"Tie-writing" is the term used to describe how we get stories to flow. We have to tie one thought to the next, and that one to what follows it, and so forth. One place within stories that this often doesn't occur is going into and coming out of sound bites. We'll address this particular concern in Chapter 9.

Conclusion

A lot goes into making a good piece of broadcast copy. In addition to the points of style we've already covered about how broadcast copy is written, we also have to be concerned with the content, what is written. We don't have the luxury of being able to spend hours on a piece of copy to make sure it's the best we can make it; at times it's a luxury to be able to review it once. So, much of what we do in terms of self-correction has to happen almost automatically. That begins to be the case only when we've written a lot. We trust that sooner than later you'll grasp how to deal with various story forms and broadcast writing guidelines as you continue writing—a lot.

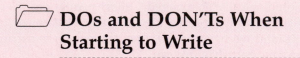 **DOs and DON'Ts When Starting to Write**

Do
- Think like a viewer.
- Be precise, accurate, germane, and equitable, with flow.
- Decide what the story is about before you start writing it.

Don't
- Let your own biases come into play.
- Let the entertainment part supersede the information part.
- Disregard the need for strong grammar and word precision skills.

WRITING GREAT LEADS AND OTHER HELPFUL TIPS

I t's a truism that "everyone knows a story written for television or radio must be conversational." But casual observation of the news in any media market shows that the skill of turning that truism into reality isn't so common. In this section, we'll use several guiding principles and some examples to show how to write conversationally while also doing a good job of delivering the news.

A well-written story will contain three basic ingredients:

- The writer captures the essence of the story in the lead.

- The copy itself doesn't sound like it's been *written* at all. It will sound, in fact, like one side of a conversation, exactly as if the anchor or reporter is talking to someone, rather than *at* someone.

- The writer presents the facts in narrative storytelling format.

In writing copy, you must always keep in mind our basic mission in broadcast news: relay needed information to the viewer or listener, making yourself clear *on the first attempt*. Remember, you get only one pass at it.

The Art of the Lead

A story "lead" is, quite simply, its first sentence. Arguably, it's also the story's single most important element. In broadcasting, the lead accomplishes much the same task as a headline in the print world. For the consumer, it's the "point of purchase." The viewer or listener will decide whether to pay attention to the story on the basis of the strength of the lead in much the same way a reader decides whether to scan through a given newspaper story on the basis of the headline. However, there's one huge difference between print and broadcast customers. If the print customer doesn't like a story headline, he or she probably won't put down the newspaper but will simply skip to the next story. A television viewer faced with the same situation is likely to pick up a remote and zap the entire newscast into oblivion. The state of oblivion is arguably a good place to visit on occasion, but who wants to live there? To avoid such a fate, when writing a lead:

- Grab the viewer's or listener's attention right away by capturing the essence of the story.
- Don't make the lead hard to digest by loading it down with too many facts! Instead, write a "nonfactual lead."
- Don't write a lead that sounds dated or stale.

In addition, you should apply the same rules and techniques in the lead that pertain to copywriting in general, including:

- Write in active voice.
- Use narrative storytelling technique.
- When appropriate, use creative techniques to make the copy sparkle. But don't overdo it!
- Write conversationally! Employ the "Mom Rule."

We'll explore each of these points in the pages ahead, beginning with the most important point of all.

Writing Conversationally: The "Mom Rule"

In the print world if a reader doesn't understand a sentence, paragraph, or story on the first attempt, he or she can go back and reread it. That's not an option in broadcasting. As mentioned, we must get it right the first time. To accomplish that, we must write the way people *listen*, a technique sometimes referred to as "writing for the ear." And to do *that*, we must write the way people *talk*. An easy way to prepare yourself for that is to remember the Mom Rule. Ask yourself: If I were sitting down at the dinner table to tell this story to my mom, what would I say? We hope you'd want to speak in sentences that are grammatically correct but not rigidly formal. You'd be friendly and conversational, using short, declarative sentences. You'd get to the point right off the bat. Apply that same rule when you're speaking to the viewer or listener. Visualize the copy as your part of a conversation with someone standing right in front of you. Keep your sentences short: take a breath! Make your tone friendly and informal, but not so informal as to be chatty, gushy, or silly.

The Mom Rule doesn't apply just to writing leads; it also applies to general copywriting. We'll talk more about the Mom Rule and see how to apply it in some of the examples that follow.

Capturing the Viewer's Attention: The Essence of the Story

The most basic definition of a newsworthy story is one that the viewers or listeners find beneficial or valuable. Remember, they're making a decision about your story (whether you like it or not) during the lead. Here's something commonly heard in writing workshops that you might find helpful: imagine that every single viewer or listener is tuned in to the same radio station. Its call letters are WII-FM, or "What's In It for Me?" If your lead doesn't answer that question *immediately*, you might lose the viewer or listener.

The lead is, in essence, a sales pitch. Make it a good one. The sale is important to you: no sale, no viewer; no viewer, no ratings; no ratings, no revenue; no revenue, no paycheck. To close the sale, you must immediately convince the viewer of the value or benefit of the story. Sometimes this is obvious and easy for the writer to do; often, it's far from it. One thing is clear: in order to capture in your lead the essence of what makes your story newsworthy, you must know it yourself.

Here's an example, loosely based on an actual news story. The scenario: Three weeks ago in Miami (a city in your state but not in your market) police arrested Kathy Newsmaker and charged her with involuntary manslaughter for the death of her baby. Kathy had left the child locked inside her car while she went inside to speak to a neighbor for "just a moment." But she was gone for more than an hour, and when she returned, the child had died from exposure to the severe heat inside the car. You've previously carried stories about this in your local newscast. Now today just before airtime a story crosses your news wire stating that the state attorney has decided to drop all charges against Kathy, saying her investigation shows that Kathy is a loving mother and that the baby's death was simply a tragic accident.

Your mission: to write a lead to this story that captures its essence and makes a connection to the viewer, without resorting to lurid writing or tabloid-style sensationalism.

This is similar to the lead that actually aired on one Florida TV station:

> TODAY IN MIAMI THE STATE ATTORNEY ANNOUNCED SHE WON'T PURSUE A
> MURDER CASE AGAINST 38-YEAR-OLD MOTHER KATHY NEWSMAKER.

Among its other sins this lead inspires a response along the lines of "So what? Who's she?" The lead does key on what happened today, but doesn't even come close to capturing the essence of what makes this story newsworthy.

Now let's apply the Mom Rule. When you open your mouth to tell Mom about this story, you won't agonize about how to begin. You'll just start talking, and you'll start with the fact that has the greatest impact on you: "Mom, can you believe it? That Miami woman who left her baby in the car got off!" What you've just expressed is the same factor that makes this story newsworthy to the average viewer: the expectation that Kathy would pay a price for her mistake, and the surprise that she won't. To be meaningful and relevant to the viewer, then, your lead must address that same issue.

It would be convenient if you could write a lead such as this:

> A LOT OF MIAMI RESIDENTS ARE SHOCKED AND OUTRAGED TONIGHT: A WOMAN
> ACCUSED OF LETTING HER BABY DIE IN A LOCKED CAR HAS WALKED FREE.

However, because this story is just breaking and no one has had an opportunity to react to it, you can't honestly say anyone is shocked and outraged. Instead, you have to focus on the *development,* which might (or might not) later lead to those outraged feelings, and get to the point right off the bat:

> A MIAMI WOMAN WHO WENT TO JAIL FOR LEAVING HER BABY LOCKED IN A HOT
> CAR IS FREE TONIGHT. THE STATE ATTORNEY SAYS THE CHILD'S DEATH WAS
> NOTHING MORE THAN A TRAGIC ACCIDENT.

There's also another way to do this. You can write *specifically* to the viewer's unspoken expectations:

> YOU MIGHT THINK THAT IF A BABY DIES WHILE LEFT LOCKED INSIDE A HOT
> CAR . . . SOMEONE WOULD GO TO JAIL. BUT IN ONE MIAMI CASE . . . YOU'D BE
> WRONG.

This last example has the advantage of being much more conversational, and because it speaks directly to the viewers' or listeners' emotions, it will be relevant to a wider circle of people. Some traditional journalists might feel that this direct viewer connection "crosses the line" toward being an editorial. However, one of the great strengths of broadcasting's conversational style of writing is that it gives the opportunity to make a personal emotional connection with the news consumer. Showcasing the relevance of a story by referencing the viewer's expectations in this manner is perfectly appropriate.

Present or Future Tense—without "TV Speak"

A very common lead style is use of the simple declarative sentence. Most producers, writers, and reporters have it drilled into them that they should never write such a sentence in past tense. The reason this rule is so universal in broadcasting is simple: if it's happening now, or will be happening soon, then it's news. If it happened hours ago, it's old news and fading fast into obscurity. Yesterday's news doesn't hold a great deal of value except to historians, otherwise no one would use yesterday's newspaper to line parrot cages. A dated newscast has even less value; you can't even wrap fish with it. The easiest way to telegraph to your audience that your newscast is fresh, new, and therefore valuable is to showcase what's happening *now* or what *will be happening* in the near future—using present and future tense, respectively.

Now here's where many broadcast news writers go astray. Many a producer will write a past-tense lead. Then, fearing the wrath of news managers, the producer simply changes the tense of the verb from past to present. The result is a nonconversational, mangled, bastardized form of English known as "forced present tense" or "TV speak." It's about as pleasant as fingernails screeching across a chalkboard.

Example Scenario

You're working in the Tucson market and are writing about a local bank robbery. The scenario: a gunman held up a bank and got away with some cash. After running out the door, for no apparent reason the gunman shot at a passerby on the sidewalk. The passerby, Otis Armstrong, was about to step into the bank to cash a check. When the shot was fired, he dived to the sidewalk and wasn't hurt. Police say it was a miracle the bullet missed Armstrong, and officers credited him for his quick reflexes in ducking for cover. The bank is processing the security film and will release it in the morning.

A traditional, unimaginative past-tense lead might read something like this:

A TUCSON BANK WAS ROBBED THIS MORNING . . . AND THE GUNMAN GOT AWAY.

But wait! It's past tense! So the producer, suffering from a sudden, acute attack of *mediocritus unimaginitivus*, simply changes "was" to "is" and "got" to "gets," and comes up with:

A TUCSON BANK IS ROBBED THIS MORNING . . . AND THE GUNMAN GETS AWAY.

The above sentence is indeed in the present tense, but the problem is that it doesn't sound natural. In fact, it's ridiculous. It's written in TV speak. The writer made a half-hearted attempt to follow the present-tense rule, but in doing so gave no thought or creativity to the effort and simply changed the tense without regard to how it would sound. Think about it. When was the last time you sat down to dinner with your mom and said, "Hey, Mom, a bank is robbed this morning?" The answer is never. No one talks that way. This style of writing might be appropriate for a tease, but not for the story itself. In "fixing" the past-tense lead, the writer actually has made the situation much worse, violating the first rule of broadcast copywriting, "be conversational." The best way to fix it is to start over, from scratch. Ask yourself three questions:

1 Who are the participants in this story?
2 What are they doing now?
3 What will they be doing later—tonight, tomorrow, or next week?

The answers to these questions will tell you how to rewrite the lead.

In this particular example, who's in the cast of characters? The list includes:

- Police
- The employees developing the security film
- The bank teller who was robbed
- Witnesses
- The gunman
- Otis Armstrong
- The viewing public (never forget the viewers and listeners!)

A list of things happening right now might include:

- Police are looking for the gunman.
- The gunman presumably is trying to avoid capture.
- The victim who was nearly shot is telling his story to friends and in general is glad to be alive.
- Police are investigating the incident.
- The bank is processing its security camera pictures.

A similar list of things that will happen in the future regarding this story might include:

- The gunman will or will not be caught.
- The bank will release its security photos.
- The bank will reopen tomorrow with business as usual.

A good writer can fashion any and all of these facts into a present- or future-tense lead. The best and most effective lead will also be the one that focuses on the most interesting human element. In this case, who in the cast of characters has the most interesting and colorful story to tell?

Present-Tense Examples

ONE TUCSON MAN IS RECOVERING FROM A FRIGHTFUL EXPERIENCE THIS
AFTERNOON.

THIS HAS TURNED OUT TO BE A DAY ONE TUCSON MAN WON'T SOON FORGET.

Future-Tense Examples

WHEN OTIS ARMSTRONG RETURNS TO WORK TOMORROW . . . HE'LL HAVE ONE
AMAZING STORY TO TELL HIS FRIENDS.

POLICE HOPE EVIDENCE TO BE RELEASED TOMORROW WILL HELP THEM
CATCH A CROOK.

OTIS ARMSTRONG'S GRANDCHILDREN WILL BE HEARING ABOUT THIS DAY
FOR YEARS.

Finally, just to show that even the past tense can on occasion be effective if it's written conversationally and employs narrative story-telling:

ONE SECOND OTIS ARMSTRONG WAS WALKING DOWN THE STREET WITHOUT A
CARE IN THE WORLD . . . THE NEXT . . . HE WAS DIVING FOR COVER.

The Narrative Lead

As we just saw in the example above, though the prohibition against "past tense" leads works as a general rule, there are some perfectly acceptable uses of past tense. Sometimes the best way to write a lead is to jump right into the story in narrative fashion. Such narrative leads don't always have to be in the present or future tense.

Example 1

THEY CAME EXPECTING FOOD . . . FASHION . . . AND FUN. BUT FOR THOUSANDS
OF PEOPLE WHO TURNED OUT FOR THE ANNUAL POETRY IN THE PARK EVENT . . .
THIS HAS TURNED OUT TO BE A DAY OF DISAPPOINTMENT.

Example 2

JOHN SMITH ALWAYS WANTED TO BE A POLICEMAN. HE NEVER EXPECTED TO BE
CALLED A HERO. BUT UNLESS SEVERAL HUNDRED OF TAMPA'S FINEST HAVE IT
WRONG . . . THAT'S EXACTLY WHAT HE IS.

Example 3

THE FIRST THOUGHT THAT RAN THROUGH HIS MIND WAS THAT IT COULDN'T BE
HAPPENING. BUT IT WAS. AND WHAT FRED JONES DID NEXT ON A RAINY
HIGHWAY ONE NIGHT LAST SPRING WOULD CHANGE SEVERAL LIVES . . .
INCLUDING HIS OWN. TONIGHT RIP REED BRINGS US THE STORY OF AN
ORDINARY MAN . . . WHO FOUND EXTRAORDINARY COURAGE.

Leads such as Example 3 that begin with a specific incident or thought are sometimes referred to as "anecdotal."

Connecting with the Viewer or Listener

The electronic media are very personal. They provide a unique opportunity to make a direct connection with the end user, and in fact work best when they make such a connection and make it effectively. One powerful way to do that is to simply ask a question of the viewer or listener.

Example 4

HAVE YOU EVER WONDERED WHY KEYPADS ON DRIVE-UP A-T-M MACHINES ARE
WRITTEN IN BRAILLE?

Example 5

HOW MUCH TIME DID YOU SPEND STUCK IN TRAFFIC THIS MORNING?

One key advantage of the rhetorical question is that it often makes a direct connection through use of the word "you," a very personal pronoun. Like any good seasoning, however, the rhetorical question is best if not overused.

Another good way to make a direct connection is to directly challenge the viewer's or listener's expectations.

Example 6

YOU MIGHT THINK IT'S NOT EASY TO GET AWAY WITH MURDER. BUT THAT'S NOT THE CASE IN BLAMVILLE. DETECTIVES THERE HAVE SOLVED LESS THAN HALF OF LAST YEAR'S KILLINGS.

Finally, you can make a direct connection by writing a statement that appeals directly to the viewer's or listener's personal experiences. A statement of this type is frequently conditional, beginning with the word "if."

Example 7

IF YOU'VE EVER DRIVEN ON THE INTERSTATE AND HAVE FOUND YOURSELF SANDWICHED BETWEEN TWO SEMIS . . . YOU KNOW HOW FRIGHTENING BIG RIGS CAN BE.

The danger of this kind of lead, of course, is that it might not appeal to viewers or listeners who haven't had the experience it references. Example 7 would be a very valid lead for residents of Los Angeles, but perhaps less valid for the subway riders of Manhattan. The key is to reference experiences that touch large numbers of viewers. Note, for this to work the topic doesn't necessarily have to affect the viewer *directly.* For instance, the subject of prostate cancer doesn't directly affect women, but it's likely to affect some of their loved ones.

Keeping It Short: The Nonfactual Lead

How many facts should your lead contain? Here's a startling thought for you: the best broadcast leads might contain *no specific facts at all.*

Many writers are tempted to launch into the body of their story right out of the starting gate. Thus we might see a lead like this:

AN AMERICAN AIRLINES 737 WITH 57 PASSENGERS ON BOARD DISAPPEARED FROM RADAR SHORTLY AFTER TAKEOFF FROM BUENOS AIRES THIS MORNING . . . SPARKING A MAJOR SEARCH BY THE ARGENTINE AIR FORCE.

It has too many facts. We don't need to know in the very first breath how many passengers are on the manifest, the airline company involved, the circumstances surrounding the disappearance, the location, and who's conducting the search. This sentence has so many facts competing for attention that the viewer can't possibly remember them all. *Keep it simple:* save the details for the body of the story. Again, ask yourself: How would you say this to your mom? Would you sit down and say, "Hey, Mom! An American Airlines 737 with 57 passengers on board disappeared from radar shortly after takeoff from Buenos Aires this morning, sparking a major search by the Argentine Air Force!" Probably not. If so, you've been watching too much bad TV news. Chances are you might say something more like, "Hey, Mom! Did you hear about that plane crash in Argentina?" Your lead should get the viewer's or listener's attention in a very similar fashion:

> WE HAVE BREAKING NEWS OUT OF ARGENTINA THIS AFTERNOON: A MASSIVE SEARCH IS UNDERWAY FOR A MISSING JETLINER.

Such a lead also serves a preview function. In essence you're saying, "Listen up. You're about to hear a story about a plane crash." With this style, when you do begin presenting the facts, the viewer or listener is prepared to accept them, instead of being clobbered over the head without warning.

Beyond the Lead: General Copywriting Tips

"Selling the story," though critically important, isn't the only purpose of the lead. It must also set up and support certain tasks and styles to be accomplished in the body of the story. The lead must begin the "preview and review" function. It must support narrative storytelling technique. And, like all copy throughout the newscast, the voice should be active, not passive.

Preview, View, and Review

Your mission, as stated, is to be clear the first time. The best way to reach any destination is to have a clear road map. When you're writing copy, that road map consists of a framework providing a clear beginning, middle, and end to the story. This is also known as "preview, view, and review," or the "Tell 'em what you're going to tell 'em, tell 'em, then tell 'em what you told 'em" rule. Exactly how to accomplish this in practical terms varies widely from story to story. A nonfactual lead written according to the guidelines we've discussed will serve as a preview for the story. In the jetliner example above, the lead makes it clear that we're about to hear a story about a missing jetliner. The body of the story should contain all the pertinent facts. Wrap up with a line that summarizes the current status of the story or looks ahead to what might happen next, such as:

> AUTHORITIES SAY THE SEARCH FOR THE MISSING JETLINER WILL CONTINUE THROUGH THE NIGHT.

Or,

IT'S NOT KNOWN WHETHER ANY OF THE MISSING PASSENGERS IS AMERICAN.

Or,

THE AIRLINE IS NOW IN THE PROCESS OF CONTACTING RELATIVES OF MISSING PASSENGERS.

Each of these sentences serves to reinforce the idea that the jetliner is missing and that concern about it is ongoing.

For a major story involving one or more **sidebars,** it's never a bad idea to write a copy story to run after the final sidebar summarizing and recapping the situation.

Narrative Storytelling

To know how to tell a story, *you must first know what the story is.* The basic definition of any story is simply this: It's something interesting, remarkable, or unusual that happened to somebody. Sounds simple enough, right? But casually glancing at or listening to many local newscasts will show that some reporters don't stop to define their stories before they sit down to write. The resulting product is confusing, incoherent, and unfocused. To prevent yourself from falling into this trap, ask yourself this simple question: What is the story *about?* If you can't answer that question *in one sentence,* you need to rethink your report and narrow the focus. In doing so, define the "something" that happened (the "What, When, Where, and Why") and the "someone" at the center of the story (the first "W," the "Who").

Usually, the best way to relate a story is to tell it the way it happened, in chronological order, preferably through the eyes of a central character (the "someone"). It's the same age-old style used in most fairy tales and novels. "Once upon a time there was a fair maiden who lived in the forest. And then yah da yah da yah da happened. And then they lived happily ever after." Narrative storytelling works because the events unfold in their natural order in a fashion that's easy to follow and comprehend. The challenges you face in your writing and the principles you'll use to approach them are not much different than what Charles Dickens, Mark Twain, or Margaret Mitchell faced. Your task, too, is to tell a story, to spin a yarn, to engage your customers in a narrative exercise that will leave them with a firm understanding of the events you're trying to relate *as if they had lived it themselves.*

But wait! When writing for TV, news directors, chief photographers, and some consultants will insist that the "best pictures should go first." Is this good advice? Not always. Putting the best pictures first doesn't always make the best story and can, in fact, make the story harder to follow. Here's an example. In the Tampa market one day all the TV stations were competing to cover a hostage situation. Two teens had broken into a house in which an elderly man lived. The police SWAT team surrounded the house. The police broke a window and threw in a telephone. The teens refused to negotiate. Eventually, police fired tear gas through the windows, broke down the door, stormed the house, and dragged the hostage takers out by their hair in full view of TV cameras. Later, police found the homeowner dead. Some reporters opened their stories in a very predictable way: They began with the dramatic video of police breaking down the door and storming the house. One reporter chose a different route. He began with video of the police surrounding the house. Then he told the story in narrative style, revealing a new fact with each sentence as it had actually occurred, allowing the drama to unfold for the viewer as it had unfolded in real life. The story won an Emmy award in spot news reporting that year. The judges found it clear and compelling. Chances are the viewers did, too.

But as with all rules, there are exceptions. Sometimes narrative storytelling principles conflict with other concerns. In most newsrooms, for instance, it's important for stories in the late evening newscast to begin with the freshest, most updated video. When such a conflict arises, go ahead and put the new pictures first, but then immediately cut to an earlier part of the story and pick it up from there in the proper chronological order. Here's an example:

(Open with natural sound, flames)

> THESE TOWERING FLAMES WERE A FIREFIGHTER'S NIGHTMARE. FOR HOURS THIS
> AFTERNOON . . . THE MEN AND WOMEN OF FIRE COMPANY 33 BATTLED THE
> RAGING FIRE. THEY BRAVED SEARING 120-DEGREE HEAT. BUT FAR MORE
> DANGEROUS THAN THAT . . . WAS THE SULFURIC ACID CONTAINED IN THE
> BURNING TANK TRUCK. THIS ORDEAL BEGAN FOUR HOURS EARLIER . . . AT THE
> U-SAVE GROCERY STORE ON BRUCE B DOWNS BOULEVARD. THAT'S WHERE TRUCK
> DRIVER MACK SIMPSON BLUNDERED INTO A HIGH-SPEED POLICE CHASE.

If you have to break from the chronology, try not to deviate from it more than once. Your viewers or listeners can probably handle one clearly defined flashback or flash-forward, but don't ask them to follow you through a whole series of them.

When writing your story, it's crucially important that you not only relate the events in chronological order, but also pick a strong central character. The best and most memorable stories are those told through the eyes of a person to whom we can all relate. In Chapter 9 about packages, we refer to this as the diamond approach. That's why in the bank robbery story outlined earlier in this chapter, passerby Otis Armstrong makes a good choice for the central character—what happened to him could have happened to any of us.

A final point about narrative storytelling: although the traditional "five W's" are very important, don't forget the "s"—the "so what?" Make sure your story contains context, perspective, and meaning. In the bank robbery, is the bank taking any extra steps to improve safety? How many other bank robberies have taken place at that branch? In that neighborhood? Are bank robberies on the rise? Are your deposits safe? Does your story show what the robbery means to the news consumer?

Write in Active Voice

As you may remember from Ms. Grundy's elementary school grammar class, a sentence is in active voice when the person or thing expressing an action is the subject of the sentence. It's in passive voice when the person or thing *receiving* the action is the subject of the sentence. There are several reasons why passive voice isn't well suited for news copy. For one, passive voice just doesn't sparkle. It's drab, stodgy, and usually cumbersome. Two or three back-to-back passive sentences can kill a story dead.

Which of the following examples sounds more crisp and memorable to you?

Example A

JOHN WAS SHOT BY FRED. FRED WAS QUICKLY ARRESTED BY POLICE. THE QUICK RESPONSE BY POLICE WAS PRAISED BY THE MAYOR.

Example B

FRED SHOT JOHN. POLICE QUICKLY ARRESTED HIM. THE MAYOR PUBLICLY THANKED THE OFFICERS FOR THEIR QUICK RESPONSE.

We hope you chose Example B. Use of passive voice can make copy sound dishwater dull. But the real sin of passive writing is that it makes your story more difficult to comprehend. Passive voice makes narrative storytelling technique difficult or impossible to carry out because it interferes with attempts to present the story in chronological order. It shows the target of the action before presenting the person or thing that initiated the action. We discover the result before seeing the cause, the exact opposite of the way it happened in real life. In our example of Fred doing evil to John, in real life the first thing that happens is that Fred acts, pulling the trigger, and then John falls with a gunshot wound. But if you write it in passive voice—"JOHN WAS

SHOT BY FRED"—then you're showing us the second action first (John being shot), the first action second (Fred pulling the trigger), and then trying to go back and piece it all together. It's confusing. Put enough passive sentences in your story and you'll make it an incomprehensible quagmire.

Finally, passive voice leads journalists to adopt lazy habits in pursuing the facts. It allows them to omit major information—such as who did it. For example, "JOHN WAS SHOT." Who did it? Maybe the reporter knows, maybe not. But if you write this sentence in the active voice, it's *not possible* for you ignore the "whodunit" question. You can write "Fred shot John" or even "Someone shot John," but it's impossible to write an active-voice sentence without some reference to the person or thing responsible for the action.

So how do you fix a passive sentence? The most common advice is to follow the classic "SVO" format: subject, verb, object. In an active voice sentence, the subject *always* will be the person or thing doing or expressing the action, and the object will be the person or thing *receiving* the action.

Perhaps an easier way to remember to put the "act" in "active voice" is through use of the acronym "ACT," as follows:

$$ACT = actor \rightarrow commission \rightarrow target$$

First, identify the "commission"—the verb you'll use to describe the action (what was committed) and write that down using the appropriate tense and conjugation. Next, identify the "actor"—the person or thing committing the action—and then write that to the left of the verb. Finally, identify the "target," the person or thing receiving the action (if there is one; not all active voice sentences must contain an object) and write that to the right of the verb. Using our example, the "commission" was a shooting. The actor who did it is Fred. The target of the action was John, whom the bullet hit. Actor = Fred. Commission = Shot. Target = John. Fred shot John.

It seems simple, but the challenge of converting a passive sentence to active stumps some people because in many passive sentences, *the actor is missing*. Consider the following passive sentence: "Thousands of dollars in bills and coins were dropped along a two-mile stretch of highway." To fix it, first thing you have to do is to identify the missing actor. In some cases this might require a little journalism, but usually it will be obvious. Suppose we know that an armored truck with a broken door dropped the money. The fix is easy: "The armored truck dropped thousands of dollars in bills and coins along a two-mile stretch of highway." Actor = truck. Commission = dropped. Target = thousands (of dollars). But what if we really don't know where the money came from? You have two choices. One, you can pick a "generic" actor, such as "someone" or "something." Or, you can abandon the sentence structure altogether and approach the statement from another angle, such as: "Sometime this morning, thousands of dollars in bills and coins appeared along a two-mile stretch of highway." The common denominator is that in every case we'll choose an actor and start our sentence or phrase with it.

Sensitivity

Let's face it: we live in a "politically correct" world. Most newsrooms have changed dramatically in recent years. Behavior that would get you canned today was common yesterday. We've all had to learn to be more sensitive in our personal and professional behavior, to think before we speak, and to filter copy for potential offensiveness before putting it on the air. Whatever your political views might be, this new sensitivity isn't a bad thing. If your copy makes a connection to 90 percent of your audience but alienates 10 percent of it because you've inadvertently offended someone, then it's 10 percent less effective than it should be. Why accept that, if you can reach more people by deleting offensive wording? It's certainly true that good journalism occasionally offends people, but here's a good rule of thumb: never offend anyone *by accident*. Make sure you're doing it on purpose and for a very good reason. On every other occasion, potentially offensive copy is simply an accidental roadblock to good communication.

Your own gut instinct, if you listen to it, will tell you about 75 percent of the time whether copy is offensive. The rest of the time, you must rely on feedback from co-workers and, most especially, from the public. Listen to what they have to say, and apply the New Golden Rule: Treat Others as They Want to Be Treated. Each case is different, of course. But to the extent that it's possible and practical for you to follow it, do so. Your copy will be that much more effective.

Basic Creative Techniques

You don't have to use a lot of creative writing techniques to write good copy for television or radio. In fact, normally you should be suspicious and wary of too much creativity. Colorful adjectives and flowery prose can, if not used properly, make a story sound contrived, hyped, and trite. Even so, some creative techniques, when used in moderation, can add to the story and make it more understandable and memorable.

Alliteration

Alliteration is the practice of taking a number of words beginning with the same consonant and grouping them together in the same sentence or phrase. For example:

POLICE ARE PLANNING TO PUT A PERSISTENT PURSE SNATCHER IN THE POKEY.

This technique has the virtue of making your sentence instantly memorable and even entertaining. The danger is that it's also a very easy technique to overdo and abuse. It's fairly safe to use with light stories but riskier with hard news. In either case use it with moderation.

Repetition

As a general rule, writers try to avoid using the same words again and again in close proximity. The idea is to find synonyms to keep the copy from sounding dull and unimaginative, which is why most writers keep a well-thumbed thesaurus close by. However, there is place for repetition. Good writers can use repetitive words, phrases, or patterns to drive home a concept or point. Typically this means constructing two or more successive sentences around the same word or phrase in a repetitive pattern.

Example 1

HE WAS ANGRY. HIS BEST FRIEND WAS ANGRY. IT SEEMED EVERYONE HE KNEW WAS ANGRY.

Example 2

FOR YEARS FRED JONES STUDIED WAR. HE LIVED WAR AND BREATHED WAR. BUT ON THIS DAY HE TURNED HIS BACK ON WAR FOREVER.

Example 3

JANE SMITH POUNDED THE PODIUM AND DEMANDED RESPECT. SHE POUNDED IT AGAIN AND DEMANDED JUSTICE. SHE RAISED HER FIST TO POUND IT A THIRD TIME, THEN TURNED AND LEFT WITHOUT ANOTHER WORD.

It's also possible to use repetitive patterns that don't involve repeating any particular word. To achieve the desired effect, the structure of both sentences must be similar.

Example 4

LAST YEAR HE WOULD HAVE PACED THE ROOM . . . WRINGING HIS HANDS IN PANIC AND SELF-DOUBT. BUT NOW HE SAT AT THE KEYBOARD, PUNCHING THE KEYS WITH CLARITY AND CONFIDENCE. COUNSELING AND THERAPY HAD MADE THE DIFFERENCE.

In the above example, notice how parts of the first sentence correspond to parts of the second, as follows:

Last year = But now

paced the room = sat at the keyboard

wringing his hands = punching the keys

in panic = with clarity

and self-doubt = and confidence

Parallel Writing with Wordplay

As you might remember from your high school English class, parallel form is the act of expressing two or more ideas by using phrases or sentences of similar construction. All four examples above are forms of parallel writing. Combine that concept with a little wordplay and you now have a creative technique that can help you get a point across in a more memorable fashion. For our purposes, then, parallel writing with wordplay is the act of linking two (or more) ideas in order to compare or contrast them, using a pun or a double meaning of one word to link them.

Example 1

IN IOWA . . . TEMPERS ARE RISING ALONG WITH THE WATERS.

This is a play off the word "rising," one verb used to place two very different but linked concepts into parallel: the act of land being flooded and people getting angry about it.

Example 2

THE SKYRISE APARTMENTS CAME WITH A SKY-HIGH COST TO THE ENVIRONMENT.

This is a play off the word "sky" or, more specifically, a play off the concept of "rising to the sky." Again, it places two very different but linked concepts into parallel: the act of building an apartment complex and the act of damaging the environment.

This technique isn't available or effective in every situation. The key is to look for two parallel actions that you can then link together with a common verb, phrase, or concept.

The Rule of Threes

The idea behind the Rule of Threes is that people remember ideas more easily if they're presented in groups of three. Examples abound in everyday conversation: "reading, writing, and 'rithmetic," "earth, wind, and fire," "Tom, Dick, and Harry," "wind, sea, and rain," "morning, noon, and night," "blood, sweat, and tears," to name a few.

The Rule of Threes is especially effective when used in conjunction with parallel writing. This involves using a group of three words or phrases to draw a comparison or contrast to a second group of three words or phrases. The danger is that this technique, like alliteration, is more difficult to bring off properly and more likely to sound contrived. When it works right, however, it can be effective. For example:

DONALD SMITH SWEARS HE BEGAN HIS DAY LIKE ANY OTHER. HE CLAIMS HE WOKE UP . . . SHAVED . . . AND HEADED OFF TO WORK. BUT THE F-B-I TELLS IT DIFFERENTLY. IT CLAIMS HE WOKE UP . . . PUT ON A FAKE BEARD . . . AND HEADED OFF TO ROB A BANK.

(Rule of Threes: waking, shaving, and heading off.)

INSTEAD OF SPENDING THEIR DAY IN SCHOOL LEARNING READING . . . WRITING . . . AND 'RITHMETIC . . . POLICE SAY THESE GANG MEMBERS SPENT IT IN A CAR RIDING . . . RACING . . . AND ROBBING.

(Combines alliteration and parallels three expected activities with three unexpected ones.)

Simile

A simile is the technique of comparing one thing to another, typically using the words "like" or "as."

Example 1

THE TORNADO TOSSED THE CARS AROUND LIKE TONKA TOYS.

Example 2

THE BOLT HIT WITH A BLAST AS LOUD AS A CANNON.

Metaphorical Writing

This is the technique of using a physical situation, thing, or activity to symbolically describe something else. A metaphor takes a comparison further than a simile does, by presenting one concept in terms of another.

Example 1

THE ATTORNEY GENERAL SAYS THE PONZEE MINING COMPANY WAS INDEED DIGGING FOR GOLD . . . BUT IN THE WRONG PLACE . . . THE POCKETBOOKS OF ITS INVESTORS.

Example 2

THE COMPANY NEVER FINISHED THE POOL. AND THE DARINS WEREN'T THE ONLY FAMILY TO GET SOAKED. THE A-G SAYS NOT ONE OF THE FIRM'S DOZEN OR SO CONTRACTS HELD WATER.

The root of most creativity is simple word association. When writing, take a minute to throw out all words and phrases you think are associated with the principal activity involved in the story. In Example 1 above, the subject is a mining company; "digging for gold" is one of many concepts one might expect to associate with that particular activity (so is "the shaft," but let's not get carried away). Similarly, in Example 2 the concepts of "holding water" and "getting soaked" are easy associations with the words "pool" and "water."

Exaggeration

This is known in literary circles as "hyperbole." A bit of well-placed exaggeration serves to paint your subject in vivid and therefore more memorable terms. This is another one that's easy to overdo; be judicious. It works best with kickers. Examples: "Roach the size of a Rolls Royce"; "Killer rabbit"; "Kamikaze pelican."

Human Terms

Stories dealing with large numbers often get lost on the average listener or viewer simply because he or she can't relate to them. It's your challenge to translate those numbers into terms people can understand. This might take a little quick arithmetic on your part, but the results are well worth it. For instance, suppose you're doing a story about oil exports and find that the gasoline usage has gone down by a million gallons a year. What does one gallon of gasoline mean to you personally? How much gasoline do you burn each week? About 20 gallons? At that rate it would take you 50,000 weeks to burn a million gallons—that's 962 years! Now you get the picture—and you can put it in just those terms for the viewer or listener:

> IF YOU BURN ABOUT 20 GALLONS OF GASOLINE A WEEK . . . A MILLION
> GALLONS WOULD LAST YOU 962 YEARS.

Personification

Personification is the technique of assigning human attributes or actions to things or concepts that aren't human. Examples: "Winter's icy breath," "hand of fate," "nature smiled," and so forth. Be *very* careful with this one. Many of the common uses deriving from this technique are so shopworn that they've passed into the land of the hoary cliché.

Exercise

At this point, we're going to use some of the principles outlined above to take apart and fix a poorly written story.

Here's an example of how not to write:

AN APPARENT ONE-CAR ACCIDENT HAS CLAIMED THE LIFE OF A LOCAL MAN.
POLICE SAY FOR SOME REASON A RED 1987 FORD TAURUS DRIVEN BY 38-YEAR-
OLD JOHN SMITH OF 1237 GONER ROAD IN TUCSON WENT OUT OF CONTROL ON
PRESTON LANE . . . FLIPPED . . . ROLLED DOWN AN EMBANKMENT . . . AND
LANDED UPSIDE DOWN IN A DRAINAGE DITCH FILLED WITH WATER FROM LAST
NIGHT'S STORMS. APPARENTLY THE DRIVER WASN'T KILLED BY THE IMPACT BUT
RATHER DROWNED AFTER BEING TRAPPED IN THE WRECKAGE. IT HAPPENED
ABOUT SIX THIS MORNING. THE WRECK WAS WITNESSED BY ANOTHER MOTORIST.
THE CAUSE OF THE MISHAP IS BEING INVESTIGATED BY POLICE.

The second sentence alone is so filled with facts, adjectives, and dependent clauses that in one breath, the writer is telling the viewer: where the facts came from (attribution); the name of the driver; the age of the driver; the driver's home town; the driver's address; the make of the vehicle involved; the model of the vehicle involved; the year of manufacture of the vehicle involved; the color of the vehicle involved; the name of the street involved; that police don't know the cause of the accident; that the car flipped and rolled; that it landed in a drainage ditch; that it landed upside down; that the ditch was full of water; and that it rained last night. That's 16 facts in one sentence!

And excessive length isn't this sentence's only sin. It also begins and ends in passive voice. In grammatical terms, the subject of this sentence is the 1987 Ford Taurus, but in fact the subject of the story is John Smith, and the story is about how our subject met his untimely end. Because the subject of the sentence doesn't match the subject of the story, the viewer is hard-pressed to figure out which is which, and thus finds it harder to understand what's going on.

Though this copy is technically accurate and grammatically correct, its style is atrocious. Yet copy just like it airs on TV and radio stations every day (this was taken from an actual example of a story that aired). How can we fix it?

For one thing, the second sentence is so loaded with facts that it can be broken up into an entire paragraph, and that's what you should set out to do. Each major fact should get its own separate sentence, rather than the writer attempting to convey several major facts in a single sentence.

Again, apply the Mom Rule. How would you relate this story if you were telling it to her? Chances are you'd say something like, "Hey, did you hear about the guy who ran off the road into a drainage ditch last night and drowned?" Why would you start that way? Because the fate of a guy who died unexpectedly while doing nothing more offensive than driving down the road is the single most interesting and memorable aspect of the story. It's something that could have happened to anybody—which happens to be precisely what makes this story newsworthy. The lead to your story therefore should accomplish the same purpose as the opening gambit to your conversation with Mom.

After you capture your mom's attention with that opening line, chances are she'd respond with a question like "No! What happened?" At this point, you'd likely continue your story, starting at the beginning and continuing in chronological order until you reach the end of your story—the outcome of which you've already revealed in your opening remark. Your news copy has to accomplish essentially the same thing. Here's one way to do it, applying the above rules:

LAST NIGHT'S STORMS ARE PARTIALLY TO BLAME FOR A TRAFFIC DEATH THIS MORNING. A TUCSON MAN DROWNED WHEN HIS CAR RAN OFF THE ROAD INTO A FLOODED DITCH. IT HAPPENED ABOUT SIX THIS MORNING ON PRESTON LANE. ACCORDING TO POLICE . . . THE CAR WENT OUT OF CONTROL . . . RAN OFF THE ROAD . . . FLIPPED . . . AND ROLLED. IT LANDED UPSIDE DOWN IN A DRAINAGE DITCH STILL FILLED WITH RUNOFF FROM LAST NIGHT'S THUNDERSTORMS. THE DRIVER DROWNED. ANOTHER MOTORIST SAW THE WHOLE THING HAPPEN . . . BUT THE CAUSE OF THE CRASH REMAINS A MYSTERY. POLICE HAVE IDENTIFIED THE VICTIM. HE'S 38-YEAR-OLD JOHN SMITH OF 1237 GONER ROAD IN TUCSON.

This particular version of the story has most of the facts of the first. The sentences are short and conversational, and each contains a smaller number of facts. Everything is written in active voice, with action following the subject rather than vice versa. Note that it doesn't contain many of the creative techniques outlined earlier; they aren't necessary in this instance. The story is much easier to understand in one take than the previous version was, and its style much more closely matches the form a two-sided conversation about the same event would likely take.

Conclusion

The single most important point to remember in writing a lead for a broadcast audience is that you must capture the attention of your viewers or listeners on the first attempt. To do this your leads must be conversational, fresh, and must capture the essence of the story. The most effective tools in your box are short, declarative, active-voice sentences and a narrative storytelling style. Consider using creative techniques to make your copy memorable and effective, but remember that the goal of your copy is clarity and brevity, not creativity. *Don't overdo it.*

 DOs and DON'Ts for Writing Leads and Other Copy

Do
- Write a fresh, updated lead.
- "Sell" the story.
- Use preview and review.
- Use the "Mom Rule."
- Make stories relevant to listeners and viewers; remember WII-FM.

Don't
- Write a stale, dated lead.
- Start writing until you decide what the story is about.
- Put too many facts in a lead.
- Write in "TV speak."
- Break from chronology more than once.

DEADLY COPY SINS AND HOW TO AVOID THEM

Four Words That Kill Good Broadcast Copy

"Allegedly"

Question: When is it safe to "call names" on the air?

Answer: Hardly ever. Not even if you say "allegedly." On-air name calling is what funds Caribbean vacations for libel lawyers.

The words "alleged" and "allegedly" are the single most abused and misused words in television. Why? Because too many writers believe the words stand as shields protecting them from litigation and freeing them to make statements they couldn't otherwise make. Unfortunately, this feeling of protection is a delusion. According to Gregg Thomas, a First Amendment lawyer with the prestigious firm of Holland and Knight, the word "has no value." Thomas says reporters who liberally sprinkle the word "allegedly" into their copy are practicing "condom journalism." "The word

is vastly overused," he says, "because somebody feels it has some pro-
phylactic effect" and allows writers to "avoid responsibility for making a declarative statement." But the word doesn't impress judges or
juries. "It offers no protection whatsoever," Thomas says.

Name-calling is one area in which writing in a conversational
style—the way people really talk—can get you into serious trouble.
Why? Because when it comes to general conversations about figures
arrested, charged, or convicted of heinous crimes, members of the public tend to assume the person involved is guilty and speak about him
or her accordingly. As a journalist, you don't have that option—not
even if you couch your name-calling with the word "allegedly" or its
cousins.

Example

Let's say you're writing a story about a high-profile child molestation
case in which the defendant, John Doe, to the surprise of many, was
able to come up with enough cash to make bail. A casual conversation
with Mom about this incident might go something like this:

CAN YOU BELIEVE IT? THAT CHILD MOLESTER GOT OUT!

A casual conversation with close friends might be even more direct:

CAN YOU BELIEVE IT? THAT DIRTBAG DOE GOT OUT!

As you sit down to write your own lead, you're faced with a problem. One, you want to write in the same conversational style, but you
realize (we hope) that you can't use the word "dirtbag" or any like it.
Also, you want to be careful not to convict the defendant on the air. So,
you write something like this:

JOHN DOE . . . THE ALLEGED CHILD MOLESTER . . . IS OUT OF JAIL.

There are several problems. One, the sentence isn't conversational;
aside from professional journalists, few people use the word "alleged"
in casual conversation. Two, it's sleazy; in this sentence, through use of
the word "alleged," we're calling Doe a really ugly name without attribution, without allowing him to face his accusers. Three, what if Doe
didn't do it? If your facts aren't straight, the word "alleged" will give
you about as much protection as an umbrella in a hurricane. Because
you didn't make an attribution, a jury is more likely to decide that you
were simply careless with the facts—and jurors might even attribute
the accusation to you *personally.*

The problem is that whenever you call some specific individual a
name—such as "criminal," "killer," "child molester," "embezzler," and
the like—essentially you're drawing a conclusion. If the facts over-

whelmingly support that conclusion, then you're probably safe. But if the facts are at all in dispute—as they almost always are in criminal cases—then that's another matter.

There's another problem with the word "allegedly." It's a lazy person's word that cheats the audience of details. It's a shortcut around the facts. Strike the word, and insert the facts. Let's take the case of John Doe, the alleged child molester, and the example lead "JOHN DOE, THE ALLEGED CHILD MOLESTER, IS OUT OF JAIL TODAY."

Which of the following conclusions can we comfortably and safely draw from that sentence?

1 The defendant's name is John Doe.
2 John Doe got out of jail today.
3 Police have charged Doe—or, at very least, have charged him in the past—with molesting at least one child.

Answer

Only 1 and 2. If you also drew conclusion number 3, you're not alone. Probably a good portion of the audience would have drawn the same conclusion. However, that conclusion can't be drawn from the lead as presented, and it's a good example of why the words "allege" and "allegedly" are so dangerous. The lead doesn't make plain who's making the allegations or give any hint as to how strong the case might be. Who says Doe is a child molester? Police? His neighbors? Sidewalk graffiti? From the lead presented above, any of the following could be true:

- The DA's office brought the charges; it's a strong case, and prosecutors are angry Doe is out.
- An individual police officer made the arrest and filled out a complaint, but the DA hasn't had a chance to study the paperwork and has no idea whether there's a case.
- Doe's next-door neighbor made the complaint and swore out a warrant for Doe's arrest, but the DA hasn't yet been able to substantiate her allegation.
- Doe is under indictment.
- Doe isn't under indictment; the grand jury hasn't heard the case yet.
- The DA privately believes there's no case and told the magistrate that he or she wouldn't be opposed to letting Doe out on bond and, in fact, plans to drop the charges after the publicity dies down.

If police have indeed charged Doe with the crime of molestation, then you're safe. But if not, then you're potentially in trouble. Even if police haven't charged Doe, you might get away with the above copy—for one story. But what happens when the 11 P.M. producer rewrites your copy for his or her newscast? He or she might draw a false conclusion from the sloppy copy you wrote. Thus you might get a lead story for 11 P.M. reading, "JOHN DOE . . . A MAN POLICE SAY IS A CHILD MOLESTER . . . IS FREE TONIGHT." This sentence is now completely divorced from the truth, and you and your employer are in trouble.

Here's another way to look at it. As mentioned, your job is to write to the facts. Take this sentence: "DOE ALLEGEDLY MOLESTED A THREE-YEAR-OLD GIRL WHO LIVES NEXT DOOR." Which fact are you trying to present here? That Doe did it? Or that someone says he did? Unless you were there personally, you can't say whether Doe did it. Therefore, you can only say that someone *says* he did. Your story, then, is about the *allegation*, not about the act of molestation. Let me say it again: you're writing about an accusation, not a crime. This is a crucially important point, and it's paramount that you remember it to clarify your thinking and writing about the matter. The molestation is, for all you know, fictional. Stick to the facts, and the fact is that someone is accusing John Doe of molesting someone. Don't structure your sentence as if Doe actually did it, with only the word "allegedly" making the difference between an accusation and an on-air conviction. Structure your sentence and story around the accusation itself. Tell us who's making the accusation, then delve as much as you can into the quality and soundness of that accusation. Bring out the players: tell us who they are, what they have to say, and how likely they are to be telling the truth. Forget the words "alleged" and "allegedly." Tell the audience what you know, with specific attribution: "SEVEN NEIGHBORS ACCUSED HIM OF MOLESTING THEIR CHILDREN. BUT TONIGHT JOHN DOE IS A FREE MAN."

Dropping the word "allegedly" will accomplish three very important goals. First, it will force you to write a much more clear, concise story. Second, your story will be much more conversational in style and therefore more understandable and memorable. And last, but certainly not least, it will stick to the facts and therefore be true. As any lawyer will tell you, the only *absolute* defense in a libel case is the truth. By taking a little extra time to present the facts, you'll be doing a better job with your audience and you will be less likely to get into trouble. The word "allegedly" stands in the way and serves no purpose. Lose it.

The threat of legal action shouldn't be your only motivation for dropping the word "allegedly." Regardless of whether you get sued, the abuses this word invites simply aren't fair to the person named. The Sixth Amendment of the U.S. Constitution gives every person the right to face his or her accuser. Journalists sometimes short-circuit the spirit of the law by hiding behind the word "allegedly." Drop the word. Come out from behind cover. Spell out who the accusers are with specific attribution. It's the fair and socially responsible thing to do.

If none of the above arguments convinces you, consider this point: As a beginning producer or reporter, you're much more likely to land a job and advance up the career ladder if your résumé reel doesn't contain eight uses of the nonconversational word "allegedly" within one 90-second period (which, so far, stands as a record among tapes I've reviewed personally).

"Suspects"

If "alleged" is the single most abused word, then "suspects" has to be a close second. A suspect is a specific, *named* individual who is charged, jailed, or wanted in connection with a specific act. There is no such thing as an "unknown suspect." It's an oxymoron, a self-contradictory phrase describing something that doesn't exist. For a person to be a suspect, police or investigators have to know who he or she is. They must have a specific name in mind or on paper.

If someone holds up a bank but police have no idea who the person is, you can refer to the perpetrator as a man, woman, bandit, robber, gunman, gunwoman, street person, or whatever (but please don't use the word "perpetrator"—see the DOs and DON'Ts at the end of this chapter). Note that in this case you *can* use red-letter, name-calling words such as "bandit" and "robber"; you're not calling anyone names on the air because *you haven't named anyone.* But if the robber is unknown, you can't refer to him or her as a suspect. The reason is simple: if police don't yet suspect anyone, then there are no suspects!

You're not convicting anyone on the air if you write words like "WITNESSES SAY THE GUNMAN FIRED TWO SHOTS . . . KILLING THE VICTIM INSTANTLY," even if police have named a suspect. But you can't substitute the word "SUSPECT" for "GUNMAN" without careful and proper attribution. If there's a dead body with a bullet hole in it, and if it was a case of murder, then there was a gunman, and you can write about him and even speculate about him. What the gunman did or didn't do isn't the dispute in this case. The dispute, and the issue to be addressed in court, is whether the suspect was the gunman.

Bottom line: if there was a crime, then there was a bad guy. You can write about him generically and call him any names you want, provided of course that your story is factual. Where you have to be extremely cautious is when you begin saying that a *specific individual* was the bad guy. "Bandit," "robber," "killer," and the like are generic terms not describing any specific individual. "Suspect" is a specific term describing a specific individual, an individual who has rights and, presumably, a lawyer just aching to sue you. But if the specific individual is unknown, then there is no suspect.

Thus you can't write a sentence such as "THE SUSPECT IS ON THE LOOSE" if police have no idea who the bad guy is. Instead, you have to write "THE BANDIT IS ON THE LOOSE."

Conversely, you can write "THE SUSPECT IS IN JAIL." But you can't write "THE BANDIT IS IN JAIL" unless you've never been sued and are curious to see what it's like.

A final point about attribution. The only truly safe stories are those that attribute the facts and accusations to an official source, such as police officers, fire officials, or prosecutors. In 49 of 50 states (South Carolina being the only exception) journalists have a qualified privilege to quote government officials and official documents. Generally speaking, you can't be sued for reporting what a police officer or prosecutor says, even if it later turns out the official was wrong or even lying. But the further you get away from official sources, the more dangerous the game becomes. Handle witness accounts very carefully when reporting accusations against individuals. In libel terms, *their* speech is *your* speech. If a witness makes an untrue libelous statement, *you* are liable and can be sued.

"Apparently"

Consider the following sentence:

APPARENTLY SMITH LOST CONTROL OF HIS CAR . . . WHICH RAN INTO A DITCH.

The only thing apparent here is that the writer doesn't have a clue what really happened. Did the steering fail? Did the driver swerve to avoid a moose? Was it a mob hit staged to look like an accident? Did the driver commit suicide? Who knows? The only thing we know for sure is that we don't know. In this case, the writer is using the word "apparently" to camouflage the fact that he or she has no facts and is just making a guess about what really happened.

Remember, it *is permissible* not to have the answers. In such cases, 'fess up. Tell the viewers or listeners you don't know. Explain what you do know, and outline the current speculation about what might have happened. Here's a fix of the above sentence using these guidelines:

THE CAR RAN OFF THE ROAD AND CRASHED IN A DITCH. BECAUSE ROAD CONDITIONS WERE DRY . . . POLICE ARE AT A LOSS TO EXPLAIN IT.

Or,

THE ROAD WAS DRY AT THE TIME. POLICE ARE NOW CHECKING TO SEE WHETHER THE CAR'S STEERING FAILED.

There *are* some perfectly acceptable uses of the word "apparent" and its derivatives. It's OK to use the word, for instance, to introduce a speculative conclusion, provided the conclusion is supported by the facts. For example:

IT APPEARS LETTUCE MIGHT SOON COST YOU A BIT MORE. WHOLESALE PRICES HIT AN ALL-TIME HIGH FOR THE SECOND WEEK IN A ROW TODAY. THE NUMBER CRUNCHERS SAY IF THAT TREND CONTINUES . . . IT WILL SHOW UP AT THE GROCERY COUNTER SOONER OR LATER.

"Undetermined"

The fourth most worthless word in television is the word "undetermined" in connection with a bank robbery or other theft. One, it's not conversational. When was the last time you turned to someone and said, "The robber got away with an undetermined amount of cash?"

Two, it's not factual—or at least, it's not always factual—and it leaves the viewer with a false assumption that the amount of money missing will be determined. Guess what, folks. Often they know *exactly* how much money the bandit got away with, for the simple reason that he probably has a "bait bag" with a dye bomb inside it and a well-known amount of bait cash. If they don't know, they'll find out very quickly. But believe this: *They might never tell you how much cash the bandit got.* There's a very simple reason for this, and it's a good one: revealing the amount of cash the bandit took is the worst form of advertising for the bank. The bandit might have escaped with a nice wad of cash. If the bank reveals the amount, it's essentially throwing out a challenge for other robbers to try to match or surpass the previous robber's haul.

As a matter of policy involving the public's safety, it makes sense for newsrooms to support this concept of not revealing the amount taken in bank robberies and other armed robberies. The exceptions are cases in which the robber got very little, or a whole lot, such as Brinks holdups running into the millions, in which case the amount taken will be well publicized.

Therefore, drop the word "undetermined." It adds nothing and isn't conversational. If you believe it's crucial to make some reference to the cash amount—and there's some indication that (1) the amount is relevant, (2) police really don't know how much was taken and are trying to find out, and (3) they're going to share this information with you—then you should write specifically to that point. For example:

POLICE DON'T KNOW HOW MUCH CASH THE BANDIT GOT . . . BUT THEY DON'T THINK IT'S MUCH. THE BANK IS COUNTING ITS LOSSES AND HOPES TO HAVE THE ANSWER BY TONIGHT.

Summary—Example of a Completely Worthless Sentence

THE UNKNOWN SUSPECT ALLEGEDLY POINTED A GUN AT THE TELLER . . . DEMANDED MONEY . . . AND APPARENTLY ESCAPED WITH AN UNDETERMINED AMOUNT OF CASH.

Miscellaneous DOs and DON'Ts for Writers

Many of these points have been made elsewhere, but we present them here in bullet form to emphasize their importance.

Do

- Do make frequent use of synonyms.
- Do make frequent use of time-specific references, such as "this morning," "this afternoon," "tonight."
- Do make frequent use of "you" inclusive words, such as "you," "us," "we."
- Do introduce the people you're interviewing. Don't rely on a super to do it for you. Hint: you don't necessarily have to give the person's proper name as long as you give us some indication of what relevance he or she has to the story. For example: "SOME RESIDENTS FEEL THE MURDER WAS JUSTIFIED" is a perfectly fine introduction to a bite with a neighbor. If you do use both the person's proper name and his or her title in your track, it's important to put the person's relevance to the story first. So give the title first, then the name.
- Do use good grammar when referencing groups. Many people confuse singular and plural when referencing a group with a pronoun. In the form of English spoken in the United States, collective nouns take the singular. So when writing for a U.S. news audience, a group is an "it," not a "they." For example: "THE UNION SAYS THEY'RE GOING TO STRIKE" isn't correct. Make it "THE UNION SAYS IT WILL STRIKE."
- Do write in active voice.
- Do make sure your words support the video, and vice versa.

Don't

- Don't begin successive sentences with the same word or words if it can be avoided—unless you're using repetition as a creative technique. Otherwise, your copy might sound dull and uninspiring.
- For the same reason, don't use the same word to describe an object again and again in close proximity.
- Don't obsess about either of the above tips. Sometimes a fire is just a fire, even on second reference, and not a blaze, conflagration, or inferno.

- Don't use clichés (such as "up in arms," "packing winds," and the like). There are exceptions. Sometimes, the cliché can serve a higher purpose, such as setting up a wordplay. For example: "RESIDENTS ARE UP IN ARMS ABOUT A CONTRACTOR UP TO NO GOOD." Sometimes you can turn a cliché around to your own purposes, in essence making fun of it. For example: "Crunching the scales" as a derivative of the cliché "tipping the scales."

- Don't use "police blotter" terms, such as "perpetrator," "at large," and the like. They're not conversational and will hamper your efforts to connect with your viewer. Plus, they'll make you sound like Dick Tracy.

- Although there are few "nevers" in this business, here's a safe one: never, ever, ever refer to a criminal or suspected criminal as a "gentleman" as a substitute for "the man." For example: "WITNESSES SAY THE GENTLEMAN KILLED THREE SCHOOL CHILDREN AT RANDOM . . . THEN FLED." Most references of this nature that wind up on the air are done live, off the cuff. Avoid this. If, on the other hand, the gunman was well-dressed, then devote a separate sentence to that fact. Don't call him a gentleman! His actions give lie to your words. Or worse than that, it sounds as though you're sympathizing with him.

- Don't present a confusing mishmash of pronouns without clear antecedents. When you use the words "he," "she," "it," "him," "her," "they," and so forth, make sure we know who you're talking about. For example: "LAST NIGHT . . . JOHN SMITH ATTACKED THE MAYOR'S CREDIBILITY. TONIGHT HE'S TAKING HIS CASE TO THE PUBLIC." Who's taking his case to the public? Smith? Or the mayor?

- Don't leave out the verb! For example: "QUESTIONS IN THE BAY AREA CONCERNING MISCONDUCT." This isn't a sentence, much less a lead. There are occasions when sentence fragments such as this one can work—provided that's the way someone would really talk. This isn't one of them. When in doubt, put in a verb.

- Don't put the allegation ahead of the attribution. For example: "ALL POLITICIANS ARE JERKS. SO SAYS BILL SMITH OF THE CITIZENS' GROUP 'TAX WATCHDOGS.'" For a split second, the anchor reading this sentence appears to the audience to be the one with the bad opinion of politicians. Don't place him or her in that precarious position.

- Don't make careless generalizations. For example: "RESIDENTS OF HUDSON BAY ARE SHOCKED ABOUT THE MURDER OF AN ELDERLY WOMAN." For all you know, she might have been a witch and they're all dancing on her grave. Unless you've talked to each and every resident, this sentence is a dangerous and possibly untrue generalization. On the other hand, if you or a colleague has talked to some shocked residents, then you can comfortably write, "THE MURDER OF AN ELDERLY WOMAN HAS SHOCKED A LOT OF PEOPLE IN HUDSON BAY."
- Don't use "TV speak." (See the extensive discussion about this subject in Chapter 3.)
- Don't begin a lead or any other sentence with a dependent clause. For example: "HIS HAIR HAVING BURST INTO FLAME, FRED BEGAN BOBBING FOR APPLES WITH NEW ENTHUSIASM."
- When using graphics, don't put words on-screen not supported in your copy.

INTERVIEWING: GETTING THE FACTS AND THE FEELINGS

Interviewing members of your community, important people visiting your community, or newsmakers you travel to visit is a vital part of the broadcast writing and reporting process. Interviews provide background information for your story, and they provide **sound bites** for your package or VO/SOT, or the radio equivalent of those television news story forms. It's important to remember that one of the unique strengths of broadcast news is its ability to transmit the experience of what happens at the scene of an event to members of your audience. The people you interview and what they say are key parts of that process.

New York City reporters who covered the 9/11 attacks against America were gratified and astonished that, in the face of such uncertainty and destruction, most people the reporters approached agreed to be interviewed about what they had just experienced. Kerry Nolan, who reports for WNYC Radio, remembers, "A triage unit had been set up right down the street from me, and I was talking to people and watching them come off these boats just covered in ash and shell-shocked." Her colleague Amy Eddings recalls, "I started interviewing people, asking, 'What did you see? What do you know?'"[1]

Interviews are essentially conversations with members of your community or those who have something to say that your viewers or listeners would find important or interesting. And when your story is broadcast, you share those conversations with your audience. So you want to let the people you interview tell about what's happening. Let them tell the story themselves from their point of view, to the degree they can. You want to let their personalities come through so that people watching or listening will feel something for them. The average person wasn't at the scene of the story and doesn't know what happened. Through your interviews, you can take the viewers or listeners to the scene to experience what happened and understand it through the words of those who were there.

The people you interview are the people whose voices will be heard in your newscast. So remember to talk and listen to a diversity of "regular" people in your community. Don't rely entirely on the experts, the officials, the usual voices. As a reporter, you can give voice to the voiceless in your community by interviewing them for your stories.

Those you choose to interview and the tone you take when you interview them will also contribute to the image your audience will have of you as a reporter and of your station as a local business. It's often the case, particularly with beginning reporters in smaller markets, that the reporters are young, single, from someplace else, and looking to move on to a larger market as soon as possible. This is the opposite of what's true of many of the members of the viewing or listening audience, who tend to be older, married with children and a mortgage, born in the community, and planning to stay in this town that's their home and workplace. So stop and think and ask who's in your audience, what their lives are like, and what their concerns and interests are.

There are several steps to take to get yourself ready to conduct an interview and to do the interview itself. These are discussed in the following sections.

Thinking Ahead

When you're thinking about which people to interview, ask yourself: "How do I make this story real for my viewers and listeners? How do I make a difference in my community? And how do I tell this story

---

1. See Judith Sylvester and Suzanne Huffman (2002), *Women Journalists at Ground Zero: Covering Crisis,* Lanham, MD: Rowman & Littlefield.

clearly and in a compelling way?" You don't want to get in an interviewing rut, going to the same experts and officials time after time, although this is easy and quick and sometimes unavoidable. Take some time to be thoughtful and creative in choosing whom to interview. Some interview subjects are given to you, not chosen, as in news conferences and emergency situations. But other situations offer you more opportunities to choose from among a broad spectrum of people.

If water rates are going up, you might think in terms of interviewing the people who come to the window at city hall to pay their bills, or the person who receives the water bill payments at the window, or the person who answers the phone and listens to comments from local residents about the rate increase. You might ask that person what people are saying to her when they pay their water bills. If the story is about the economy, you might first ask your neighbors and colleagues, "Do you know anybody who's out of work, who's been laid off, or who's looking for work?" People who are out of a job and looking for work will have firsthand knowledge about the state of the economy as it affects their lives. These individuals can add depth, perspective, and context to your story, which "official sources" may not be able to provide.

Interviews with affected individuals "humanize" your stories. For example, if the welfare allowance for a woman with two children is raised from $188 a month to $201 a month, a mother of two can put a human face on the story by telling you what $13 more a month will buy.

Being Prepared

You want to prepare for your interview by learning as much as possible about your subject in advance. That means research. Read what you can about the subject so that you'll be familiar with it. Ask other people in your newsroom and station what's important to ask about the subject. Brainstorm with them, to the extent that time constraints allow. The person you'll spend the most time with on any given TV story is your photographer. He or she can help you prepare by suggesting questions and offering perspective. Talk with your photographer as you plan each story, and work together as a team.

You want to have some idea what you're going to ask and in what order before you go out on a story. Prepare at least a few questions, and write them down to use as a memory jog if you get nervous or draw a blank. You don't want to be "married" to these questions and follow them blindly in spite of what the interviewee says, but you do want to have a focus beforehand for your story. Too often, students and young professionals go into an interview with a list of questions and essentially read them to their interviewees. When that happens, it *isn't* a conversation. But a list can be helpful, because you don't want to be fishing around and asking questions about everything in the hope of getting a usable sound bite. Interviews have a dual purpose. They're a way for the reporter or writer to gather information, and they're a way to gather usable sound bites. Do the information-gathering part of the interview off-camera and the sound bite–gathering part on-camera.

In the information-gathering part of the interview, what people tell you provides details and even language you can use in your story. NBC correspondent Bob Dotson was one of the many reporters who covered the Union, South Carolina, story about Susan Smith, who drove her car into a lake with her two young sons strapped into the back seat. One of the recovery divers told Dotson that the first thing the diver saw in the submerged car was "a tiny hand pressed against glass." Dotson used that detail and those words at the top of his report.

When you're writing your TV news package or radio wrap, you'll be weaving together the words in your narration track with natural sound and with sound bites (and video in the case of television) you've gathered in the field. So the writing for your story actually begins in the field as the interviews and natural sound are being recorded. Before you go out into the field, you want to be prepared and know your subject so that you'll know what you're talking about and asking about.

If your interview is part of a spot news story, and there's no time to prepare, you'll be drawing on the base of knowledge you've accumulated from reading your local newspaper, reading news magazines and books, surfing the Internet, meeting people in your community, and keeping up with their topics of concern and conversation. So always pay attention to what's in the news, and pay attention to what the controversies and disagreements and issues are within your community. These are daily habits you want to cultivate. They'll serve you well over time. Remember, in situations such as the 9/11 terrorist attacks, reporters have no time to prepare—just react.

Interviewing is equal parts art, craft, and science. And the first question you ask can dictate the entire experience. If people are offended by what you ask them or by the tone in which you ask it, it will color the whole interview. If people feel they know and can trust you, things will go more smoothly. So, people skills are essential. Tell the person up front who you are, which station you represent, and what you're doing. For example, "I'm Jane Smith from Channel 2. We're doing a story about the heat. We'd like to talk with you about how it's affecting your company, family, business, health"—whatever the focus of your story is. Don't tell the interviewee beforehand what the specific questions will be. That leads to rehearsed answers. Just tell him or her the topic of the questions. Use a professional and conversational tone of voice.

You must also remember to ask questions that can be answered, and that can be answered with something *other* than yes or no. What made the Chris Farley interview skits on "Saturday Night Live" so hilarious was Farley's own bumbling, nervous attempt at being an interviewer. He would ask long rambling "do you remember when" questions. All his interviewees could answer was yes or no. We learn nothing from such interviews.

Knowing the Mechanics of Interviewing

Remember to look straight in the eyes of the person you're interviewing and maintain eye contact with him or her. Strong eye contact seems to help divert the person's attention away from the equipment, which makes for a less nervous interviewee. Don't fidget with your notes or with your hair or wave the microphone around. When possible, use a clip-on microphone. When interviewing for TV, ask the person you're interviewing to look at you, not at the camera. Your back will be to the photographer, who will get a shot over your shoulder of the interviewee's face. Stand very close to the camera. Never chew gum.

The microphone should point toward the interviewee and be about six inches below his or her mouth in normal situations. In a situation in which there's loud ambient noise, such as a cheering crowd at a football game, put the microphone closer. (Clip-on mics don't work well in these situations.) As you ask your questions, point the mic at yourself and record your own questions because you might want to use them in the edited piece. However, be sure to have the mic directed at the interviewee for all of his or her comments. If the mic is moving back toward the interviewee as he or she begins to answer, the audio might not be usable.

As often as possible, conduct the interview at the scene of the event or in the setting of the story, whether in a factory or a classroom or an orange grove. Be sure to find out your interviewee's full name, how to spell it, and how to pronounce it correctly. Write down his or her phone number in case you need to call back later. If the person is an "official," get a title.

In the interview itself, you want to be direct, clear, straightforward, empathetic, and respectful. You want to be frank, sincere, and courteous. You want to ask precise, specific questions, one at a time. You want to show interest in what the person is saying by looking directly at him or her. And you want to actively listen to what the person is saying to you. That's the only way you can come up with logical follow-up questions. In many ways, this kind of active listening is really watching, for you must pay attention to any nods of the head, frowns, clenching of

Reporter Steve Andrews and photojournalist Gordon Dempsey of WFLA-TV in Tampa, FL conduct an interview.

the teeth, or tightening of the facial muscles that may tell more about the interviewee's true reactions than what he or she is saying to you. Also keep in mind that people sometimes lie or "shade" the truth.

Your questions should be direct, simple, and open-ended. Asking people open-ended questions allows them to show what they know. You want to get them talking by asking questions that start with why, how, and what. Ask them, "What is the proposal designed to accomplish?" Or "What is your understanding of how the accident happened?" Or "Why do you love your hobby?" Or "How does the agency's report fall short?"

You must also understand what the interviewees mean by what they say, and you might need to ask for clarification to make sure. You might need to say, "What do you mean when you say . . . ?" Or "Tell me a little bit more about that." Or "Give me an example of that."

Ask questions that cause the person to think, to reflect, to search and, if necessary, to clear up any discrepancies in earlier statements he or she may have made about the same subject. Challenge the interviewee to respond to different viewpoints or to answer critics by asking, "How do you respond to Councilman White, who says this is only a short-term fix and won't solve the problem long-term?" Or "Why are you so determined to push this legislation through when there's so much opposition to it from the teachers' union?" Attribute challenges such as these so that it doesn't sound like you're the one making them.

You might also need to ask the people you interview to summarize what they've just said in one or two sentences, especially if they tend to ramble on or talk in long run-on sentences. You might need to interrupt them and re-ask the question if they go way off track. You need short answers—sound bites—you can use in your story. Because you'll be using audio or videotapes or disks to record your interview, and you or someone else will be editing it later, you can ask the question a second time if the interviewee flubs up the answer the first time. Or you can ask the question another way. Or you can ask it a third time. Take the time to get the most understandable, succinct statement you can. Tape is inexpensive and reusable. After you've asked all of your questions, ask if there's anything the interviewee would like to add. Then wait. For television interviews, also ask the photographer if there's anything else he or she would like to ask. Remember, you and the photographer are a team.

Leave some editing "space" during the interview. Let the person you're interviewing finish answering each question, then pause for a couple of seconds before you ask the next question or interrupt the speaker in some way. This can be tough to learn, but it becomes important in the editing booth when you're working on a deadline. You don't want to "step on" the sound bites. Also, don't listen out loud by saying "OK" or "Uh-Huh" in response to everything your interviewee says. You don't want to sound as if you're agreeing (or disagreeing) with what the person is saying. If you're off-camera, you can slightly nod or tilt your head to confirm to the person you're interviewing that you're listening and paying attention.

You want to stay in control of the interview and not let yourself be used. This is particularly important in live situations. One California TV reporter, interviewing a member of the Hell's Angels motorcycle gang, live, was shocked when the biker grabbed the microphone and began swearing during the 6 o'clock news. In hindsight, perhaps the reporter should have anticipated such an outcome. But once the biker had the microphone in his hand, the reporter was helpless to end the interview. It was up to the director and producer in the control room to end it instead and for the anchor to apologize. Remember, you hold the microphone. You stay in control. There are other, less extreme situations to watch out for. At times, politicians and others who are accustomed to being interviewed frequently won't answer the question you ask; instead they'll respond with something they want you to use in your story. You might ask the governor what's being done to curb illegal immigration, and the answer he gives you may be that he's working hard to provide tax relief for home owners this year (a part of his campaign platform). So pay close attention to what he's actually telling you. If you think a politician is avoiding a question, ask it again. And again. Then ask him why he's avoiding the question.

If you're writing a 90-second TV story, you'll be looking for sound bites that run about 10 seconds in length; that's about one sentence long. If you're writing a documentary, you'll be looking for sound bites that may run 20 seconds in length; that's about two or three sentences long. Radio sound bites range from about 5 to 15 seconds in length and are usually in the lower end of that range. Sometimes you'll be looking for a long series of quick sound bites from your interview subjects. If you're interviewing college students about where they'll be traveling for spring break, you might just ask them that one question, "Where are you going for spring break?" When the sound bites are edited together into the final piece, the answers will then be: "Cancun . . . Austin . . . home to Miami . . . London . . . Phoenix . . . I'm staying here to study." In this case, one- or two-word answers are all you're looking for.

If your station has cameras or audio recorders with time code, it's helpful to set your watch and the camera or recorder time to real time, so that you can just glance at your watch and make a note of the time when you hear a sound bite you're pretty sure you'll want to use. This makes the editing process go more smoothly and quickly. It's particularly important when you're working on a daily deadline or when you're covering a trial, for example. You may wind up with four or five field tapes.

It's also helpful for television reporters to carry audio recorders with them to their interviews. This way, reporters can pick out their sound bites by listening to the audio while they're riding back to the station. When choosing a sound bite, remember to listen to the phrasing of the sentence. You want to cut the sound bite at the end of a phrase or the end of a sentence when the voice falls. You don't want to cut someone off in midsentence, when the voice is rising.

Because you or someone else will most likely be editing these interviews later, it will be important for your photographer to shoot some **cutaways** of you (in TV interviews) when the interview is finished. These are essentially shots of you listening to your interviewee. When the photographer is shooting these, ask your interviewee another question so that you can look at her knowledgeably and listen attentively. Hold the mic as you did for the actual interview. Don't nod your head, shake your head, laugh, smile, or talk while the photographer is shooting these cutaways. Just listen attentively. The cutaways will be used in the editing process, and you want to be shown listening, not agreeing or disagreeing or laughing at what your interviewee is saying.

Most interviews are conducted with both you and your interviewee standing or with both of you seated. The point is that you want your eyes to be on the same level. If you're interviewing a person in a wheelchair, you sit in a chair. If you're interviewing children, be extra patient with them, and get down to their eye level by sitting in a chair or getting down on your knees. If you're interviewing an NBA center, you might need to stand on a step stool or have him sit while you stand!

Dressing Appropriately

Let caution and restraint be your wardrobe watchwords. It's very important that you dress modestly and professionally, especially if you're on TV. The only logo you should ever display on your clothing while on the job is that of your station or network. Also, safe and traditional styles are much wiser selections than are fashion-forward and true-to-the-trend choices. Be sure you're not attracting too much attention for what you wear; you want viewers to concentrate on what you say.

If you're going to interview a U.S. senator in her Washington, D.C., office, wear a suit. If you're going to interview a West Texas rancher, jeans and boots would be appropriate. If you're doing a live television report outside in Minnesota in the winter, you might want to wear as much clothing as you can scrounge up. Sometimes, informal attire for celebrities can give the interview a casual feel, and conversely, semi-formal attire for people not usually the subject of interviews might be viewed as a sign of respect. Wear something sensible to work every day, and keep a pair of khaki slacks and some hiking boots in a suitcase by your desk for those times you're sent at a moment's notice to cover a fire or flood or chemical spill.

For both men and women, jewelry should be kept to the barest of minimums. Necklaces, bracelets, and large earrings can be distracting if they reflect light, and they can clang against microphones. Also, busy patterns and pastels tend to create havoc for sensitive cameras.

Though this advice speaks primarily to the on-camera talent among you, please know that radio reporters, videographers, and other field personnel also have standards to meet. Wear clean clothes, without logos, suitable to step into a place of worship if you have to get a quick bite from a clergy member.

"Managing" the Interviewee

The camera or audio recorder intimidates many who aren't accustomed to it. And most "regular" people have never been interviewed or been on-camera before. You may need to put your interviewees at ease and "warm them up" by asking a few easy questions to begin interviews. You don't want to start immediately with the toughest question you have, the one most likely to end the interview once it's asked in confrontational situations. The photographer or sound tech can use this "warm-up" time to double-check that the microphone is working and to help the interviewee get comfortable.

In the case of TV, remind the person you're interviewing to look at you during the interview and to ignore the camera and crew as best he or she can. It will then be up to you to be fair with this person and to establish your own rapport with him. No one wants to look "bad" during an interview or to stumble over words or to lose composure. No one appreciates leading questions. No one wants you to put words in her mouth. And no one likes to feel he's been "tricked" by the media. If the interviewee is in a tough spot, she might be anticipating a tough question, so don't wait *too* long to ask it. Often, people will rise to the occasion when they're asked really pointed questions. You don't have to ask hard questions in nasty, vitriolic ways. Overly aggressive, rude, dishonest reporters have left some members of the public with a wary attitude toward media practitioners, and they might be defensive until they get to know you individually as a member of the media in your market. Winning their trust can take some time.

Keep in mind also that not everyone wants to be interviewed and not everyone is good at it. And, because of company policy, some employees are essentially forbidden from talking with members of the media, and they'll be putting their jobs on the line if they talk to you. That's a powerful deterrent for them.

Your goal as a reporter is to inform the people in your community, not to panic or titillate or mislead them. When you're working on your story, you're working to answer the basic journalistic questions of who, what, when, where, why, and how. When you're in the field and conducting interviews, you want to find out all the information you can about the story you're writing. If this is a conflict story, you want to identify spokespersons for all sides of the issue and talk with as many of them as possible.

But keep in mind that you absolutely do *not* want to turn your photographer's gear into a hundred-pound pencil and notepad. You're going to have to listen to this tape later and log all of it, and you don't need or want 60 minutes of interview for two quick, 10-second sound bites. Many questions are for background information, and you can take written notes about those off-camera: information such as how old the person is or how long she's worked for the company. But others are for sound bites, and you want those to be sharply focused, narrow questions done on camera. You want to ask: "What did you see?" "What did you hear?" "What did you think?" "What did you feel?" "What led you to make that decision?" "What will you accomplish with this new program?" "What bothers you about that?" "How did you . . . ?" "What was it like to be . . . ?" These questions are open-ended and don't presuppose an answer. In contrast, it isn't informative to ask someone, "Isn't it about time we begin to clamp down on these violators?" That leads to a one-word yes or no answer and makes it appear the interviewer already has an opinion about the matter.

If at all possible, you want to avoid questions that result in yes or no answers. For example, if you ask someone, "Is it hot enough today?" his answer might be yes or no. But if you say to him, "The weather's so hot today, how would you describe it?" you'll get a sound bite you can probably use. This is especially true when interviewing children. If you ask a child, "Are you having a good time in preschool?" her answer might be yes or no or simply a nod of the head. But if you ask her, "What do you like best about preschool?" you'll get an answer such as "playing with computers" or "coloring in my coloring book" or "playing with my friends." In some cases, such as stonewalling by a politician or local official, if yes and no are the only answers the individual will provide, it can be effective to edit a string of them together into one long sound bite. Next time, the politician might give you more of an answer.

Also, some people will avoid you because they have something to hide. One controversial style of interviewing is the "ambush," wherein a reporter runs up to someone as he's leaving his home for work, for example, and starts firing questions unannounced. This might be all you can do if the person consistently refuses to agree to a scheduled interview, but it catches the person off-guard and the answers might not be particularly informative.

Telling Their Stories

Reporters can relay details more succinctly than "average" people can, because reporters are trained storytellers. What reporters can't relay as effectively are the thoughts, feelings, attitudes, and reactions of the people they interview. That's what sound bites are for. Your interviews are a way to get at what's in a person's mind, expressed in his or her own words. As often as possible you want to look for people who are *telling* this story, rather than people who are telling *about* this story. In other words, look for eyewitnesses you can interview. Look for those people who are directly affected by an action or event. Look for those who can provide the color, the details. Then let these people tell you what they went through, what it was like, what they see as the problem. (We'll have more about this in Chapter 9 as we look at the diamond approach to structuring a package).

As a reporter, you're the one who can best summarize the *objective* information in the narration **track** and **stand-up** of your story. Those you interview are the ones who can best tell the *subjective* information about how they felt, about what they experienced, about how they live on $201 a month. They can tell you the ideas, the reactions, the opinions, the feelings, the fears, the challenges.

Being Sensitive

Beware of asking "how do you feel" questions when interviewing those in shock or in grief. Members of the audience often *know* how the grief-stricken feel. They can see how the person feels by looking at her face in your video, or by remembering a tragedy in their own lives. You'll appear immature at best and insensitive at worst for not knowing how it feels to lose a family member or neighbor or friend to a violent or sudden death. Think of something more informative to ask. "Give sorrow words," said Shakespeare, and many in grief can articulate their loss. But they and those around them may be in a daze, struggling to retain their composure and to understand what you're asking. Kindness and tact and patience will serve you well in these situations. You might want to approach someone in this situation without the camera or recorder. Any crew members with you can stand back a bit while you go up to introduce yourself. You might say, "What's happened is awful. And we're sorry to bother you right now. But we'd like to talk with you about what's happened."

Most people will do it, if approached in the right way. It's actually easier to get a "yes" response in person than by phone, so go ahead and approach people in this situation in person. If the person's son has been killed in an automobile accident, you might say, "We're so sorry about what happened. We'd like to talk with you about your son. What was he like? What did he like to do? We'd like to tell our audience what he was like as a person. Do you have any pictures you could share with us?" Or "What happened is a tragedy and I know you must be devastated." Sometimes people will just pick up on such a statement and start talking about what their son was like. If they're comfortable with you, they'll open up. But keep in mind that people know their rights—they know that they don't have to talk with you—and if you're standing on their private property, they know they can ask you to leave and expect you to comply.

Be sensitive to people and their situations. Many spot news stories are tragic, traumatic. They involve fires, murders, fatal accidents. Your interviewees are human, and you're in their faces with a microphone and maybe a camera too. This is their family or livelihood you're asking about. This is their home or business you're in. People are perceptive. If you're sincere and caring, your interviewees will pick up on that. If you're merely feigning sympathy, they'll pick up on that too. The interviews you've already conducted will have shaped your reputation as a reporter in the community. People will remember you from your previous work. Many will feel they know you and might already like and trust you. Of course, if this is your first interview, you're just starting to build your reputation in the market. How you handle those first few tough interviews will go a long way toward setting your reputation with the viewers or listeners in the market you're in.

Diane Pertmer has been a news reporter at WFLA-TV in Tampa, Florida (www.wfla.com), for more than 20 years. She knows from personal experience how much common courtesy and human kindness matter in these situations. Her most memorable interview wouldn't have ever happened had she not extended a simple courtesy on the worst day of one man's life.

She and her photojournalist partner arrived at the scene of a violent murder. A killer had somehow slipped inside the home of a young teenager, savaged her, and escaped. Her family discovered the horror, and never set foot in the house again. Detectives on the scene told the news crew the parents were with the next-door neighbor. So when a man who fit the description of the anguished father walked to a car, Diane asked if he was the victim's dad. He said no, a relative. She asked if anyone in the family, considering the terrible circumstance, was available to answer a couple of questions. He said no. As he turned away, Diane told him she and her partner were sorry they had to be there and asked that he express their sympathies to the girl's parents.

Diane later learned that the man was the girl's father. He agreed to an exclusive on-camera interview, because he said the news crew respected his family's grief and placed it above the demands of TV news. Diane says her experience underscores an important truth in reporting: compassion is part of fairness. Both values create a foundation of trust usually necessary to negotiate an interview. Television is intimate. People in grief should believe that sharing their loss on TV won't be exploited.

But ordinary people thrust into extraordinary circumstances often have their own reasons to speak publicly in an interview. The father of the murder victim pleaded for help in finding the killer. He also shared memories of his daughter, an important acknowledgment that her life, however brief, mattered to others and should be recognized. Family members managing unwanted media attention after suffering a loss will often agree to an interview, if only to talk about what the loved one meant to them. It's helpful to request that the family designate a spokesperson if emotions are especially raw.

Diane believes the most successful interviews come from demonstrating genuine interest in the person and the subject, no matter what the story is. In answering Diane's questions after his daughter was murdered, the victim's father offered a warning made compelling by his courage in going public: watch your children, warn them of the dangers out there, and never fail to tell them you love them.

Knowing the Power of Silence

Reporters can sometimes concentrate so much on the questions they're asking that they forget to *listen* to what their interviewees are saying. So this is a reminder to listen to the words your interviewees use. Listen carefully to the language they use to describe something. And remember also to *wait* during those "pregnant pauses." If you ask someone a question and she doesn't answer it right away, stay quiet and continue to look at her. Don't be too eager to jump in with the next question just to fill the silence and to keep the conversation going. Let the person you're interviewing pause and think for a moment, and then let her finish speaking. Sometimes the silences and the pauses themselves are as telling as the answers you thought you'd get. Sometimes the nonanswers and the evasions are more informative than the answers are. In a memorable Barbara Walters interview with one of O. J. Simpson's attorneys, there was an excruciatingly long pause before the attorney finally answered Walters' question about whether he believed O. J. Simpson is an innocent man. He never answered yes or no, but instead made a long statement that sometimes the guilty go free to prove a greater point and to right a greater wrong.

Checking Your Bias

The people you'll be interviewing are who they are: they look the way they look, and they are the age they are. Don't assume every business tycoon is a man. Don't assume every nurse practitioner is a woman. Don't make similar assumptions about race or age or anything else. Don't derail your interview by making inappropriate opening remarks, such as "I had no idea you would be. . . ." That says more about you than it says about the person you're supposed to interview. Just ask your questions. And don't assume that all men or women or teenagers or Christians or motorcyclists think alike about any given topic. You're interviewing *this* person about what *this* person thinks or saw or experienced.

Reading between the Lines

As we alluded to before, people in the spotlight who are frequently interviewed sometimes develop a style of answering questions that allows them to use the media for their own purposes. You might find yourself in the position of asking a politician, for example, what he or she plans to do about a specific situation. Rather than answering the question, the person might respond with a sound bite about a totally different (but favorite and popular) subject and might then leave the room, pleading time constraints. This leaves you in the position of having only the one sound bite the person gave you, a sound bite that is completely off the subject but one the politician wants on the air.

Also, listen to what politicians don't say. The politician might say, "I categorically deny being in Laos on July 17th." The truth might be that the senator was in Laos on July 16th, and you'll have to read "between the lines" for your answer. So be prepared, be persistent, and pay attention to what's being said to you. Remember that there's a difference between persistence and rudeness. You want to be persistent in searching for answers. Being rude won't help you find them. You want to be *assertive but not abrasive*. You'll be working in this market for some time, and you don't want to burn too many bridges before moving on to another market, if that's the career path you follow. You're in a high-profile job. People will remember how you treat them, or someone close to them, or they'll hear about someone else's experience from neighbors or friends.

"The Get"

In the 1990s, an aggressive style of interview pursuit appeared and was quickly dubbed "the get" by veteran reporters. This term describes the aggressive pursuit of someone—the get—for an exclusive interview. In this situation, there's ferocious competition from other reporters in the market or at the other networks.

Jill Rackmill knows how tough it can be to get an interview that everyone is after. She's a producer for ABC's investigative unit. One of the most sought-after groups following the 9/11 terrorist attacks—as much as family members and friends of those who lost their lives and the police officers and firefighters who survived rescue attempts—were the air traffic controllers handling the doomed flights. Jill's knowledge about the profession and professional contacts with controllers helped her get one of the most compelling interviews to come out of the months of coverage that followed the tragedy.

Unknowingly, seven years earlier she began laying the ground-work that resulted in that interview. One of her first assignments as a green 24-year-old was to attend a national convention of air traffic controllers in Tampa, Florida, and gather information about their safety and equipment concerns. At the time, she knew next to nothing about aviation. The only advice she was given was that air traffic controllers are an intense bunch with a notoriously high tolerance for stressful situations. She says that as a journalist who shares some of the same personality traits, she was in heaven.

She spent four days interviewing dozens of controllers from across the country. A "tough-guy" attitude permeated the smoke-filled convention rooms as they swapped one harrowing story after another about radar blackouts, weather disturbances, pilot errors, and worst of all, near midair collisions because of faulty equipment.

But beneath all the controllers' tough talk was a passionate and deeply personal commitment to a job in which a single wrong decision could mean life or death for strangers flying at 30,000 feet. Sure, they made a lot jokes about "pushing tin" around the sky and getting paid for "playing a video game" but they realized the gravity of their mission and took pride in their skills and training. The "controllers" were just that: control freaks whose worst nightmare was losing sight of a plane—even for a split second—because of mechanical or human error.

Soon, she began to speak their jargon and laugh at their inside jokes. During the next seven years Jill stayed in touch with many of the controllers. Sometimes she called for off-the-record guidance or background about an aviation story, but often, it was just to say hello.

On September 11, 2001, like most Americans, Jill watched as the horror unfolded live on television. And, like most journalists, she recognized instantly that this would be the biggest story of our time. Because of her past reporting experience, her thoughts immediately turned to the air traffic controllers who were working the hijacked flights. Someone somewhere in a darkened room had watched the events unfold on a radar scope, had lost radio contact with the pilot, had seen the green blip go off course. The controllers *had* to know before the rest of the world that something had gone terribly wrong—but for once, it was beyond their "control" to do anything but watch. The thought was chilling.

Immediately she knew in her heart that she would tell this story. She knew controllers; she understood their mentality. They had a story to tell and she would be the one to tell it. And maybe in some small, small way, she says, she could contribute to our shared national understanding of what had happened.

By 10:30 A.M., she was driving to Boston, where two of the four hijacked flights had originated, with the hope of meeting the controllers directly involved in handling those flights. All of New York City's bridges and tunnels were shut down, and she spent nearly five hours sitting in traffic, listening to radio reports and wondering if the car trip had been such a good idea. The phone lines were jammed, but after repeated efforts, she finally reached one air traffic controller who, in the years since they had met, had been elected to an office in the national union representing controllers. The source was furious, telling her that thousands of people were dead, we were in the middle of an intense law enforcement investigation, many of the nation's controllers were in hysterics and finally, that her call was *not* appreciated. (Only the source didn't say it quite so nicely.)

Still she drove on. Late that night she arrived at the Boston Air Route Traffic Control Center, which is actually in Nashua, New Hampshire. The facility, which even in normal times is highly secured, was under full alert. Police cars surrounded the building and it appeared that no one was coming or going. So she sat in the bar right next door to the center, hoping some controllers would wander in for a beer. No luck.

She stayed in Boston for five days helping ABC News with other reporting, but she struck out with the Boston controllers. The national union had decided that no controllers would speak to the media.

When she returned to New York, she redoubled her efforts, and was one of many journalists trying desperately to get the same story. (In fact, the National Air Traffic Controllers Association logged 475 interview requests.)

Through sheer desire and persistence, long-established contacts, and a sincere respect for the controllers' profession, she finally managed to get an interview with a remarkable woman named Danielle O'Brien, who on the morning of September 11th handled American Flight 77, the plane that hit the Pentagon.

Jill is quick to point out that the Danielle O'Brien interview, which aired on "20/20," was much more than "a get" for her. It was a labor of love, born in a time of tragedy. She says there's no substitute for the hard work of cultivating sources, combined with a true, heartfelt sincerity of wanting to be a responsible and thoughtful conduit for someone else's voice. Through the years, she had gained the respect and trust of air traffic controllers by learning how to speak their language and by consistently honoring their needs for confidentiality when they spoke on background. And most important, she had maintained regular contact with her sources, even when there was no "big get" to get. And that's what made the difference.

Live from Iraq

As this book was going to press, the United States was involved in a war against the regime of Saddam Hussein in Iraq. For the first time, hundreds of journalists "embedded" with U.S. and British troops were able to broadcast images and interviews live from an active battlefield. TV "embeds" were equipped with the latest technology to transmit reports back home. Satellite videophones, digital cameras, and wireless laptops allowed them to capture pictures and sounds and instantly edit and send them out. These stories demonstrated the mesmerizing power of television, live television in particular. Even though some of the video was green and shaky, the timeliness and "realness" of it was both eerie and compelling. Viewers who watched those early stories remember NBC's David Bloom reporting from atop a tank at it rumbled through the Iraqi desert and later describing what it was like trying to work in the middle of a sandstorm that briefly delayed the forward movement of his unit. They also remember Bloom's untimely death from natural causes as he was covering the war. They remember Peter Arnett describing for NBC the bombs falling on Baghdad and lighting up the night sky in what the Pentagon called a campaign of "shock and awe." They also remember Arnett's swift dismissal from the network after he agreed to be interviewed on Iraqi TV and used the opportunity to question the effectiveness of the U.S. war plan. They remember the "night vision scope" video of a young Army private, Jessica Lynch, on a stretcher as she was rescued from the Iraqi hospital where she'd been held as a prisoner of war. They remember reports from Umm Qasr early in the war that showed a chaotic scene of coalition soldiers scrambling to the top of sandy berms and firing repeatedly on Iraqi positions. They remember that an "embed" happened to be on hand when a U.S. soldier from one airborne division attacked his comrades by throwing grenades into a command tent.

U.S. and BBC reporters on the scene were able to get reactions from commanders and front line troops minutes after military actions began. State-run stations in the Middle East and Arab-owned cable networks were also broadcasting in real or close-to-real time, carrying statements from Iraqi officials contradicting what the American and British commanders were saying and running video of dead coalition soldiers and interrogations of U.S. prisoners of war. And viewers remember watching live as a large statue of Saddam Hussein came tumbling down from its pedestal in Baghdad, the joint work of U.S. forces and Iraqi citizens. While U.S. Secretary of Defense Donald Rumsfeld called these "embedded" reports "only slices" of the whole story about what was happening on the battlefield in Iraq, they did provide an unprecedented look at the chaos of war in real time and what eyewitnesses had to say to reporters about it.

Conclusion

As a reporter, you'll find there are competing values within your newsroom. Think about them when considering whom to interview and how to go about it. Here's a list of news values that most can agree with: integrity, accuracy, fairness, responsibility, sensitivity, and accountability. But these news values compete and conflict with others that are equally important and valid to your news director: being competitive, being timely, being compelling, being commercially successful in the ratings, being marketable, being promotable. If your organization has a mission statement, it might provide some guidance to you about what's really important at your station. If the mission statement declares, "We will seek every opportunity to destroy our competitors," you'll be moving in one direction with your interviews and your reports. If the mission statement pledges the newsroom "will bring to light the good news, so we can celebrate, and the bad news, so we can work together to correct the problems we encounter," then you'll be going in a different direction and can explain to your interviewees the reasons behind some of your questions.

Get out in your community and listen to what "real" people are saying. You can listen to what people are saying when they're standing behind you in the grocery store checkout line. You can listen to what people are saying when they're talking with each other at high school basketball games. You can listen to what people are saying when they're talking with each other at the gym, at the gas station, at the table next to yours in the restaurant or coffee bar, or in the chair next to you in the beauty salon or the barber shop. Many people complain that media types rarely go out to community events to find out what average people are up to. You get the idea. Get out there, and wherever you are, listen. You'll learn what's important to people in your community. And you'll increase your list of people in the middle, not just those on the fringe or in "official" positions, whom you can call for interviews. You'll then have enterprise story ideas and interview subjects for your newscast, stories that will differentiate your station, and you, from competitors.

News directors and assignments editors love enterprising reporters who come up with many of their own story ideas. Let people in the community help in this regard. In big markets, the community isn't just the city of license. It might be the surrounding beach communities, or communities of commuters, or certain demographic communities. As a reporter, you're a contact person, a conduit to put informed people in your community on the air so that others can hear their voices, thoughts, and opinions. You have the power to do that. Use it wisely.

Also, don't forget to listen to the people who work at your own station in departments other than news. Ask the receptionist, members of the sales staff, the engineering staff, or the housekeeping staff about news story ideas and interview possibilities. These people have most likely been at your station and in your community much longer than you have. They all have networks of family and friends and business associates. As a group, they're most likely more diverse than your circle of friends. They can help you decide whom to interview and what questions to ask, especially when you're just getting started in a market.

We've covered a number of points in this chapter, from planning the interview to managing the interviewee to actively listening to what's being said. Here's a quick checklist of things to remember when you're getting ready and when you're conducting a news interview.

 DOs and DON'Ts When Interviewing

Do
- Think ahead.
- Be organized and prepared.
- Research the topic and the people.
- Dress appropriately.
- Be courteous.
- Maintain eye contact.
- Interview in a conversational tone.
- Leave editing space after answers.
- Attribute charges to the person making them.
- Read between the lines (especially when interviewing politicians).
- Listen.

Don't
- Ask yes or no questions, especially of children.
- Be "married" to your questions.
- Give up control.
- Show agreement or disagreement.
- Tell the interviewee what your specific questions will be.
- Forget to ask for clarification.
- Ask really tough questions right away.

WRITING RADIO NEWS

Radio is the fastest and most widely dispersed mass medium. It's ubiquitous. It's everywhere. Because you can listen to the radio in places where you can't watch TV or read a newspaper, it's the medium through which much of the public is first informed when big news breaks.

Listening to radio reports is how many people first heard of the September 11, 2001, terrorist attacks against the United States. Beth Fertig is a reporter for WNYC Radio in New York City. She was two blocks north and one block east of the World Trade Center complex when the first tower collapsed on September 11. She remembers, "I heard this huge rumbling noise like an elevated train above my head. . . . I just held my microphone out to get the sound of it and, after a few seconds, started narrating what I was seeing" (see *Women Journalists at Ground Zero: Covering Crisis* by Judith Sylvester and Suzanne Huffman). Beth worked all day and through the night of September 11. She did a feature that **NPR** (National Public Radio) ran of her tape and colleague Marianne McCune's tape, just recounting their experiences at Ground Zero. There's no written script of the story. Beth's feature was recorded off-site under very trying circumstances and there's no copy of it remaining. The audio of her story is archived on the WNYC website (http://www.wnyc.org) for September 12, 2001. It's titled "Witness to Collapse" and runs 4:14. Here's her script, reconstructed from the archived audio.

BETH: IT STARTED WITH ONE PLANE CRASH. THEN ANOTHER. AND THEN . . . THE BLAST. (BACKGROUND SOUND OF BUILDING FALLING)

NAT (NATURAL) SOUND OF BETH ON TAPE, RUNNING: (GRUNTING) THE BUILDING IS FALLING RIGHT NOW. PEOPLE ARE RUNNING THROUGH THE STREET. SMOKE IS EVERYWHERE.

BETH: THIS REPORTER AND OTHER BYSTANDERS WERE STILL TAKING IN THE SURREAL VISION OF TWO FIERY HOLES IN THE TWIN TOWERS . . . WHEN WE WERE NOW RUNNING FOR OUR LIVES. AS POLICE URGED THE CROWD TO HEAD NORTH, MANY STOPPED AT A SAFE DISTANCE A FEW BLOCKS AWAY TO WATCH THE GIGANTIC CLOUD OF SMOKE AND DEBRIS. LORETTA WILLIAMS SAT WITH A COLLEAGUE FROM THE PORT AUTHORITY, WHOSE OFFICE WAS IN ONE OF THE TOWERS. THEY HAD WALKED DOWN 82 FLIGHTS OF STAIRS. (CAR HORNS AND STREET NOISE IN THE BACKGROUND)

LORETTA: WE JUST SHOOK UP. (SOBBING)

BETH: TELL ME WHAT YOU SAW WITH, WITH THE PEOPLE. WERE PEOPLE OKAY? TELL US ABOUT THAT.

LORETTA: NO, A COUPLE OF PEOPLE, THEY GOT BURNED. THEIR SKIN WAS COMIN' OFF. THEY GOT BURNED. WE WAS JUST TRYING TO GET OUT SAFE. THAT'S ALL WE WAS CONCERNED ABOUT.

BETH: SEVERAL WITNESSES INCLUDING DENNY SEE-TOE SAID THEY SAW PEOPLE JUMPING OUT OF THE BUILDINGS. (SOUNDS OF FIRE ENGINES IN THE BACKGROUND)

DENNY: AS THE FIRE WAS PROGRESSING, I SAW PEOPLE JUMPING OFF THE TOWER, LITERALLY JUST JUMPING OFF THE TOWER WITHOUT ANY GROUND SUPPORT WHATSOEVER. IT WAS NOT A PRETTY SIGHT. (SOUNDS OF FIRE ENGINES IN THE BACKGROUND)

BETH: EVERYWHERE PEOPLE WERE TRADING STORIES, GAZING SOUTH IN SHOCK. AND THEN, WHAT WAS LEFT OF THE FAMILIAR SKYLINE VANISHED COMPLETELY WHEN THE SECOND TOWER COLLAPSED LESS THAN AN HOUR AFTER

THE FIRST. . . . I WAS WITH MY COLLEAGUE MARIANNE MCCUNE WHEN WE HEARD THE BLAST. WE WERE REPORTING LIVE ON THE AIR AND WERE ASKED TO DESCRIBE WHAT WE SAW.

NAT SOUND OF MARIANNE AND BETH ON TAPE: THAT'S WHAT WE WERE SEEING BEFORE. YEAH. IT'S GONE. IT'S GONE. MARIANNE, CAN YOU SEE IT? MARIANNE, I CAN'T SEE ANYTHING. I CAN'T SEE ANYTHING. WE CAN'T SEE ANYTHING OF TOWER TWO.

BETH: IN A NEARBY FOUNTAIN, FIRE MARSHALS WASHED OFF THE SOOT COVERING THEIR CLOTHES. SUPERVISOR THOMAS WILLIAMS SAID THEY WERE TRYING TO RESCUE PEOPLE BUT WERE FORCED TO EVACUATE. (STREET NOISES IN THE BACKGROUND)

THOMAS: THE TOP HALF OF THE BUILDING COLLAPSED AND STARTED FALLING DOWN. THAT'S WHEN WE EVACUATED THE AREA. WE STARTED RUNNING. AND SMOKE CAME DOWN AND ENGULFED US IN SMOKE. AND, AND, AND DEBRIS HERE. AND I JUST GOT LOST. AND I RAN TO THE WINDOWS. AND I JUST THANK GOD I JUST GOT OUT. I JUST DIDN'T KNOW WHERE I WAS.

BETH: HUNDREDS OF FIREFIGHTERS ARE BELIEVED TO HAVE DIED. HE SAID HE DIDN'T KNOW WHERE SOME OF HIS COLLEAGUES WERE.

THOMAS: I HAVE NO IDEA. I, I, I, I, I PRAY TO GOD THAT THEY'RE SAFE AND ALL RIGHT.

BETH: LATER AT THE SAME FOUNTAIN, VOLUNTEERS ASSEMBLED TO HELP THE EMERGENCY CREWS. CARPENTERS RIPPED DOWN BLUE SCAFFOLDING FROM A CONSTRUCTION SITE TO MAKE STRETCHERS. PAUL NEV-IS HAD BEEN WORKING NEARBY AND WANTED TO HELP. (STREET NOISES IN THE BACKGROUND)

PAUL: EVERYBODY JUST STARTED ORGANIZING. ALL THE UNION MEMBERS. WE PUT MILITARY, MEDICAL. AND WE PUT BLOOD DONATIONS. AND WE SPOKE WITH THE COPS, CORRESPONDED WITH EVERYBODY. THERE'S BEEN A LOT OF BLOOD DONATIONS THAT WAY. THERE'S BEEN MILITARY PEOPLE ON STANDBY. ALL OF THESE PEOPLE ARE ON STANDBY FOR WHATEVER THE CITY NEEDS. (CROWD NOISES IN THE BACKGROUND, SHOUTING, SOMEONE WHISTLES)

BETH: AT AN OUTDOOR TRIAGE CENTER JUST NORTH OF THE WORLD TRADE CENTER, DOCTORS, NURSES, POLICE, AND FIREFIGHTERS ALL HELPED WITH RELIEF. FILM COMPANIES EVEN PROVIDED LIGHTS WHEN THE SUN WENT DOWN. MEDICAL STUDENT ROBERT DIRK STANLEY CAME FROM BROOKLYN HOSPITAL TO HELP SET UP. (CROWD NOISES IN THE BACKGROUND)

ROBERT: THESE PEOPLE ARE GOING TO BE OUR TRIAGE PEOPLE. THEY'RE GOING TO ASSESS THE PATIENTS. WE HAVE A, WE HAVE SOME SURGEONS SET UP IN THE BUS OVER THERE. THEY'RE GOING TO DEAL WITH SURGICAL, SURGICAL PATIENTS, THOSE ARE PEOPLE WHO ARE IN DIRE NEED OF SURGERY. WE HAVE CRITICAL CARE SET UP OVER HERE. UH, BEHIND THAT IS LESS CRITICAL CARE. ON THE OTHER SIDE IS NONCRITICAL, TRAUMA. (CROWD NOISES IN THE BACKGROUND, SHOUTING)

BETH: LATE IN THE AFTERNOON, AS WORKERS WERE PREPARING TO TREAT THOSE PULLED OUT OF THE RUBBLE, ANOTHER HUGE BOOM RUMBLED THROUGH THE STREETS. SEVEN WORLD TRADE CENTER, ANOTHER PART OF THE COMPLEX, HAD COLLAPSED. A NEW CLOUD OF SMOKE HAD FORMED. WORKERS AT THE TRIAGE CENTER WORRIED AS IT HEADED THEIR WAY. BUT THE DANGER PASSED. . . . MEANWHILE THE WOUNDED POURED INTO LOCAL HOSPITALS. STEVEN MALSKY EMERGED FROM N-Y-U'S DOWNTOWN MEDICAL CENTER WITH GAUZE OVER HIS EYES. HE SAID HE'D GOTTEN TRAMPLED WHILE RUNNING FROM THE WORLD TRADE CENTER, BUT SOMEONE CAME TO HIS RESCUE. (SIRENS IN THE BACKGROUND)

STEVEN: I DIDN'T GET THE PERSON'S NAME. BUT, UH, SOMEBODY HELPED ME AND BROUGHT ME TO THE HOSPITAL . . . AND WHOEVER THAT PERSON IS, I'M GRATEFUL.

BETH: MAYOR RUDOLPH GIULIANI MARVELED AT THE ABILITY OF NEW YORKERS TO PULL TOGETHER. BUT HE ALSO WARNED THAT THE NUMBER OF CASUALTIES WILL BE MORE THAN MOST OF US CAN BEAR. FOR N-P-R NEWS, I'M BETH FERTIG IN NEW YORK.

Notice how the background noises in the recorded interviews add to the sense of mood and place. Sound is the driving force of radio, and good-quality audio is very important. The voices of the reporters and anchors, the natural sounds from the scene of events, and the eyewitness sound bites with those who are there are the essential ingredients of radio news.

It's important for the radio journalist to remember that sound itself attracts. Just ask any eavesdropper. Sounds have a romance. Consider how the sound of a cricket at night establishes mood in a radio drama. Or think about the sound of thunder or of rain. (See "Empire of the Air [video recording]: The Men Who Made Radio"; a film by Ken Burns; a production of Florentine Films; produced by Ken Burns, Morgan Wesson, Tom Lewis; written by Geoffrey C. Ward; PBS Home Video; Turner Home Entertainment, 1991, 1996.) Radio is a medium that employs the magic of sound. Radio made America a land of listeners in the early 1920s. And America remains a nation of listeners today, a captive audience commuting to and from work each day.

High-Energy News

Radio news is a high-energy production of highly condensed information. Some radio newscasts might run only four minutes, but contain a dozen to 15 stories.

"Hyperkinetic" best describes radio news on many commercial stations these days. Short, rapid-fire stories, a high story count, and a driving rhythm are what one hears most often on the car radio during morning and evening drive times. Radio news at the top of the hour is often followed by traffic and weather reports, sports updates, medical reports, commentary, possibly a syndicated piece or a business report, and then the cycle repeats itself on the quarter-hour and the half-hour. Most stories are only a few seconds long.

KFWB (980 AM) is an all-news radio station in Los Angeles. There, news is on a 20-minute cycle—"You give us 20 minutes and we'll give you the world!"—although the station also does headlines and promos at the bottom of the hour. This station (as part of the old Group "W" stations) was one of the pioneers of the all-news radio format and is now one of two all-news radio stations in the market (KNX 1070 AM is the other). As a result of merger mania, however, these two former arch rivals are now both owned by the same company.

Here are two scripts from one of KFWB's newscasts. The first is a straight "reader"—to be read live by the newscast anchor. Its **slug**—or title—is Dog Mauling and it runs :26.

```
SLUG: DOG MAULING

COPY:          0:26


     THE MONTEREY COUNTY DISTRICT ATTORNEY'S OFFICE SAYS CRIMINAL
CHARGES WILL MOST LIKELY NOT BE FILED AGAINST A WOMAN WHOSE
GRANDDAUGHTER WAS MAULED BY THE FAMILY DOG. SPOKESMAN RANDY TAYLOR
SAYS THE ATTACK WAS A SURPRISE AND THERE WERE NO INDICATIONS OF
PREVIOUS NEGLIGENCE. THE GRANDMOTHER WAS WALKING WITH HER 5-YEAR-
OLD GRANDDAUGHTER, HER 10-YEAR-OLD GRANDSON, AND THE FAMILY'S TWO
ROTTWEILERS WHEN THEY WERE STARTLED BY A LIZARD. IN THE COMMOTION,
ONE OF THE DOGS ATTACKED THE GIRL, WHO DIED HOURS LATER. THE DOGS
HAVE BEEN IMPOUNDED.
```

The second script is also a "reader"—but with a sound-on-tape open. Its slug is Watching BinLaden. The audio cart containing the sound-on-tape open is #041 and runs :07. The copy runs :22. That makes the cumulative time of the story :29.

SLUG: WATCHING BINLADEN

CART: #041

SOUND: 0:07

COPY: 0:22

CUME: 0:29

INSTRUCTIONS: PLAY CART TO OPEN STORY, THEN FADE DOWN

#041

(ARABIC SPEAKING OPENS . . . SAME CLOSES)

:07

U.S. AUTHORITIES SAY THE LATEST VIDEOTAPES OF OSAMA BIN LADEN WERE PROBABLY MADE A YEAR AGO. THEY BELIEVE THE FOOTAGE WAS CRAFTED TO KEEP BIN LADEN'S WORDS AND IMAGE BEFORE THE PUBLIC WHILE HIS FATE IS IN DOUBT. DEFENSE SECRETARY DONALD RUMSFELD CLAIMS THE LATEST VIDEOS ARE A COMPILATION OF OLD VIDEO CLIPS. ONE TAPE SHOWS BIN LADEN CRITICIZING ARAB GOVERNMENTS AND THE PRESENCE OF U.S. SOLDIERS IN THE GULF REGION.

Technology and Terminology

The technology and terminology can vary from station to station. Some use carts; others use cassettes, tapes, or disks. The script formats can vary too. Some are written in all caps, some in caps and lowercase. In some stations, one story is an entire paragraph. In others, each sentence is a paragraph. Some writers indent; others don't. Some double-space their copy, some single-space. So you have to be flexible and willing to learn. You're going to have to adapt to your station's format, news "style," and audience.

There are two basic kinds of radio news stories: **reader/actualities (RAs)** and **wraps.** An RA will be read by the anchor, who will read the opening copy, punch a cart or disk, which is the audio recording of the actuality or sound bite, and then read the closing copy. A wrap includes the anchor lead and a voiced report from the reporter along with an actuality (sound bite); a wrap is the equivalent of a news package in television. In some newsrooms, a reader or "R" means the anchor reads the copy, a sound bite or "S" means the anchor reads a story that includes a sound bite, a voicer or "V" means a reporter delivers a story that includes a sound bite or bites and is prerecorded with the reporter's voice. Many stations are digital now and play the audio cuts right out of a computer or from a mini–disk player. But some stations still use cart machines, which are essentially audiotape players.

Most radio news stories on commercial stations are *very* short. As a writer, think in terms of 30 seconds for each story; that's about five sentences long. A story that runs 35 seconds will raise an eyebrow at the editor's desk in some stations. Generally speaking, each radio news story opens with a couple of sentences of copy, followed by a sound bite or clip of natural sound that runs between 5 and 10 seconds, and ends with a closing sentence or two. Write the bare minimum you need. You have to be clear, but you also have to be concise.

Mike Rogers has made his career in radio news. Here are two scripts written by Mike at KRLD News Radio (1080 AM), Dallas/Fort Worth, Texas. KRLD is a CBS-owned-and-operated station; its format is News/Talk with Top-40 overtones. Mike's stories are often delivered with more "attitude" than regular news stories are. He often calls his reports "The Other Side of the News." The two scripts are two versions of the same story. These are reader/actualities, designed for the on-air talent to read, hit play on the actuality cart or disk, and finish reading. Notice how short the stories are, how succinct the writing is, how tight the sound bites are.

6DEGREE1

AIR DATE = 9SEPT 98

TALENT = RMR

CART = W-01

KILL = 7PM

SIX DEGREES IN CYBERSPACE

EVER HEARD THE THEORY THAT EVERYONE ON EARTH IS SEPARATED FROM EVERY OTHER PERSON BY NO MORE THAN SIX RELATIONSHIPS??? IT'S CALLED THE SIX DEGREES OF SEPARATION . . . AND NOW THERE'S A WEBSITE THAT ALLOWS US TO FIND OUT IF IT'S REALLY TRUE. ANDREW WEINRICH (WINE-RICH) IS PRESIDENT OF SIX-DEGREES-DOT-COM.

CART = W-01

OUTCUE = " . . . CONNECTING THEM ALL TO EACH OTHER"

RUNS = :13

[VERBATIM] THE GOAL IS TO PROVIDE INTERNET USERS WITH TOOLS THAT ALLOW THEM TO NETWORK . . . TO INTERACT . . . TO BUILD WHAT WE CALL THEIR PERSONAL VIRTUAL COMMUNITIES. WE DO THAT BY GIVING THEM CONTACT MANAGERS AND CONNECTING THEM ALL TO EACH OTHER.

THE SIX DEGREES WEBSITE NOW HAS ONE MILLION MEMBERS . . . EACH CATEGORIZED BY NAME . . . ADDRESS AND OCCUPATION. WEINRICH SAYS HE'D EVENTUALLY LIKE TO FORM A NETWORK OF EVERY INTERNET USER IN THE WORLD. . . .

6DEGREE2

    AIR DATE = 9SEPT98

    TALENT = RMR

    CART = W-02

    KILL = 7PM

    NETWORKING ON THE NET

KEVIN BACON'S NOT A MEMBER . . . BUT A MILLION OTHER PEOPLE HAVE JOINED A NEW WEBSITE THAT TESTS THE SO-CALLED "SIX DEGREES OF SEPARATION" THEORY. IT STATES THAT EVERY PERSON ON EARTH IS NO MORE THAN SIX RELATIONSHIPS AWAY FROM ANY OTHER PERSON. ANDREW WEINRICH (WINE-RICH) IS PRESIDENT OF SIX-DEGREES-DOT-COM . . . WHICH TAKES A LIST OF YOUR FRIENDS AND ACQUAINTANCES . . . AND PROVIDES YOU WITH A LIST OF "BLIND DATES." . . .

    CART = W-02

    OUTCUE = " . . . A TREMENDOUS AMOUNT OF POWER."

    RUNS = :15

[VERBATIM] A BLIND DATE IS BY DEFINITION WHAT WE CALL YOUR SECOND DEGREE. IT'S NOT SOMEONE I KNOW. IT'S SOMEONE THAT KNOWS SOMEONE I KNOW. IF WE CAN BUILD A DATABASE WHERE WE CAN CAPTURE ALL OF THIS INFORMATION AND ALLOW PEOPLE TO IDENTIFY RELATIONSHIPS TO THE PEOPLE THEY DON'T KNOW THROUGH THE PEOPLE THEY DO KNOW, WE CAN PROVIDE THEM WITH A TREMENDOUS AMOUNT OF POWER.

WEINRICH SAYS THE SIX DEGREES WEBSITE CAN BE USED FOR ONLINE NETWORKING . . . BECAUSE EVERY MEMBER IS LISTED BY NAME . . . ADDRESS AND OCCUPATION. . . .

In the preceding examples, you'll notice that the directions accompanying the stories are fairly straightforward. Those at the beginning of the stories include the slug (title, with the number at the end of the slug giving us which version of the story it is), the date, who the reporter is, which cart to use, and the time at which to "kill" the story. These stories are scheduled to be killed or dropped after 7 P.M., which is the expiration time the writer has given them. The directions in the middle give the cart or disk number again, give the **outcue** (final few words) of the sound bite, and indicate the length of the bite, that brief portion of the interview that the reporter chose to include in the story. You'll notice that all the copy to be read live is in uppercase, but this can vary from newsroom to newsroom.

Life in the "Biz"

Radio news keeps its writers and reporters busy. One reporter says, "It's like feeding a shark. You keep feeding it, or it eats you." It's a high-energy job, and you need lots of stamina to do it. The hours are long, and there are constant deadlines. You have to be fast, you have to be organized, and you have to write short.

Writing short is a challenge. It's much tougher than writing long is. It takes practice because there's so much you have to leave out. That increases the burden of deciding what the important details are that you must put in. A radio story is reminiscent of the old "Dragnet" Sergeant Friday statement: "Just the facts, ma'am." There's no time for any more than that.

The radio news writer needs to remember: (1) to write in the present or future tense—this news is being heard in the current moment; (2) to write with a sense of urgency or a sense of the event itself; and (3) to choose the sound bite with the most "zing." The shorter the sound bite in radio, the better. Three seconds is long enough *if* the bite delivers the message. For example, the opening copy reads "U.S. Senate candidate Ron Kirk is pleased." Then bring up the sound bite: "Boy! Howdy!" Then continue the copy for the story and explain why the candidate is so happy.

As is the case in television, a good lead can make a radio news story. It's what gets the listener's attention in the first place. So think carefully about the words and sounds you're planning to use at the beginning of each story.

It's almost always necessary for the radio news writer to identify the person speaking in the sound bite or actuality. For example, write "Prime Minister Tony Blair said the death of Princess Diana is a great loss for the nation" leading into his sound bite. In radio, the idea is to let the listeners hear the voices and the sounds in the news. It's up to the writer to explain to the listeners why those voices and sounds are important.

Radio reporters work in relative anonymity compared with television reporters, because a lot of radio interviewing is done using the phone. If you can get someone on the phone, you can probably get that person to agree to a taped interview. Radio reporters can locate possible interview subjects by using city directory cross-referencing systems. If a man is holding children hostage at a day care center in town, the radio reporter can cross-reference the address of the house across the street from the day care center, look up the phone number and name of the people living in that house, call them up, and ask them to describe for the listening audience what activity they can see going on across the street. Most people are willing to do this. If these eyewitnesses don't want their names used on the radio, the reporter can identify the person speaking as a "neighbor" or "someone who lives directly across the street from the day care center."

In a large-market radio newsroom, there are news editors, news reporters, and anchors/personalities. In other radio stations, one or two people may wear all the hats, serving alternately as anchors, reporters, and editors. The news editors are similar to assignments editors and producers in television. They're concerned with the newscast itself, the individual stories in it, and how the stories fit together. They're also consciously concerned with getting and keeping listeners, the audience for their advertisers. The editors both assign stories and produce the newscasts. Producing includes putting the stories in order, lining them up so that they flow together naturally. News editors are interested in story count; the more stories in the newscast, the better. That means the shorter the stories, the better. Editors will edit reporters' copy to make the newscast as a whole flow together; they'll add segue lines to some stories; they'll rewrite and cut where necessary. (See Chapter 10.)

Some radio news reports are assigned, some come from the "futures" file, and others come from reporter enterprise. Radio news is a team effort; it's collaboration. Radio reporters have to produce a lot of copy. They have to "crank it out" on deadline. This pressure to produce, to get stories on the air as quickly as possible, is enormous. And it's relentless, because the clock is always ticking.

Radio reporters are often expected to write four or five different news stories a day. And they're often expected to write multiple versions of each story, using different audio cuts or sound bites. This may add up to 20 different stories a day. That's 20 different pieces of copy. So radio reporters have to be able to write fast and to write a variety of leads for their copy. Their days are long and unpredictable. It's hectic, concentrated work. There are few breaks, and there are no long lunch hours. Radio news reporters often eat while they work, or they eat while they drive. As they drive between assignments, they're rethinking the story they just covered, deciding on definitive leads and choosing which audio cuts to use.

Radio reporters rarely know what they're going to be doing as the day progresses. When spot news happens, they go there, and they *stay* until they get the story—whether it's to the river where searchers are looking for a body or to a day care center where a gunman is holding children hostage and police are set up to wait him out. Live reports from the scene of such events can be called in using a phone. Many radio stations have microwave trucks equipped with a transmitter called a **Marti unit.** Engineers can hook up "the Marti" and have studio-quality sound over the microphones. But this takes time and planning, so most reporters call in their daily radio spot news stories using a landline phone or a cell phone.

To help keep up with what's going on in the world, news editors and reporters listen constantly to the police scanners in the newsroom, and they keep an eye on the television monitors on the wall. The newsroom phones are set on speed dial for calls to the police dispatcher, the sheriff's office, the fire department, or other agencies when a story breaks.

Radio reporters say they love "being in the know" about news events. They have access to the rich, the famous, and the infamous for interviews. They travel and have front row seats at many history-making events. And the job is different every day. After all, the "unexpected" is what makes news. Radio reporters meet world leaders, national leaders, and celebrities. They go places, see people, and have access to people and places they normally wouldn't have. If you like to observe, it's the perfect place to be. It's fun, it's interesting, it's exciting, and there's not as much equipment to lug around as in TV. The everyday tools of the trade are portable: a writing pad or laptop computer or word processor, audiotape or mini–disk recorder, cell phone, beeper, and "patch" cords for audio jacks on public address systems. Other helpful equipment includes an umbrella, a ball cap, extra shoes, sunscreen, and a big water jug. (The umbrella can even serve as a makeshift sound booth on the scene.)

NPR–Style News

Although many commercial radio stations do a rapid-fire, high-story-count brand of news with very short stories at the top of the hour, there are alternatives for those who want more.

News Director/Anchor Kyle Kellams of KUAF-FM in Fayetteville, Arkansas,
delivering the morning news.

Here's the entire script of one morning's two-minute newscast from
the NPR station (KUAF, 91.3 FM) at the University of Arkansas in
Fayetteville. It aired at 8:33:

THIS IS K-U-A-F. I'M KYLE KELLAMS WITH THIS NEWS . . .

RAISING THE MINIMUM WAGE IS ONE OF THE ISSUES THAT ARKANSAS
CANDIDATES FOR SENATE ARE USING TO ILLUSTRATE THEIR DIFFERENCES. THE
MATTER CAME UP IN LAST NIGHT'S DEBATE BETWEEN REPUBLICAN INCUMBENT
TIM HUTCHINSON AND DEMOCRAT CHALLENGER MARK PRYOR. PRYOR SAYS HE
FAVORS RAISING THE MINIMUM WAGE, WHILE HUTCHINSON SAYS HE'S AGAINST
THE MOVE. HUTCHINSON SAYS RAISING THE MINIMUM WAGE MIGHT HELP
TEENAGERS BUT WON'T AID WORKING FAMILIES. THE CANDIDATES ALSO
DISAGREED ABOUT THE BEST WAYS TO ADMINISTER WELFARE AND ABORTION.

PRESIDENT BUSH WILL BE MAKING ANOTHER TRIP TO ARKANSAS
TOMORROW. THE PRESIDENT WILL VISIT A LITTLE ROCK HIGH SCHOOL, THEN
PARTICIPATE IN A FUND RAISER FOR ARKANSAS G-O-P CANDIDATES TOMORROW
NIGHT AT THE STATE HOUSE CONVENTION CENTER.

ARKANSAS STATE POLICE SAY THEY WILL STEP UP, AGAIN, THEIR
ENFORCEMENT OF TRAFFIC LAWS AROUND CONSTRUCTION ZONES. AND THE STATE
HIGHWAY AND TRANSPORTATION DEPARTMENT SAYS IT WILL STEP UP EFFORTS

TO INFORM OUT-OF-STATE DRIVERS ABOUT THE WORK ZONES ALONG ARKANSAS INTERSTATES. DEPARTMENT OFFICIALS SAY ABOUT TWO-THIRDS OF THE FATAL ACCIDENTS AROUND ARKANSAS HIGHWAY WORK ZONES INVOLVE OUT-OF-STATE DRIVERS.

FUNDS FOR MOSQUITO ABATEMENT PLANS WILL BE DISTRIBUTED TO EACH COUNTY IN ARKANSAS. THE MILLION-DOLLAR PACKAGE, SPLIT AMONG THE COUNTIES, CAN ONLY BE USED TO HELP ERADICATE MOSQUITOES AND FOR PUBLIC EDUCATION. THE MONEY IS PART OF A PLAN TO HELP SLOW A POSSIBLE SPREAD OF WEST NILE VIRUS.

THE FORT SMITH REGIONAL AIRPORT WILL DEDICATE ITS NEW TERMINAL TODAY. THE 20-MILLION-DOLLAR STRUCTURE WAS MADE POSSIBLE BY A GRANT FROM THE FEDERAL AVIATION ADMINISTRATION.

THE UNIVERSITY OF ARKANSAS FOR MEDICAL SERVICES IS SET TO RECEIVE A 500-THOUSAND-DOLLAR DONATION FOR A HIGH-TECH RESEARCH AND DEVELOPMENT PROGRAM. THE CONTRIBUTION, FROM ENTERGY ARKANSAS, WAS ANNOUNCED YESTERDAY AT A GROUNDBREAKING FOR U-A-M'S ARKANSAS BIOVENTURES, A THREE-POINT-NINE-MILLION-DOLLAR FACILITY.

IT'S 25 MINUTES BEFORE NINE.

Sam Baker is an assistant news director and morning host for KERA (90.1 FM), an NPR station in Dallas, Texas. He writes his own scripts and anchors the station's "Morning Edition" program. Here are two versions of a story he wrote about a nationwide system that's been developed to help find missing children.

YOU'VE HEARD A NUMBER OF RECENT STORIES ABOUT THE SUCCESS OF THE AMBER ALERT PROGRAM IN FINDING CHILDREN IN OTHER STATES. BUT THE TEXAS OFFICER WHO HELPED SET UP THE PROGRAM WORRIES THAT AUTHORITIES ACROSS THE COUNTRY MIGHT OVERUSE THE RESCUE TOOL. TARRANT COUNTY SHERIFF DEE ANDERSON TOLD THE DALLAS MORNING NEWS THE PLAN WORKS, BUT IT'S NOT EASY. HE SAID AGENCIES NEED TO UNDERSTAND THE POWER OF IT, AND THAT IF YOU USE THE AMBER PLAN TOO OFTEN, YOU CAN LOSE IT. ANDERSON WAS SPOKESMAN FOR ARLINGTON POLICE WHEN THE ALERT PROGRAM WAS CREATED TO TRY AND HELP FIND 9-YEAR-OLD AMBER HAGERMAN. SHE WAS LATER FOUND DEAD. NORTH TEXAS POLICE HAVE ISSUED ABOUT 50 ALERTS SINCE 1997. THE PLAN HAS BEEN CREDITED WITH SAVING 8 CHILDREN FROM HARM.

THE AMBER ALERT SYSTEM THAT BEGAN IN TEXAS IS BEING CREDITED FOR THE SAFE RETURN OF TWO TEENAGERS IN CALIFORNIA. THE STATE IMPLEMENTED THE SYSTEM LESS THAN A MONTH AGO, AND USED IT FOR ONLY THE SECOND TIME YESTERDAY TO ANNOUNCE THE GIRLS HAD BEEN ABDUCTED AT GUNPOINT FROM A REMOTE AREA OF LANCASTER, CALIFORNIA. THEY WERE FOUND LATER THE SAME DAY. AN AMBER PROGRAM SPOKESMAN IN THE D-F-W AREA SAID THE ALERT SYSTEM HAS BEEN CREDITED WITH THE RETURN OF 17 YOUNG PEOPLE AROUND THE COUNTRY SINCE 1997.

Sam says, "With each newscast limited to two minutes minus weather, sports scores, and a national underwriter credit, I'm lucky on any given day to get three or four stories in. However, I must admit it's also my fault. Over the years, I've constantly heard the rule for newscasts on commercial radio is about two to three lines per story. I fail to see how anyone can do that and provide the depth of information that public radio listeners want. Therefore, I take the liberty of making the story as long as necessary (within reason) to have the listener come away with a basic understanding of the story, including answers to 'why' and 'how' whenever possible. I'll mention one writing tip and it's easier said than done—eliminate use of the verb 'to be' as often as possible. In time you'll find yourself using stronger verbs and writing more concise sentences."

Glenn Mitchell is also a reporter at KERA in Dallas, and he freelances for NPR. The shortest pieces he writes run about three and a half minutes. Some go more than seven minutes. He says that what he writes is determined by the quality of the sound he gets in the field. (Remember how compelling the background sounds were in the opening story from September 11.) He advises beginning writers to think in advance about the best questions to ask so that the end result will be good-quality sound.

Before he writes his final scripts, Glenn listens to the sound he's recorded and then he writes the script. He wants sound that's going to tell a story. Most of it will be interview sound, but some will be natural sound. If he's doing a story about a factory, he'll talk to the person who runs the factory, people who assemble the product, the engineer who designed the product, and he'll also get ambient sound of the factory machinery so that the final piece isn't just words. The ambient sound is the radio equivalent of natural sound in TV. It enhances a story and puts the listeners in the place where the story occurs.

Glenn says in order to get good quality sound, he has to get a lot of audio. His ratio is 5-to-1: He'll record 15 minutes for every three minutes he actually uses, and he's a veteran at this. As a beginner, your ratio might be 10-to-1 or 15-to-1. The turnaround time for Glenn's reports varies. It might be a few hours, or a few days. Sports stories are usually due the next morning after the game. He might have as long as a week to put together a feature story about the arts. It's the time devoted to stories that makes NPR news unique. Three to seven minutes is a luxuriant amount of time for a single radio news story. NPR reporters have that luxury because public radio station newscasts might run a half-hour or more in length.

National Public Radio stations feature long-form, thoughtful pieces that might run 8 to 10 minutes in length. If NPR reporters can make it a good "sound" story, they can turn in a long piece with lengthy interviews and lots of natural sound. For example, a bridge in Austin, Texas, has become known for the colony of bats that lives in its girders. A reporter for NPR once did an eight-minute piece about the bats and the bridge. He included the natural sound of the bats beating their wings as they flew out of the bridge at sunset, interviews with people who had come to watch the bats fly out, interviews with bat experts, and interviews at the bridge with T-shirt vendors selling a variety of books, bat caps, and other bat paraphernalia. The reporter was able to create a "word picture" of the scene for his radio listeners.

Such word pictures are what radio journalists strive to create. And we remember those written by such legendary reporters as Edward R. Murrow. This is part of a script Ed Murrow wrote and broadcast on the CBS Radio Network on April 15, 1945, the day Allied troops liberated the Buchenwald concentration camp from the Nazis: "As I walked down to the end of the barracks, there was applause from the men too weak to get out of bed. It sounded like the hand clapping of babies; they were so weak." You, the listener, can "see" the condition of the men Murrow is seeing through the words he has written in this script. Good writing is in the details, the language, and the choice of words.

Conclusion

It doesn't matter if you listen to NPR or the local all-news radio station, one of radio's strengths is that it's portable. You can take it with you and hear it while you jog or while you drive your car. Another strength is its intimacy. You can hear the person speaking, hear the inflection in his or her voice, the tone, the emotion. You get to use your mind's eye. A child was once asked whether he preferred radio or television. He said radio. When the father asked why, the child answered that he preferred radio because the pictures are better. (See "Empire of the Air [videorecording]: The Men Who Made Radio.")

It's up to the radio writer to create those word pictures. The best writers become "wordsmiths." They know what words mean, and they choose the appropriate words, the most descriptive words for the story they're telling to the listening audience. Some television writers and reporters have started their careers in radio and will tell you "if you want to get into television, start in radio." There, the pictures don't get in the way.

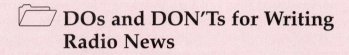

DOs and DON'Ts for Writing Radio News

Do
- Write short.
- Use descriptive language.
- Create word pictures.

Don't
- Forget to get good ambient sound.
- Forget to write in present or future tense.
- Let the shark get you.

TELEVISION NEWS STORY FORMS— THE VO

In television news, there are five basic story forms: **readers** (or "tell" stories), **voice-overs (VOs), voice-over to sound on tape (VO/SOTs),** reporter **packages,** and **donuts.** Beginning writers and associate producers are the people primarily responsible for taking information from story notes and compiling it into story form to be read by an anchor as a reader, a VO, or a VO/SOT. If a story involves no video or other visual over the face of the anchor, then it's called a reader. Sometimes, the viewers can see the anchor's face for the duration of a story and also see a graphic over his shoulder. That story would still qualify as a reader, because the viewers see the anchor for the entire story. Because there's not much production value associated with reader stories, they're usually quite short and might include a promise of video once it becomes available.

Midday anchors Gayle Guyardo and Bill Ratliff on the news set at WFLA-TV in Tampa.

A voice-over is any story that's read by the anchor and also incorporates video, a full-screen graphic, or some other visual. The term "voice-over" simply indicates that the anchor's voice is heard "over" some visual. The acronym VO usually indicates that she's talking over a piece of video. If she's talking over a graphic, many news operations label the story a VO/g to distinguish between the two. Later, we'll get to the longer story forms, such as VO/SOTs and packages. In this chapter, we'll concentrate on VOs.

Voice-over stories serve an important role in a newscast. They help the producer vary the pace of the show, while allowing us to deliver useful and interesting information in short form. VOs work very well when we cover events and a comment from someone at the event really wouldn't add that much to the story, when there's no real issue involved, or when there's only a limited amount of interesting information to impart to the viewers. A downtown street fair would probably warrant VO coverage only. It would involve nice colorful video and would be a way to highlight a part of the community; however, there's no controversy, and someone saying "I enjoyed the petting zoo" doesn't add anything, so a 20- to 30-second VO would suffice. The street fair isn't as important as other stories in the newscast are, so less time would be devoted to it.

The relative importance of the story isn't the only reason for assigning the story VO status. We might be getting late-breaking video from the satellites and have no time to put together a longer piece, so we would quickly edit some of the compelling video and give the few details that are available. Perhaps a trial has generated a couple of important bits of interesting information, but not enough to warrant more than 20 or 30 seconds. The information might be good, but there just isn't much of it.

Also, what might be a full-blown reporter package on a slow news day can be reduced to VO status simply because other news takes precedence. A producer might feel compelled to include the story, but simply can't give up the time in a packed news show to make it a long piece. Something a reporter has been working on all day might occupy only 30 seconds of news time when all is said and done.

The flip side of that is what's known as "trying to make chicken salad out of . . ." (you fill in the rest). Some days, the news managers are sitting around trying to figure out what to cover, especially as the lead story, because it seems *nothing* is going on. On those days, a compelling VO can give the show a kick start and perhaps even lead to a short series of related reports. Matt Morin is a producer at the NBC affiliate in Plattsburgh, New York, and remembers just such a day.

Because it was *so* slow, the news managers were considering a story about a stolen exotic bird as the lead story on the evening newscast. But they decided to take a look at what was happening in world and national news before making the decision. About the only thing worthwhile was the outpouring of support for victims of an earthquake in Turkey. However, to that point they knew of no local groups organizing relief efforts, and no one was aware of a large population of people of Turkish ancestry in upstate New York. They decided to do some digging though, and a reporter learned that there were a few Turkish students at a nearby university and at another small college in the area.

As the day progressed, the death toll from the earthquake continued to rise. The news team learned from the Turkish students that there were other Turkish people living in the area, and the story of what they went through waiting to hear of the fates of loved ones and friends made a solid story for the reporter. So the newscast opened with compelling video of the quake site as a VO, progressed to the reporter package about how the local Turkish community was dealing with news of the tragedy, moved on to a VO/SOT about the local Turkish students and the impact on them, and then moved to a quick VO/graphic about how local residents could help through the Red Cross. The first VO included the latest information about the death toll and tales of survival, and served as a "scene setter" to pieces 2 and 3. The second VO put a wrap on the segment. The two short stories added both pace and context. By the way, the stolen bird story wound up as a VO, item number 11.

The Mechanics of a VO

Information for a VO can come from a number of sources, such as story notes compiled by a reporter or videographer, news releases, wire services, video feed services, and the like. Story notes might be very brief, requiring the writer to expand on what's provided either by incorporating related information or by contacting the reporter or videographer (who might have gone on to another story assignment) for more information. The writer might also contact a source indicated in the story notes for clarification or additional information. In the case of news releases, the writer's primary task is taking the information and boiling it down to the essential elements. In the case of a script sent by a wire service or feed service, the primary task is to rewrite the information, putting a local "angle" on the story.

Writing from Video

The basic facts gathered at the story site or from newsmakers obviously give us a good starting point for what we should write. Who, what, when, where (and when we know them, why and how) are important elements in any news story. But if that's all we write, then we've created news print with wallpaper video over the top of it. In television, it's vital that we write from the video. In other words, what we see on the video should lead us to mention specific things in the script.

Now, we're not talking about play-by-play, as in "here's the mayor leaving her office, and here she is entering the council chambers" kind of stuff. But there should be a definite connection between the video and the words. If we mention the mayor, we should see the mayor. Some in the business call not having a picture to go along with a mention of someone or something specific the "not-seen-here syndrome," as in, "Mayor Smith, not seen here. . . ." So if we don't have a shot of the mayor we might want to refer to the project or the meeting rather than to the mayor—whatever it is we have video of.

Likewise, if we have a shot of a child jumping up and down, we might not write "little Jane Brown was jumping up and down," but instead, perhaps we would write something about the excitement of the moment. The video and the script should always match *thematically*. So let's be sure if we mention Jane specifically we have a shot of her, and if we write about her painting a picture (or say something about artistic expression), we don't see her reading a book. If we have a shot of the coach sweeping out the dugout, maybe we could make reference to the concerns he had coming into the season "being swept away." *The visuals should drive the writing, and then how the story is written will logically drive how the visuals are edited.* News Director Dan Dennison of KHON-TV in Honolulu calls it having stories that are high on the **SWAP** scale—working toward *synchronized words and pictures.*

Here are some examples:

Example 1

GAS PRICES—Version 1

On cam	FIGHTING IN THE MIDDLE EAST IS PUSHING UP GAS PRICES HERE IN THE U.S.
:00 Take tape snd under (VO) [Editor: show invasion video]	(vo) ISRAEL SENT TROOPS AND TANKS INTO THE WEST BANK DURING THE WEEKEND. THAT HAS SOME ANALYSTS WORRIED THE ARAB STATES MIGHT RETALIATE WITH A CUTBACK OR EVEN A SHUTDOWN OF OIL PRODUCTION. IT HASN'T HAPPENED YET BUT FEAR OF SHORTAGES HAS SENT PRICES AT THE PUMP SOARING. IN SOME AREAS THE PRICE OF GASOLINE JUMPED 25 CENTS A GALLON OVERNIGHT.
:30 Tape out	

What's wrong with this story? Our short VO about how fighting in the Middle East is affecting oil prices begins well enough with "generic" video of soldiers in battle. But it continues to show combat long after the copy has turned to what's happening at the pump. Our video has become **wallpaper**—pictures shown for the sake of showing pictures without a direct connection to the copy. In television, we use pictures to support the copy, but in the example above, after the third sentence the pictures actually *conflict* with the copy. What sense does it make to show video of tanks rolling through streets when we're talking about people filling their gas tanks?

Here's another example.

Example 2

FIRE ECONOMY—Version 1

On cam	AS IF PROPERTY DAMAGE WEREN'T ENOUGH . . . NOW THIS SUMMER'S WILDFIRE SEASON IS HURTING ARIZONA'S ECONOMY.

:00 Take tape	(vo)
snd under (VO)	DURING THE PAST FEW WEEKS
	FOREST FIRES HAVE CONSUMED THOU-
	SANDS OF ACRES AND BURNED DOZENS
[Editor: at :00 show flame video]	OF HOMES IN SOUTH AND CENTRAL
	ARIZONA.
	SOME OF THOSE FIRES ARE STILL
	SMOLDERING.
	THE SUMMER TRAVEL SEASON IS
	VERY IMPORTANT TO THE STATE'S
	ECONOMY.
	BUT TOURISM OFFICIALS REPORT
	VACANCIES ARE UP BY 75 PERCENT.
	THE GOVERNOR HAS PROMISED
	DISASTER RELIEF.
:30 Tape out	

This VO begins appropriately with fire video as the copy discusses the recent history of the fires, but when the story switches gears to discuss the effects on resorts, motels, and restaurants, the video continues to show towering flames.

So how can we solve this problem? A step in the right direction is to choose the correct visuals to go with the copy. In the gas prices example, the problem began when the copy switched to prices while the viewer was still seeing video of warfare. Could the producer have solved the problem by substituting "generic" pictures of people pumping gas? Not totally. Certainly, a quick shot of people gassing up would have been appropriate—for a sentence or two. But if it drags on too long then that video, too, will become "wallpaper." What about the fire story? Would "file" video of hotels and restaurants at the appropriate point have solved the problem? Again, such video would have improved the situation—but if it drags on too long, it becomes a new problem.

The general problem in both cases is that we have only "generic" video to support the copy—generic warfare, generic gas pumps, generic hotels, generic restaurants, and so on. These "generic" pictures are like the repeat patterns on wallpaper—hence the term. The best solution is to provide *specific* video. In the gas prices example—do we have pictures of people pumping gas *today*—including shots of the *current* prices at the pump? In the fire story, do we have pictures of empty resorts, motels, and restaurants shot *today*? (And while we're at it, can we get some interviews with people today who are affected by these stories? Maybe these items are worth more than a VO!)

If we get the "fresh" *specific* video, then copy should reference it in some way, *specifically.* Below are examples of how both of these stories might look with wallpaper removed.

Example 3

GAS PRICES—Version 2

On cam	FIGHTING IN THE MIDDLE EAST IS PUSHING UP GAS PRICES RIGHT HERE IN THE BAY AREA.
:00 Take tape	(vo)
snd under (VO)	ISRAEL SENT TROOPS AND TANKS INTO THE WEST BANK DURING THE
[Editor: at :00 show invasion video]	WEEKEND.
[Editor: at :03 show oil field video]	THAT HAS SOME ANALYSTS WORRIED THE ARAB STATES MIGHT RETALIATE WITH A CUTBACK OR EVEN A SHUTDOWN OF OIL PRODUCTION.
[Editor: at :09 show pump vid]	THAT HASN'T HAPPENED YET. . . BUT FEAR OF SHORTAGES HAS SENT PRICES AT THE PUMP SOARING.
	WE CHECKED SEVERAL STATIONS HERE IN TOWN THIS MORNING . . .
[Editor: at :15 show price]	THE LOWEST PRICE WE FOUND WAS A BUCK FIFTY AT THIS SUNMART STATION AT THE CORNER OF HAWTHORNE AND FIRST IN TAMPA.
[:30 tape out]	(on cam)
On cam	THE OWNER TELLS US THAT'S 25 CENTS MORE THAN YESTERDAY. OTHER STATES ARE REPORTING SIMILAR HIKES.

Example 4

FIRE ECONOMY—Video Match Version

On cam	AS IF PROPERTY DAMAGE WEREN'T ENOUGH . . . NOW THIS SUMMER'S WILDFIRE SEASON IS HURTING ARIZONA'S ECONOMY.
:00 Take tape	(vo)
snd under (VO)	DURING THE PAST FEW WEEKS FOREST FIRES HAVE CONSUMED THOUSANDS

[Editor: at :00 show flame video]	OF ACRES AND BURNED DOZENS OF HOMES IN SOUTH AND CENTRAL ARIZONA.
[Editor: at :06 show last year resort vid]	THE SUMMER TRAVEL SEASON IS VERY IMPORTANT TO THE STATE'S ECONOMY . . . AND LAST YEAR . . . BUSINESS WAS BOOMING AT THIS RESORT IN VISTA FLAMANTE.
[Editor: at :14 show today video, starting with empty parking lot]	TAKE A LOOK AT THAT SAME RESORT TODAY: THE PARKING LOT IS MOSTLY EMPTY.
	THE STATE SAYS IT'S LIKE THIS ACROSS THE AREA WITH VACANCIES UP 75 PERCENT.
:30 Tape out	(on cam)
On cam	THE GOVERNOR IS PROMISING DISASTER RELIEF.

In both cases, the "nonwallpaper" versions of these stories are more interesting because the copy is about specifics, not statistics. Also note that in both instances, part of our solution for getting rid of the wall-paper video was to come back on camera for the final line. There's nothing dishonorable about an on-camera shot—and some operations prefer to end stories with an on-camera tag, particularly if a different anchor will read the next story.

Literal Video

One sin almost as bad as failing to match the copy to the screen is that of taking the video *too* literally. Your pictures should support your copy, but that doesn't mean your copy has to be a slave to the pictures. You're writing a story, not a slideshow and certainly not a video catalog. For instance, if you begin your story with a shot of the sunrise, you don't have to write, "The sun burst over the horizon in a huge orange ball of flame at 5:15 A.M. this morning." You can use the picture to support in a general way the idea that your story is about a new day or what it might bring. "Sunrise was not a welcome sight to dozens of weary volunteers who faced another grueling day of battling the wildfires."

Here's another example. Imagine that you have a shot of a woman crying, with tears rolling down both cheeks. You don't have to write, "Tears rolled down both cheeks as Linda Jones began her press conference." You can write, "It was with uncommon bravery that Linda Jones approached the podium this morning to share her grief with the community."

In neither case are we using the video as "wallpaper" because it's specific, and we're referencing it specifically in copy. In both examples we're using the video to support our copy thematically, rather than literally.

"Thematic" video can be used in other ways. Let's revisit a paragraph from our fire season story:

> TAKE A LOOK AT THAT SAME RESORT TODAY: THE PARKING LOT IS MOSTLY EMPTY.
>
> THE STATE SAYS IT'S LIKE THIS ACROSS THE AREA WITH VACANCIES UP 75 PERCENT.

With the words "take a look," we began showing video of a specific item, which in this case was the empty parking lot. It's okay to continue showing video of that same specific resort to cover the next sentence, even though that sentence is general in nature, because it's about what's happening at *other* resorts. Use of sustaining video to support a general theme in this way is permissible, but don't let it drag on for too long.

The fire story also provides an example of the same process in reverse: starting general and going to the specific, as follows:

> THE SUMMER TRAVEL SEASON IS VERY IMPORTANT TO THE STATE'S ECONOMY . . . LAST YEAR . . . BUSINESS WAS BOOMING AT THIS RESORT IN VISTA FLAMANTE.

In this case, we'll cover the first sentence with video of the resort packed with tourists last year. This supports the theme of "travel" in a general way. The second sentence transitions from a general statement to a very specific one about the very resort we're seeing. This is also an acceptable use of video.

The key to these examples, and what sets both of them apart from "wallpaper" video, is the fact that both contain specific references—and we move quickly to other video once we've made our point.

Writing from File Footage

Sometimes, despite your best efforts, all you have is file footage. There's no prohibition against using file, especially if it shows something specific. Often, we have to use file because we're writing about something in the past. So if you mention last year's record snowfall, you'll have to get file footage of that. Also, even in the cases when we know the tape doesn't show what the script is mentioning, there are ways to downplay the discrepancy. For example, let's assume that Johnny Famoussinger was killed in a plane crash half an hour before airtime, and no video of the crash site is available yet. We might choose to use file tape of a recent concert, but of course that has no direct relation to today's story. Making a reference to the specific video we have at the beginning of the story makes the use of this piece of file tape more acceptable. The story would begin something like this:

<u>**Singer**</u>

	(Gayle)
On cam	POP SUPERSTAR JOHNNY
	FAMOUSSINGER IS DEAD.
:00 Take cass snd under (VO)	(vo)
	SHOWN HERE AT A CONCERT LAST
	MONTH . . . FAMOUSSINGER WAS
	RETURNING TO GOTHAM CITY FROM THE
	WEST COAST EARLY THIS MORNING . . .
	WHEN HIS PRIVATE JET WENT DOWN
	IN A REMOTE PART OF THE ROCKY
	MOUNTAINS. . . .

Making a reference to the video we're seeing makes it more acceptable for use in relation to a story that has nothing to do with the concert. It's important to write from the video throughout, but in cases like this we have no video to go with today's story other than the file tape. So, a direct video reference at the top is about the best we can do. Failing to reference the video can lead to some confusion. In this example, we'd be talking about Famoussinger returning when the footage is of him singing. Giving the viewers the visual reference at the top alerts them that what they see is what they're going to get.

Improper Use of Video—or, "When Wallpaper Strikes Back"

When a producer or reporter uses video as wallpaper, file tape frequently is part of the equation. One good cure, as we saw above, is to make specific reference within copy to the pictures. If you can't figure out a way to write such a reference into the copy, then this is a strong clue that you shouldn't be using the tape. The rule is particularly important when it comes to use of file tape containing identifiable faces.

The truth is that television news has a horrible habit of turning real human beings into objects for the purpose of illustrating general problems or issues. For instance, to cover a story involving the latest report about the number of people with sexually transmitted diseases, an assignments editor might say to a photographer, "Go out and spray some video of people walking around downtown." Chances are, you've seen a story just like this: The copy mentions a general health problem such as obesity, AIDS, heart disease, or whatnot, while the video shows throngs of "generic" people. If the shot is very wide, the storyteller might get away with it (although that doesn't mean it's right). But what if it's not so wide? What if there are recognizable faces in it?

Using pictures of people in this way is a form of wallpaper video. But it's worse than other forms of wallpaper because instead of using generic pictures to illustrate a story, we're using *specific* pictures. There's no such thing as a "generic" person. Every face has attached to it a real person with a real name and a real address and real rights, who's real likely to hire a real good lawyer to hit you real hard with a real ugly lawsuit. If there's a recognizable face in your video, then that video is *specific,* not generic—and some might construe your story to be *about that individual.* So if you're using a "crowd shot" to illustrate a story about something negative or embarrassing such as STDs, and Ethel Icetea recognizes herself in your video, she isn't going to be happy. If she gets a call from her neighbors kidding her about it, she's going to be less happy. You might then get a call from the law firm of Ketchum and Cheatham that will negatively affect *your* happiness.

Some assignment editors who are savvy enough to realize the danger of having specific faces in generic video might say something like this to the photographer: "We're doing a story about juvenile delinquents hanging out at the skateboard park downtown. Go spray me some pictures of some kids—but no faces." So Joe Grabbenshoot brings back video of hands, feet, and torsos, which then hits the air covering portions of your juvenile delinquent story. Trouble is, your video shows the only kid hanging out downtown today who happened to be wearing a barbed wire bracelet in combination with a Marilyn Manson T-shirt and a bicycle chain belt—and he recognized himself. So did his friends. Phone call holding for you on line two.

This kind of video misuse gets on the air in other ways, too. Imagine your medical reporter is doing a piece involving the latest statistics about the problem of babies being born addicted to crack. She says to the editor, "Grab some of that delivery room video we shot last month." In goes the video to cover part of your track, and guess what? Ethel Icetea was delivering her baby the day you shot that video, and now thanks to you her friends are calling her to ask whether she's gotten over her little crack problem.

Here's an even more common example. You're the crime beat reporter. You're doing a story about the latest crime stats. Drug arrests are way up. This doesn't surprise you because you've been on four really cool crack dealer roundups in the past year. So you say to the editor, "Cover this with some of that great arrest video we got last summer." The editor pulls up a dramatic shot of police slamming some handcuffed guy against a cruiser and slaps it into the story. Trouble is, little did you know that prosecutors had dropped the charges against this particular guy a few days after his arrest. He was innocent. And by the way, the guy is in the lobby and would like to have a word with you.

It's possible to victimize businesses in this way as well. An assignment editor in one medium market reportedly once sent a photographer out to "get **b-roll** of banks" to support a story about financial trouble in the state's banking industry. At least one of the banks the photographer shot was in perfectly good financial shape, and its managers were none too pleased to suddenly see its sign flashed in a story about failing banks. It's said that money exchanged hands because of that one.

The cure for each of these scenarios is the same one we applied earlier in this chapter: Make a specific reference to the video. If you're showing a group of people walking down the street, then you should tell us what that specific group of people has to do with your AIDS story. If you can't make the link then drop the video. Similarly, if you're showing some guy being thrown up against the hood of a car in handcuffs for your story about street crime, your copy should tell us who that person is and how he's related to your crime story. Chances are that a year after this video was shot, you either don't know who the guy is or don't know what happened to his case, or both—which means you shouldn't use the video.

Bottom line: The viewer has a right to expect that the pictures you're showing are directly related to the words you're speaking. Such is the visual language of television. If those pictures are specific and show a particular and recognizable individual, business, or organization—then the audience will believe the story is about those individuals or institutions. It's worth noting that the word "recognizable" sits on a slippery slope. The individual doesn't have to be recognizable to the public at large—only to the individual or that person's friends. The same is true of businesses. So check your video very carefully. Raise red flags if your pictures portray (or appear to portray) any individual or organization in a less than favorable way. If the story is *supposed* to be about those people or places, then proceed. But make sure the connection is deliberate, not accidental.

And by the way, the word "spray" as it's commonly used in newsrooms can be an indicator that something bad is about to happen, because it's commonly taken to mean the act of pointing the camera in a general direction and capturing video in a quick, sometimes indiscriminate fashion. The act of capturing video for use in a television newscast should always be very deliberate.

Poster Children

Let's say you've done your homework and you're absolutely certain of the identity of the person you plan to use in your file tape. You're also certain that the person does have a direct connection to the story you're trying to illustrate, and you plan to make this connection plain in your copy. You're free to proceed, right? Actually, you should pause for just one more question: Is it *fair* to use this person in the fashion you're proposing?

If the mayor throws an ashtray at a citizen during a city council meeting, then that video is fair game every time you do a story about the mayor's temper. But what about the guy in your arrest video? Do you really want to drag this man out and parade him around every time you do a story about street-level drug busts? Even if he was guilty, how many times does his family deserve to be subjected to those pictures of him being thrown up against that car hood? Similar considerations apply to the victims of crimes and accidents. If you've been in television very long at all, chances are you've had a discussion like this one: "Jane, we're doing another piece about the Death Ramp tonight. We'll need the pictures of that great accident from last December." So tonight on your newscast some poor schlub who spent weeks in the hospital after that accident gets to see himself being pried out of the burning wreckage of his car and then wheeled out on a gurney for the 18th time. Typically, when charity organizations choose a poster child, it's a voluntary arrangement. Releases are signed. Money might change hands. Who wants to be poster child for Fatal Accident Week? Or Crime and Violence Week? No one. But in television news, we don't ask. We just do it—and we'll use those same pictures again and again.

The next time you propose to do this to someone in a story for which you're responsible, give it some thought. How many times has this particular person been used as "file tape"? Is it really necessary? Are there viable alternatives? Approach these questions with a sense of humanity.

Graphics

But what, you ask, do I do if I need to mention something for which I have no appropriate video, file or otherwise? The use of graphics has become increasingly important in television news for that very reason. It's particularly difficult to visually depict a lot of numbers using video, but it's fairly easy to do so with a graphic. Your story might be about crime figures: assaults are down, armed robberies are up, property crime is down, other types of crime have remained constant. You probably won't be able to get your hands on video of each of those crimes taking place, but you can ask a talented (and VERY valuable) graphics person to put together a **full-screen graphic (FSG)** titled "Crime Statistics" that shows the numbers of each type of crime as compared to a previous period of time. Or maybe you need to write about the effects of gas leaking out of underground storage tanks. You're probably not going to persuade your shooter to go dig a hole and crawl down into it to get some shots, and besides, that wouldn't be as effective as an animated graphic showing the storage system and how a leak can occur. So when you don't have video of something specific, either don't write specifically about it, or consider using a graphic as your visual support.

When you use graphics, make sure the elements match the script from top to bottom or from left to right, depending on how the graphic is designed. Also, don't try to cram too much information onto an FSG. When that's the case, the graphic is "too busy" and difficult to read. Use bullet points that the anchor might read as bullet points, or might elaborate on. Having each new bit of information "reveal" as the anchor gets to it also adds to the pacing and look of the piece, and keeps the viewer from "reading ahead" and thereby paying less attention to the anchor than to what's on the screen. The idea is that as the anchor is saying "the number of armed robberies in the Hooverville metro area increased 17 percent compared to last year," the viewers see something such as "ARMED ROBBERIES UP 17%" on the screen. Just as is the case when we're writing from video, what the viewers hear and what they see must match when we're using graphics. The "matching" theme applies to **over-the-shoulder (OTS)** graphics as well. You'll want to find the single frame of video (a close-up shot) that best illustrates your story for the OTS, and then make sure that the wording at the bottom is wording the anchor will actually use during the on-camera lead. So if you pick a cute shot of a kitten for the OTS for your story about the animal shelter and ask someone in graphics to add the words "Furry Friends" to the bottom of the graphic, we should hear the anchor say the words "furry friends" at some point before we go to video.

Following are examples of some of the most common ways stations use graphics.

Bullet Points

A bullet point consists of two or three words of text summarizing a statement or point presented in copy, usually set off by an asterisk, circle, square, or some other form of demarcation at the beginning of the line. Reporters or producers typically use bullet points when they need to cover a difficult passage and no specific video is available to support the copy. For example, imagine the city council is ordering the police chief to take a series of steps to reduce expenditures. When you're explaining those steps in your copy, you can either show video of city council people sitting around or video of cops at shift change. Both would be "wallpaper" used in this way. The better option is to extract bullet points from the specific steps the council is ordering, then present those points on-screen over a color background, preferably one that an artist has composed with your station's logo and artwork or an icon to support the theme of the story.

Quotes

This technique is similar to the use of bullet points described above, except that in this case instead of extracting bullet point summaries we'll excerpt full quotes. This is useful in a number of scenarios, including:

- Presenting excerpts from a formal statement given by someone who is either unwilling or unable to go on-camera
- Pulling quotes from a document used in an investigative story
- Quoting court testimony
- Giving text support to a hard-to-understand audio track, such as a 911 tape, undercover audio introduced as evidence in court, a phone conversation, and so forth.

In such instances, we would typically use quotation marks on-screen.

Charts and Graphs

When presenting complex statistics, simply flashing the numbers on-screen can be confusing. Good old-fashioned bar charts, line graphs, and pie charts often do a better job of showing the meaning of numbers in relation to one another.

Locator Graphics

Viewers often find it difficult to relate to addresses or to the names of small towns or obscure locations. Full-screen maps do an excellent job of making such locations meaningful.

General Information

When your copy contains lists, numbers, or general information such as the name of someone who's giving an interview by phone, full-screen graphics support will help the viewer grasp the information.

Weather Graphics

Weathercasts make use of a wide range of full-screen graphics, everything from maps showing weather fronts and radar images to "list" graphics supporting the forecast.

Explanatory Graphics

Sometimes you find yourself needing to explain a concept for which there just aren't any good pictures. In such cases you'll need original artwork. Probably the most common use of original artwork in local television is in the area of medical reporting. For instance, if you're giving an explanation of how a quadruple bypass works, b-roll of doctors and nurses bending over a patient on the operating table isn't going to provide much help. Quite literally, you'll need to draw the audience a diagram. It's the only good way to show the problems of restricted blood flow to the heart and how the bypass operation resolves that.

Graphics of this sort are useful in many situations when you need to provide an explanation of something involving something about which pictures don't tell the story of the larger concept involved or where cameras can't go. All of us saw this type of graphic use in action in the days following the terrorist attacks against the World Trade Center; virtually every news organization everywhere used graphics to show how the fuel-fed fires inside the buildings weakened the support girders and ultimately caused them to fail. In a story about corrosion inside the Sunshine Skyway Bridge, WFLA-TV reporter Mark Douglas found himself needing to explain a method of construction that uses steel tendons under tension to hold concrete columns together. For this purpose he asked a graphics artist to render a cross-section of a bridge column. (It's worth noting that in the station's converged environment, the artist who did the work happened to be a graphic artist for the *Tampa Tribune*, who generated the artwork for the newspaper version of the story. A television artist then adapted the artwork for use in the broadcast report.)

Sophisticated graphics suites also have animation capabilities to show effects progressing over time. Again, the more sophisticated the technique, the longer it takes to render. Reporters and producers are well advised to keep this in mind when asking for graphics.

Thematic Graphics

This category involves the use of art to establish an overarching visual "theme" for a story. This visual theme then appears on all graphics for the entire story. In many cases these "themed" graphics can support the story in all the ways outlined above—extracting bullet points, giving quotes, presenting explanations, and so on. Sometimes themed graphics have no purpose other than to give visual support to the theme or tone of the story.

Branding

No discussion of graphics use would be complete without some mention of "branding." Almost every full-screen graphic has the *potential* to support the news organization's brand. Some TV newsrooms pay little or no attention to branding. Others, such as WFLA-TV, are passionate about it. Most of the station's full-screen graphics will bear the "Eight On Your Side" logo somewhere on them.

It's also quite common for stations to use full-screen graphics or animations for the sole purpose of carrying out a branding function. Thus a station's top story might be preceded by a flashy graphic bearing the words "BIG story," usually accompanied by some cheesy "swooshing" sound effect. Many stations have "franchises" of various sorts—medical, consumer, investigative, and so forth—and will often precede such reports with a full-screen "stinger" flashing the station's logo with a few notes of its station music or a sound effect of some sort. Branding style and usage vary dramatically from station to station—and as always, there's no accounting for taste. But the goal is always the same: to achieve a uniform station "look" and to impress that look on the mind of the viewer.

A Final Thought about Graphics

Of course, graphics are used in VO/SOTs as well as VOs, and are pre-produced for insertion in packages too. Good graphics are a big help when illustrating stories that are "video poor" or when we need to use numbers or other statistics, but don't use graphics as a substitute for good pictures. When you do have good video, take advantage of it. Videographers are told to concentrate on *tight shots of people doing things*, because that makes for compelling video. Writers need to look

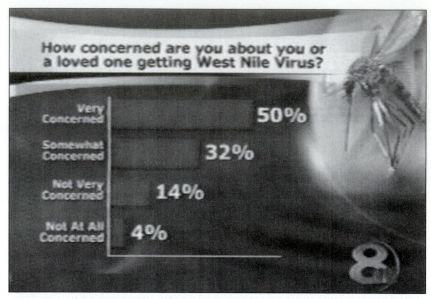

Bar chart: This graphic helps support a story about a viewer poll measuring concern about a public health threat.

Branding graphic: The sole purpose of this visual, which was part of an animated package open or "stinger," is to brand the story.

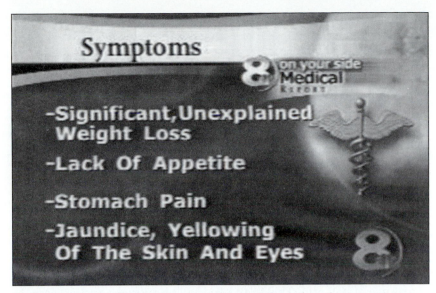

Explanatory graphic: This graphic uses bullet points drawn from the story script to provide visual support for storytelling.

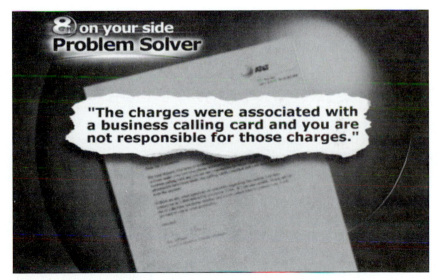

Quote graphic: This graphic excerpts an exact quote from a document referenced within the story.

for those compelling pictures when **logging** tapes (making a list of the shots, including a description of each usable shot and where it's located on the tape) and let those shots drive the story. Utilize your video to its full extent, and do the same with the natural sound you have.

Use of Natural Sound

What we hear is just as important as what we see. A VO about a fund-raising concert can be more effective if the anchor pauses for a few seconds when we go to the tape to allow for some "nat SOT full" to let the viewers hear one of the bands. Then she can tell us more as the sound of the band continues "under" her voice. Pieces that have no **natural sound** are "flat." When we go somewhere, we experience sights AND sounds. The news crew serves as a surrogate for the viewers, and needs to give audience members as much of the ambiance of the scene as possible. That means incorporating natural sound, including frequent use of nats full. This is an especially important pacing element in packages, and we'll discuss it further in Chapter 9. In radio and in TV, the liberal use of natural sound makes the difference between mundane pieces and really good broadcast journalism.

A Lot to Say in 30 Seconds or Less

Although there's no set length for any broadcast story, VOs on local news programs typically run about 20 to 30 seconds. In a series of back-to-back VOs, some might be as short as 10 to 12 seconds, and in rare circumstances a VO might run as much as 40 to 45 seconds. Generally though, you can expect a VO to be about 20 to 30 seconds in length. It's not uncommon for viewers to see the anchor briefly at the beginning of a VO and perhaps again at the end. However, it's still a VO and not a reader because at some point in the story we see something other than the anchor's face.

Writing from the video is so important that we'll mention it several times throughout this book. Having the video to tell part of the story helps, but in many cases, we can't fit all the information that's available into the time limit we're given. Information *will* be left out. The key is not to leave out any major information. VOs are challenging because television news writers must capture viewer attention, impart the most relevant information of the story, and perhaps even transition to the next story, all in 20 to 30 seconds.

It's difficult to be very creative in such a short amount of time, and many of us making the transition to broadcast are caught in the "flowery words and phrases" mind-set we learned when writing much longer stories and essays. The creativity in broadcast writing doesn't come in how many dependent clauses and rarely used words we can stick in one sentence. Instead, creativity is often evident in the ability to tell a story so that people who don't know anything about what happened can understand what we're telling them right away. As with any good piece of broadcast writing, an informative VO gives viewers the most pertinent information and relates to what the pictures are showing.

Broadcast writers do have room to get creative with their writing, depending on the type of story they're dealing with. This is frequently the case with soft news or feature stories. We still have to use clear, understandable words and short sentences, but the English language is a wonderful tool, even when you're operating within severe time constraints. Chapter 4 contains a lot of information about writing creative news copy, but here's a quick example of how to change a lackluster story into a better one. The following very average copy is taken from an actual newscast that hit the air exactly as presented below. Note that the available video consists entirely of a giant pumpkin and the farmer who grew it. A suggested rewrite follows. We'll explain what the markings on the left side of the page mean in the "Providing Directions" section that follows the examples.

Pumpkin (Early Version)

	(Ted)
On cam	IT'S ALMOST TIME FOR HALLOWEEN . . . AND WHAT WOULD HALLOWEEN BE WITHOUT PUMPKINS?
:00 Take tape	(vo)
nat snd under (VO)	FOLKS ACROSS THE COUNTRY ARE GEARING UP FOR THE HOLIDAY, MAKING COSTUMES . . . BUYING TREATS . . . AND HARVESTING PUMPKINS FOR THIS SEASON.
	MILTON BARBER MAY NOT WANT TO BUTCHER HIS PUMPKIN BECAUSE IT'S A WORLD RECORD PUMPKIN.
	THE WINNING PUMPKIN WEIGHS A WHOPPING 743 POUNDS.
	BARBER SAYS HE'S NOT SURE WHAT HE'LL DO WITH THE PUMPKIN BUT HE DOES PLAN TO SELL THE SEEDS.
:40 Tape ends	

The story as written contains all the pertinent information, but it certainly isn't very memorable. The following example takes the same set of facts, presents them in a different way, and still takes only 40 seconds to read. After reading both, decide which of the two you prefer.

Pumpkin (Later Version)

	(Ted)
On cam	EVERY OCTOBER SOME PERSON
OTS	PRETENDS TO HAVE PRODUCED THE
	PLANET'S MOST PRODIGIOUS PUMPKIN.
	THE PERSON MAKING THAT CLAIM
	THIS YEAR MIGHT HAVE A CASE.
:00 Take tape	(vo)
nat snd under (VO)	MILTON BARBER OF PITTSBURGH IS
	PLEASED AND PROUD TO BE THE OWNER
	OF AN OUTRAGEOUSLY OVERSIZED ENTRY.
	IN FACT . . . MILTON'S PONDEROUS
	PRODUCE WEIGHS ROUGHLY FOUR
	TIMES MORE THAN MILTON HIMSELF.
	IT'S A VERITABLE VEGETABLE ON
	STEROIDS . . . THIS PUMPKIN CRUNCHES
	THE SCALES AT A STAGGERING 743
	POUNDS.
	THAT'S ENOUGH TO GIVE A FOUR-
	OUNCE SERVING TO EACH OF ABOUT
	THREE THOUSAND PEOPLE!
	WHAT'S HE GOING TO DO WITH ALL
	THAT POTENTIAL PUMPKIN PIE?
	WELL, HE COULD TURN HIS ENTRY
	INTO THE JACK-O-LANTERN THAT ATE
	PITTSBURGH.
	BUT WHETHER HE DOES THAT OR
	NOT . . . MILTON DOES HAVE ONE THING
	IN MIND.
	HE MAY WELL WIND UP TURNING
	THE WORLD'S BIGGEST PUMPKIN INTO
	THE WORLD'S BIGGEST PUMPKIN PATCH.
	MILTON PLANS TO SELL THE SEEDS.
:50 Tape ends	

Providing Directions

Writing a VO so that viewers can understand the story (and perhaps even get a kick out of it) is only part of the writer's responsibility. Other people in the news operation also have to understand what the writer has in mind in relation to the video or other visual elements of the story. If the story is structured so that viewers are supposed to see the anchor and an over-the-shoulder (OTS) graphic for the first sentence, the script has to indicate that.

Television news scripts are set up in split-page format. The right side of the page is what the anchor is supposed to read. It also includes a bit of information to help cue the anchors as to who reads the story and when the video appears. That information is placed in parentheses and isn't in uppercase, so the anchor knows not to read it. (Some stations do it differently, putting the anchor copy in upper/lowercase and directions all uppercase. The key is to set directions and copy off from one another somehow.) The left side of the page contains directions for the control room personnel. If those directions are incomplete or missing, the show director has to guess at which point to incorporate the tape, or if there's even a tape associated with that particular story. Having the tape appear too soon or too late throws off the flow of the story. Anchors can adjust their read rate when the tape is a second or two early or late, but several seconds of discrepancy almost always result in noticeable errors on the air. You don't want your anchor to be talking about "this little boy" at the time that the tape is showing a female police officer.

In the pumpkin example above, the writer intends for the viewers to see the anchor (Ted) for a brief period of time before the video appears. That's what the "on cam" marking means. There would also be a small graphic over one of the anchor's shoulders. The director will then "take" the video at the point indicated on the script. The anchor knows that his face is no longer on the screen at this point, because of the (vo) indication on the right side of the page. So, he can read directly from the hard copy of the script and keep an eye on a video monitor at the same time to make sure the script and the video are matching. If they aren't, he can vary his read rate.

We line up the directions on the left with the place in the copy at which the directions are supposed to be applied. Go back and look at the pumpkin example. We've asked the director to take the video when the anchor is saying "folks across the country" in the "before" example and when the anchor is saying "Milton Barber of Pittsburgh" in the "after" example. We've also indicated on the script that the video is accompanied by natural sound, the sound of the people in the pumpkin patch, for example, and that the natural sound is to be played "under" the anchor's voice. When the director calls out "take

VTR three" (in this example, let's say the tape in question is being played through machine three), she also indicates to the audio person to "track" it, meaning to play the accompanying sound.

All tapes start at :00, so when the director takes the tape he or she also resets a timer in the control room. Writers also indicate how much time is on the tape. In that way, if the timer is up to :38 on a piece accompanied by a 40-second tape and the anchor still has two sentences to read, the director knows it's time to quickly cut back to the camera shot of the anchor before the tape goes to black on the air. In an effort to keep this from happening, writers and producers time the part of the script intended to be "under" video beforehand and ask tape editors to provide 10 seconds of tape beyond what's needed.

So, if someone read the "before" pumpkin example and it took :30 to read it, the tape editor would be asked to provide :40 seconds of tape. That video **pad** is critical, and we indicate the amount of tape provided including the pad. This alleviates a lot of panic in the control room. A quick production note: The 10 seconds of pad isn't a new shot but a continuation of the shot that covers the final seconds of the VO. Just as we don't want the video to run out, we also don't want the shot to change just before the director punches out. So the final shot on a 40-second piece of tape would run from about :25 or :26 all the way to :40—or as close to :40 as that one shot will get you.

Also, notice where the "tape ends" marking is positioned. It comes at the bottom of the script. This indicates that once we've taken the tape, it's supposed to continue until the end of the script. If instead we had wanted to see the anchor for the final sentence of the script, we would have positioned the "tape ends" marking at the end of the preceding sentence and added an "on cam" marking at the beginning of the final sentence. It's very important to include these directions, and we'll introduce you to others as we discuss other television news story forms. Remember, television is a visual medium and news writers have to provide information to the folks on the technical side so that the pictures and the words will match up.

Now let's look at a few more examples. First, a reader story.

Boys Ranch
_____

(Colleen)

SS: BOYS RANCH   ARIZONA BOYS RANCH HAS FILED
                                  AN APPEAL TO KEEP THE STATE FROM
                                  SHUTTING DOWN THE PROGRAM FOR
                                  DELINQUENT YOUTHS.
                                      THE BOYS RANCH ACCUSES THE
                                  STATE OF WRONGLY REFUSING TO RENEW

ITS CHILD-CARE LICENSE.

THE GROUP'S ATTORNEY CLAIMS
THE STATE SINGLED OUT THE MARCH
DEATH OF 16-YEAR-OLD NICHOLAS
CON-TRER-AZ BECAUSE IT DOESN'T
LIKE THE PROGRAM.

THE BOYS RANCH HAS BEEN IN
OPERATION FOR 49 YEARS.

The only marking we've provided for the director on this example (other than the title of the story) is the notation "SS: BOYS RANCH." That lets the director know that the story begins with the anchor (Colleen) on-camera and an image out of the still store machine appearing over her shoulder. Because no other markings appear, the director knows no tape is involved and that we'll see the anchor's face for the duration of this short story. "SS" stands for still store, and this particular image will include the written title "BOYS RANCH." Colleen knows not to read her name even though it appears on the right side of the page because it's in parentheses and is in upper- and lowercase. The procedure at this station is to put the script in all uppercase.

Now we'll look at a few examples of different ways of dealing with VOs, either as individual stories or as part of a story set.

Periodontal
_____

	(Colleen)
On cam	THERE'S A NEW WEAPON TO HELP KEEP YOUR TEETH HEALTHY.
ENG NATVO	(vo)
LENGTH :30	THE FOOD AND DRUG ADMINISTRATION HAS JUST APPROVED AR-TI-DOX . . . A NEW, PAINLESS TREATMENT FOR PERIODONTAL DISEASE.
	IT COMES IN THE FORM OF A TOPICAL GEL AND IS CONVENIENT TO USE.
	THE CURRENT TREATMENT USED TO FIGHT PLAQUE PROBLEMS AND BACTERIA REQUIRES ANESTHESIA AND CAN BE PAINFUL.
ENG OUT	

Notice that some of the markings we've provided for the director on this script are a bit different from what we've used before. All stations in this country speak the same language; it's just that the dialects can vary. The wording used for the various directions is usually a function of the newsroom computer system used in that particular station. Some of the more common software programs for writing television news are NewsStar, AP NewsCenter, EZNews, and Basys. In our earlier examples, we noted the place where the tape is supposed to start with the marking "take tape." This station uses the marking "ENG NATVO." In the next example, that point will be indicated by the marking "M2/VO." They all mean the same thing: this is the place to start the tape. The way we indicate the place at which the director should punch out of the tape in this story is with the marking "ENG OUT," which means the same thing as "tape ends." In one station, "ENG" means a videotape; in another, that's indicated by "tape," and in others, it's indicated by the particular type of videotape the station uses, such as "M2," "beta," "SVHS," and the like.

You'll notice that the time for the tape is indicated near the beginning of the script rather than at the end. It's simply a matter of getting accustomed to the conventions used in a particular station. Although the wording and the positioning of the director cues are sometimes a bit different, we give the director the same information in all of these examples: whether or not the anchor appears on-camera, if a tape is involved, and if so, where it starts, where it ends, and how long it is.

Daviscourt
_____

	(Gayle)
SQ/SS	(SQ/SS)
	ADAM DAVIS AND JOHN WHISPELL
	HAVE NEW ATTORNEYS TONIGHT.
	BUT THEY STILL HAVEN'T ENTERED
	PLEAS TO THEIR MURDER CHARGES.
M2/VO	(M2/VO)
	THE 19-YEAR-OLDS ARE CHARGED
	WITH MURDERING CARROLWOOD
	REALTOR VICKIE ROBINSON LAST MONTH.
	ROBINSON'S 15-YEAR-OLD
	DAUGHTER VALESSA IS ALSO CHARGED
	... SHE'S ENTERED A NOT GUILTY PLEA.
	THIS MORNING, A HILLSBOROUGH
	JUDGE ASSIGNED BOTH MEN

COURT-APPOINTED LAWYERS.

THEIR ARRAIGNMENT WAS DELAYED

UNTIL THE NEW LAWYERS GET

FAMILIAR WITH THE CASE.

M2/ENDS :35

This example is essentially the same as the one that came before it. We begin with Gayle on camera and an image from the still store (SS) squeezed (SQ) to fit over her shoulder. We then punch up the tape at the indicated spot, and it continues until the end of the story.

Orimulsion

	(Bob)
SS/CK/WALL	(SS/CK/WALL)
	THE FIGHT TO BURN ORIMULSION AT A PARRISH POWER PLANT IS OFFICIALLY OVER TONIGHT.
	TODAY, FLORIDA POWER AND LIGHT CALLED IT QUITS.
M2/VO	(M2/VO)
	FOR YEARS THE POWER COMPANY HAS TRIED TO GET PERMISSION TO INTRODUCE THE CONTROVERSIAL FUEL.
	ORIMULSION IS A MIX OF WATER AND A TAR-LIKE SUBSTANCE THAT'S MINED OUT OF A RIVER IN VENEZUELA.
	IT DOESN'T FLOAT AND MIXES WITH WATER.
	THAT MAKES IT MUCH MORE DIFFICULT TO CLEAN UP IF THERE'S A SPILL.
M2/ENDS :35	

At the beginning of this VO, we're doing something a little different. Instead of having something out of still store squeezed over Bob's shoulder, we're going to position him in front of the **chroma key (CK) wall** and electronically place the still store image on the wall behind him. This is how weather maps, radar, and satellite images are projected behind the weathercaster. As a way to enhance the pace of the program and show off other parts of the news set, many stations (and network newscasts) have begun using the chroma key wall for much more than weather.

Let's look at one final example of how VOs are used. Often, a number of related stories are placed back-to-back, and we transition from script to script without seeing the anchor between stories.

World Tonight

	(Colleen)
	MAKING HEADLINES IN THE WORLD TONIGHT . . . TWO RIVALS TEAM UP . . . TO FLY AROUND THE GLOBE . . . AND HISTORIC TALKS IN NORTHERN IRELAND . . .
ENG NATVO	(vo)
	FOR THE FIRST TIME EVER . . . THE POLITICAL LEADERS OF THE PROTESTANT AND CATHOLIC COMMUNITIES IN NORTHERN IRELAND SAT AND TALKED . . . FACE TO FACE.
	DAVID TRIMBLE AND GERRY ADAMS SPOKE OF WIDE GAPS BETWEEN THE TWO SIDES . . . AND SAID THEY'D USE THE TALKS TO GET TO KNOW EACH OTHER.
	THEY'VE PLANNED MORE MEETINGS.
WIPE ENG NATVO	(wipe vo)
	(Colleen)
	(vo top)
	STEVE FOSSETT AND RICHARD BRANSON ARE TEAMING UP . . . TO TRY TO FLY A BALLOON AROUND THE WORLD.
	BOTH MEN HAVE FAILED SEVERAL TIMES TRYING TO MAKE THE FLIGHT ON THEIR OWN . . . BUT SAY TEAMWORK WILL GIVE THEM AN ADVANTAGE.
	THEY SAY THEY'LL TAKE TURNS FLYING THE BALLOON.
WIPE ENG NATVO	(wipe vo)
	(Colleen)
	(vo top)

> A FRESNO, CALIFORNIA, CORNFIELD
> HAS TOURISTS TRYING TO FIND THEIR
> WAY OUT OF A MAZE . . . THE MAZE IS
> IN THE SHAPE OF THE STATE OF
> CALIFORNIA . . . WITH A STAR TO SHOW
> FRESNO'S PLACE IN THE STATE.
>
> THE WALLS ARE 10 FEET HIGH . . .
> AND THERE ARE 85 PLACES WHERE
> VISITORS HAVE TO TRY TO FIGURE OUT
> THE RIGHT WAY TO GO.

ENG OUT

In this example we start with Colleen on-camera and give a brief idea of the stories coming up. We get to the first of the three stories in standard fashion, but then transition to the subsequent stories by wiping from one tape to the next. Colleen continues to read, with video starting right at the top of stories 2 and 3. Some of the markings here might seem redundant, because if we're wiping to a new VO, it stands to reason that the second VO will start right at the top. But it's better not to look confused, and often in a series of stories like this, each is on a separate page. So it helps to reiterate at the beginning of tape 2 what the instructions were at the end of tape 1.

Conclusion

By now it should be clear that we have much more to deal with than just the words we write. The copy must support the video and vice versa, and there are other considerations as well. Some have called it writing in 3-D—having to consider the words, the pictures, and the sounds we have to work with. This is true even when structuring one of the most basic television story forms—voice-overs. The challenge of incorporating those elements effectively and of providing the script cues that go along with them becomes a bit more extensive when we get to VO/SOTs and packages. The production element of what we do is also important, but the bottom line is still the ability to craft the written part of the story. Use of over-the-shoulder inserts, chroma key, wiping between tapes, and other production techniques can add to the presentation of stories. But no amount of jazzy production can rescue a poorly written piece.

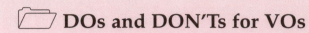 **DOs and DON'Ts for VOs**

Do

- Write from the video.
- Grab viewer attention right away.
- Make sure everyone on the team knows what we're doing.

Don't

- Leave out times and other cues.
- Write generic copy for generic video.
- Leave out any major information.

TELEVISION STORY FORMS—THE VO/SOT

As the acronym implies, a VO/SOT begins as a VO, which you're quite familiar with by now. But, as also implied, the VO/SOT involves an additional element, the SOT (sound-on-tape) portion. The SOT (often called a **sound bite,** or simply a bite) is a brief snippet of an on-camera interview that's edited to follow a certain amount of voice-over video. So, the VO/SOT involves more than one voice: the anchor's voice and one or more brief comments from an interview source or sources. Some news operations use the acronym VO/B rather than VO/SOT so that they can indicate if more than one bite is included. So, a VO/B/B would include two different bites. However, many operations still use VO/SOT because the number of sound bites on the tapes isn't what's really important to the people in the control room. What's really important is the length of the SOT. More about that when we discuss marking VO/SOT scripts.

The Role of a VO/SOT

A VO/SOT lets producers vary the pacing of a news program and allows us to give a little more airtime to a story than if it were a VO, but not as much as to a package. A VO/SOT should be used when we're covering an event and something a participant or observer has to say carries some emotion or impact that would be lost if we paraphrased the comment for an anchor to read.

Melissa Antoccia is a producer in Las Vegas. One of the photographers at her station covered an overnight house fire and got a few comments from the public information officer (**PIO**) for the fire department. (It isn't uncommon for a photographer to shoot and conduct brief interviews by himself or herself.) The video was compelling—the house completely in flames, firefighters working hard to put out the fire—but most of what the PIO had to say was general information about what happened, so Melissa was thinking VO.

However, one comment stood out when Melissa was logging the tape, and she decided to make the piece a VO/SOT. The PIO said that the people in the house were very lucky to get out and credited some neighbors who knocked on the windows of the house and woke up the sleeping occupants, probably saving their lives. The emotion in the voice of the PIO was sincere and imparted a sense of how truly lucky the people in the house were. Some of that emotion would have been lost had the anchor told that part of the story.

This raises a concern that Melissa is quick to point out. Generally, an official spokesperson isn't as emotionally involved in a story like this as the people affected are, and a bite from one of the neighbors or one of the occupants would have been better still. Many news operations are overly dependent on "official" comments. Work to get bites from the people who are directly affected. PIOs are generally very helpful to news crews, but there's no way they can share the emotion that someone else experienced because of losing a home or suffering some other tragedy.

Joe Kovacs is an assignments manager in Miami, and he echoes Melissa's thoughts about the importance of good bites. In South Florida, tanker truck rollovers are all too common, and it seems the more deadly the cargo, the more likely the truck is to crash during rush hour. On many occasions, Joe has had to drop all preparations for other stories (including some for which he had ordered satellite time) to get a crew to the scene of a rollover. These stories are often covered as a live reporter toss to a VO/SOT, because the crew doesn't have time to produce a package before hitting the air live. However, it's important to get a sound bite into a breaking news piece such as this, whether the bite is from a highway patrol trooper who explains what the agency thinks happened or from a motorist who narrowly missed being caught up in the flaming accident. Such a bite can enhance a story tremendously.

One word of caution from Joe. He says just because you do an interview, don't think you *have* to use a portion of it on the air. If the bite isn't compelling, it's just taking up air time. Sound is good, when the sound *is good*.

Scripting a VO/SOT

When we decide to make a story a VO/SOT, there are a few more steps in the scripting process than when we're working with a VO. Because a VO/SOT begins as a VO, everything that applies to scripting and marking a VO applies to the first part of a VO/SOT. It's still very important to write from the video and to follow all the other guidelines listed in earlier chapters. But with the VO/SOT story form we incorporate an SOT, and we need to do a couple of extra things with the script. As noted in Chapter 1, we believe that it isn't enough to place a super over the bite to identify the speaker. Many people are doing other things while the news is on and aren't paying close attention to the screen. If we don't verbally identify the speaker, many viewers won't know who the person is or why what that person is saying is relevant to the story. However, some writers and instructors will tell you this breaks the flow of the story, so this isn't a practice followed in every newsroom, although we think it should be for the reasons stated above.

The VO portion of the script needs to accomplish several things relevant to the SOT that the viewers are about to hear. The writer should identify the person who's about to speak by name and give the person's title, which usually is enough to explain why what the person has to say is relevant. The writer should then set up the bite by giving the viewers an idea of what the speaker is about to say. A super is a supplement to this spoken information, not a replacement for it.

Setting Up the Bite

The key to an effective setup of an upcoming bite is to give the viewers a sense of what to expect the speaker to say without parroting what we're about to hear. Let's say we've selected a bite from the mayor of a small town in our market. In the bite, the mayor talks about the give-and-take that occurred during an all-night bargaining session she's just wrapped up with the police union. We wouldn't lead to a bite like that by saying something about the mayor's being glad the impasse is over, because that leads the viewer to expect the mayor's comment to have something to do with her relief rather than the bargaining session itself. Equally bad is to lead into the mayor by saying something like "Hooverville Mayor Jane Smith says the deal involved concessions from both sides" if that's followed by the mayor saying "the deal involved concessions from both sides" or even "both sides made concessions." When the bite repeats what the anchor has just said, it sounds foolish indeed.

Another common mistake is to lead into a bite by writing something along the lines of "and Mayor Smith had this to say" or "we asked Mayor Smith about that" or "Mayor Smith commented about the issue." These are very weak ways to lead to a bite. We need to write something specific that sets the stage for the specific bite we're about to hear.

How do we know what to write to set up bites? Our interviewees often provide the words we need, and there's no shame in borrowing liberally from your sources to flesh out your scripts. After all, it's *their* story we're telling. Using our example with Mayor Smith, let's look at a typical question and answer from an interview about this subject.

> **Reporter:** "How would you characterize last night's bargaining session?"
>
> **Mayor:** (in typical politi-speak) "We are indeed gratified that an amicable solution has been reached and that a new contract seems imminent. We believe the union negotiators to be tough, but fair. Neither side got everything it wanted, but the deal we have arrived at proves that when people work toward a common goal and consider the ramifications of various scenarios, agreement is possible." (At this point the mayor slips up and begins to talk like a real person.) "The bottom line is, the city wanted to come to terms before the deadline and so did the union. The officers didn't want to go without paychecks and we didn't want to face the possibility of having no police on the streets. That would have brought the city to a standstill."

Because you're a sharp reporter, your sound bite antennae immediately send a message screaming to your brain. Sound bite! The final part of the mayor's 45-second answer to the question is a nice succinct 12-second sound bite. In general, you look for bites in the 8- to 12-second range. They can be shorter, but need to be at least 5 or 6 seconds long to give the people in the control room time to get the super in and out. Bites can also be longer than 12 seconds, but it has to be truly compelling information to warrant going beyond 15 seconds or so.

The mayor has provided us with what we were after—a good bite of the sought-after length in the language of real people. But what about all that stuff she said before the bite? It isn't totally useless. She gave us a good phrase to use to lead to her bite when she said the agreement involved concessions from both sides. Based on the bite we've chosen and the additional information we've decided to incorporate in the VO portion of the script, we can write the story. But even after we write, we're not finished with this story.

Marking a VO/SOT Script

Just as we have to take a few more things into consideration when writing a VO/SOT script, we also have to add some information for the director and his control room crew that we don't include on VO scripts. With a VO, all we have to do is indicate when the tape is supposed to start and how much time is on the tape so that the director knows how much tape remains as the anchor nears the end of the script. But with a VO/SOT, we have to indicate when the tape is supposed to begin, when the audio on the tape switches from natural sound under the anchor's voice to stand-alone sound from a bite, and when the bite ends. You might wonder about the pad video that goes at the end of a VO. It's still necessary to add video pad when editing the tape, but we don't indicate the pad on the script for a VO/SOT when both the VO and the SOT are edited on the same tape. Here's why.

Let's say that we write a script that includes 25 seconds of voice-over and a 15-second bite. That tape is supposed to end at 40 seconds, regardless of when the tape was rolled or what the anchor's read rate is, because the end of the SOT determines the end of the tape. We don't want to see the interviewee just sitting there after the bite ends. We delete the audio and let the video of the interviewee continue to avoid going to black or snow just in case there are problems in the control room, but we definitely want the director to punch out of the tape right after the interviewee finishes her comment. Just in case, though, there's that silent shot (continuation of the shot of the interviewee's face) to cover us.

Reading Up to the SOT

Editing an SOT on the end of a VO creates an additional problem, because the anchor has to stop speaking at a specific time so as not to talk over the top of the SOT or leave a long pause before the SOT begins. There are two ways to keep this from happening. Someone in the control room can count down in the anchor's ear and tell her to slow down or speed up so that the VO read comes out the right length. As an alternative, many news operations place the VO and the SOT on separate tapes. That gives the director a little more latitude for dealing with discrepancies in how long it takes to read the VO. By putting the

SOT on a separate tape, we can wait until the anchor is finished read-ing the VO (with no one distracting her by talking into her ear while she's trying to read) and then transition to the other tape. The same guideline about including pad video is true if the SOT is on a separate tape. The first tape has no definitive out point, but the second tape does, so we indicate the pad on the VO script but not on the SOT script. We put pad on both tapes, and on both it's a continuation of the shot with which we ended. Again, we put pad on the end of the SOT *just in case*, but the plan is for the director to punch out as soon as the bite ends, and that's the time we give the director.

Let's return to our friend Mayor Smith and look at a couple of exam-ples of marking a VO/SOT script, followed by explanations of how we arrived at the times indicated and what the new markings mean.

New Contract

	(Dave)
On cam	HOW DOES HOOVERVILLE MAYOR JANE SMITH SPELL RELIEF? C-O-N-T-R-A-C-T.
	(vo)
:00 Take tape and snd under (VO)	AFTER AN ALL-NIGHT BARGAINING SESSION AT CITY HALL, THE MAYOR AND POLICE UNION REPRESENTATIVES HAVE COME TO TERMS ON A NEW CONTRACT FOR HOOVERVILLE'S FINEST.
	NEGOTIATIONS HAD STALLED IN PAST WEEKS AND THE JULY 1ST DEADLINE WAS LOOMING.
	THE 25 COPS REPRESENTED BY THE UNION THREATENED TO WALK OFF THE JOB IF THEY DIDN'T GET A 10 PERCENT PAY RAISE AND TAKE-HOME USE OF THEIR PATROL CARS.
	THE MAYOR SAYS THE AGREEMENT INVOLVES CONCESSIONS FROM BOTH SIDES.
:25 Tape cont. vid and snd full (SOT)	(sot)
:26 Super: Jane Smith/Hooverville Mayor	
:40 Tape out	Outcue: "the city to a standstill"

On Cam

> IF THE CONTRACT IS APPROVED BY
> UNION MEMBERS, OFFICERS WILL GET A
> 5 PERCENT RAISE AND WILL BE
> ALLOWED TO TAKE THEIR SQUAD CARS
> HOME EACH NIGHT.

The first few directions on the left-hand side of the script are familiar. But at some point we transition from the anchor's voice to sound on tape, which is new for us. We have to let the director, the audio person, and other control room personnel know when to make those adjustments. How do we determine that 25 seconds is the time in this example? Simply by reading and timing the portion of the VO from the time the tape starts until the anchor stops talking. In this example, that goes from "After an all-night bargaining session" to "concessions from both sides." So at 25 seconds the anchor stops reading and someone else starts speaking on tape. As soon as possible after that transition has occurred, we put up a super identifying the speaker. Then the director waits to see :40 on his control room timer and to hear the final few words of the mayor's comment, called the **outcue.** How do we figure 40 seconds? When the videotape editor was given the script, she was told to put down 25 seconds' worth of pictures to go along with the VO portion of the script. The writer would then indicate the bite that had been selected, and the editor would add that to the tape. In this case let's assume the bite was 15 seconds long as indicated by the editing machine timer, making the whole piece 40 seconds long. The editor would end the mayor's audio at the appointed time but allow the video to continue for an extra 10 seconds to give the director some pad, but the intent is to have him get out of the tape right at 40 seconds. When the director sees :40 and hears the outcue, he goes back to a studio camera shot of the anchor, who wraps up the story by relaying one final piece of information.

It's important that the story end with the anchor and not with someone else speaking. The anchor comes back on camera (or we could choose to add more VO after the outcue, making the piece a VO/SOT/VO) to wrap up that story and transition to something else. The stories wouldn't flow together very well if an SOT ended and the anchor started immediately reading a different story. The anchor's role is to end one story and transition the viewers to the next one.

Here's one final note about the script markings on our example. You'll notice that there's a big gap on the right side of the page. When the anchor sees nothing, that means stop reading. You'll also notice that the outcue is listed on the right side of the page. That's so the anchor can also listen for it and be ready for the next on-camera portion of the script. We also add a blank line or two after the outcue, leaving the outcue "floating out in space," to lessen the chance that the anchor might read it as part of his next line. Now, we'll set up the same story using two videotapes rather than one. Again, this is done so that the anchor's read of the VO portion doesn't have to come out at exactly a certain time. You might have noticed that each sentence on the right side of the page is indented. This makes it easier for the anchor to know where one thought ends and another begins and makes for a smoother read.

New Contract

	(Dave)
On cam	HOW DOES HOOVERVILLE MAYOR JANE SMITH SPELL RELIEF? C-O-N-T-R-A-C-T.
	(vo)
:00 Take tape vid and snd under (VO)	AFTER AN ALL-NIGHT BARGAINING SESSION AT CITY HALL, THE MAYOR AND POLICE UNION REPRESENTATIVES HAVE COME TO TERMS ON A NEW CONTRACT FOR HOOVERVILLE'S FINEST.
	NEGOTIATIONS HAD STALLED IN PAST WEEKS AND THE JULY FIRST DEADLINE FOR A NEW AGREEMENT WAS LOOMING.
	THE 25 COPS REPRESENTED BY THE UNION THREATENED TO WALK OFF THE JOB IF THEY DIDN'T GET A 10 PERCENT RAISE AND TAKE-HOME USE OF THEIR PATROL CARS.
	THE MAYOR SAYS THE AGREEMENT INVOLVES CONCESSIONS FROM BOTH SIDES.
:35 Tape out (the remaining part of this script would go on a separate page) :00 Wipe to tape 2 snd full (SOT) :01 Super: Jane Smith/Hooverville Mayor	(sot)

:15 Tape out	Outcue: "the city to a standstill"
On cam	IF THE CONTRACT IS APPROVED BY UNION MEMBERS, OFFICERS WILL GET A 5 PERCENT RAISE AND WILL BE ALLOWED TO TAKE THEIR SQUAD CARS HOME EACH NIGHT.

The difference between this example and the first one is that we end one tape and transition to another within the same story. Our VO should take 25 seconds to read, but if the anchor's read is a little short or a little long, it's not a problem because we have 35 seconds' worth of tape. Whenever the anchor reaches the end of the VO, the director rolls and transitions to the next tape, which is now only 15 seconds long because it contains the SOT only. The time for the super is different because it's now based on the start time of the second tape, not the first one. Also, the two parts of this story appear on separate script pages.

Stand-Alone SOTs

Let's assume that for some reason, we don't have any video to use with the VO portion of a story. We could set up the story as a straight SOT and use the same markings that we used in the second half of our second example of the contract story. However, straight SOTs are pretty rare. Because this is a visual medium and head shots aren't all that compelling, the preference is to use some sort of video to get into the bite—video from the meeting, a photo opportunity with the mayor and union officials, file video of cops on the beat, or something else that goes along with our script. Still, on occasion we might script an SOT with no VO—simply an on-camera introduction from the anchor that leads directly into the bite. The same guidelines apply to that type of lead to a sound bite as to a sound bite lead accompanied by video. We still need to introduce the speaker, tell why his or her comments are important, and set up the bite.

The Need for Good Communication

As you can tell, television news writers have a lot more to worry about than just the words they put on the page. It might seem that we've placed too much emphasis on the directions you add to television

A production worker uses a touch-screen computer interface to control robotic cameras during a WFLA-TV newscast.

news scripts, but the most beautifully written piece can quickly turn into a nightmare on the air without the correct markings. Now that we've added SOTs to the mix, the directions take on added significance. Communication with all the other people who will have something to do with how that story appears on the air is critical. Many news workers have noted that the biggest problem in the communication business is a lack of communication. Never assume that others in the news operation know how you want a story to play. You have to tell them by marking the script appropriately.

Be aware that just as we might write a straight SOT story, there are variations on the VO/SOT setup to a story. We might have an SOT/VO or a VO/SOT/VO—starting with the bite and then going to voice-over or adding some more voice-over after the bite ends. The order of the elements doesn't matter, as long as everyone involved clearly understands what's going on.

Now let's look at a few more examples of how to script VO/SOTs. The first is actually a VO/SOT/VO.

Duck Folo
_____

	(Colleen)
SS: Adoption	HAVING DUCKS AS PETS IS
	CATCHING ON IN TUCSON.

ENG NATVO   (vo)

THE HUMANE SOCIETY HAS
ADOPTED-OUT 160 DUCKS SO FAR.
WE BROUGHT YOU THIS STORY
EARLIER IN THE WEEK.
BIOLOGISTS ROUNDED UP THE
DUCKS FROM THEIR HOME IN KENNEDY
PARK.
WE WERE THERE WHEN DONNA
AVERY PICKED UP HER NEW FINE,
FEATHERED FRIEND.

DISSOLVE ENG SOT

(sot)

ENG SOT 12 sec.   "I would take as many ducks,
CG: Donna Avery\Animal lover   turkeys, geese, anything . . . chickens.
                                   They just run wild at my house, they
                                   love it. They come to the door and beg
                                   for food and they have food outside
                                   (laugh)."

ENG NATVO   (vo)

CITY OFFICIALS SAY THERE WERE
JUST TOO MANY DUCKS AT KENNEDY
PARK.
THEIR WASTE WAS CAUSING A
VIRTUAL TOXIC SOUP FOR THE FISH . . .
AND WAS ALSO HARMING OTHER BIRDS.

ENG OUT

In this example, we start with the anchor on-camera with a graphic
from the still store machine over her shoulder. Notice that she's on-
camera for only a few seconds before we go to the video. The anchor
then reads over video for about 15 seconds before reaching the (sot)
marking. She knows that this notation means that a source is about to
speak on tape, so she remains silent during the SOT.

On the left side of the page, we've told the director to dissolve (a
different transition than a wipe) from the VO tape to the SOT tape at
that point and have indicated that the sound bite lasts for 12 seconds.
We've also indicated "CG," which means character generator and is
another way of saying "super." At this point the written name of the

person speaking is supered (superimposed) on the lower third of the screen. The sound bite is written on the right-hand side so that both the director and the anchor can follow it and listen for the outcue. Many news operations write out the bite like this for closed-captioning and also so that the anchor can summarize the comment if something goes wrong with the tape. The anchor knows not to read this part of the script because it's in quotes and *isn't* uppercase.

When we reach the outcue, the second tape continues with more VO video following the SOT. The director cues the anchor, who then reads the remaining script over the video. She knows that she won't have to look at the camera during the VO and will probably choose to read from the hard copy rather than from the prompter. This will allow her to pay closer attention to how her read rate is matching what we're seeing on tape. VO/SOT/VOs obviously give us an opportunity to use a few more shots than we'd use in a VO/SOT. Remember, this is a visual medium, so when you have good video, think VO/SOT/VO rather than VO/SOT.

Be aware that most of the time, the two parts of a story like this are on separate pages and occupy two lines on the show rundown (see Chapter 10 about producing). So in this example, everything from "ENG SOT 12 sec." would be on a second script page. This helps the director grasp that the VO and SOT are edited on separate tapes and that the producer is calling for some type of transition between the two. The second bit of VO video is on the same tape as the SOT, so no dissolve or wipe is indicated; we merely continue with the second tape.

Blood Testing

	(Colleen)
SS: BLOOD TESTING	A TUCSON HOSPITAL IS PIONEERING NEW BLOOD TESTING TECHNOLOGY.
ENG NATVO	(vo)
	KINO COMMUNITY HOSPITAL'S BLOOD BANK IS THE FIRST IN THE U-S TO HAVE THIS NEW TECHNIQUE, CALLED GAMMA REACT SYSTEM.
	NORMALLY, BLOOD TESTING TAKES UP TO AN HOUR AND A HALF . . . BUT THIS TECHNIQUE TAKES ONLY ABOUT 25 MINUTES.
	HOSPITAL SPOKESWOMAN BRENDA PARKER SAYS THE HOSPITAL CAN NOW CHECK FOR INCOMPATIBLE BLOOD MORE QUICKLY.

DISSOLVE ENG SOT	(sot)
ENG SOT 15 sec.	
CG: Brenda Parker\Kino Hospital	"In a crisis situation when you need blood in a hurry you've got to be able to find compatible blood fast . . . and this method enables us to identify the antibody fast and get compatible blood much, much faster than the previous method."
ENG OUT	(out)
LIVE	OFFICIALS WITH THE UNIVERSITY OF ARIZONA MEDICAL TECHNOLOGY PROGRAM PLAN TO VIDEOTAPE KINO TECHNICIANS DEMONSTRATING THE NEW TECHNIQUE FOR CLASSROOM USE.

This example is very similar to the duck folo story, except that we've set this one up to have the director punch back to the studio camera at the end of the SOT rather than having the anchor read over more VO tape. The (out) tells the anchor that the tape has ended and she should be ready to go back on-camera. As with the previous example, everything from "ENG SOT 15 sec." will be on a separate page. Any time there are two tapes, there are two script pages.

In the following example, we'll look at a story designed to follow a related piece about reputed drug kingpin Charles Miller. The first story details charges that Miller has threatened to harm U.S. students at a veterinary school in the Caribbean if the U.S. government continues to crack down on what it terms his illegal drug operation. That story leads us to this one:

Miller Details

	(Bob)
2SHOT	(2shot)
	TONIGHT, WE'RE LEARNING A LOT MORE ABOUT CHARLES MILLER . . . THE MAN WHO'S MAKING THE THREATS.
Gayle	(Gayle)
	HE HAS A LONG HISTORY OF VIOLENCE BUT HAS BEEN ABLE TO AVOID ARREST ON THE ISLAND OF SAINT KITTS.

SS/CG

Super: Charles Miller

(SS/CG)

AN ARTICLE IN THE WASHINGTON
POST GIVES A LOT OF DETAIL ABOUT
MILLER.

Add: smuggled drugs from
Miami to New York

(add)

AT ONE POINT, MILLER WAS
SMUGGLING MORE THAN A TON OF
COCAINE AND MARIJUANA A MONTH
FROM MIAMI TO NEW YORK.

Add: immunity, witness protection
program

(add)

DESPITE THAT, HE WAS GIVEN FULL
IMMUNITY AND A PLACE IN THE U-S
GOVERNMENT'S WITNESS PROTECTION
PROGRAM IN EXCHANGE FOR
INFORMATION ABOUT A DRUG
SMUGGLING RING.

Add: admitted to participating
in murders

(add)

MILLER ADMITTED IN COURT TO
TAKING PART IN THE MURDERS OF FIVE
PEOPLE IN A MIAMI CRACK HOUSE IN
THE 1980S.

add: State Department: still dangerous

(add)

STATE DEPARTMENT OFFICIALS SAY
MILLER IS STILL DANGEROUS . . . THEY
WANT HIM TO FACE SMUGGLING
CHARGES . . .

Add: Warning U-S citizens

(add)

AND THEY'RE ALERTING PEOPLE ON
SAINT KITTS TO BE CAREFUL.

M2/SOT UP FULL

Super: James Rubin/State
Department Spokesman

(SOT)

("We know of this individual and
consider this threat, this person,
sufficiently violent to justify taking
these steps.")

RUNS: 08

TAG

(tag)

THE STATE DEPARTMENT IS HINTING
THAT U-S AUTHORITIES WILL RETALIATE

AGAINST MILLER IF HE HARMS U-S
CITIZENS.

THERE ARE 250 AMERICAN STUDENTS
AND 50 AMERICAN FACULTY MEMBERS
AT ROSS VETERINARY UNIVERSITY.

In this example, we start with a 2shot to let the anchors play off one another as they lead to this story. The news operation has no video of Miller and certainly has no video that supports the particular points to be made in this story. So the producer calls for a picture of Miller from still store (SS) and information to be superimposed over that image. That information comes from the character generator (CG). We've indicated to the director the specific places at which new information is to be added. The anchor has this information as well, so that she can pace herself to read something as it's being added to the screen. The entire VO portion of this script is read over a graphic rather than over video.

When we reach the end of that section of the story, we go to a sound bite on M2 (a particular type of videotape) from a State Department spokesperson, and the director adds a super (name and title of the person speaking) on the lower third of the screen. The SOT lasts for eight seconds; then the director punches back to the studio camera for the anchor to read the **tag.** "Tag" is the term used for the final bit of information that the anchor reads to wrap up a story before moving on to something else.

Conclusion

As we noted in Chapter 7, the wording of the directions provided to the director often varies slightly from one news operation to another. But, again, the basic information provided on VO/SOTs is the same: Do we start on camera? Where does the VO begin? Where do we transition to SOT? How long is the bite? Does the anchor finish the story on-camera or by reading more VO copy? We reiterate a point made several other times in this book. The markings are important. Television news is very team-oriented, and everyone on the team has to know what's coming next for the script and the visual elements to work together as we intend.

DOs and DON'Ts for VO/SOTs

Do
- Write specific leads to bites.
- Put VO and SOT on separate tapes.
- Leave room for error (pad) in case of control room mayhem.
- Pick compelling bites.

Don't
- Parrot what the interviewee will say.
- End a VO/SOT without re-establishing the anchor.
- Assume other people know what's supposed to happen unless you tell them.

TELEVISION STORY FORMS— THE PACKAGE

Kelli Durand wanted to be a reporter badly enough to leave a pretty good engineering operator's job in a large market television station to go to one of the nation's smaller markets in an on-air position. After being in a small Ohio market for a while, Kelli was assigned to cover a show at the county fairgrounds featuring entertainer Bill Cosby. Sounds like an interesting (and relatively easy) assignment. It didn't turn out that way.

As is often the case with big-name celebrities, the news crew wasn't granted a one-on-one interview with Cosby and was limited to a total of three minutes of video and natural sound of the show. No more than 15 seconds of continuous show video could be used during Kelli's package. She figured out a way around these two minor hurdles: just get interviews with the people enjoying Cosby's performance and use her script to start the joke and let Cosby deliver the punch line, easily within the 15-second time limit.

But then the problems started. A major rainstorm hit the fair-grounds, quickly turning the area into a massive mud pit and delaying the start of the show. It was after 9 o'clock when Cosby came on. The people in the floor seats (the more expensive tickets) were drenched and weren't very interested in being interviewed. The rain was caus-ing the microphone to short out. The cameraperson had to wipe off the lens continually to get a usable image. Kelli and her cameraperson were dripping, and their clothes were clinging to them. It was cold.

Still, Kelli had time to get the package ready, if that was all she had to do. It wasn't. She's also the 11 P.M. weathercaster. She and the cam-eraperson arrived at the station about 10:15. She quickly wrote the story (she started writing it in the car) and went into an edit booth. She recorded her audio track. It was difficult to get whole sentences out, because she was still shivering uncontrollably and her heart was beat-ing so fast she could hardly catch her breath. At her station, the reporter is responsible for editing the voice track and the bites, and she finished that at about 10:45—leaving the cameraperson 15 minutes to edit in the video from the performance. Her boyfriend had dashed to her apartment to get her a dry suit, so she changed, created her new weather maps, set up the sequence for the weather segment, and was ready to go when weather came on at 11:12. The Cosby story was the lead story, and it was ready on time.

Viewers got to see a hairstyle they'd never seen on Kelli before that night, and she has no idea what she said during the weather. She says she was so unprepared to go on live that she felt as though she was going to be sick right there on the weather set. She wanted to make the Cosby story memorable, and many viewers probably do remember it, but not for the reasons she had in mind. This is the reality of television news reporting. It isn't all glamour. It involves long hours, hard work, sometimes miserable conditions, intense deadline pressure, and, in many markets, less pay than you'd earn in most other professions. But it's fun (sometimes), you get to do a lot of interesting things and meet a lot of interesting or important people, and beating a deadline can be a real adrenaline rush. Kelli Durand can certainly attest to that.

Kelli was able to get her story ready in such a short time because she has a real command of the mechanics of putting a package together. Now that we've gained some experience writing VOs and VO/SOTs, *we* can move into reporter packages. As the name implies, packages involve reporters and are "packaged," meaning that they're fully self-contained pieces. You'll recall that VOs and VO/SOTs are read by the anchors. Their involvement in a package is to set up the story in general terms and introduce the reporter. The anchor should also wrap up the story at the end with some additional fact that the reporter was unable to fit into the package itself. This is called the tag. As is the case coming out of VO/SOTs, the flow from one story to another isn't what it could be if the anchor doesn't come back on-camera and wrap up a package before going on to another story. Additionally, it's important to have an anchor say something more than "Thank you, John" at the end of the package. If that's all the anchor says, he or she has no "ownership" of the story. We suggest giving anchors active roles in packages, and that would come in the package lead and the tag.

Other than the introduction and the tag, however, an anchor doesn't have anything to do with the presentation of a package. Once an anchor has introduced the reporter, the reporter takes over and relays the information relevant to the story. So, a package is the first story form we've discussed that involves a reporter's voice. A reporter might gather information for a VO and conduct the interview for an SOT, but neither of those story forms involves the reporter putting his or her voice on tape. A package does.

Stand-ups

In most cases, a package also involves a stand-up. A stand-up is when the reporter appears on-camera in the field and delivers a line or two. A stand-up can appear anywhere in the package—either at the beginning or end or somewhere in the middle. When it's placed somewhere in the middle, it's referred to as a "stand-up bridge." Bridges are more common than opening or closing stand-ups. That's because we want the beginning and end of packages to be visually compelling, and the stand-up usually isn't the most compelling video we have to work with.

When a reporter does a stand-up, he or she has to have written a portion of the story so that what's said in the stand-up flows with what comes before it and what comes after it. Usually that doesn't involve actually putting a portion of the story on paper; reporters quickly develop the ability to write in their heads, coming up with good 8- to 12-second stand-ups that will flow with the rest of the script that will be written later.

Why Stand-ups Are Important and How to Do Them Right

Stand-ups are important for several reasons. First, they're the reporter's opportunity for face time. News directors and other managers strive to have the viewers "identify" with newscasters, both anchors and reporters. Though it isn't essential that every package have a stand-up, it would be strange indeed to hear a reporter's voice day after day and never see that reporter's face. Also, stand-ups give you a good opportunity to talk about something for which you have limited or no video, and *when done right*, stand-ups can help draw the viewer into the story by illustrating something. We put emphasis on the phrase *when done right* because we see lots of stand-ups that are just painful to watch. When you do a stand-up, try not to look like you just had surgery to implant a metal rod in your back, and please try not to make a very unnatural turn at the waist (turning away from the mic in the process) to refer to something behind you.

Remember the Mom Rule? If you brought mom to the scene, would you stand there in front of her, at attention, and turn *away* from her to point something out? Of course not. You'd take dear ole mom by the hand and walk her over to something, and explain what she was looking at. Though you can't literally take the viewers by the hand, figuratively that's what you need to do. Work toward involved stand-ups. If your stand-up doesn't pass the chroma key test (you might as well have been standing in front of an image of the scene projected on the chroma key wall), then why be at the scene at all? DO SOMETHING! This will require (dare we say it?) a bit of choreography to make the stand-up look and feel natural.

Think of it this way. You want your stand-ups to be interactive. The viewers can't become part of the scene directly, but can do so through you. If all you do is stand there looking and sounding stiff, you haven't done anything to engage the viewers. You want to be animated and

Reporter Brooke Baldwin of WVIR-TV in Charlottesville, VA, doing an interactive stand-up for a piece about chainsaw sculpting.

make your stand-up interesting and informative, without being goofy (unless the story calls for that approach). Then, you have to match the energy level you projected on-camera when you get to the sound booth to record your package narration. If you sound uninterested or uninteresting, guess what's going to happen? TV news reporters write conversationally in order to sound as natural as possible when delivering those lines.

Live Stand-ups

In Chapter 10, we discuss live reporting at length, from a producer's standpoint. The producer should be involved in how the reporters plan live shots. Where will we go live? What will be happening at the time? Is there any opportunity to be interactive? The reporter and producer should discuss these and other related questions for every live shot. Keep in mind that just because your stand-up is live, it doesn't mean the rules for making it interactive don't apply. Actually, they apply even more because chances are you're doing live at both the beginning and end of a taped piece, and we certainly don't want to see you twice looking like you're at boot camp and are terrified of the drill instructor.

Logging

Once he or she has a good stand-up to work with, one key thing a reporter can do to make writing a package easier and quicker is to log the tape back at the station or in an edit bay in a remote vehicle at the story site. Even if the reporter has been on the scene with a videographer the whole time, the reporter still doesn't know exactly what the shots show or exactly what all the possible sound bites and natural sound segments are. The reporter's sound bite antennae might have alerted him or her to several potential sound bites during the interview, but most people can't memorize things well enough to allow them to write a good package without reviewing the tape. You can start to get an idea of the bites you have if you use a mini–audio recorder and listen to the interview in the car on the way back to the station (assuming someone else is driving).

During logging, the reporter looks at the tape to pick out specific shots to write from, specific sound bites to use in the story, and snippets of natural sound to incorporate. Natural sound is what the microphone picks up when you're not in an interview situation. It could be bells ringing, parts of a conversation, or any other naturally occurring sound. It's important for the reporter to have specific shots, bites, and natural sound in mind when writing the package. We have to write words that are supported by the video we have, and the sound bites are the backbone around which any package is built. The natural sound clips that are incorporated give body to the story. So, a reporter has to note all three elements on the story log and use that material to craft an informative and interesting story. You can write a story without going through the logging process, but chances are it won't be nearly as strong as it could have been had you taken a few minutes to familiarize yourself with what's on the tape.

Leading into and out of Bites

In Chapter 8 we discussed the importance of setting up the SOT by indicating who the bite is coming from and why the speaker is important to the story, and giving the viewer an idea of what will be said. We need to do the same thing in a package every time a new speaker is introduced. If we use the same speaker more than once, all we need to do to introduce the second or third bite from the same person is give the viewers an idea of what will be said. It's not necessary to give the person's name or title again. So getting into the SOTs is the same in a package as in a VO/SOT, but because the SOT in a package is followed by more narration from the reporter, we now have to be concerned about how we get out of the sound bite as well as how we get into it.

Let's say that several of the bites we're considering using are listed on the log sheet as follows:

Bob Jones—Concerned Citizen

25:30 "I think it's strange"

25:40 "no public input"

27:14 "any elected official"

27:28 "disservice to the constituents"

28:12 "what the city is trying to do is an outrage"

28:24 "we'll speak at the polls"

28:50 "in this day and time"

29:05 "government of, by, and for the people"

Note that during the logging process, we don't write down every word in the bites. Transcribing an entire interview takes a lot more time than news reporters typically have. Later, after we've selected specific bites to use, we'd go back and get the verbatim of those bites for closed-captioning. But there's no need to write down every word of a bite until we know we're going to use it. Also note that we've indicated the time on the tape at which Jones says the first few words of each comment, called the **incue,** and the time at which the bite concludes along with the last few words he says, called the **outcue.** We do this for two reasons. First, when we time the narration parts of the package and add in the times for the SOTs and the stand-up, we know if we've hit the overall time allotted for the piece by the producer. Second, adding the times helps the videotape editor find things quickly. Whenever we can save ourselves or someone else some time, we need to do so. In this example, let's say we choose to use the third bite listed. The log shows we're dealing with a 12-second bite, and the videotape editor knows exactly where to find it—28 minutes and 12 seconds from the beginning of the tape. The portion of the script that would include this bite would look something like this:

> . . . To say that Bob Jones and his neighbors are concerned would be an understatement.
>
> Jones incue: "what the city is trying to do is an outrage"
>
> Jones outcue: "we'll speak at the polls"
>
> But city elections won't be held until 18 months from now. In the meantime, the citizens' group has other plans. . . .

We've set up the bite by letting the viewers know to expect Jones to say something about being upset, and we've led out of the bite by picking up on the voting theme. In other words, our narration is a continuation of the thought that Jones started in his bite. As with all other tips we'll pass along, don't overdo this one, but these types of transitions, called tie-writing, can be very effective in keeping the flow of the story going. Let's look at a sample package script, and see how we can work for flow into and out of bites and how we can incorporate natural sound.

> JURASSIC PARK
>
> nat snd full from movie: "Can I touch it?"
>
> In the make-believe world of Jurassic Park, scientists used D-N-A to recreate living dinosaurs. In real life, much of the work done by the Jurassic Park scientists is possible, and in some cases, commonplace.
>
> nat snd full: "Take a look at this strand."
>
> Gene sequencing takes place at this lab and other sites around the country every day. Project director Rob Ferl says what happened in Jurassic Park might be possible one day.
>
> Ferl incue: in terms of basic

Ferl outcue: very rapid rate

But not quite as fast as the fictional scientists do it. In reality, scientists can extract D-N-A . . . even that of extinct animals.

Stand-up: Reproductive biologist Tim Gross is learning a lot about the diets and reproductive systems of mastodons by analyzing ancient, well-preserved mastodon droppings. Getting D-N-A is one thing, but it's the next step that science hasn't reached yet.

Gross incue: once you have DNA

Gross outcue: form an embryo

Scientists agree that it's just a matter of time before they gain that knowledge and something like Jurassic Park is a reality.

Ferl incue: certainly, once you have

Ferl outcue: reconstructing an animal

Gross incue: 20 years ago

Gross outcue: a reality today

Still, it's easier to re-create dinosaurs in Hollywood than it is in the halls of science . . . for now. In Hooverville, I'm Joe Reporter, Newswatch One.

Working with Available Video and Natural Sound

There are several things to note about how the script above is put together. First, think about the video we have to work with. If we didn't have clips from the movie, all we'd have would be shots inside a lab filled with beakers and test tubes and other shots of scientists huddled over petrified mastodon dung. Not exactly compelling stuff. But our friends in Hollywood often send out clips (they call them "trailers") of movies that are about to be released. It's good publicity for the movie-makers and good video for us to use if we have a story that lends itself to using clips from a particular movie. In this case, that's exactly what we have. After looking through the trailers, we're struck by a line from the movie as a very good way to immediately capture the viewers' attention. The two kids and their scientist friend are stuck in a tree, and the little girl asks if she can pet the friendly dinosaur that's eating some of the leaves. So, that brief clip becomes the beginning of our news story. We can then get into the facts about what real-life scientists are doing in terms of gene sequencing and the like. Notice also that we've incorporated natural sound full (nat snd) in two spots. First, there's a clip from the movie at the beginning of the story, and then a comment made by one researcher to another as she looks into a microscope. Remember that natural sound is any sound recorded other than in an interview setting. So snippets of conversation, a car horn, a sheep bleating, and other sound can be used as pacing elements and to add body to your pieces. Use natural sound liberally, as it fits. If a horse neighing has nothing to do with the story, don't use it just because you have it. But if you're doing a story about new train service in your area, maybe you can work in the conductor shouting out "All aboard," or the wheels screeching, or the whistle blowing, or all of those things.

Tie-Writing

Now let's look at some of the transitions. We know from the preceding narration that the project director is going to talk about how his work parallels what happened in the movie "Jurassic Park." He finishes the bite by talking about how rapidly gene sequencing takes place, and we follow that up with another comparison with the movie scientists. Moving on to the second bite, we know that Gross will talk about some "second step" in the re-creation process, and we follow that up with a note about the inevitability of reaching that second step. That leads us into what needs to happen for scientists to reach the point of being able to re-create an animal. Notice that Ferl's bite about that subject is followed immediately by one from Gross with no narration between the two. It isn't needed because one comment leads naturally into the next one. That's called "butting sound bites." We finish the story by following up on Gross' comment about things that would have been unthought of 20 years ago being commonplace today, by noting that the real scientists can't do everything the movie scientists can—at least not yet. So, the goal is to have the parts of the story flow together as seamlessly as possible to support the central theme of the package.

Two Scripts for Packages

Now this part of our script is ready to go to a videotape editor, who puts the pieces of narration and the SOTs together and places the appropriate video over the top of the sound track. The first script we provided gives the editor the order of things and is called the **editing script.** The next step for the reporter is to put together what's called the show script (at some stations it's called the **producer's script**). That script includes what the anchor is supposed to say to get into and out of the piece (the lead and the tag) and the directions for the director and other control room personnel. That script would look like this.

Jurassic Park
_____

	(Anne)
On cam	IT TAKES A HEALTHY DOSE OF
	SCIENCE FACT TO MAKE A GOOD WORK
	OF SCIENCE FICTION.
	AS JOE REPORTER TELLS US, THE
	BOOK AND MOVIE JURASSIC PARK
	MIGHT CONTAIN MORE SCIENCE FACT
	THAN WE REALIZE.
:00 Take tape vid &	
snd full (PKG)	(pkg)
Supers:	
:01 Courtesy: Universal Pictures	
:25 Rob Ferl, geneticist	
:42 Joe Reporter, Newswatch One	
1:00 Tim Gross, biologist	
1:31 Tape out	Outcue: standard
On cam	THE SCIENTISTS SAY THAT AS WE
	GET CLOSER TO UNDERSTANDING LIFE
	AND MAYBE ONE DAY RE-CREATING
	IT, THERE WILL BE MANY ETHICAL
	QUESTIONS TO BE ANSWERED ALONG
	THE WAY.

You can see that the producer's script contains none of what the reporter will say, only what the anchor will say to get us to the reporter's taped piece. The director really doesn't need to know anything about the content of the piece. She just needs to know when to transition to the tape, when to put in supers, and when the tape ends so that she can come back to an on-camera shot of the anchor.

You might be wondering how we arrive at the times listed on the producer's script. Once the videotape editor has finished assembling the piece, the reporter looks back at it and notes when each person first appears and, in this case, when a clip from the movie appears so that we can give credit to our Hollywood friends. Those are the times given to the director for insertion of the supers. The reporter also notes the time at which he finishes his final piece of narration and lists the final few words that he says or, in most cases, simply writes the word **standard** (or "SOQ" for standard outcue). In this case, we've told the director to be looking for 1:31 on the control room clock and to be listening for the reporter to say the line that's standard at the end of packages. In that line the reporter gives the name of the city or location where the story was shot, his name, and the name of the news organization. That's called the **signature outcue,** or **sig-out** for short. We place the outcue on the right side of the page so that the anchor can also be listening for it. As you can see from the editing script example, in the sig-out we say "I'm Joe Reporter" rather than "This is Joe Reporter." "I'm" is more conversational and helps convey the personal relationship we try to build with viewers.

So, in essence, a reporter is responsible for two scripts for a package. One of those goes to a videotape editor, who assembles the story (in many small markets and even some larger markets, the reporter *is* the tape editor), and the other goes to the producer and director. The editor puts together the self-contained part of the story, the package itself, and the producer and director deal with the live elements of the story—the lead and tag and the supers.

The Importance of Audio

All too often, the only sound reporters think about while writing is the audio captured during the interview process. But to forget about nat sot is a mistake. The best stories always make good use of nat sot—and to make that happen, reporters must work with the photographer to capture it and write to it.

The best photographers don't leave nat sot to chance, and go out of their way to make sure they do a good job of getting it on tape. You can tell a tape that's been shot in this fashion. For instance, video of a quiet wooded setting will come with sound of birds, bees, frogs, crickets, the rush of wind through the trees, and so on. If the story is about a search through the woods, then you might hear the barking of dogs, the crunch of searchers' footsteps through the leaves, the chatter of two-way radios, and so forth. Hopefully in *neither* case will you hear instead audio of the photographer gossiping with co-workers.

If the hallmark of the good photographer is that he or she takes care to accurately capture nat sot, then the hallmark of the good reporter is that he or she works with that photographer to use the nat sot to its maximum effect. The photographer will lay in nat sot "under" the reporter's audio track, but sometimes the best use of nat sot requires more than that. It requires a nat sot break. Sometimes this can be as simple as writing a pause into the script. Sometimes it requires specific showcasing in the writing. Following are examples of both.

Reporter Diane Pertmer and photojournalist Maurice Capobianco of WFLA-TV in Tampa, FL discuss their assignment as they return from an interview.

Example 1

	DEPUTIES WERE DETERMINED TO FIND THE LITTLE GIRL. NO ONE WANTED TO GIVE UP.
nat sot up full, shot of deputy jumping off log and splashing into puddle. Runs :01	(nat sot)
	BUT BY MIDDAY . . . SEACHERS HAD BEEN SLOGGING THROUGH THESE SOGGY WOODS FOR 14 HOURS . . . AND THE STRAIN WAS BEGINNING TO SHOW.
nat sot up full—deputy on radio. Runs :03	"Hey. We've got to get some relief out here. This is nuts."
	BUT NO RELIEF WAS COMING.

Example 2

	IT ALL CAME DOWN TO THIS PITCH IN THE BOTTOM OF THE NINTH.
	KELLY LOCKED EYES WITH THE PITCHER . . . AND HER GAZE NEVER WAVERED AS THE BALL SOARED TOWARD THE PLATE.
nat sot, crack of bat. Runs :02	(nat sot)
	KELLY DIDN'T PAUSE TO SEE WHERE THE BALL WAS GOING. AS SHE DASHED TOWARD FIRST THE CROWD ROSE TO ITS FEET. WHEN THE BALL CLEARED THE FENCE . . . IT WAS INSTANT PANDEMONIUM.
nat sot, crowd screaming Intersperse with shots of backslapping, etc. Runs :04	(nat sot)
	THE TEAM NOBODY BELIEVED IN HAD DONE THE IMPOSSIBLE.

Effective use of natural sound is essential for great storytelling. Good photographers will find ways to sneak it in without being told. But the great teams work together to make it happen.

Other Audio Elements

Music

The use of music isn't uncommon in television news, although policies vary from station to station. A sports story about car racing might include hard-driving, high-energy music. A story about a little girl battling cancer might include sad piano music. A sweeps piece about teen drinking in an urban bar district might feature hip-hop music. The first question you should ask when proposing to use music is, "Why are we doing this?" Chances are your main interest in music will be to set a mood. In the sports story above, you're using music to say, "This is exciting." In the story about the little girl, you're telegraphing to the audience, "You should be sad." In the drinking story, the music contributes to an electric, contemporary atmosphere.

Some might ask whether it's appropriate for a journalist to suggest to the viewer how he or she should feel. You'll have to make up your own mind about that, taking into account your standards and those in your newsroom. Use of music in a sports story is probably relatively safe; sports activities are, after all, a form of entertainment. Laying sad music into a "sad" story is slightly more problematic. You are, in essence, taking deliberate steps to create sympathy for the subject of your story. Is that appropriate? Is the subject of your story truly deserving of sympathy, and is it up to you to say so? In the case of the little girl cited above, it's probably okay. But then you also have to ask, "Is it *necessary*?" And while you're at it, be careful not to make it too sappy. The bar scene example above might be the most troublesome. Hip-hop music might indeed create a contemporary atmosphere, but the "cool" music might also suggest to the wrong people that underage drinking is cool, too.

Music is used most appropriately when it's a natural part of the scene you're documenting and the photographer records it as nat sot.

If you decide to use music, as with any other communication tool make sure you know the message you're trying to deliver with it. The message must be appropriate and not subject to misinterpretation.

Sound Effects

Be very, *very* careful with these. Sound effects used in place of natural sound that you wish you had but don't are a form of unlabeled re-enactment and therefore ethically suspect. The only safe uses of sound effects are in instances when there can be no doubt that the sound effect *is* a sound effect. It's usually not possible to pull this off when showing video, because the viewers will tend to believe that any sound they hear is nat sot. But you can do it with graphics. For instance, if you're showing a graphic animation of a beating heart and wish to dub in a heartbeat, there's no harm done. Bottom line: Don't mislead the audience.

The Diamond Approach

In Chapter 1 we mentioned that broadcasters don't use inverted pyramid style. For packages, we sometimes use the diamond style. The diamond style is especially useful when writing packages in which we're dealing with something that affects a large number of people. Some examples might be the marriage penalty tax, changes in one of the city's zoning ordinances, or a promising cancer treatment. In each case, the tendency is to hit the viewers with a bunch

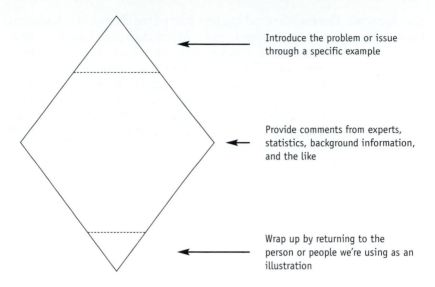

Introduce the problem or issue through a specific example

Provide comments from experts, statistics, background information, and the like

Wrap up by returning to the person or people we're using as an illustration

of numbers and statistics: Married couples pay 10 percent more in taxes than unmarried people living together do, the zoning change would result in the closing of 20 local businesses, the new treatment would help the 400,000 Americans suffering with a particular type of cancer.

Don't misunderstand. Using some supporting numbers and statistics is important. But we want to "peopleize" stories—to tell them in human terms through the eyes of an individual, a family, or a small group. We can then use the experiences of the people who are our examples to make the stories more interesting. The three stories we just mentioned might start something like this:

BEING MARRIED COSTS MIKE AND JAN PARKER AN EXTRA 500 DOLLARS IN TAXES EACH YEAR.

THIS HARDWARE STORE HAS BEEN IN KEITH ROLLYSON'S FAMILY FOR 60 YEARS. BUT A CHANGE IN A HOOVERVILLE ZONING ORDINANCE MIGHT FORCE THE FAMILY TO CLOSE THE STORE FOR GOOD.

SAM SMITH PLAYED COLLEGE TENNIS . . . BUT NOW HE CAN BARELY WALK. HE HOPES A NEW CANCER DRUG HELPS HIM GET BACK ON THE COURT SOME DAY.

Remember, we have to catch the viewers' attention right away. Personalizing the lead sentence helps us do that, and the example of how the issue affects a person, family, or small group forms the top part of the diamond. The middle (and bigger) part of the diamond is for numbers, statistics, comments from experts about the subject, and the like. The bottom of the diamond is where we come back to the person or people we're using as an illustration. Using the three stories we've been talking about, that approach would allow us to close by mentioning what the Parkers hope the tax code changes would mean for them, what the future holds for the Rollyson family hardware business, or what the prognosis for Sam Smith might be and whether he'll be hitting backhands any time soon.

Donuts

In local television news today, lots of stories include the reporter live on the scene. Sometimes, the reporter appears on camera for a minute or more to update the viewers about a breaking story that has just occurred, and there's been no time to shoot and edit video. More often, however, the reporter has had time to put together a taped piece, which she introduces live from the field. This type of report is called a **donut** in some newsrooms and a "sandwich" in others. A donut is a special type of package and is a bit more involved than a regular package is.

With a donut, the anchor still sets up the story in general terms and introduces the reporter. But rather than introducing the reporter's taped package, the anchor "pitches" to the reporter in the field, who is live on-camera. The tone of the introduction changes a bit, and of course the script markings change some as well. The reporter further sets up the story and introduces the taped portion.

The way the package part of a donut is structured is a lot like a regular package, but there are a few differences. First, because of the extra time it takes for the live reporter segments before and after the package, the tape will have to be a little shorter for a donut than it might be if no live elements were incorporated. Second, because we see the reporter before and after the package, there's no reason to use a stand-up within the piece. That would mean seeing the reporter three times in one story. Some large-market stations take that approach, but we think that's too much reporter and not enough other video. Third, because the reporter is going to come back on-camera after the package, there's no need to include a sig-out at the end of the tape. It would sound silly to hear "In Hooverville, I'm Joe Reporter, Newswatch One" and then switch to a shot of Joe saying something else. Let's take our Jurassic Park story and set it up as a donut. We'll assume that we're airing the story to coincide with the big opening of the movie at the Hooverville Metroplex. The first showing is at 7 P.M., and by the time we go on the air with this story at 6:11, the ticket line already stretches out the door and halfway around the block. Here's how we set the story up to incorporate live reporter presence at the scene.

Jurassic Park

	(Bill)
On cam	IT TAKES A HEALTHY DOSE OF SCIENCE FACT TO MAKE A GOOD WORK OF SCIENCE FICTION. JOE REPORTER IS STANDING BY LIVE OUTSIDE THE HOOVERVILLE METROPLEX WHERE A LOT OF PEOPLE ARE WAITING TO SEE THE NEW MOVIE JURASSIC PARK. JOE, WE UNDERSTAND THIS MOVIE MIGHT CONTAIN MORE SCIENCE FACT THAN WE REALIZE.
Take LIVE	(Joe ad lib)
	Roll cue: "dinosaurs running loose"
:00 Take tape vid & snd full (donut)	(pkg)
Supers:	
:01 Courtesy: Universal Pictures	
:25 Rob Ferl, geneticist	
1:00 Tim Gross, biologist	
1:21 Tape out	Outcue: "halls of science . . . for now."
Take LIVE	(Joe ad lib)
On cam	THANKS, JOE. SCIENTISTS SAY THAT AS WE GET CLOSER TO UNDERSTANDING LIFE AND MAYBE ONE DAY RE-CREATING IT, THERE WILL BE MANY ETHICAL QUESTIONS TO BE ANSWERED ALONG THE WAY.

The story is essentially the same as in the previous example, except that Joe is now live on-camera outside the movie theater before and after the package runs. Also, we don't write down what Joe says in the field, except for his final few words leading to the tape. The **roll cue** lets the director know when to roll the tape. The outcue is different, because the reporter will come back on-camera briefly after the package, so there's no sig-out.

There are two other types of packages that we'll mention briefly. Anchor packages are voiced by an anchor, and because the anchor is on the set, anchor packages typically don't include a stand-up or a signature outcue if they appear on the same show he or she is anchoring. Nat snd packages include no narration at all—just bites, natural sound, and perhaps a bit of music or other sound.

Conclusion

Remember when you're writing a package that your job is to provide the glue to get the viewers to the next sound bite or piece of natural sound. Get to that point as expeditiously as possible. You aren't paid on the basis of how many words you cram into your narration, but on the basis of how well you tell stories. Some of the best stories have limited narration and some (nat snd packages) include no reporter voice at all. You aren't the focus of the story. The people you're reporting about are.

Remember also that your story script is only part of what you're responsible for. The producer script contains vital information and the reporter is responsible for making sure that information is complete and accurate. If one person in the chain isn't "on the same page," the package you worked so hard on can wind up looking terrible on the air. Because the reporter, videographer, and editor have done most of the work on a package and it's very close to being fully self-contained, the people in the control room can take a bit of a breather while the package is rolling and "gear up" for what's ahead. But that happens only if all the needed directions are on the script.

 Package DOs and DON'Ts

Do
- Give the anchor an active role.
- Work for flow from track to bites and back to track.
- Incorporate natural sound breaks.
- "Personalize" stories.

Don't
- Stand stick-straight on stand-ups.
- Leave out *any* cues on the producer's script.
- Become the focus of the story.
- Forget that reporting can be hard work.

PRODUCING TV NEWS

If you're reading this chapter, then chances are (1) you've decided to pursue a career in TV newscast producing, (2) you're thinking about it, or (3) you're reading this as a classroom assignment. If the first two reasons apply, this chapter will give you a good understanding of what the job entails. We'll discuss how to carry out the basics of building a television newscast, how to fill out a production rundown, how to write leads to enhance story flow, and how to write good **teases.** If, on the other hand, you have no intention of becoming a producer, then this chapter will still be of value if you plan to work in the field of television news. No matter what you do in broadcast journalism, if you aren't a producer, you'll be dealing with them. This chapter will give you a good understanding of what drives them, what their needs are, and why they act in the sometimes mysterious ways they do.

What Is a Producer?

Simply put, news producing is the art and science of filling a broadcast with news content. There's not much glamour in it and, as a consequence, most of the public at large has only a vague idea, if any, of what a producer does or even that producers exist. Yet the producer is one of the most important people, if not *the* most important person, involved with the newscast. Whereas newsroom managers hover about trying to look important, the producer is the point person responsible for getting the broadcast on the air. One good way to judge the importance of a producer is to watch what happens when one falls ill and has to call in sick: instant panic! It's guaranteed that someone will have to be called in as a replacement; just as a plane can't take off without the pilot, the newscast won't air without a producer.

Though the viewer doesn't know it, few people in the newsroom are more critical to the viewer than the producer is. The producer, through the decisions he or she makes, is the viewer's window to the world. It's up to the producer to decide which stories are important to the viewer, and to choose those stories and present them in a newscast in such a way as to showcase context, meaning, perspective, and, above all, relevance. This requires news judgment and a sense of mission. It also requires technical expertise. Often producers don't get much training in the latter, and it's not unusual for producers to find themselves "thrown in, sink or swim." Therefore we'll go into a great deal of technical detail in this chapter.

The producer has an alter ego and partner in crime: the director. Whereas the producer is in charge of the content and timing of the newscast, the director leads a production crew that's responsible for executing most of the technical and some of the aesthetic aspects of the plan.

Why Be a Producer?

When interviewing intern candidates, it's not unusual for news directors to hear, "I want to be an anchor." There's certainly nothing wrong with this goal. But obviously, there are only so many high-paying anchor jobs. Competition for them, or on-air jobs of any kind, is fierce.

On the other hand, competition for producer jobs isn't nearly as intense. The typical reporter opening might attract anywhere from 50 to 150 tapes. The typical producer opening might attract 10 to 15 tapes. Do the math. If you're a good producer, you can write your own ticket. These days in many stations, an experienced producer of a major newscast often makes as much as, if not more than, most reporters.

If you're a good writer, have excellent people skills and excellent news judgment, enjoy leading teams of people, and prefer to be involved in the "big picture" rather than just a piece of it, then producing might be for you. But producing isn't for everybody. Most people either really like it or really hate it. There's little middle ground.

Producer Duties

The producer's shift normally begins with an editorial meeting. The editorial team consists of the newscast producers, the assignments editor, the executive producer, and other senior managers. In many (if not most) stations, reporters and photographers sit in on the editorial meetings as well. The group discusses the stories available for coverage and then assigns coverage resources. Afterward, the producer goes back to his or her desk, sorts through the local and regional news feeds, wire material, and the like, and decides which stories will go into the day's broadcast, in what form, and in what order. Producers write some or all of their own copy and also supervise other copywriters who may be assigned to the newscast. Producers edit reporter copy (at least, they're supposed to). They order or supervise the ordering of all graphics for the newscast. They sit in the control booth to time the show and deal with breaking news.

In carrying out those duties the producer must accomplish the following tasks, arranged here in roughly descending order of priority:

- *Precisely time the broadcast.* The newscast must end at the appointed time. It can't run long, and it can't run short. Some kind of content must separate the commercial breaks; they can't "bump together!"

- *Choose the right mix of stories.* The producer, working in concert with the assignments editor and newsroom managers, must make sure that coverage and newscast resources are devoted to the right stories. "Right stories" has a broad range of definitions, but normally it means those stories that are most newsworthy on the given day, in light of the community's needs and the station's coverage philosophy.

- *Place the stories in the correct order.* This is an activity also known as "filling the rundown" or "completing the lineup." The **rundown** or **lineup** (different stations use different terminology) is a spreadsheet-like form listing the stories in the chronological order in which they'll air. This information typically includes, for each story, the page number, the slug (title) of the story, the anchor who'll be reading it, the type of camera **shot** or shots to be used, the form of the story, basic production elements that will be needed, the running time, and so on. We'll discuss story placement in greater detail later.

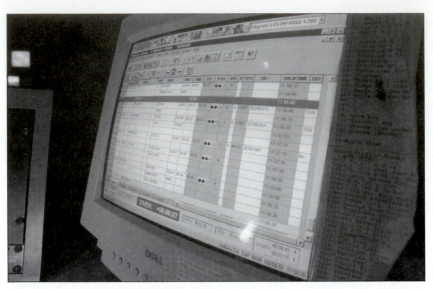

A typical newscast rundown displayed on a computer monitor at WFLA-TV.

- *Work with the director and production crew to get the newscast on the air.* A good producer never loses sight of the fact that the director is an equal partner in the newscast. Good communication and cooperation between the producer and director are absolutely essential!
- *Write copy.* Most producers write at least some copy, and some producers write *all* the copy, with the exception of reporter packages. This function varies from market size to market size, depending on whether writing assistance is available to the producer. Simply put, good producers must write well according to the principles outlined elsewhere in this book.
- *Edit the copy.* Good producers always carefully read any and all copy written for their newscasts. They work with the reporters to assist and help direct the development of their stories. They edit copy for accuracy, fairness, balance, comprehension, and storytelling, as well as for libel and privacy concerns.
- *Order the graphics.* Generally, the more sophisticated the product, the more sophisticated the graphics. Many stations have good art departments and place a high priority on graphics. The producer orders graphics for his or her show and works with the reporters to ensure they make good use of graphics within their packages.
- *Scan the wires and feeds.* Good producers continually scan the incoming wires and feed services to ensure that the best, freshest, and most updated material is included in the broadcast.

- *Work with the desk.* Good producers work closely with the assignments desk to be on top of and react appropriately to breaking news.
- *Show leadership.* The producer is a "big picture" person. He or she sees how all the individual parts fit together and, like a symphony conductor, must orchestrate everyone's efforts to achieve a satisfactory, high-quality product. In doing so, the producer works with many people whose primary responsibilities pertain to a much smaller part of the picture. In order for all of this to come together, the producer must have excellent leadership skills and must contribute to a positive and productive work environment.

Despite the "descending order" nature of this list, none of these tasks and responsibilities is unimportant. Failure to properly time a show will get you in trouble with your news director very quickly. Failure to show good leadership will get you in trouble more slowly. For a producer to be truly excellent and successful, he or she must earn an "A" in each of these categories.

The Rundown

Anchors generally read their copy from scripts, which are available to them in printed form on the news set and electronically on a prompter. If the scripts are a book, then the rundown is a table of contents. But it's more than that, because it also gives the director and production crew much of the information they need to execute the newscast from a technical standpoint.

Rundown design, use, and implementation vary widely from station to station. These days, most news operations are computerized. But whether the rundown is contained on a computer screen or on a printed form, its use is the same: to list the stories, story formats, running times, and other information needed to get each newscast element produced and on the air. Below is a sample of the most important columns contained in a typical rundown, followed by detailed explanation of each.

PAGE #	SHOT	RUNS
SLUG	TYPE	BACKTIME
ANC	WR	

PAGE #

Most stations make use of page numbers to assist in the process of keeping the scripts in their proper order. The page number is similar to, but not exactly the same as, a page number in a textbook. Most stations label individual blocks of stories with letters of the alphabet. A news **block** is usually defined as a segment of news content sandwiched between commercial breaks. Thus the first segment of the newscast, containing all of the stories between the newscast **open** and the first commercial break, is often referred to as the "A" block. The next news segment, lying between the first commercial break and the second, is the "B" block, and so on. Page numbers frequently begin with the block number. So, the first story in the newscast is generally given a page number of A1. The second story is A2. However, many stations number their stories in increments of 10—A10, A20, and so on. This allows producers to insert new stories into the middle of the rundown later without having to renumber every story.

Some stories take up more than one line on the rundown in order to accommodate production information. In such cases the page number usually is subdivided with decimals or trailing letters, depending on the capabilities of the newsroom computer system. Example 1: A10, A10A, A10B, and so on. Example 2: A10.1, A10.2, A10.3, and so on.

SLUG

The **slug** is a short description that serves as a daily title for the story. Different stations have different conventions for slugging stories. Some have no convention. The purpose of the slug is to make sure that all scripts, graphics, tapes, live remotes, and other production elements associated with the story are labeled properly and consistently. This is a critically important function. For instance, an incorrect slug on a videocassette can often lead to someone losing a tape or miscuing it, causing major problems on the air. (Anchor: "Apparently we don't have that story. We'll try to come back to it in a moment. In other news . . .")

As mentioned, sometimes stories have more than one element, causing them to take up more than one line on the rundown. Often these different lines require individual slugs. Again, different stations have different conventions, but normally the sub-lines contain similar slugs along with a differentiating character or words. For instance, a typical package might require three scripts: the **lead** or **intro,** the package verbatim, and the package **tag.** Typical slugs for the three package elements associated with a murder trial might be:

SMITH TRIAL (LEAD)

P-SMITH TRIAL (PACKAGE VERBATIM)

T-SMITH TRIAL (TAG)

Depending on the limitations of the computer system or rundown form, some stations simply use the whole term, as follows:

SMITH INTRO

SMITH PACKAGE

SMITH TAG

ANC

This column would simply contain the name or initials of the anchor reading the story.

SHOT

The shot column generally contains information about how many people will be framed in the camera shot for a given story, and whether a graphic will be part of the camera shot. Typical basic choices might include:

- *1shot.* One anchor on camera, centered, no graphic. Sometimes known as the "head and shoulders" or "H&S" shot.
- *2shot.* Two anchors on camera, centered, no graphic.
- *OTS.* One anchor on camera, framed to accommodate a corner or side graphic positioned "over the shoulder."
- *3shot.* Three anchors on camera.
- *Wide.* All anchors on camera.
- *CK.* One anchor at the chromakey board.
- *Dblbox.* "Double box" shot, typically with an anchor framed in one box and a reporter framed opposite, for Q&A.
- *3box.* Same as above, with three boxes—typically, an anchor and two reporters or interview guests.
- *Wipe.* Not a shot at all, but rather an indication that we'll go to the next story without coming back to an anchor, by use of a production technique during which video of the preceding story will "wipe" off the screen, to be replaced by video of the next story.

There are many other possibilities, depending on the capabilities of the station and set design. In addition, terminology tends to vary from station to station. For instance, a graphic shot known as an over-the-shoulder or "OTS" in one station might be a "1box" in another. There is no universal list of terms, and producers must re-learn some of these terms every time they change jobs. However, the principles are usually the same.

TYPE

A number of different terms might go here to help describe the type and format of the story. Again, specific terms used vary widely from station to station depending on technology and newsroom custom. Some basic possibilities include:

- *Intro.* Anchor- or reporter-read copy preceding a package.
- *Tag.* Anchor- or reporter-read copy following a package.
- *Tossback.* Similar to a tag, but usually includes two or more people with a question-and-answer opportunity.
- *Reader.* An anchor on camera reading copy without video support or full-screen graphics. Normally, this implies a stand-alone story, not a package or **live shot** intro.

- *VO.* For voice-over. This indicates that the anchor will read copy and that for portions of the narrative the audience will see video while hearing the anchor's narration.
- *VOB (also VO/SOT or VOBITE).* For "voice-over with sound bite" or "voice-over with sound on tape." This indicates that the anchor will read copy, that for portions of it the audience will see pictures, and that the anchor will pause while the audience hears a portion of an interview with "sound up full."
- *BITE* or *SOT.* Same as above, except that no pictures will precede the interview.
- *VONATS.* Same as a VOB, except that the anchor will pause for "natural sound"—sound recorded in the field of something other than an interview (the crack of a bat, the roar of the crowd, a space shuttle countdown, and the like).
- *PKG.* For "package." Indicates a preproduced tape element that typically includes interviews, pictures, and reporter narrative in one contained unit.
- *LIVE.* Indicates the use of a live remote by microwave, satellite, fiber optic line, and so forth. Some stations specify here which mode will be used: "LIVE/SAT" for a satellite shot, "LIVE/REM" for a local microwave shot.
- *SS/CG.* "Still store with character generator." Indicates the use of a full-screen graphic with text to be inserted electronically live on the air. Almost all SS/CGs are voiced-over live by an anchor.
- *SS/FULL.* Same as above, but the text is pre-pasted on the graphic rather than inserted live on the air.
- *ENG.* For "electronic news gathering." Some stations use this as a designation for whatever standard format they're using to record and play back news video. For example: eng/pkg. Some news operations list the specific format, such as "beta," "svhs," "editstar," and the like. Still others omit a tape or server designation for news stories, with the assumption that all such elements will be played from a standard news video machine unless otherwise designated. In our examples we'll also omit the use of this term.
- *VTR.* Similar to ENG, but usually denotes a production department video device other than one normally used to play back news video, such as an open-reel 1-inch tape machine used for newscast opens, teases, and other standard elements.

WR

This column contains the name or initials of the writer assigned to the story.

RUNS

This column contains a running time for the story or story segment. (An example of a story segment, as opposed to a single story, would be "weather." Weather might contain many elements, but on most rundowns it's listed with a single slug and running time.) Ideal running times for various story formats vary from station to station, but the following examples are typical:

Reader:	:10–:15	Pkg:	1:20–1:30
VO:	:15–:25	Tag:	:05–:10
VOB:	:35–:45	Tossback:	:05–:10, or longer if
Intro:	:10–:15		there's a Q&A session

BACKTIME

The **backtiming** column is critically important. Prior to the newscast, it shows the producer whether the show *appears* to be properly filled. During the newscast, a constant check of this column tells the producer whether the show is light (not enough material to stretch to the off-time) or heavy (some material might have to be dropped to conclude on time). In some stations this is also described as being "short" or "long."

In the old days it was said that "all good producers could tell, add, and subtract time backward." These days most modern newsroom computer systems automatically figure the backtimes based on the information the producer enters into the "RUNS" column. If not, the producer will have to figure this information by hand (oh, joy).

Building a Newscast

Now that you have a good understanding of what kinds of story elements are available, we're ready to learn the basics of designing a newscast.

Newscast Formats

There are as many varieties of newscast as there are news organizations. The basic principles we'll discuss here apply to all formats and newscast lengths. But for the purposes of this lesson we'll build a newscast based on a typical half-hour news format.

All newscasts are defined in part by the number of commercial breaks they contain. Our sample newscast will have four commercial *breaks* of two minutes duration each. It will contain news, weather, and sports in the traditional order. It will end with an external commercial break, usually known as a "terminal break." For the purpose of this exercise, this will be a 6 P.M. newscast, and we'll title it "Rumor Has It News at Six."

Here's the format: *"Rumor Has It News at Six" with Fred Feelgood and Jane Jabberon—Basic Format*

A Block—Hard News

Break One 2:00

B Block—Softer News

Break Two 2:00

C Block—Weather

Break Three 2:00

D Block—Sports

Break Four 2:00

E Block (Kicker Block)

Terminal Break 1:10

News Hole

Before we can fill our newscast, we must first determine how much time is at our disposal. The basic amount of time available for news generally doesn't vary much from night to night. The total amount of time required every night to run all the commercials, teases, sports, weather, and chitchat is sometimes called the **skeleton time** or "filler time." When you subtract this from the total available time, you're left with what is usually known, with a certain lack of elegance, as the **news hole.**

Let's figure out the news hole for our sample newscast. First, let's add in *all* the standard features that will appear every night. Typically, this will include the open, the close, the teases, the tosses, and so on.

"Rumor Has It News at Six" with Fred Feelgood and Jane Jabberon—Skeleton Rundown on Scratchpad

Element	Running Time
Newscast Open	0:20
A Block—Hard News	
Tease One	0:20
Break One	2:00
B Block—Softer News	
Tease Two	0:15
Break Two	2:00
C Block—Weather	
Toss to WX	0:10
WX	3:20
Tossback from WX	0:15
Tease Three	0:15
Break Three	2:00
D Block—Sports	

(continued)

Element	Running Time
Toss to Sports	0:10
Sports	3:20
Tossback from Sports	0:15
Tease Four	0:10
Break Four	2:00
E Block—Kicker	
Tease for 11 PM	0:25
Close	0:30
Terminal Break	1:10
Total Running Time	**18:55**

This is the "newscast skeleton"—so called because it's the bare bones that we must flesh out with news content. Adding up all of these times, we come to 18:55. Wise producers might wish to add in another 30 seconds of time for miscellaneous slippage because of package overruns, unscheduled chitchat, and the like.

Total Running Time	18:55
+ Pad Time	:30
= Skeleton Time	19:25

Thus the skeleton time of 19:25 is the time that's already prefilled in this particular newscast before the producer even sits down to begin work. The obvious next question is, How much work will the producer have to do? How much time must he or she fill?

Our sample newscast begins at 6:00 P.M. and ends at 6:30, giving us one-half hour's time. We must now subtract the skeleton time from the available time to get the news hole, as follows:

Total Available Time	30:00
− Skeleton Time	19:25
= News Hole	10:35

That's our news hole: 10 minutes and 35 seconds. It ain't much, is it? Nevertheless, your job for the day is to fill it. Note: the news hole *is* adjustable. It might expand or contract depending on the length of the commercial breaks. It can also expand or contract depending on the amount of time devoted to sports and weather. For that reason, producers are known to frequently ask sports anchors and weathercasters to "donate time," which sports anchors and weathercasters really hate to do. Wise producers don't abuse the privilege.

These days it's a rare newsroom indeed that's not computerized to some extent. With most (if not all) newsroom computers, the producer has to enter and save the skeleton rundown just once. On each subsequent day, the computer prefills the daily rundown based on this stored skeleton information. (This stored skeleton information is sometimes referred to as the rundown filler.)

An "empty" computerized rundown prefilled with the skeleton information we just derived might look something like this:

"Rumor Has It News at Six" with Fred Feelgood and Jane Jabberon—Skeleton Rundown on Computer

Page#	Slug	Anchor	Shot	Type	WR	Runs	Backtime
A00	Newcast Open			vtr/sot		:20	11:05
Alast	1-tz		2shot	vo		:20	11:25
Break One						2:00	11:45
B10							
Blast	2-tz		2shot	vo		:15	13:45
Break Two						2:00	14:00
C10	WX toss		3shot			:10	16:00
C10A	Weather					3:20	16:10
C10B	Tossback		3shot			:15	19:30
C20							
Clast	3-tz		2shot			:15	19:45
Break Three						2:00	20:00
D10	Toss to Sports		3shot			:10	22:00
D10A	Sports					3:20	22:10
D10B	Tossback		3shot			:15	25:30
Dlast	4-tz		2shot	vo		:10	25:45
Break Four						2:00	25:55
E10	11 Teaze			ss/cg		:25	27:55
E20							
E30	C ya/Close		wide			:30	28:20
Terminal Break						1:10	28:50
	Totals					18:55	6:30:00
	Over/Under					−11:05	

Most modern computerized rundowns will automatically total the story times and figure a backtime. For the moment, take a look at the total running time for all the stories together. Ideally, it should read "29:30"—which would leave us with 30 seconds of pad time. But the total in this case is 18:55. This is our skeleton time, the amount of news content time prefilled with the standard time typically used every night for weather, sports, teases, commercial breaks, and so on. Add in :30 for pad and the total is 19:25—exactly the amount we earlier figured by hand.

Take a look at the over/under clock. We're under by 11:05. This is the amount of time we must fill with news. Subtract that 30 seconds of pad time we talked about, and the total is 10:35. That's the "news hole" for the day.

Now look at the backtiming figure at the top of the right-hand column. It reads "11:05." The computer is showing you that if you don't add any more content to the newscast, but you want the newscast to end at 6:30:00, then you must *start* the newscast at 6:11:05. Obviously, we *are* going to add some content. We'll discuss backtiming in much greater detail later.

A note about computerized rundowns: they're only as good as the people configuring them. It's in your best interests not to always blindly trust the computer, especially if you're producing a newscast with which you aren't familiar. In such cases you're well advised to sit down and figure out your news hole by hand as a way of verifying what the computer is telling you.

Ordering Stories—The Three Factors

Now comes the fun part, the puzzle you're paid the humongous, hairy bucks to figure out. You must choose the stories you want to put in your newscast and the order in which you'd like them to run.

The first thing you'll do is come out of the morning meeting and write down the stories that have been assigned to your newscast. Make at least tentative decisions about the format you might like for those stories—which will be "straight packages," which will be live remotes, which will be newsroom-anchored pieces, and the like. This will leave you a certain amount of time you must fill from other sources. You'll want to spend the next hour or so scanning the wires, looking at the feeds and feed rundowns, and working with the desk for updates and follow-ups in order to develop a list of potential extra stories for your newscast.

At some point you'll want to begin sketching out a rundown. How does one decide the order in which the stories should run? This is one of the most difficult tasks a producer faces. The answer will vary from individual to individual and from station to station. But every producer should have a rhyme and a reason for the order of the show. In the trade magazines you'll occasionally see job ads for producers that declare, "Show stackers need not apply." "Show stacker" is an epithet for a producer who either stacks stories seemingly at random or stacks them in the order of perceived priority without any flow from one story to the next. A good producer doesn't just stack stories, but instead takes three major factors into account when ordering them: *priority (newsworthiness), flow,* and *pace.*

Priority

Though you usually won't stack stories strictly in descending order of their importance, generally you'll *begin* with the top-priority story. Choosing the lead might well be the most important decision you make during the day. Why? News research suggests that news consumers base their viewing decisions on the lead, which they know should be the "most important story." If this most important story isn't important to them, they might switch in search of another story, and often, they don't come back. So the ratings battle for the day is often won or lost on the strength of the lead story.

It sounds simple, right? Your lead should be the most important story of the day. That shouldn't be too hard to determine, should it? Actually, it can be maddeningly difficult. You might have several stories of more or less equal importance, none of which stands out as the clear lead. Your newscast might be competing with another newscast airing on your station an hour later or earlier, leaving you to duke it out with your fellow producer about the choice of a lead. In addition, there are other factors to consider besides the basic news value of the story. In many stations producers are required to take the station's mission statement and coverage philosophy into account when choosing leads and stories. The process can get complicated. That's why in many stations this decision isn't left to the producer alone, but rather becomes a team decision.

Flow

Once you've chosen the lead, the next step is to choose story number two. This seems logical enough. You might be tempted at this point to place the *second* most important story of the day in that slot. But stop and think a moment. Placing the second most important story second isn't always the best choice. Good producers usually group stories somewhat according to theme, then group the themes in logical order, taking newsworthiness into account. Thus, if you're leading with a story about city council raising taxes, your second story might be a VO or VOBITE about an action some other governmental body took today. Your third story should be some subject that flows logically out of the second story. It might or might not be the third most newsworthy story of the day.

This sounds difficult, but it's easy to get the hang of it. Suppose your first story is about city council raising property taxes and the second story is about the county commission taking action to fix a problem-plagued intersection. You have a story you haven't yet placed about a bad accident. Where should it go? Chances are it will "flow" best out of the story about the intersection, flowing with the "traffic" theme. Then if you have other police- and fire-related matters, these would flow well out of the accident story, and so on.

Pacing

The third critically important factor is pacing. Many inexperienced producers make the mistake of cramming all their packages into the top of the news block, then running the "less important" VOs and VOBITEs at the end of the block. This is terrible for pacing.

Remember, your greatest enemy is the remote control. If your viewer loses interest, zap, you're the history channel. One way to keep your viewers' attention is to keep a fast pace. Ideally, something should be changing every few seconds: reveal a new fact, change the camera shot, change the video, put in a new edit, change the graphic, and so on. Back-to-back packages tend to slow the pace. Break up the pace by inserting tags, VOs, VOBITEs, or readers.

A good, cheap, and easy way to keep the pace going is to tag every package on-camera, or to tag every VO or VOBITE on-camera prior to changing anchors. The latter has other benefits as well. If the anchor begins every reading sequence on-camera and ends it on-camera before the second anchor speaks, it brings a sense of closure and also boosts the anchor's image as being in control of the sequence. This enhances the authority, professionalism, and teamwork of your anchor team, which will make your news director and news consultant happy—and in the process make your newscast better and more competitive. We'll discuss tags in more detail later.

Filling the Rundown—The Scratchpad Method

There are two methods for drafting a rundown, and we're going to look at both. Some producers like to begin by immediately sketching out their first draft on-screen in the computer rundown. We'll see how that process works in a moment. But some find it more useful to order stories by hand on a piece of scratch paper first. This method has two advantages. One, computers will sometimes lie to you; hand calculations give you a way to verify what the computer is showing you. Second, the old-fashioned tools of pencil-and-eraser allow you to easily tinker with a handwritten rundown, moving the elements around fairly quickly and conveniently. Once you've found a draft rundown that appears to make sense in terms of story order and total running time, you can then enter it into the computerized rundown.

For the scratchpad method, you need only write down the slug of the story, a note about its type, and the proposed running time. We'll add up these times and get a quick estimate of the total running time of the stories, then compare it to our available news hole.

So, with a list of available stories on my desk and the above principles of story ordering firmly in mind, I'm ready to scratch out a proposed plan of action. Here's draft 1 of my proposed rundown. Note, by this method we write down only those stories that are *not* part of the skeleton time of the newscast. This means we're temporarily omitting opens, teases, the running time for sports and weather, and other elements that appear in the same place with the same running time every day. We'll draw a short line to separate blocks.

"Rumor Has It News at Six" with Fred Feelgood and Jane Jabberon—Rundown Draft 1 on Scratchpad

Council Taxes	live/pkg	2:10
Intersection Repair	vo	:25
4-Car Pileup	vobite	:40
Apartment Fire	live/pkg	2:10
Fire History	ss/cg	:25
Housefire Update	vo	:25
Robbery Attempt	vo	:25
Suspect Caught	vo	:25
Robbery Trial	pkg	1:40
Murder Trial	vo	:25
Legislature/Crackdown	vo	:25
_____		
Truck Recall	pkg	1:40
Recall Info	ss/cg	:25
Toaster Lawsuit	vo	:25
Stock Market	ss/cg	:20
_____		
Weather		
Waterpark Opens	vobite	:45
_____		
Sports		
_____		
Skiing Squirrel	vonats	:35

This rundown looks great, and I'm happy as a clam. So I add up all my times and get—13:45. But wait; didn't we say our available news hole was only 10:35? We're over by 3:10!

Now you begin to understand the heartbreak of producing. You can rarely, if ever, produce your ideal newscast. We're going to have to cut some content.

First I go back and re-examine my rundown. OK, I guess I don't need that house fire update that I had planned to run updating a fire from the day before. It's a shame, too, because I was going to run a "follow-up" over-the-shoulder graphic with it, and my news director loves those. Oh, well. It's toast.

Do I really need to run a bite on the water park opening? Nah. That gives me another :15 back. I'll write tight; another :10 saved.

The stock market is slow today. I'll need only :15 to give the results. There's another :05. But I'm still 2:15 too long.

My VOs are going to have to be more tightly written. I think I'm going to need the full :25 to explain the intersection story, but the rest of the VOs can be cut by at least :05 apiece. That gives me back :35. I'm still 1:40 long.

That apartment fire story has good visuals but isn't a complicated story. I'll ask the reporter to keep her lead, tag, and tape time tight and give me back :10.

I'm still long by 1:30.

Now, I go to sports, hat in hand, and find out how busy a sports day this has been. The sports anchor, because he's a heck of a guy, admits that there have been more active sports days, and agrees to donate :30 to the cause. So sports will run 2:50 today, instead of the normal 3:20. I'm still 1:00 long.

Second, I head to the weather office. But wait a minute. I know the weathercaster really hates giving up time even on a slow weather day, and that she always checks my rundown to verify that the time is really needed. The first thing her eye is going to land on is that "Skiing Squirrel" kicker. So I change the slug to "Kicker" and knock the time down to :20 instead of the :35 I had hoped to run. This will cost me the ability to take natural sound up full within the story, but what the heck. I take those steps, walk into the weather office, and make my pitch. She's unhappy about giving up a full :30 because there's a severe weather system in the Midwest she wants to talk about. But she owes me because I gave her 15 extra seconds on Wednesday and again on Thursday. She gives in and donates 30 seconds. So, weather will run 2:50 today instead of 3:20.

That still leaves me :15 long. But with a 30-second close and 30 seconds of pad time, I still have a safety margin left of :45. That should still be enough to give me a "loose" show, which my bosses like. (Anchors always complain to the boss if they have to rush through their tosses.)

So, the final rundown on scratchpad might look something like this:

"Rumor Has It News at Six" with Fred Feelgood and Jane Jabberon—Rundown Draft 2 on Scratchpad

Council Taxes	live/pkg	2:10
Intersection Repair	vo	:25
4-Car Pileup	vobite	:40
Apartment Fire	live/pkg	2:00 (was 2:10)
Fire History	ss/cg	:20 (was :25)
(Housefire Update deleted)		(was :25)
Robbery Attempt	vo	:20 (was :25)
Suspect Caught	vo	:20 (was :25)
Robbery Trial	pkg	1:40
Murder Trial	vo	:20 (was :25)
Legislature/Crackdown	vo	:20 (was :25)

(continued)

Truck Recall	pkg	1:40
Recall Info	ss/cg	:20 (was :25)
Toaster Lawsuit	vo	:20 (was :25)
Stock Market	ss/cg	:15 (was :20)
Weather		(minus :30)
Waterpark Opens	vo (was vobite)	:20 (was :45)
Sports		(minus :30)
Kicker	vo	:20 (was :35)
Total		10:50
News Hole		10:35
Over		:15

Filling the Rundown—The Computer Method

Rather than draft out a rundown on paper, some producers prefer to begin entering a draft directly into the computer. Using that method, the first draft we came up with earlier might look something like this when entered into a typical computer rundown:

"Rumor Has It News at Six" with Fred Feelgood and Jane Jabberon—Rundown Draft 1 by Computer

Page#	Slug	Anchor	Shot	Type	WR	Runs	Backtime
A00	Newscast Open			vtr/sot		:20	57:20
A10	Council Taxes			live/pkg		2:10	57:40
A20	Intersection Repair			vo		:25	59:50
A30	4-Car Pileup			vobite		:40	0:15
A40	Apartment Fire			live/pkg		2:10	0:55
A50	Fire History			ss/cg		:25	3:05
A60	Housefire Update			vo		:25	3:30
A70	Robbery Attempt			vo		:25	3:55
A80	Suspect Caught			vo		:25	4:20
A90	Robbery Trial			pkg		1:40	4:45
A100	Murder Trial			vo		:25	6:25
A110	Legislature/ Crackdown			vo		:25	6:50
Alast	1-tz		2shot	vo		:20	7:15
Break One						2:00	7:35
B10	Truck Recall			pkg		1:40	9:35
B20	Recall Info			ss/cg		:25	11:15

(continued)

Page#	Slug	Anchor	Shot	Type	WR	Runs	Backtime
B30	Toaster Lawsuit			vo		:25	11:40
B40	Stock Market			ss/cg		:20	12:05
Blast	2-tz		2shot	vo		:15	12:25
Break Two						2:00	12:40
C10	WX Toss		3shot			:10	14:40
C10A	Weather					3:20	14:50
C10B	Tossback		3shot			:15	18:10
C20	Waterpark Opens			vobite		:45	18:25
Clast	3-tz		2shot			:15	19:10
Break Three						2:00	19:25
D10	Toss to Sports		3shot			:10	21:25
D10A	Sports					3:20	21:35
D10B	Tossback		3shot			:15	24:55
Dlast	4-tz		2shot	vo		:10	25:10
Break Four						2:00	25:20
E10	11 Teaze			ss/cg		:25	27:20
E20	Skiing Squirrel			vonats		:35	27:45
E30	C ya/Close		wide			:30	28:20
Terminal Break						1:10	28:50
	Totals					32:40	6:30:00
	Over/Under					+ 2:40	

Note that the total running time is 32:40. The over/under clock confirms it: we're over by 2:40, and would have to start the show 2:40 early (at 5:57:20 as the backtiming column on page 180 shows) to get everything in. Because the computer doesn't automatically add in the pad time, we're actually over by 3:10. More about backtiming in a bit.

Now, let's repeat the horse trading we did earlier. To recap, we shortened all but one of those VOs by five seconds; we deleted the Housefire Update; we shortened the Apartment Fire story by :10; we stole :30 apiece from sports and weather; we shortened the Stock Market story by :05; we took the sound bite out of the Waterpark story and shortened it by :25; and finally, we took the nat sot break out of the Skiing Squirrel story and shortened it by :15. With those changes, draft 2 now looks like this:

"Rumor Has It News at Six" with Fred Feelgood and Jane Jabberon—Rundown Draft 2 by Computer

Page#	Slug	Anchor	Shot	Type	WR	Runs	Backtime
A00	Newscast Open			vtr/sot		:20	0:15
A10	Council Taxes			live/pkg		2:10	0:35
A20	Intersection Repair			vo		:25	2:45

(continued)

Page#	Slug	Anchor	Shot	Type	WR	Runs	Backtime
A30	4-Car Pileup			vobite	:40		3:10
A40	Apartment Fire			live/pkg	2:00		3:50
A50	Fire History			ss/cg	:20		5:50
A70	Robbery Attempt			vo	:20		6:10
A80	Suspect Caught			vo	:20		6:30
A90	Robbery Trial			pkg	1:40		6:50
A100	Murder Trial			vo	:20		8:30
A110	Legislature/						
	Crackdown			vo	:20		8:50
Alast	1-tz		2shot	vo	:20		9:10
Break One						2:00	9:30
B10	Truck Recall			pkg	1:40		11:30
B20	Recall Info			ss/cg	:20		13:10
B30	Toaster Lawsuit			vo	:20		13:30
B40	Stock Market			ss/cg	:15		13:50
Blast	2-tz		2shot	vo	:15		14:05
Break Two						2:00	14:20
C10	WX toss		3shot		:10		16:20
C10A	Weather				2:50		16:30
C10B	Tossback		3shot		:15		19:20
C20	Waterpark						
	Opens			vo	:20		19:35
Clast	3-tz		2shot		:15		19:55
Break Three						2:00	20:10
D10	Toss to Sports		3shot		:10		22:10
D10A	Sports				2:50		22:20
D10B	Tossback		3shot		:15		25:10
Dlast	4-tz		2shot	vo	:10		25:25
Break Four						2:00	25:35
E10	11 Teaze			ss/cg	:25		27:35
E20	Kicker			vo	:20		28:00
E30	C ya/Close		wide		:30		28:20
Terminal Break						1:10	28:50
	Totals					29:45	6:30:00
	Over/Under					− :15	

This will work. Now that we have the basic newscast down, it's just a matter of filling out the details.

Newscast Production: Sweating the Details— Graphics, Artwork, and Visual Pacing

We've decided how to fill our newscast. Now it's time to make decisions about the production of the stories. Sets, production techniques, and available artwork vary widely from station to station. But in every station, producers have to ask themselves questions such as:

- Where will I use wide shots?
- Where will I use 2shots?
- Where will I use 1shots?
- Which anchor intros will make use of artwork?
- How will I get into and out of live shots?
- Will I have a reporter on the set? At the chromakey board? In a debriefing area?

The answers to these questions will depend on the resources available, on your philosophy, and on the philosophy of the managers to whom you report. Resources and philosophies vary, but one factor is nearly universal: When changing from one story to another, producers should *almost always* make a visual change as well. For instance, if an anchor is on camera reading a story on a 1shot, don't have her begin a second story on that same 1shot! That's one of the most common mistakes inexperienced or untalented producers make. You must keep up a good visual pace.

Examples of techniques that can be used to make a visual change between two stories include, but are not limited to, the following:

- Changing from a 2shot to a 1shot.
- Any change of anchors.
- Changing from a 1shot "H&S" (head and shoulders) to an "OTS" (over-the-shoulder graphic shot) with the same anchor, or vice versa.
- While on an OTS shot, changing from one OTS graphic to a different graphic.
- Changing from an on-camera shot to a tape or graphic, or vice versa.
- Wiping or dissolving from one tape to another.
- Wiping or dissolving from a tape to a graphic, or vice versa.

How Do I Know When to Use an OTS Graphic?

Generally speaking, in any newscast, artwork and graphics are desirable. Lots of bland 1shots are not. A newscast filled with artwork tends to look sharper and more sophisticated. Good, aggressive producers seek ways to use plenty of artwork. OTS graphics work best at the beginning of stories, during the anchor leads. Tags generally are best done on a 1shot without graphics.

That said, the artwork should have a purpose. It should add to the meaning of the story in some specific way, containing a picture or piece of art and a slug line specifically related to the story at hand. Otherwise, the graphic tends to distract from the anchor's presentation. One mistake you often see in television is the use of completely generic graphics. Thus, you'll find an anchor reading a story about a robbery and murder while sharing the camera shot with a graphic of a generic pistol and a slug that reads "Murder." It's probably the exact same graphic the audience saw in the past 57 murder stories the station aired. To add insult to injury, the pistol's probably pointing at the anchor's head. Drop the graphic. It's worse than useless; it's distracting. If, however, the graphic includes some kind of image specific to this particular case and a specific slug ("1st St. Murder"), it has more use.

If you work in a station that has strong branding, you should treat all graphics as an opportunity to express that brand. In other words, if the story is investigative in nature, the OTS graphic should include your station's investigative logo; medical news should contain the logo of your station's medical unit, and so forth.

When Should I Use a 1shot? When Should I Use a 2shot?

Another mistake inexperienced producers often make is to produce the entire newscast on a 2shot. In some cases this stems from a lack of resources—not enough cameras or camera operators on the floor. Just as often, it stems from a misguided effort to show the anchors as a "team." There are more effective ways to showcase teamwork than by always showing them on a 2shot for every single story. Remember: *The most powerful shot in television is the head and shoulders 1shot.* Why? The 1shot is so powerful because it provides the best opportunity for eye contact. (This is another reason you should choose your graphics judiciously; OTS shots provide less eye contact because the anchor is, in essence, competing with the graphic for the viewer's attention.) 2shots are appropriate for establishing shots at the beginning of a newscast, as tease shots at the end of news blocks, and as transition shots.

The 2shot Transition

The 2shot transition, when used properly (and quickly), is a good tool for showcasing teamwork. The basic idea is to use the 2shot to change anchors between *related* stories.

In our sample newscast above, the Robbery Attempt story and the Suspect Caught story provide such an opportunity. Suppose we had originally planned to change anchors here, and anchor "A" is tagging the final line of Robbery Attempt on a 1shot. Make it a 2shot, and write the copy for the two stories with the transition in mind, in such a way as to enhance teamwork. The first anchor will "hand off" to the second one.

Robbery attempt tag

2shot   (Fred reads/Jane is looking at him)
                                         THE ROBBER LEFT EMPTY HANDED
                                         BUT HE DID GET AWAY.

Suspect caught intro

(Jane reads, addressing Fred)

NO SUCH LUCK FOR THE MAN

WANTED IN YESTERDAY'S HOLDUP.

(Jane addresses camera)

Push to 1shot   JUST A LITTLE WHILE AGO POLICE

SLAPPED CUFFS ON A SUSPECT.

When Should I Use Tags?

Tags serve two purposes. One primary purpose is pacing. Every time you change a visual element, you add to the pacing. Tags are one more visual element you can change for the purpose of picking up the pace.

Tags also serve to bring "closure" to a story or, just as important, to a story sequence or pod. For our purposes a **pod** is a set of consecutive stories read by the same anchor. In a sense the person reading that story pod "owns" it. Usually, he or she will begin the pod on-camera, making eye contact with the viewer, and end the pod the same way: on-camera, making eye contact with the viewer. This brings a sense of closure to the pod and underscores the anchor's ownership of it. This, in turn, serves to enhance the anchor's image and authority. Because the viewer relates to your product primarily through your anchors, anything that helps their image helps you. This is known in some circles as the "anchor in command" theory of producing. It works.

How Often Should I Alternate Anchors?

There's no hard-and-fast rule, but you should avoid anchor "ping-ponging," a technique wherein we see a different anchor every 20 seconds. Inexperienced producers use ping-ponging for the purpose of driving an audience nuts. Generally, you should *not* always alternate anchors between every story, and certainly not between every 20-second VO. A pace of alternating every 45 to 70 seconds, or between reporter pieces, is about right.

Not every newscast has the luxury of dual anchors. In a solo newscast, you shouldn't alternate anchors at all. (Just checking to see if you're paying attention.)

How Do I Know When to Wipe between Tapes?

Another mistake inexperienced producers often make is to throw in wipes between VOs apparently at random, thinking they "look cool." Generally, they just look confusing. Wiping from one VO to a different, completely unrelated VO can throw off the audience. To be effective, wipes should take place only between related stories. For example:

- Wiping from one crime story to another
- Wiping from one fire to another
- Wiping from one consumer story to another

- Wiping from one environmental story to another
- Wiping from one weather damage scene to another
- Wiping between "thematically" related stories (back-to-back stories in state or national round-ups, newsreels, or miniblocks)

Putting It on the Air

So. You've chosen your stories, filled out the rundown, written all the copy for which you're responsible, and edited all the reporter copy to your satisfaction. You're done, right? Wrong. Now you have to get your show on the air and, equally as important, *off* the air *at the appropriate time.* To do so requires a skill set that's different from the one you've used so far to build your show.

Backtiming

As you'll learn, unexpected, terrible, and traumatic things can happen in the course of producing live TV. Live shots crash; tape machines eat stories; editors don't finish stories in time; reporters ad-lib information in their tags that you weren't expecting; anchors throw in ad-libbed questions you don't have time for; weathercasters go short or long; sportscasters go short or long; packages go short or long; chitchat goes short or long. Don't look now, but there are about a thousand and one things that can ruin the timing of a perfectly timed show, and you must react to all of them in the control room, while the show is live on the air. So it's crucial that you always know precisely how your show is timing out at any given moment. This is done through backtiming.

The concept is simple. Given the length of each story remaining in the newscast, at what clock time must each story begin for the newscast to end on time? In order to keep your newscast on track you must backtime every single story. Most modern news computers will take care of this function for you. If not, you'll need to do it by hand.

In backtiming a show, you begin at the end, with the off-time to the newscast. In our sample newscast the program following news begins at 6:30:00. Therefore, the off-time for news is 6:30:00. Next, look at the last element in the newscast. It's a terminal break, which runs 1:10. Subtract the running time of the terminal break from the off-time to get the backtime for the terminal break, as follows:

$$6:30:00 - 1:10 = 6:28:50$$

6:28:50 is the *backtime* for the terminal break. In other words, for the newscast to end exactly on time, the terminal break must begin at *exactly* 6:28:50. We say "exactly" because the running time of the terminal break is a "hard" time; it will run exactly 1:10, no more, no less. Now repeat this for the story element preceding the terminal break, the close, which is scheduled to run :30:

$$6:28:50 - :30 = 6:28:20$$

For your newscast to end on time, the close must roll at exactly 6:28:20. This assumes your canned close music runs exactly :30 and ends with some kind of music **stinger** or recognizable ending. However, note that just because you *roll* the close at 6:28:20 doesn't mean you have to *air* the close at that time. Chances are you don't really intend to run the full :30 of available music while sitting on a wide shot of anchors filing their nails on the set. Being up to 25 seconds "late" taking that wide shot with music up full is no problem; in fact, it might be desirable, given that you're paid to put news on the air, not music.

Now repeat the process for the kicker. The kicker runs exactly :20 seconds:

$$\textbf{6:28:20} - :20 = 6:28:00$$

The kicker must hit at approximately 6:28:00 for you to be on time. Don't forget, though, that being :15 late won't kill you because, as we discussed, the running time for the close is negotiable.

Repeat this process for every element in the newscast, and you'll find that your backtiming calls for your newscast open to roll at 6:00:15. Of course, it will actually roll at 6:00:00, a difference of 15 seconds. This is another way of saying that you are going into the newscast :15 light or short. However, remember that the computer doesn't figure in any "pad" time for you. To be perfectly on time with a desired "pad" time of :30, we'd need to go into the newscast :30 light, for a start time of 6:00:30.

By this point in our day we've "fleshed out" the rundown, using the principles outlined above to number all the pages, insert the shots, assign anchors to the stories, add in the tags and 2shots, and so on. Here's how the final rundown appears, with backtiming.

"Rumor Has It News at Six" with Fred Feelgood and Jane Jabberon—Final Rundown

Page#	Slug	Anchor	Shot	Type	WR	Runs	Backtime
A00	Newscast Open			vtr/sot		:20	0:15
A00A		f/j	2shot				
A10	Council Taxes	j	OTS	intro		2:10	0:35
A10A	p-Council Taxes			live/pkg			
A10B	t-Council Taxes	j/f	2shot	tag			
A20	Intersection Repair	f	OTS	vo		:25	2:45
A30	4-Car Pileup	f	wipe	vobite		:40	3:10
A30A	4-Car Pileup tag	f	1shot				
A40	Apartment Fire	j	OTS	intro		2:00	3:50
A40B	p-Apartment Fire		dblbox	live/pkg			
A40B	Tossback		dblbox				
A40C	t-Apartment Fire	j/f	2shot	tag			

(continued)

Page#	Slug	Anchor	Shot	Type	WR	Runs	Backtime
A50	Fire History	f	OTS	ss/cg		:20	5:50
A70	Robbery Attempt	f	OTS	vo		:20	6:10
A80	Suspect Caught	f	wipe	vo		:20	6:30
A80A	t-Suspect Caught	f	1shot	tag			
A90	Robbery Trial	j	OTS	intro		1:40	6:50
A90A	p-Robbery Trial	j		pkg			
A90B	t-Robbery Trial	j	2shot	tag			
A100	Murder Trial	f	1shot	vo		:20	8:30
A110	Legislature	f	OTS	vo		:20	8:50
A110A	t-Legislature	f	1shot	tag			
Alast	1-tz	j/f	2shot	vtr/vo		:20	9:10
Break One						2:00	9:30
B10	Truck Recall	f	OTS	intro		1:40	11:30
B10A	p-Truck Recall	f		pkg			
B10B	t-Truck Recall	f	2shot	tag			
B20	Recall Info	j	OTS	ss/cg		:20	13:10
B30	Toaster Lawsuit	j	OTS	vo		:20	13:30
B30A	t-Toaster Lawsuit	j	1shot	tag			
B40	Stock Market	f	OTS	ss/cg		:15	13:50
Blast	2-tz	j/f	2shot	vtr/vo		:15	14:05
Break Two						2:00	14:20
C10	WX toss		3shot			:10	16:20
C10A	Weather					2:50	16:30
C10B	Tossback		3shot			:15	19:20
C20	Waterpark Opens	j	1shot	vo		:20	19:35
C20A	t-Waterpark Opens	j	1shot				
Clast	3-tz	f/j	2shot	vtr/vo		:15	19:55
Break Three						2:00	20:10
D10	Toss to Sports		3shot			:10	22:10
D10A	Sports					2:50	22:20
D10B	Tossback		3shot			:15	25:10
Dlast	4-tz	j/f	2shot	vtr/vo		:10	25:25
Break Four						2:00	25:35
E10	11 Teaze	f	OTS	ss/cg		:25	27:35
E10A	t-11 Teaze	f	1shot				
E20	Kicker	j	1shot	vo		:20	28:00
E30	C ya/Close		wide	vtr/sot		:30	28:20
Terminal Break						1:10	28:50
Totals						29:45	6:30:00
Over/Under						− :15	

In the example, we've listed the running time of each story in one lump sum. For instance, story A10, the Council Taxes live shot, should run 2:10 including lead, package, and tossback. Some producers prefer instead to time each story element individually, for example listing :15 for the lead, 1:20 for the package, :35 for the tossback, and so on. Either method is valid.

The important thing to remember about backtiming is that it's a constantly shifting target. Some newscast elements such as the open, packages, and commercial breaks have "hard" running times. But the running time of many stories or segments are *estimates*. They're soft times, not hard. It's extremely doubtful that every element in the newscast will run the exact amount of time you've budgeted for it. While the newscast is on the air, you must keep a constant vigil on the clock and on your backtiming, adjusting your newscast where necessary as stories go short or long.

Here's an example of how this newscast might actually play out. The perfectly timed rundown is finished, all the stories are written, and the tapes are ready. The open rolls, and we're on the air. Your first two live shots take more time than you allotted, and your anchors talk longer than anticipated on the 2shot at the end of the first block. Your backtiming tells you that you're supposed to be hitting the first break at 9:30, but you actually hit it at 10:10. What does this mean? It means your newscast is now in a bit of trouble. The commercial break began 40 seconds later than planned, meaning that you're :40 heavy. You've blown your safety margin and then some. Even if you don't roll *any* close music, at this rate you'll be :10 late hitting the terminal break. If that happens then your newscast will then **upcut** (run over the top of) the next program by 10 seconds. This is simply not allowed. You *must* get the show off on time, which means you're going to have to make up some time. The only course of action at this point is to begin looking for stories to drop or segments to shorten.

What if you're supposed to hit the break at 9:30, but actually hit it at 9:00? The break began 30 seconds early, meaning that you are 30 seconds light or short. You'll need to add 30 seconds worth of content to your newscast to end on time. The single easiest way to add content is to ask the sportscaster and/or weathercaster to use it. The second easiest way is to ask all the anchors to burn up a little extra time as chitchat. For really serious shortfalls, a wise producer always has a backup package in mind, such as a piece off one of the daily feeds that an associate producer can grab for you quickly. Some veteran producers are known to keep "evergreen" feature tapes squirreled away for such eventualities.

Forward Timing

Forward timing is the opposite of backtiming. It's useful for newscasts in which certain stories *must* air at a certain time. It asks the question, if a particular story must air at a given desired time, at what time must each preceding story hit for the newscast to be on time?

To figure forward times, begin with the start time of the newscast, then add the running time of the first element to get the desired start time of the next element.

As an example, let's pretend the Apartment Fire story contains a live shot we'll receive by satellite, and that the satellite **window** (the time you've leased from a satellite broker) opens at 6:05 and not a second sooner. Let's see if we'll hit it.

The calculation for the forward time of the newscast open is quite simple: it begins when the newscast starts, at 6:00:00. Now let's figure the forward time of our lead story. To get it, we simply add the running time of the newscast open to its forward time, as follows:

$$6:00:00 + :20 = 6:00:20$$

So our lead story will hit at exactly 6:00:20. We know this time is exact because the running time of the open is in stone; it runs exactly 20 seconds, no more, no less.

Now let's figure the forward time of the following story, Intersection Repair. To do so we'll add the running time of the lead story to the lead story's forward time:

$$6:00:20 + 2:10 = 6:02:30$$

This tells us the Intersection Repair story will hit at approximately 6:02:30. This time is "approximate" because the 2:10 running time is the producer's estimate. The actual live shot and package could go long or short when it actually hits the air.

Repeating this process for each story preceding the Apartment Fire story, we find that Apartment Fire will hit at about 6:03:35. This is too soon; we'll miss our window. Either we must lengthen the running times of the existing content elements, or we'll have to add new content to the rundown ahead of the Apartment Fire story, thereby moving the story down in the newscast.

Here's what the first block of the newscast looks like, with forward timing:

"Rumor Has It News at Six" with Fred Feelgood and Jane Jabberon—First Block with Forward Time

Page#	Slug	Anchor	Shot	Type	WR	Runs	Forward Time
A00	Newscast Open			vtr/sot		:20	0:00
A00A		f/j	2shot				
A10	Council Taxes	j	OTS	intro		2:10	:20
A10A	p-Council Taxes			live/pkg			
A10B	t-Council Taxes	j/f	2shot	tag			

(continued)

Page#	Slug	Anchor	Shot	Type	WR	Runs	Forward Time
A0	Intersection Repair	f	OTS	vo		:25	2:30
A30	4-Car Pileup	f	wipe	vobite		:40	2:55
A30A	4-Car Pileup tag	f	1shot				
A40	Apartment Fire	j	OTS	intro	2:00		3:35
A40B	p-Apartment Fire		dblbox	live/pkg			
A40B	Tossback		dblbox				
A40C	t-Apartment Fire	j/f	2shot	tag			
A50	Fire History	f	OTS	ss/cg		:20	5:35
A70	Robbery Attempt	f	OTS	vo		:20	5:55
A80	Suspect Caught	f	wipe	vo		:20	6:15
A80A	t-Suspect Caught	f	1shot	tag			
A90	Robbery Trial	j	OTS	intro	1:40		6:35
A90A	p-Robbery Trial	j		pkg			
A90B	t-Robbery Trial	j	2shot	tag			
A100	Murder Trial	f	1shot	vo		:20	8:15
A110	Legislature	f	OTS	vo		:20	8:35
A110A	t-Legislature	f	1shot	tag			
Alast	1-tz	j/f	2shot	vtr/vo		:20	8:55

Writing Notes

Copywriting issues are well covered elsewhere in this book, but two bear further exploration here: story ties and teases.

The "Cheap Tie"

Having had it drilled into their heads that all good newscasts have good story flow, many producers try to create flow artificially with really bad plays on words. Thus you might see a producer lead with a story about a protest at city hall, then follow with a story about a house fire. What's the tie? There is none, but the producer vainly attempts to create one by using cute copy like this:

WHILE HARSH WORDS ENFLAMED THE DEBATE AT CITY HALL TODAY, FLAMES QUITE LITERALLY ERUPTED AT ONE LOCAL APARTMENT COMPLEX.

Don't do that, please, else that strange noise you hear in the distance will be the clicking of thousands of tuners. You should almost always avoid the temptation of tying events together that weren't tied together in real life.

Another heinous producer practice involves the use of the words "while" or "meanwhile" to link unlinkable stories, *without* wordplay. Thus you might hear an anchor read the following script.

OTS = Tax Vote	THE CITY COUNCIL WILL VOTE ON THE TAX INCREASE NEXT WEEK.
OTS = Pileup	MEANWHILE IN SOUTH WHADDADUMP TONIGHT, PARAMEDICS ARE STILL ON THE SCENE OF A FOUR-CAR PILEUP.

Unless that pileup was caused by a reckless motorist madly rushing to escape the city council meeting, there's no tie and therefore no "meanwhile."

The only difference between these two forms of cheap tie is that the former is an amateurish mistake, whereas the latter is an artless amateurish mistake. Story flow is important. However, the fact is that stories don't always flow together. In such instances it's perfectly permissible to use an audible change of gears such as, "In other news." It's not creative, but it serves the purpose. Think of it as verbal punctuation for the viewer (but don't overuse it).

Conversely, if two stories *do* flow together perfectly, this might be a good place for a 2shot transition from one anchor to another, as discussed earlier.

Teases

Teases are some of the most important pieces of copy you can write for your newscast. They are, however, a double-edged sword. Research suggests people *do* base their viewing decisions on the teases—and sometimes the decision they make is to switch off. So you must make those teases compelling.

Provide Viewer Benefit

It's important to remember that teases are *not* news stories. You can't write them the same way. They're sales pitches, and you must treat them as such. In writing them you have a lot in common with any salesperson: You must try to convince the potential customer that the benefits of consuming your product are worth the price. The key word here is *benefit:* Your tease must promise the viewer benefit *without* delivering it just yet. Remember, you're trying to "make a sale" here, and the price you're asking is that the viewer stick around and devote his or her personal time to the story. That won't happen if you give your product away for free in the tease.

What is a viewer benefit? It's anything of value to the viewer. If you go to Fred's Taco Stand and shell out your hard-earned cash for a taco, you expect to get a tasty treat in return. You're trading value in the form of cash (the price) for value in the form of something nutritious, or at least enjoyable, to eat (the benefit). A similar transaction takes place between a newsroom and the news consumer. The consumer pays a price by giving us his or her time and attention, an *extremely* valuable commodity for which advertisers are willing to pay top dollar. In exchange, the viewer expects to *receive* something of value. You'd better deliver if you plan to keep that viewer as a consumer. No excuses: just cough up the viewer benefit.

Generally, for a viewer to obtain a benefit from a story, the story must affect him or her in some way the viewer finds valuable. This includes a wide range of possibilities. Some examples:

- Information of any kind that is useful or that addresses a viewer need or desire
- Reassurance or resolution of a fear
- Entertainment
- A surprise
- Affirmation of personal values
- Confirmation of personal beliefs
- An emotional connection or stimulus
- Anything interesting, enjoyable, or diverting

Stories without viewer benefit are, by definition, a waste of the viewers' time. If you air enough of them, the viewers will say good-bye to you and your product and, as it were, go elsewhere for their tacos. You shouldn't run stories devoid of benefit, and you *certainly* shouldn't *tease* them. An overhyped tease for a story that doesn't deliver is less than worthless; it is in fact *harmful* because it draws the viewers' attention to and might even cause them to stick around for a bad story. You've probably seen it yourself: a TV station teases a story about a basketball-shooting chimp once or twice in prime-time teases, then twice more within the newscast. When we get to the story itself, we find it's a 15-second VO showing a chimp from some roadside attraction in Dogs Barking, Mississippi, sinking one lousy basket. Further, by the time the story airs, we will have spent more airtime promoting the story than we spent airing the actual story. This really grinds your viewers' gears. They don't like being tricked. If they stick around for a story—or, in the case of a late newscast, stay up for it—and the story doesn't deliver the value the tease promised, they're going to feel misused. This common practice is a sore point with viewers. They frequently complain about hyped, sensationalistic teases and promotions in viewer calls, e-mails, and focus groups.

Deliver What You Promise

Don't abuse the viewers' trust. It helps to think of it this way. Your newscast presents an array of products of varying worth. Your job, as product manager, is to set the appropriate price for each one. In TV terms, the price is the time we're asking a viewer to devote to a story. For instance, a good lead story for a 10 P.M. newscast should be worth asking the viewer to stick with us through prime time and tune in just to see it; therefore, it's a good candidate for inclusion in prime-time teases. A good third-block medical package might be worth the same price. Or maybe it's at least good enough to ask the viewer to sit through two commercial breaks to see it, and therefore would be a good candidate for inclusion in tease 1, preceding the first commercial break. We'll assess our basketball chimp story the same way: Is it worth asking the viewer to tune in at 10 o'clock just to see it? Absolutely not. Is it worth asking the viewer to sit through four commercial breaks to see it? No. Is it worth asking the viewer to sit through *one* commercial break to see it? We hope it's at least worth that, or we shouldn't run it at all. Therefore, it's a good candidate for a quick mention at the end of the preceding block, but not suitable for "deep" teasing beginning with the first commercial break. The bottom line is this: Viewers are keenly aware of the value of their time. The "price" we set for each story must accurately reflect its value. When the price and value don't match, viewers feel cheated and tend to call news directors and give them a piece of their mind, as well they should.

Don't Bore the Viewer

Teases that undersell or promote boring stories in a boring way are just as bad (if not worse) than hyped teases. Every producer tries to put together compelling newscasts, but let's face it: not every story is tease material. Yet some producers feel compelled to tease even the most routine of stories, especially if those stories appear later in the newscast. Why would you show a meeting video and write a tease to go with it that says, "AND LATER: DOZENS TURN OUT TO HEAR A TOP ECONOMIST SPEAK TODAY IN TOWN. WE'LL TELL YOU WHAT HE HAD TO SAY."? The viewer might rightly assume that you're teasing the best story you have left to offer—and if the best you have isn't that good, why stick around? Yet you can see writers inflicting teases like this on viewers time and again in almost any TV market. It's the equivalent of our aforementioned Fred's Taco running a commercial that says, "Our tacos are as dry as dust and might even make you sick, but come on down anyway!" It's better just to say "BACK AFTER THIS" than to tease a boring story just for the sake of running a tease.

Tease the Right Stories the Right Way

In planning teases, first identify the stories still to come that have the most viewer benefit. (One important producing technique is to make *sure* you save stories for the lower news blocks that *do* provide benefit—otherwise known as "teasable" stories.) Identify that benefit. Then write to it, making the viewers understand that if they don't change the channel during the commercial break, we'll reward them with a benefit—without actually *delivering* that benefit in the tease!

Please don't make the mistake of beginning your tease copy with the words "Coming up next." This is an instant turn-off. "Coming up next" is TV-speak that, roughly translated, means "It's time for a commercial now." Start that way, and the viewer will zone out and probably leave the room to go to the bathroom or whatever. Instead, begin your tease as if it were a story. Instead of giving the full story, however, you'll hook the viewer by promising viewer benefit, thereby motivating the viewer to stay for the rest. Make use of the "you" connection wherever possible. Use narrative storytelling and/or the rhetorical question whenever possible. Use the imperative voice when appropriate to literally command attention. And it can't be said enough: clearly focus on the viewer benefit!

Example 1—How Not to Do It

	COMING UP: THE LATEST INFORMATION ABOUT DIABETES FROM THE U-S GOVERNMENT.
[VO video showing doctor examining patient]	
	THE STATS SHOW 25 PERCENT OF ALL PEOPLE DON'T KNOW THE SYMPTOMS. DETAILS WHEN WE RETURN.

The tease practically gives the story away but still manages to leave the viewer benefit unclear. Video is generic. How am I affected? Plus, the final line isn't a strong suggestion that the viewer return. Click. See ya.

How to Do It

	DID YOU KNOW YOU COULD HAVE DIABETES . . . AND NOT KNOW IT?
[Video of patient with very concerned expression listening to doctor]	

> THE LATEST STATS SHOW YOU OR
> SOMEONE YOU LOVE COULD BE IN FOR
> A FRIGHTENING SURPRISE. FIND OUT
> HOW TO TELL FOR SURE . . . NEXT.

The benefit is very clear: watching this report could improve my health. In fact, I can't afford *not* to watch it. Video and copy make the "you" connection. The imperative voice in the final line *commands* me to return in terms that show it's in my own best interests to do so. You can bet I'll hang with you. And by the way, if you promise the story is "next," don't break the promise. The story should be right there when you come back from the commercial break.

Example 2—How Not to Do It

> STILL AHEAD: BRUSH FIRES
> CONTINUE TO RAGE OUT OF CONTROL
> IN MEXICO.

[VO video of dramatic fires]

> DRAMATIC FOOTAGE WHEN THE
> NEWSHOUR CONTINUES.

The benefit is weak, though I might stick around to see the pictures. But the fire is a long way away. Frankly, you don't sound like you're that interested in my watching this, anyway. Gotta go.

How to Do It

> BRUSH FIRES CONTINUE TO RAGE
> OUT OF CONTROL IN MEXICO.

[VO video of dramatic fires]

> AND NOW THERE'S A DISTURBING
> NEW DEVELOPMENT TO THE DISASTER . . .

[Cut to VO video of asthma patient coughing or using inhaler]

> . . . ONE THAT COULD AFFECT OUR
> HEALTH HERE IN THE BAY AREA.
> LEARN HOW . . . AND WHAT YOU CAN
> DO ABOUT IT . . . NEXT.

Benefit is clear: brush fires in Mexico might affect me. You're asking me to find out how and what kind of action I might need to take. I'd better listen up.

Example 3—How Not to Do It

	COMING UP NEXT ON THE NEWSHOUR:
[VO video of washing machine in operation]	
	NO ONE LIKES TO DO LAUNDRY . . . RIGHT?
[Cut to VO video of unhappy-looking reporter sorting clothes]	
	WE MADE REPORTER JANE DOE DO IT EVERY DAY FOR A WEEK!
	AND SHE MADE A SURPRISING DISCOVERY.
	WE'LL TELL YOU ABOUT IT . . . NEXT.

Copy is semi-cute and somewhat creative—but there's no real viewer benefit other than the hint of some possible entertainment value. Yawn.

How to Do It

	DIRTY LAUNDRY. NO ONE TALKS ABOUT IT. NO ONE WANTS TO DEAL WITH IT.
[VO video of laundry going into washing machine]	
	BUT AT LEAST YOU KNOW WHAT GOES IN DIRTY . . .
[Cut to VO video of clean laundry coming out of dryer]	
	COMES OUT CLEAN . . . RIGHT? WRONG!
[Cut to VO video of germs under microscope]	
	NEW LAB TESTS PROVIDE A NASTY AND DANGEROUS SURPRISE. LEARN WHY AND WHAT IT MEANS TO YOU IN A REPORT YOU WON'T WANT TO MISS . . . NEXT.

OK, you have me. My laundry comes out dirty? This I gotta see!

Tease Tips

A question producers often ask about writing teases is, "Should I use my best video?" Photographers and reporters sometimes pressure producers not to "give away" the best pictures in a tease. Usually this is a mistake. Remember, you're *selling* the story to your audience. Your best pictures normally will be your strongest selling point. Use them! Note, this doesn't mean the package you're teasing has to begin with those pictures; sometimes narrative storytelling concerns will lead the reporter and photographer team *not* to lead off their story with the most dramatic pictures. That decision should not apply to the *tease*, however. Use your best material.

Also remember that video isn't your only option. Another effective technique you might consider is the "menu tease." Using this method, the tease writer gives a list of stories or segments and the *time* at which each will air. Example: "NEW FINDINGS MIGHT CHANGE THE WAY DOCTORS TREAT SOME WOMEN FOR MENOPAUSE. MEDICAL REPORTER STACY STETHOSCOPE EXPLAINS WHY AT 6:18. WE'LL HAVE WEATHER AT 6:20 AND TRAFFIC AT 6:23. STAY WITH US." Such teases might or might not use video and typically will make use of on-screen text to reinforce the hit times. The idea here is that some viewers will flip around when the commercial break hits, no matter what. This style of tease gives them a reason and a *time* to come back. In essence, you're making an appointment with the viewer.

When you conclude the tease, finish in the imperative voice. Make a command. Or as a sales executive might put it, "Ask for the order." Phrases such as "find out, "learn why," "see why," and so forth, stand a much better chance of engaging the viewer than do simple declarative statements such as, "That story next."

One common tease technique is use of the rhetorical question. "Did you know you could have diabetes and not know it?" is an example of that. The power of this technique is that posing a question but not giving the answer can create a hunger for information. But don't overdo it. Not *every* tease should contain a question.

Here's a final thought and a challenge about producing teases. There's been plenty of experimentation through the years but despite that, most newscast formats remain pretty basic—30 minutes to an hour filled with news, weather, and probably some sports, punctuated by commercial breaks and teases. In many stations tease formats haven't changed in years if not decades—a 2shot of the anchors, quickly followed by video of one or two upcoming stories with "news music" slipped underneath. Often you'll find the video preproduced with station graphics and a "coming up" banner or the equivalent, sometimes with a cute slug line, sometimes not, and you'll see them done the same way day in and day out. Weather teases are the absolute worst. How many times have you heard two anchors blabbing the following: "The weather today was really [fill in the blank] but what will it be like tomorrow? Jane Isobar is next with the forecast!" Does it really have to be that way? What rule book says that every tease must begin with a 2shot? In fact, who decreed that every tease must always involve *both* anchors? Who says every tease must have music? Or video? Through the years newscast formats have become so familiar to viewers that we've created what amounts to a visual language of sorts. When the viewer sees that tease 2shot and begins to hear the tease music, regardless of what the anchors are saying the *first* message the viewer gets is, "It's time for a commercial." To combat that, WFLA-TV recently began experimenting with "the stealth tease." The concept is simple: throw away the rule book, forget format, and write a tease that best accomplishes the goal of hooking the viewer. There's no ban on the traditional 2shot tease, but it's become just one option in the tease toolbox. Other tools in that box might consist of a 1shot, or an OTS shot with a graphic, or a single anchor standing at a chroma key wall, or a single anchor standing by a monitor with video rolling, or a single anchor standing by a monitor showing bullet points or a graphic, and so on. A tease might include video. It might not. It might include music. It might not. Imagine a single anchor sitting on-set, making eye contact while holding up a piece of paper, and saying, "What's in this document could change the way doctors treat some women for menopause. Find out why and what it means to you next." The point is to sell, and to choose the tool that works best for the job at hand.

Perhaps many producers won't feel empowered to take it upon themselves to "break the format" when it comes to teasing. But you can certainly propose changes to your supervisor. Don't be shy about it. Whatever you do, don't let yourself get caught in a rut, and don't write teases just so that you can get your "tease ticket" punched.

A Final Thought about Producing TV News

We've spent several pages detailing how to produce a newscast, but we haven't addressed the question of *why* you should produce one. Only you can answer that. Every producer has a different set of drives and motivations. Some produce because they love writing. Others like the excitement of calling the shots, especially in control room environments. Still others enjoy being newsroom leaders and having the ability to shape the "big picture." One thing is for certain: To do well as a producer, you must have passion. Whatever passion brings you here, don't lose sight of it. Nurture it. Cherish it. Never let it go. You'll need it to keep you going during the tough times. As we discussed in other chapters, our medium is incredibly powerful. On the best days, producing television news can be very fulfilling. Enjoy yourself. But don't squander the opportunity to do some good.

Conclusion

In this chapter we've discussed in detail how to use a rundown form to build a television newscast, time it correctly, and get it prepared for air. We've provided a producing exercise, which you can find on the Web site at *www.mhhe.com/tuggle*. The exercise includes a final rundown as put together by a producer in a top-20 market. In the next chapter we'll discuss a producer's role in the booth and how to handle live shots and breaking news.

 DOs and DON'Ts for Producing TV News

Do

- Remember that a producer's job is one of the most critically important in a television newsroom.
- Arrange stories to create a good story flow.
- Consider scripting an on-camera tag when changing anchors.
- Leave some pad time in your rundown.
- Understand how a computerized rundown works.
- Write teases that "sell" the viewer benefit of a story.
- Make the "you" connection when writing teases.

Don't

- Forget that being a good producer requires not only technical skills, but also leadership skills.
- Stack stories simply in order of descending priority.
- Forget that good pacing also is an essential element in ordering a rundown.
- Start a newscast "heavy" if you can avoid it.
- Blindly trust the computer to time your newscast.
- Give away the story in the tease.
- Be shy about "breaking format" or using your creativity.

THE CARE AND FEEDING OF TELEVISION LIVE SHOTS

Being a newscast producer is like having two jobs for the price of one. Once the rundown is complete, the show written, and the video elements finished, the producer goes to the control booth. There, the role changes completely. The producer removes his or her production design hat and takes on a role more like that of an airplane pilot. A good grasp of the station's technical systems and an ability to make cool, calm-headed decisions under fire are essential. In this chapter, we'll discuss two of the toughest booth challenges: the art of juggling live remotes, and coping with live, breaking news.

Live Shot Philosophy

What makes a good live shot? TV critics love to debate that point, and they often accuse stations of "going live for live's sake." To some stations and news directors, a mediocre live shot is better than no live shot at all. We won't settle that argument here. But clearly some live shots are better than others. The rule of thumb for any good live shot is similar to the standards for a good stand-up. It's not just about face time, although that's important too. Rather, all good live shots are interactive in nature. The audience can't be at the scene, so the reporter goes there for us, taking us by the hand and giving us a guided tour. He or she demonstrates something, touches something, picks something up, kicks something, opens or closes something. Walk-throughs can be effective, but not if they're "walks to nowhere." If the reporter is going to move through the scene, then there should be a point to the trip; it shouldn't simply be a journey down five feet of sidewalk. Often the reporter can give this trip purpose by simply gesturing to the surroundings and explaining what we're seeing. In general, the effectiveness of the live shot rises in proportion with its interactivity. Conversely, the less the reporter has to do on the scene of the live shot, the more it's going to seem like "live for the sake of live."

Immediacy is also a factor: Is this story legitimately late-breaking, or was it done and over with hours ago? Breaking news stories can make compelling live shots. Cold, dark crime scenes or empty buildings where something happened hours ago don't make good live shots. In most stations, there won't be enough live units for every reporter, so the producers have the luxury of deciding which stories are most suited for live shots on that particular day.

One element even a mediocre live shot adds to a newscast is the "people" factor. Broadcasting is all about sight and sound, to be sure, but it's also about *people.* It is, in fact, an intensely personal medium. Even if a live location is visually weak, the live reporter can provide that "people" connection.

For whatever reason you choose to go live, the idea is to get your live shots on the air cleanly. The best TV stations put resources and systems in place to make sure that happens.

Command and Control

Picture the following scene. It's election night. Reporter Jane Sittenfijit notices that the incumbent mayoral candidate she's covering is coming to the podium to declare victory. Jane needs to get this on the air *right this very second!* First, she tries shouting into the microphone, hoping that someone back at the station is listening to the live feed. Nothing happens. Next, she disconnects her cell phone, which she was using to monitor the station's off-air **signal,** and dials the producer's direct line. As the seventh caller, she wins a free ticket to Voice Mail Hell, where a recorded voice invites her to leave a message. With mounting panic, she calls the assignments desk, and a polite but clueless intern promptly puts her on hold and leaves in search of someone who can make a decision. Now completely desperate, Jane writes the words "PLEASE TALK TO US" in huge block letters on her reporter's notebook and begins waving it at the camera. As the mayor begins speaking, she finds herself resorting to "the jumping jacks," waving frantically and springing and bouncing in front of the camera like a poodle begging for table scraps in a desperate attempt to get someone's attention.

Meanwhile, back at the ranch, the intern talks to the assignments editor, who talks to an associate producer, who talks to the executive producer. The executive producer reads between the lines and realizes the urgency in Jane's message. She orders the associate producer to run to the control booth and tell the producer that the mayor is declaring victory and to get Jane live on the air right this very second.

In the control booth, producer Timmy Timex gets the message. He presses the **IFB** button, which pipes his voice into the anchor's ear, and orders, "Fred, toss out to Jane in the field; the mayor's at the podium."

On air, viewers see Fred put his finger to his ear and say, "I'm told Jane Sittenfijit has some breaking news for us. Let's go live to her now." Viewers are then treated to the spectacle of Jane jumping up and down in front of the camera, waving and shouting, "Hey! Can you hear me? You guys need to come out to me now! Can you hear me? Hey! You idiots, you're not listening to me!"

This goes on for what seems like an eternity but really lasts only 10 seconds. The program cuts back to Fred, who says, "Sorry about that folks, we're having some problems. In other news tonight . . . "

The scenario described above might seem extreme, but this kind of on-air train wreck happens all the time in TV news. In live TV a certain amount of error is inevitable. But wise newspeople keep that error rate to an absolute minimum by designating a *live coordinator,* also sometimes called an *ENG coordinator* (ENG being an abbreviation for electronic news gathering). Many large-market stations have employees whose sole job assignment is to coordinate live remotes and tape feeds. Smaller stations might distribute these duties among associate producers, desk assistants, or tape editors. Stations with the smallest staffs might not be able to pull anyone aside at airtime to coordinate live shots; in such cases, the producer will have to juggle live coordination along with everything else.

The live coordinator has three primary duties:

- Facilitate communication with the crew in the field, the producer, and the engineers tuning in the live shot.
- Supervise to make sure that each live remote is ready at the appropriate time.

- Make sure the producer is fully apprised of the status of all live remotes—*especially* if the live shot is in trouble.

Of those three points, the last is the most important. *The absolute number one most important task of any live coordinator is to ensure that bad live remotes don't get on the air!* In a well-run station the producer never, ever attempts to air a live shot unless the coordinator has specifically pronounced the live shot ready. For a live shot to be ready, five elements must be established and verified. They are:

1 *Signal.* Is the microwave, satellite, or fiber signal strong and airworthy?
2 *Video.* Obviously, we have to see a camera picture.
3 *Audio.* We must be able to hear the reporter.
4 *IFB.* The reporter must be able to hear program audio from the television station.
5 *Readiness.* The reporter and photographer must be standing by and ready for the live shot!

The concept of IFB merits further discussion. In some stations "IFB" has become a generic term used to describe all methods by which a reporter in the field can hear some or all of the television station's off-air signal. IFB is an abbreviation for "interruptible feedback." With true IFB the producer or live coordinator can open a mike, interrupt the program audio going to the field, and speak to the reporter. Stations have various ways of delivering IFB. A common method is to route all or a portion of the station's program audio to a phone line, then have the reporter dial into that line using a mobile phone. The connection is "one way"; most stations use an "auto-answer" system that connects the reporter's call to the IFB system automatically, without human intervention. The reporter can't speak, only listen. The live coordinator hears the reporter not by telephone, but rather by way of the reporter's live microphone. The disadvantage to that, obviously, is that the live coordinator can't hear the reporter's microphone unless the live signal has been established. IFB can also be delivered by way of a subcarrier on the station's broadcast signal, which is monitored in the field by way of a special receiver. Some stations deliver IFB through a two-way radio system. IFB can also be delivered by satellite signal.

In the absence of IFB, a producer can still salvage a live remote *if* the IFB failure is caught in time. **Talent** in the field sometimes can receive cues by various other methods. For instance, a field producer or photographer who's on the telephone or 2-way radio with someone back at the station can relay cues by hand signal. Or talent in the field can monitor the station's on-air signal by way of a portable television receiver. None of these alternative methods is ideal because none allows the producer to communicate directly with the talent, but each will do in a pinch. In fact, the use of a TV monitor *in addition* to IFB often is necessary for sports or weather remotes, during which the talent needs to see the program in addition to hearing it.

However IFB is received, no live shot can air without it or a substitute method of communicating cues to the talent in the field. Otherwise, the reporter has no way of knowing when or whether he or she is on the air. Lack of IFB is one of the most common causes of live shot failures. In our example, the live shot crashed primarily because the reporter had disconnected her IFB line, and no one at the station noticed. It's easy to see how this can happen. A failure of live video or audio normally will be very apparent to an alert live coordinator, who will then take immediate steps to alert the producer and director not to take the shot. But a sudden failure of IFB isn't so obvious.

Live shots can also fail through *improper* IFB. With traditional IFB, the station simply feeds program audio to the reporter in the field. The reporter hears everything, including his or her own voice retransmitted by the station. This isn't a problem because the retransmission happens at the speed of light, and the reporter's words return by way of IFB as they're spoken. However, traditional IFB will *not* work with a satellite remote. In such cases the reporter's video and audio signals travel far into space, bounce off a satellite, then return to earth. The round-trip covers tens of thousands of miles—and even at the speed of light, the journey is *not* instantaneous. There's lag. If the station feeds the satellite audio back down the IFB to the reporter, the talent's words arrive a noticeable fraction of a second after they were spoken. This creates an "echo" effect in the ears of the talent that can throw the reporter off balance and even cause slurred speech.

Typically, the way to correct this is with a form of IFB known as **mix-minus.** Using the mix-minus method, the reporter's home station sends a special feed down the IFB line that consists of some or all of the station's program audio *minus* the reporter's microphone. Through this method, the reporter hears what's going on back at the TV station without receiving a distracting echo of his or her own words. (The "lag effect" is so distracting that some stations habitually feed mix-minus IFB for *all* live remotes as a matter of course.)

It's the job of the live coordinator—or, in lieu of a coordinator, the producer—to verify all five elements of a live shot, as follows:

- *Signal readiness.* Typically, a station engineer will tune in the signal and approve it as airworthy.
- *Video readiness.* The live coordinator, usually in cooperation with an engineer, will visually check the camera picture, noting stability, lighting, white balance, framing, and the like.
- *Audio readiness.* The live coordinator will listen to the audio. Usually an engineer will check it through a VU meter to make sure it's within acceptable limits.

- *IFB.* This is a simple but important task. The live coordinator merely has to open the microphone and ask, "Can you hear me?" and then listen for the reporter's response on the live feed from the reporter's microphone. A wise live coordinator asks the reporter for a *visual* confirmation, such as a "thumbs up." Otherwise, the live coordinator can't always be sure the reporter didn't nod in response to something someone else said there on the scene. (For satellite remotes, the coordinator should verify with the audio director that the talent is receiving mix-minus IFB. If not, the problem won't be apparent until the reporter starts speaking.)

- *Readiness.* The coordinator verifies this by giving time cues to the talent. Many news operations give the field talent time warnings at 5 minutes, 2 minutes, 1 minute, 30 seconds, and 15 seconds. Some reporters like more cues, some like fewer. The practice in some stations is also to alert reporters when they're live in a double box, when they're in a VO, and to give time cues for the running times of packages or sound bites within the live shot. Most crews like to be told when the live shot has ended and they're clear to tear down.

Special Live Coverage

On certain big coverage days, live coordination can become very complicated. For instance, on a major election night even a small-to-medium-market television station might have four or five live shots, including some from other cities. More than one live coordinator might be needed to keep track of all of them.

Ideally, each remote location will establish *two* lines of communication with the station: one line to the live coordinator, and one to the auto-answer IFB. During the live shot, the live coordinator keeps in two-way contact with the photographer or field producer on one line while also speaking to the live talent by way of the IFB. A very good rule of thumb is to set up a system ensuring that when the crews call the station to talk with the live coordinator, they never get a busy signal! One solution is to surround the live coordinator with a bank of telephones, with a dedicated phone line assigned to each remote location. Or the live coordinator might choose to have just two phones—one to be used to accept calls, the other used for a "rolling conference call." The way the latter system works is that a crew calls in on line A and then is immediately transferred to the ongoing conference call with the coordinator on line B. It's possible to pull this off with handsets, but many stations have very sophisticated communications panels set up for handling live remotes in this fashion.

In either scenario, ideally each remote crew will also have a pre-assigned number to call for IFB. This helps sort out confusion, because crews won't have to call in frantically at the last minute to learn their IFB assignments. Pre-assignment also allows the coordinator to physically label the phones or control panels with the names of the crew members who'll be using them, thus making it unnecessary for the producer to punch six buttons to discover which one is connected to Jane at the mayor's headquarters. In major coverage situations, even large-market TV stations might not have enough IFB lines to go around. Some crews will have to double up. This will require close coordination so that crews dial the right line at the appropriate time, and no one gets a busy signal.

Now let's go back to Jane Sittenfijit, covering our hypothetical mayoral race. If our system works as it should, Jane is standing by, already dialed into the IFB line. When she frantically needs to get onto the air, all her photographer or field producer has to do is pick up the phone, alert the live coordinator, and remain on the line. The live coordinator calls the newscast producer in the control room. The producer gets the message, quickly finds a spot for Jane's report, tells the live coordinator to have Jane stand by, and within seconds, Jane is on the air—calm, collected, and kicking the competition's rear.

Contingency Plans

Count on it: if your station does live shots, it *will* experience live shot failures. The main idea behind live coordination is to make sure bad live shots never get on the air and the audience never knows about your technical difficulties. Even with the best live coordination, however, occasionally a live shot will go bad before your very eyes, live during your newscast: the microwave transmitter will blow a fuse, the camera will die, a short will suddenly develop in a microphone, the IFB line will disconnect without warning, a video cable will fail. A thousand and one things can go wrong with live television, and the broadcast corollary of **Murphy's Law** states that you'll experience each and every variety of live shot failure during the course of your career, probably multiple times.

There are three major steps you can take to prepare yourself. First, at all times be prepared to have your anchor apologize for technical difficulties and move on. Second, *always* know what your next step will be! Never go to the control booth without a viable "Plan B" that you can execute quickly in case of live shot failure. Make sure that your director and everyone else who needs to know about the plan is informed. Third, see to it that all taped elements that can be fed back in advance *are* fed back in advance. That way, if the live goes south, the failure won't take every coverage element with it. (For instance, you can always roll the reporter's package even if the reporter's live signal dies at the last minute—but only if you have the package already in hand.)

One legendary coverage anecdote in Florida serves as a cautionary tale about what can happen if the above rules aren't followed. A coastal station decided to send most of its staff to cover an approaching hurricane. The satellite truck rolled and just about everyone rolled with it—anchors, reporters, photographers, everyone except the producer and a couple of editors. All day the crew worked to cover the hurricane. The tapes were to be played on the air live from the satellite truck; the crew fed back nothing in advance. Can you guess what happened? The truck croaked at the last minute. The poor producer back at the station, as legend has it, was left with 30 minutes to fill, and no way to fill it. Ow.

Now here's an example of a backup plan that worked. A Texas station rushed a crew to cover a major spot news story in a nearby city. Not long before airtime, managers learned their satellite truck was having problems. There had been no opportunity to feed back tape, but another affiliate of the same network had managed to uplink about two minutes of rough-cut video. So, moments before the newscast open rolled, a producer ran a stack of Associated Press wire copy to the set and asked the anchors to ad-lib over the rough-cut video and narrate what they saw on the tape. The open rolled, and the anchors proceeded to do exactly that. While this was going on, the station managed to get in contact with its reporter and put her on the air by phone for a **Q&A** with the anchors. Shortly after that, the satellite truck operator resolved the technical problems, and the reporter went live. It wasn't elegant, but it worked, and the audience never suspected the station had encountered a technical problem. When all was said and done, the station actually had more and better coverage than its competitors—not bad for a newscast that started with a failed live shot.

What other options might that station have employed as a backup to the satellite shot? What if there had been no video in-house at all? If you have information and an anchor, you can do television. In an absolutely worst-case scenario, you can have your anchors sit and read wire copy right off the wires. With a little prep time, you can prepare graphics support in the form of a map and full-screen bullet points. You can usually arrange a live phone interview with officials on the scene or at a command post. While you're doing that, you can have a producer or reporter put together a backgrounder or perspective piece using file video of similar stories from the past.

One option you definitely do *not* have: When a big story erupts, you can't hold it and push it lower down into your newscast while you get your act together. When the newscast open rolls, you *must* be there with the lead story. Period. It's your job to make sure it gets on the air with as much information as you have, in the best format you can prepare.

If you have to implement a backup plan, don't wait too late to execute it. Remember that you need time to get word of any changes to the director, anchors, editors, engineers, and everyone else affected! Many newscasts have crashed and burned with anchors looking lost and confused on-camera, while a producer was still trying to issue instructions. Always think *two steps ahead*. In the event of live, breaking news, your audience will forgive you for all kinds of technical glitches, provided that you handle them smoothly, fully explain what's going on, and step quickly to your next coverage element. The audience will *not* forgive you for looking lost, confused, or unprofessional, which is likely to happen in the absence of contingency plans or if those plans are triggered too late. Wise producers have backups for everything and know precisely when to execute them.

The Anchor Question

One hotly debated aspect of live shots is the anchor question. Most producers secretly (or openly, as the case may be) hate the anchor question because it takes time they'd rather devote to something else. When the newscast gets "tight," anchor Q&A often is the first thing producers toss out. Usually this is a mistake. Anchor questions provide an opportunity to showcase the expertise of both the anchor and the reporter, which is important from a competitive standpoint. Much more important than that, however, is the opportunity the Q&A provides to add context, meaning, and perspective to the story.

Until recently, conventional wisdom said no factor was more important in winning the ratings wars than a station's prowess in covering breaking news. Many believe this is no longer true. In the 21st century it's a sorry station indeed that doesn't know how to cover spot news. The future will belong to those stations doing the best job of providing context, meaning, and perspective. A well-done Q&A can accomplish this very effectively. Adding perspective is so important that a Q&A alone might be reason enough to justify a live shot. Conversely, a live shot without Q&A is a wasted opportunity.

Obviously, to get a meaningful answer, the anchor question itself has to be meaningful. Here is an example of a nonmeaningful, wasted Q&A opportunity:

[Rip N. Reed]	THAT'S THE SCENE FROM THE COURTHOUSE. BACK TO YOU, FRED.
[Fred Feelgood]	RIP . . . HAS THE DATE BEEN SET FOR THE NEXT HEARING?
[Rip N. Reed]	YES . . . FRED . . . IT WILL TAKE PLACE TWO WEEKS FROM NOW ON THE 10TH OF OCTOBER.

In the above example, the question didn't elicit any meaningful information. The anchor simply prompted the reporter to give information he would have given anyway, had he not saved it for the "question." This is an example of airing a question for the sake of airing a question.

Now, here's an example of a more meaningful Q&A:

[Rip N. Reed]	THE NEXT HEARING IS SCHEDULED FOR OCTOBER 10TH. FRED?
[Fred Feelgood]	RIP . . . IS THE DELAY NORMAL FOR A CASE OF THIS NATURE?
[Rip N. Reed]	NO . . . IT'S NOT. THE PROSECUTOR ISN'T TALKING. BUT THE DEFENSE ATTORNEY TELLS ME IT'S MORE PROOF THE CASE IS WEAK. HE BELIEVES THE PROSECUTOR IS STALLING . . . HOPING TO FIND NEW EVIDENCE IN THE WAKE OF TODAY'S SETBACK.

In the above example, the anchor asked a meaningful question, and the answer gives perspective and meaningful insight to what's happening in the trial. In the process, the anchor also comes off as a journalist who has a brain and is paying attention to what's going on.

One question that often arises in discussions about anchor questions is, "Should the question be scripted?" In most cases, it's preferable for the anchor and reporter to have a discussion prior to airtime to talk about material that might be suitable for a Q&A. This doesn't mean the question has to be precisely scripted, but the both the reporter and the anchor should have an understanding of what will be asked.

What if there's no opportunity for an advance discussion? In that case the reporter is fair game for a random question. Some reporters really hate it when anchors play "stump the reporter." But there's no shame in getting hit with a question you can't answer. Just say so—and promise an update later.

In some cases producers might decide to tightly script questions and their answers. Risky investigative reports involving lawyers who vet, approve, and lock in every word are a good example of that.

If the question is scripted in advance, it's important to write Q&A as a natural interchange. Do *not* script video, graphics, or other show-and-tell material as the answer to a question! It's amazing how often TV producers do this. Preproduced answers of this type lead to some of TV news's silliest moments. "Fred, I'm glad you asked me that question, because I just happen to have some video, graphics, and bullet points to help answer it." The audience probably suspects we prepare Q&A material in advance, but let's not be insulting about it.

Whichever method you choose, don't lose sight of your goal, which is to provide context, meaning, and relevance in a way that makes a personal connection to the viewer.

Common Live Shot Pitfalls

Live television is an incredibly complicated affair. Any successful live shot amounts to a near-miraculous escape from Murphy's Law and the dozen of pitfalls that conspire daily to defeat live reporting. Here's a list of common traps and how to avoid them.

Problem: Live reporter hears "echo" in the ear.

Cure: Make sure the live coordinator flags any satellite remotes for the audio director so that he or she will send a "mix-minus" IFB signal to the field. Even better, the station should feed mix-minus IFB for *all* remotes.

Problem: Live crew gets a busy signal when trying to call the live coordinator.

Cure: When juggling several live remotes, designate phone lines for each crew. For routine coverage days, many live coordinators prefer the use of 2-way radio.

Problem: Live crew gets a busy signal when trying to dial IFB.

Cure: The live coordinator should pre-assign IFB numbers for each crew. If there aren't enough lines to go around, the crew should contact the live coordinator to request clearance before dialing IFB. Some systems require a technician to manually reset the IFB line after the crew disconnects; the live coordinator should help ensure this happens promptly.

Problem: The reporter in the field has lost IFB and isn't in immediate contact with the live coordinator by phone or radio.

Cure: The reporter should step away from the camera. Otherwise, if the producer and director see the reporter standing by looking ready, they might be tempted to punch up the shot.

Problem: You're going live in five minutes, you have a two-minute tape to feed, but when you call the station, you find some other crew is feeding tape via the same microwave receiver you need to access.

Cure: This problem is incredibly common in breaking news situations. The station will have three or four live vans out in the field gathering news, and each crew will expect to feed tape at

4:55 P.M. for a 5:00 P.M. broadcast using the same microwave receiver. The only solution is for the live coordinator to anticipate this problem and work with crews to pre-assign their tape feed **windows.** Crews that miss a window get dropped from the newscast. The live coordinator might allow some live crews to feed tape from the van *during the live report,* but this is very risky, requiring close coordination and the right equipment in the field.

Problem: You're producing a newscast and you learn as the open is rolling that your lead live shot isn't ready.

Cure: This problem is also very common. It represents a total breakdown in communications on the part of everyone. Sometimes producers, having heard nothing to the contrary, will sail along "assuming" the live shot is OK. Good producers *never* do that. The only correct assumption until you hear to the contrary is that the live shot is *not* ready. Further, don't be passive in your live communications. Set a deadline by which you expect confirmation—say, five minutes before airtime—and hold the live coordinator and field crews to it. Always have a contingency plan in case the live shot fails and make sure everyone understands what it is. Don't wait until too late to implement it! If you're a reporter, photographer, or producer in the field, realize that a good producer and director can handle almost any live emergency, but last-second live surprises are the hardest to deal with smoothly. If you run into technical problems in the field that jeopardize the live shot, call in to report them immediately—*even if you'd rather spend the time working on the problem.* The producer and live coordinator *must* know what's going on, and to learn that they have to hear from you. No other consideration is more important.

Problem: You're on the air live giving a report from the State Fair when a drunk stumbles into the camera and knocks it off the tripod.

Cure: There isn't one. Welcome to live TV.

Are You a Breaking News Warrior?

Compared with any other medium, local television news has two major strengths: pictures and immediacy. Combine them, and you have a live shot. The most successful television station will be the one prepared to go live with breaking news at the snap of a finger.

Are you prepared to win in this game? Let's find out. Consider the following scenario. You're sitting in the control booth a few minutes into your newscast when you get a frantic call from the assignments desk: one of your live weather cams has caught a tornado on the ground! You punch up the remote on your router and sure enough, there it is—no audio, but spectacular live pictures of a huge black tornado now looming over the downtown skyline. You check the program monitor and find that your anchor is now reading the lead to a long medical report, which your station has been promoting heavily all day.

Which of the following would you do?

1 Climb under the control desk and whimper.
2 Get on the IFB and tell the anchor to stop reading and listen. When she stops reading, tell her to toss to live pictures of a tornado on the weather cam and ad-lib over it.
3 Allow the anchor to continue reading the lead to the taped medical report. Once the report is on the air, use the time to find out more information about exactly where the tornado is and where it's going, and to get the weathercaster to the set.
4 Do nothing; wait for the National Weather Service to issue an official tornado bulletin.
5 Run outside and roll up your car window.

If you answered 3, your heart's probably in the right place but not your posterior, which is about to be kicked by the competition. If you answered 2, you're the one who will be doing the posterior kicking.

"But wait a minute," you object. "I can't talk to my anchor while she's on the air. She can't handle it. She'll choke on-air, then hunt me down and harm me!"

If it's true your anchors can't handle breaking news, it's not necessarily their fault. Anchors can handle breaking news situations such as the one described above if they're trained for it and, more important, if they understand they'll be asked to do it this way. It's up to the news managers to set the tone and direction. Stations that can handle such situations are ready to do battle in the TV news wars of the 21st century.

A Final Word: What If It All Goes to Hell, or "Why Are We in This Handbasket, and Where Are We Going So Fast?"

If there's one universal factor about live television, it's that occasionally it will crash and burn. Count on it. Murphy's Law has several television corollaries, including:

- If a live shot can crash, it will.
- If an editing machine can jam, it will.
- If this is the worst possible day for one more spot news story to erupt, it will.
- If a tape might not make it, it won't.

- If the president of your company's broadcast division is in town, all of the above will occur simultaneously.

Your only defense is to remember the Boy Scout motto. If the lead story is in jeopardy of not being finished in time because the reporter was late with the copy, you'd better have a Plan B that's better than "I'm going to kill the reporter." As discussed above, have a backup plan and don't hesitate to use it.

Even with good contingency plans, the worst will sometimes happen even to the best of producers. When it does, don't lose sleep because of it. Simply learn from the experience, and come fighting back the next day. Don't let the occasional TV production tragedy get you down. No matter how bad it was, tomorrow is another day. And the same can be said in the aftermath of excellent newscasts as well! An often-heard saying in this business is, "You're only as good as your most recent newscast," and there's a great deal of truth to that. The best way to cope with that reality is to try to bring a fresh sense of energy, enthusiasm, and determination to the beginning of every day.

Conclusion

The best live shots are those in which the reporter is able to interact with the surroundings in some way. Live shots require strong communications support from the television station. The producer must verify that the signal is strong; that the remote has good video, audio, and IFB—and that the talent is ready. A good producer always has a contingency plan ready in case the live shot fails. The best producers are aggressive in their handling of breaking news and can get live shots on the air quickly and seamlessly.

 Live Shot DOs and DON'Ts

Do	Don't
• Make live shots interactive.	• Just stand there!
• Have a strong and reliable system for communication with crews in the field.	• Air a live shot without verifying its full readiness.
• Seek Q&A opportunities that add context and perspective.	• Go into the booth without a live-shot backup plan.
• Realize the importance of breaking news.	• Let a fear of production mistakes make you timid about getting breaking news on the air.
• Trust and expect your anchors to be able to stop what they're doing to handle breaking news.	• Let a bad live shot or on-air mistake get you down.

WHY WE FIGHT

My father was 25 years old when Japan bombed Pearl Harbor. He and most of his generation went to war. I graduated from college in 1980. Most of my generation went to work. During World War II the government gave director Frank Capra the job of explaining the war effort to Americans and getting them behind it. The result was the famous *Why We Fight* documentary series. There's no similar effort to motivate modern Americans to fight the office wars of the 21st century. But that doesn't mean we don't need it—*especially* in the field of journalism.

In the post–9/11 world, our job is more difficult than ever—and more important. The question that has been asked many times of journalists since the attacks is: "What has 9/11 taught us?" There's probably no consensus and some believe it taught us nothing. But at the local news level, arguably the stations that had established strong reputations for honesty and credibility were the ones that fared the best. In the post–9/11 world, people came to television news looking for reliability and for context, meaning, and perspective—not for the car crash or police shooting of the day. To those viewers, the craft of journalism was suddenly important again. Those of us who'd never lost faith in our craft were glad to welcome them back. We must continue to serve them well in the future. And that will require a firm commitment to the concept of ethics.

Up to this point, this book has been largely technical in nature. We've discussed the mechanics and style of broadcast copywriting, news gathering, and news production at length, but we haven't delved as much into its substance or purpose. For the next few pages we'll put aside the *how* of journalism and concentrate on the *why*. It's our intention to give a broad overview and summary of the ethical process at both the newsroom and the individual levels. We'll also explore a topic not often addressed in the available literature about ethics, and that's the motivational challenges, professional disappointments, and on-the-job frustrations that can adversely affect a journalist's ethical focus, commitment, and quality of work.

In discussing ethics we'll rely heavily on work, wisdom, and inspiration from the Poynter Institute and on the expertise of Poynter faculty members Bob Steele, Al Tompkins, and Jill Geisler.

Building the Ethical Newsroom

Let's assume for a moment that you work in an average newsroom. Most if not all the journalists within consider themselves ethical. They probably have above-average intelligence and abilities and at least average motivation. Now, imagine that an ugly episode plays out in the community, a news coverage challenge that strains emotions to the breaking point and severely tests the newsroom's decision-making processes. Would your newsroom rise to the occasion?

On Tuesday, April 20, 1999, two heavily armed students walked into Columbine High School in Littleton, Colorado, and opened fire. More than a dozen people died. With no warning, local media found themselves having to cover what turned out to be the bloodiest school rampage in U.S. history. Some stations performed better than others. Many made mistakes, some of them spectacular. Consider the following:

- While the gunmen were still presumably roaming the halls, some stations aired live cell phone interviews with students. One anchor went so far as to urge students to call the TV station instead of 911 (advice that was quickly retracted). One purported student cell phone call, which also aired live on a network news service, turned out to be a hoax.

- By contrast, at least one other local TV news producer took such a student call and handled it far differently. Realizing she wasn't trained as a crisis counselor or hostage negotiator, she didn't even consider putting the caller on the air. Instead, she urged the student to call 911 and then disconnected the call.

- Stations aired emotional interviews with extremely distraught juveniles at their most vulnerable moments, interviews that wound up being replayed again and again on the national news media.

- Almost every station showed, to at least some degree, live helicopter pictures of police positions and student escape routes, which of course might have been of extreme interest to the gunmen inside the school, who did have access to televisions.

Clearly, different ethical and decision-making processes were at work here among the various newsrooms and journalists. In the aftermath of Littleton, the local and national media endured intense criticism. But there was some praise as well for the self-restraint and balance some of the journalists showed.

Now picture this happening in your newsroom. Would your team handle it well? Even if the people in your newsroom are ethical, if your newsroom has had no training in ethical decision making, the outcome is doubtful. A newsroom filled with ethical people isn't necessarily an ethical newsroom! The Poynter Institute's Bob Steele says that our individual ethical principles "compete with each other and may compete with other people's principles. So we have to have the skills of ethical decision making, the process and tools to work through conflicting principles and colliding values."

Geisler, Tompkins, and Steele of Poynter speak frequently about the issues of ethics and decision making. Their view is that ethics isn't something you *have;* it's something you *do*. Ethics isn't simply an injunction to "do right." It's a process for achieving that goal. According to Steele, Tompkins, and Geisler, the decision-making processes in most newsrooms come in three flavors. They are:

- Gut reaction
- Rule obedience
- Reflection and reasoning

Reliable, ethical decision making is likely to take place only on that third level.

Gut Reaction

It's probably safe to say that most journalists consider themselves ethical. If pressed to justify that claim, many of them might say they "go with their gut" or "trust their instincts." But according to Steele, Tompkins, and Geisler, gut-level reactions, though important, are just the first step. The problem with your "gut" is that it's unique to you. It's shaped by an entire lifetime of personal experiences and past incidents, both pleasant and unpleasant. Your gut feelings can be emotional, prejudicial, unreasonable, strongly set, even irrational. Steele puts it this way: "Too strong of a gut reaction can prevent reflective and reasoned thinking. Too strong of a gut reaction can keep us from hearing the contrarian thoughts of others. Too strong of a gut reaction can trap us in the rigidity of rules and keep us from seeing the gray that always exists between the black and the white." Steele says you *should* listen to your gut, but don't completely trust it. Your gut reaction *will* have value, though, if it gets a conversation going—provided that conversation doesn't stop at the "gut level."

Rule Obedience

If you're talking about an ethical issue, you're already ahead of some newsrooms. What sometimes happens, however, is that conversation proceeds to the next level, rule obedience, and then stops there. According to Steele, Tompkins, and Geisler, at this level the participants recognize there's an issue, but they're not sure how to proceed. So, they open the station's policy manual—or, if there isn't one, they discuss the issue in light of the station's known rules, regulations, and precedents. They pick the rule or regulation that seems to fit (examples: "We don't cover suicides" or "We don't show bodies") and then proceed accordingly. The problem with this, of course, is that no rule book can possibly cover every situation. Blind obedience to rules precludes reflection and reasoning. At this level the best courses of action might never even come up for discussion.

Reflection and Reasoning

In healthy newsrooms most rules are really *guidelines* meant to provoke further discussion, not end it. In such a newsroom, the decision-making process will now proceed to the third level. At this stage, participants attempt to find the proper course of action in light of the given facts while taking into account the station's guidelines and policies. Such discussions work best if they include a wide range of viewpoints, especially when working through major crises. Participants must ask certain questions, and the discussion might make use of formal guidelines for ethical decision making, which we'll discuss in a moment.

What Is Ethical? A Case Study

So how does one decide whether a given course of action is ethical?

One of the best ethical codes is the one adopted by the Society of Professional Journalists (SPJ), *www.spj.org*. It contains four basic points. Ethical journalists should:

- Seek the truth and report it
- Minimize harm
- Act independently
- Be accountable

When newsrooms fail to act ethically, often it's because the decision-making process either got hung up on or never got to that second point. The concept of minimizing harm suggests that the end does *not* always justify the means, and that not every fact or fact-gathering tactic is worth the collateral damage it might cause to people or organizations. Working these problems through isn't easy. It requires a *process*. Mistakes are likely to occur when the process fails or none is in place to begin with.

In a workshop presented by the Radio and Television News Directors' Foundation (RTNDF), Geisler, Tompkins, and Steele discussed a fascinating case study that shows how this can happen. A station in Denver wanted to interview a victim who had suffered burns and other injuries in a building explosion. First the reporter tried an open front-door approach; she sought the interview through the hospital's public relations department. A spokesperson denied permission for the interview, telling the reporter the family didn't wish to talk. The reporter contacted the family directly and discovered, as she had suspected, that this wasn't true; the victim and his wife very much wanted to talk. Angered that the P.R. spokesperson had misled her, the reporter decided to sneak up to the hospital room and obtain the interview on the sly. Accordingly, the photographer stuck the camera under his coat. The two of them made it up to the hospital room unchallenged, grabbed the interview, and presented a compelling exclusive story on the next newscast.

Would you have a problem with this course of action? At this point none of the 40 or so participants in the RTNDF workshop, which included some veteran news managers, objected. Many said that if the reporter and photographer were in the hospital room at the invitation of the patient, then they had a legal right to be there.

The problem with the law is that it tells you what you can get away with, not what you *ought* to get away with. Or, as Tompkins put it, "The law tells you what you can do. Ethics tells you what you *should* do."

In this case, the television station's actions might have been different had the decision makers stopped to thoroughly discuss the proposed course of action before taking it and had asked any of the following questions during that discussion:

- Will the crew's presence in the room interfere with the patient's medical treatment?
- Will the crew's presence in the room adversely affect the patient in any way?
- Is this the type of environment where the crew would need to be wearing caps and gowns?
- What if the crew plugs in its lights and blows a circuit?
- Are there any considerations we should be thinking of or might be missing because of lack of expertise? Is there someone who can guide us on this?

As it turns out, burn patients require special germ-free environments. The crew's entry into the room *was* potentially dangerous for the patient. In the aftermath, the hospital raised a hue and cry. This led to a public relations problem for the TV station, which had to apologize for its actions. The journalists weren't aware of the medical danger, of course, in part because they didn't have the expertise to know about it. In cases like this, newsrooms are wise to seek what Geisler likes to call a "rabbi," a teacher or expert who can advise the decision makers.

The concepts of seeking the truth and minimizing harm go hand in hand. But of the two, the duty to seek the truth and report it is primary. As Steele puts it, the idea is to minimize harm while maximizing truth-telling. Decision-making processes fail if they don't include prudent steps to reduce the harm a story might cause. But they fail even worse if they minimize harm by eliminating needed truth-telling.

In the case study above, the television station would have been well served to consider other options. Among the possibilities:

- Confront the P.R. spokesperson with the truth about the family's willingness to talk and enlist her help in setting up a safe interview.
- Consider a phone interview with the hospitalized patient.
- Interview the wife separately outside the hospital.

These options might have preserved the station's ability to tell the truth of what happened while minimizing the harm that getting the interview might have caused.

Doing Ethics: Excerpts from the Poynter Guidelines

In a healthy newsroom environment one or more people, perhaps making use of a gut reaction, will red-flag ethical issues or challenges for discussion. The discussion will proceed to that third level, reflection and reasoning. Steele has a list of questions participants should ask. Among them, paraphrased below, are:

- What do we know? What more do we need to know?
- What is our journalistic purpose?
- What are our ethical concerns?
- Which organizational policies and professional guidelines must we consider?
- Which other voices, people with diverse perspectives and ideas, should we include in the decision-making process?
- Who are the stakeholders—those who will be affected by our decisions? What motivates them? How would we feel if we were in their shoes?
- What are the possible consequences of our actions?
- What are our alternatives?
- Will we be willing—and *able*—to publicly explain our actions?

One might reasonably question whether there's *time* to go through all of these steps in a crisis situation, given the deadlines a typical television or radio news operation faces. The answer is yes. A station's news operations do not have to grind to a halt during the decision-making process. The desk can still dispatch crews and begin the process of getting the news on the air. It is possible even in such situations to convene quick meetings, either in a nearby conference room or in the middle of the newsroom, to seek staff input for identifying issues and discussing options. Nor does the process have to stop when the formal planning meeting ends. Some stations have ongoing ad-hoc conferences, in the news director's office or some other central location, which people can join and leave as their deadlines permit. Regardless of the method, if a news organization believes ethical decision making is important, it will find a way to do it.

Acting Independently

The SPJ's admonition to "act independently" isn't as complicated or hard to interpret as the injunction to "minimize harm." Though the code contains several bullet points of advice under this heading, the gist of it is simply this: the only item on your news-gathering agenda should be the intent to gather the news. You should steer clear of any influences that might call that agenda into question. Hordes of people are out there trying to influence your reporting and swing you over to their point of view with tactics ranging from the subtle to the extreme. Land mines and pitfalls litter the journalistic landscape. If you step in one, the best course is to simply back out of it—and, if necessary, disclose the conflict, apologize for it, and take corrective action.

Accountability

That fourth ethics point—"be accountable"—is relatively new to the SPJ code, having been added in 1996. The RTNDA's (Radio-Television News Directors Association) revised code of ethics, adopted in 2000, contains similar language. Journalists are still struggling with it. Most television and radio stations do a fairly poor job with it.

The text of the code itself speaks of abiding by high standards, promptly correcting mistakes, and the like. But it also urges journalists to "invite dialogue with the public over journalistic conduct." Television and radio stations are in the position to do this much better than any newspaper is; after all, we're actually *capable* of the speech the word "dialogue" implies. Some television stations have viewer mailbag segments that include comments from the public received by way of telephone and e-mail. This is a good start. Segments that specifically solicit viewer feedback about the station's news coverage decisions are better. Segments that invite such feedback and respond to it sincerely are the best. Very few television or radio stations have such segments. Fewer still—as of this writing, only two or three—have viewer representatives or ombudsmen to facilitate this process.

If a television station, radio station, or network news operation truly wishes to hold itself accountable to the public, it should clearly state what it stands for and provide a mechanism for soliciting, airing, and, most important, *responding* to public feedback openly and sincerely.

It takes a bit of courage to do this. A commitment to public feedback implies a commitment to own up to mistakes. Journalism is difficult; few of us are completely without ethical sin. Mistakes are inevitable. History suggests the public can be very forgiving—*if* forgiveness is requested. On the other hand, the public has nothing but contempt for people and institutions that ignore or deny their mistakes or, even worse, defend them as if they were some kind of virtue.

Many in our industry don't feel we should have to explain ourselves. That attitude is evident in the reply a network news executive once gave to a reporter when the executive said that yes, the network does have a policy about privacy but no, it's not going to share it. Journalists frequently wrap themselves in the First Amendment, but don't always stop to recall where those First Amendment rights came from. They came from the American people, who decided to give our industry constitutional protections granted to no other. In return we owe it to our public to share and explain our methods and motivations.

Remember that final point on Steele's questions for ethical decision making: has the newsroom reached a decision it is able and willing to explain? Newsrooms and journalists unwilling or unable to explain themselves cannot claim to be ethical. It's really that simple.

An Ethics Barometer

We've seen that newsrooms can't rely on the collective gut instincts of their employees for ethical decision making. They need a process, and that process requires training, implementation, and maintenance. Newsrooms with such a system in place will create a culture characterized by some or all of the following:

- Training in and frequent discussion of the ethical decision-making process within the newsroom.
- Frequent "red-flagging" of ethical issues by employees or managers for discussion.
- Management and rank-and-file attitudes that cultivate, encourage, and respect "contrarian" viewpoints. Such an atmosphere is characterized by employees who aren't afraid to speak up, and by managers who encourage them to do so.
- Special in-house workshops or staff discussion groups to talk about ethical questions the station might have encountered or case studies of ethical issues other stations have encountered.
- Regular staff meetings, one-on-one or in groups, to critique stories and discuss the issues.
- Frequent dialogue with members of the public affected by coverage decisions.
- On-air acknowledgment of viewer feedback and public discussion of major coverage decisions.

Summary

Why is all of this so important? According to Steele, Geisler, and Tompkins, when faced with a crisis such as Littleton, television news can't merely be good. We owe it to our viewers to be *excellent*. Says Tompkins, "It is not possible to be ethical without being excellent."

And vice versa.

Building the Ethical Journalist

To conduct yourself ethically on a personal level, you'll need two items. The first is your bag of decision-making tools as described above, which you'll put together and continually sharpen through training and experience. The second is that most elusive ingredient of all: a good attitude, made up of energized spirits, respect for your co-workers, a determination to make a positive difference for your viewers and community, and a passion for what you do for a living. Much has been written about the basic tools for ethical decision making, but much less is available about the subject of how to keep your personal energies properly focused. In the pages ahead we'll talk about both: how to keep a good ethical balance in the face of the tough personal and professional challenges you'll encounter, and how to keep yourself focused, motivated, and energized.

Practice, Practice

In the first part of this chapter we noted that without the proper training, a newsroom filled with ethical journalists nevertheless might fail to act ethically. The same is true at the individual level.

Ethical challenges and choices big and small face individual journalists every single day. Each choice you make—ranging from the stories you elect to pursue, the people you choose to interview, and the way you treat the people you encounter—has ethical implications and potential pitfalls. Sometimes the choices aren't clear. More frequently, it's not always clear there *are* choices. You might find yourself blindly pursuing a course of action without having stopped to even question whether there might be alternatives. In such cases you might traipse along blindly, not worried about anything—until you suddenly step on an ethical land mine. At that point, of course, the damage is done and the only real question is how to make repairs and clean things up.

How can you steer through the sometimes treacherous waters of journalism? A heart of gold isn't enough. Even if you're kind to children and animals, pay your taxes, and don't rob banks, this doesn't mean you're ethical. If you want to play the piano, you have to practice, practice, practice. The same is true of journalism. To hone your ethical sense you'll need training in the art of ethical decision making and critical thinking, and experience doing it.

We hope that, by the time they've landed their first job, most journalists will have had some exposure to ethics concepts in college. If not, they'll have to learn the ethical process on the job. But even if you *have* had some training in ethics, you can't stop there. Says Bob Steele of Poynter Institute, "Journalists should be in a life-long learning mode." It's been pointed out that journalists get less continuing education than members of any other profession. Chances are you'd be shocked if you were to discover that a surgeon who's about to perform heart surgery on you hasn't brushed up on the subject since leaving medical school 10 years ago. Journalists are no different. According to

Steele, "You should always be searching for new information. We should always be challenging our own assumptions by adding knowledge to our noggins. We should be constantly sharpening the tools in our professional bag, including the skill-based tools of writing and interviewing and reporting, but also the decision-making tool."

The single best way to learn every day is through interacting with your colleagues, asking many questions, looking for mentors, and, as Steele puts it, for "models of excellence in our colleagues and in other newsrooms." You should constantly observe and analyze the effects of your actions and words on colleagues and on the public. Another good learning tactic is to read books and trade publications to discover the ethical challenges others have faced and how they've dealt with them. Finally, formal ethics training is available through seminars and workshops sponsored by the RTNDF, the Poynter Institute, and others.

If the process works as it should, you'll still be learning about journalism and ethics the day you retire.

The Importance of Being Earnest

When you get that first job, chances are you'll be excited, pumped, filled with good intentions, and eager to get to work. You might assume your new co-workers feel the same way. If so, you could be in for a shock. It's probably true that most journalists begin the same way: We're optimistic, determined, eager, and idealistic. But here's a disturbing truth: Often, something ugly happens along the way. We start out as people not too different from our viewers and listeners. But after a few years many of us are profoundly different. Some of us become cynical, jaded, distrustful, and bitter. We don't react to stories and situations the same way our public does. We develop an attitude of "Been there, done that." Stories have to be bigger, more sensational, and more splashy to get our attention. We begin to think we're smarter than our viewers and listeners and have a right to decide for them what is and isn't worthy of public discourse. We're less respectful of people and of each other. Of course, this isn't true of all journalists. But you can walk into almost any newsroom in the country and see these forces in action—forces that do little to create a healthy environment for good journalism or ethical behavior.

It doesn't have to be this way. Plenty of journalists find a way to keep themselves energized and their spirits renewed in the face of the inevitable on-the-job frustrations, disappointments, and disagreeable bosses. The probability that you'll be a capable and ethical journalist rises in direct proportion to your success in keeping a healthy attitude and maintaining your ability to enjoy your work.

Journalism isn't just a job. It shouldn't be something you decided to do because it sounded more appealing than becoming an accountant or a tax attorney or a meter reader. Journalism is a calling. As with most callings, the only truly successful players will be those who have a passion for it. Why else would you be willing to work holidays? Or be on call 24 hours a day, seven days a week? Or work the long hours we're often required to work? If you don't have a passion for it, not only will you not succeed, but you might be standing in the way of someone who does. As NBC anchor Brian Williams told news directors at the 1999 RTNDA convention, if you don't have a passion for this business, then please get out of the way of those who'd be willing to crawl over broken glass to get here.

So, you've arrived on the journalistic scene, fresh out of college, with a microphone in one hand, a notepad in the other, a heart burning with enthusiasm, and a passion for the business. How are you going to keep those fires burning? All professions sometimes lead to burnout, but ours—with its unique combination of high ideals, grueling deadlines, and profit pressure—is more susceptible than many. The most ethical journalists will also be those who've done the best job of coping with these forces and remaining true to their ideals.

How to Immunize Yourself against Disillusionment

That first disillusionment can come very quickly. Newsrooms are filled with cynics, and pretty soon you find they're having an effect on you. You notice that no one around you seems to be working as hard as you feel you're working. You further notice that management doesn't seem to care. Then you begin to examine your station's news product with a more critical eye. What news is the station covering, and why? Is there a larger meaning or purpose to what the newsroom is doing? Does anyone in management articulate an overall vision, or does the news product seem to you to be a random bag of car chases, shootings, and petty crimes? Who's paying attention? Budget issues begin to bug you. Lack of leadership begins to bug you. The daily confusion begins to bug you. Pretty soon you've concluded that no one cares but you, that managers and co-workers are just phoning it in, and that the company ownership cares about nothing but the bottom line. The day arrives when you suddenly decide you can't stand it for another moment.

What are you going to do about that?

You basically have two choices. One, you can give up. "Giving up" can take the form of quitting outright, but more likely such mental surrender will manifest itself in the form of you deciding to join the cynical masses, adding to the group bitterness while going through the motions of doing your job. Giving up has the virtue of being really easy to do.

The second choice is more difficult. You can vow a mighty oath *never* to give up, to keep slugging, and to always do your part to make a positive difference, no matter how small that difference may seem on a daily basis. So management is driving you nuts? Become what the Poynter Institute sometimes refers to as a "contrarian," someone who makes it a point to be the "loyal opposition" in challenging (diplomatically, if possible) management and co-workers. Network. Let co-workers and managers hear from you. Find ways to express yourself and to nudge people in a different direction.

For this second choice to work, you'll need to focus on the positive. Don't let yourself fall into the pit of relentless negativism where many cynics dwell. The best way to immunize yourself against disillusionment is to concentrate your attention on the things you enjoy that drew you here to begin with. Did you get into the business because you love to write? Guess what—even on the worst possible day, you're still writing, and you're still getting paid for it. Are you doing this because you like the excitement of having your finger on the pulse of the world? The world is still there, it still has a pulse, and your finger is still on it. Did you become a journalist because you want to make a difference? No matter what you do in a newsroom—every time your fingers dance across a keyboard, or your hands adjust a camera or an editing machine, or you clear your throat to begin tracking a package, or you pick up the phone to talk with a contact or source, you have a chance to change the world, if only a little bit. Focus on what you enjoy. Throw your arms around it. Don't let the negatives distract you from the realization that you fought hard to be here for a reason, and that those reasons haven't gone away.

Much has been written about "youthful idealism." But idealism doesn't have to be the province of the young. There's no reason that you can't hang onto your ideals and fight the disappointment and disillusionment that strike so many. But to be successful, you must not be so idealistic that you can't cope with the reality of the daily grind. More important, you have to cope with the fact that others have ideals, too, and they're likely to be different from your own. Says Steele, "I think we can be both idealistic and pragmatic. I believe that high ideals help us search for excellence. But I also believe that we have to search for the common ground that allows for differences, that respects and tolerates opposing ideas, that accepts that there is a great deal of gray between the black and white of ethical decisions."

Disillusioned journalists tend to think no one cares. An idealistic journalist knows that if he or she cares, that's one, and it beats the hell out of none. One caring journalist can find or inspire others. It just takes persistence and a little faith.

You and the Stockholders

It's common to come away from that first disillusionment disgusted about your station's profit motive. Don't. Profit is a perfectly honorable motive for any business. In fact, the profit motive, along with the underlying work ethic that makes it possible, forms the bedrock of our society. If you work for a commercial television or radio station, then you're in the business of providing news and information for profit. You expect to be paid for your services, do you not? So do the owners and investors who make it possible for you to do your job. It's a simple equation: Profit provides resources for journalism. No profit, no journalism. (Even if you work for a public broadcaster, then contributions and taxes from people and institutions who work for a profit fund your efforts.)

If your station appears to be taking inappropriate steps in the pursuit of profit, that's not necessarily an indication that something is wrong with capitalism or the profit motive. More likely it's just bad management.

Chances are you didn't get into television or radio news because you have a burning desire to make stockholders rich. Conversely, it's a good bet the stockholders didn't invest in your station because they wanted you to have a job. It's possible that many of them don't give a rat's patoot about journalism, though doubtless some of them do. Yet the two of us—journalists and stockholders—can get along just fine if we remember one key principle: We can't live without one another! The relationship will be mutually profitable if we create value for one another. Good journalism will increase shareholder value. Growing shareholder value will make more good journalism possible. Mutual benefit is the foundation of any viable business relationship. As long as your interests complement those of the stockholders, and vice versa, you can continue doing business.

An already cynical age is even more cynical in the post-Enron world. Cynics love to decry the death of journalism at the hands of uncaring corporations that seem concerned about nothing but the bottom line. Some companies clearly are better than others, but here's a little secret that applies to almost all of them: The stockholders financed the bus, built the bus, and own the bus. But they're too busy to drive the bus. They gave the bus keys to *us*. *We* get to drive it—and we can take it anywhere we want, within reason. It's a precarious relationship, to be sure. Journalists and news managers get bounced off the bus, or under it, all the time. But many of us just hop right back onto the next bus. The system will function unless those of us doing the actual work stop caring.

Bottom line: don't let contempt for the profit motive of stockholders adversely affect your attitude, performance, or ethical balance.

The Ratings and You

The popular media, especially those in Hollywood, like to portray journalists as evil, ratings-grubbing sensationalists. This tends to paint an honorable aim, the pursuit of ratings, with the brush of a dishonorable tactic, sensationalism. Too many of us journalists tend to agree with the critics that the pursuit of ratings is somehow wrong or at least distasteful, and because of that we lose respect for our industry and, in essence, for what we do for a living. To say the least, this is *not* a morale booster. You can see the detrimental effects of this constant criticism on the morale and attitude of journalists every day in trade magazines, on the Internet, in journalism forums, and in electronic publications such as *ShopTalk.*

But as with the pursuit of profit, there's nothing wrong in and of itself with seeking to enhance ratings. For one, you want your station to be profitable, for all the reasons we've already discussed. Second, you want your journalism to be *effective.* If a storyteller shouts to the woods and no one hears, did the message get out? No. The best story in the world will have no effect if no one sees or hears it.

It *is* true that the thoughtless pursuit of quick ratings sometimes leads broadcasters to take actions that are unethical or, at the very least, tasteless, silly, and counterproductive. This is where journalists need to be on guard. But don't sneer at the basic desire to grow ratings and profit, not unless you're willing to show you mean it by giving up your paycheck and working for free. An honest craftsperson provides honest value for payment received. An honest broadcaster provides honest benefit for viewership or listenership received. Ratings and profit are the measures by which we're judged, and in a free market society this is as it should be. Concentrate on providing the viewer and listener benefit, and your viewers and listeners will reward you.

Your Public Covenant

No matter how discouraged you might sometimes become on the job, and no matter how much respect you might lose for your employer, there's one key factor that ought to keep you going: your viewers or listeners.

A colleague once described to me his frustration caused by poor conditions at the competing station where he worked—few resources, questionable ethics, little leadership. But he claimed he still did the best job he could day in and day out *despite* his feelings. "My viewers are counting on me," he explained. "I can't let them down."

He's exactly right. Your viewers count on you. If you can't motivate yourself to do a good job for your employer, then do it for your viewers or listeners.

You should always keep your viewers or listeners in mind whatever you do. Some (if not most) newsrooms have a thinly veiled contempt for news consumers. How many assignments desk personnel refer to the newsroom's published telephone number as the "nut line" or "idiot phone"? To be sure, members of the public can be quirky, cranky, and sometimes downright abusive. Often they ask dumb questions. Still, we're there for them. They're our reason for being. If you can't embrace that concept, then you really should find something else to do in life.

A respect for members of the public and compassion for their feelings in your personal conduct should be a basic part of your ethical makeup. In an interview situation, which do you prefer: a confrontational question designed to show how aggressive and smart you are, or an even-toned question designed to elicit information? Which is better: to jump out of the bushes with microphone in hand and ambush someone on camera, or to make an attempt to schedule an appointment to interview that person? Which would you rather do: ask, "How do you feel?" or say "Tell me about yourself?" If you picked the second answer to each of these questions, you're beginning to get the idea.

Broadcast journalism, especially at the local level, is all about serving people and serving the community. The best reporters seek out the unheard voices, listen hard, and tell those people's stories. The best television and radio stations reach out to all segments of the community. They establish a dialogue with community members and might even formalize it on the air through a feedback segment or community reporting beat or both. Their reporting will address community needs and reflect community values.

You'll face many ethical challenges in your career. Sometimes the process of weighing your journalistic duty against the potential harm a story might cause is very difficult. The options can be murky. Your ethical compass stands the best chance of remaining true and pointing you in the right direction if you energize it with the goal of providing service and value to your viewers or listeners and to the community. Though public distrust of the media continues to grow, the basic presumption still is that journalists should be telling the truth and serving the public interest the best they know how. It's the covenant our industry, and you personally, have formed with the public. Take it to heart.

When You and the Boss Disagree

It's bound to happen sooner or later, and odds are it won't be later: you and the boss will disagree. Like individuals, organizations tend to have a personality of sorts, and like people, some organizations are more skilled and likable than others are. There are as many different news philosophies as there are journalists. The chances of your personal news philosophy being in perfect harmony with that of your employer aren't great. Perhaps you're a "high-road" producer working for a "flash and trash" newsroom, or vice versa. Perhaps you find that you're a conservative working in a liberal environment, or vice versa. How are you going to cope while keeping your sanity, your sense of ethics, and, we hope, your job?

Realize that no matter what kind of environment you find yourself in, on-the-job clashes are inevitable. Don't expect to win every battle. Do make sure your voice is heard. Never lose sight of the fact that you *do* have influence. Have the courage to present your ideas. Most important, work to develop the skills you need to *properly* present them. Says Steele, "A young journalist will have a much better chance of achieving her own ethical standards if she can make clear, concise principled arguments to her boss as well as to her colleagues." The good news, according to Steele, is that the best news organizations not only listen to their youthful members but also value them. "The most thoughtful counter-intuitive idea might come from one of the youngest and newest members of the organization, those fresh eyes and new perspectives that might drive the decision-making process. The chance of that happening is enhanced when the young and/or new person makes a clear, concise argument that will get other people saying, 'Uh, huh, I hadn't thought of that.'"

It must be acknowledged, however, that even in the best newsrooms your voice won't be as strong and respected or have as much leverage as those of the more experienced journalists. To make yourself heard you'll need to network with people and form alliances. Says Steele, "Even if you don't have a stripe on your sleeve because of your youth or shortness of tenure, you can influence people through your intelligence, through your commitment, and through the questions you ask and the knowledge you bring to the discussion." And he adds, if you want change, "you can only get the change through influence."

What if you have an urgent problem or a strong ethical objection in a given situation? First of all, do *not* be a hothead. Don't pitch a fit. Don't storm out of the room or seek some big confrontation. Steele says the proper tactics are essential. "There are a number of ways for a young journalist to raise concerns with a news director or executive producer. You can pose it in writing, raising three or four questions about a particular dilemma and how it's being handled. You can ask for a private conversation in which you raise some questions and state your beliefs." It does take a little courage to speak up. It also takes patience. It's not reasonable to expect that you'll be able to single-handedly change your newsroom's policies, ethics, and values. It is reasonable to expect to be able to *influence* them, however, and have an effect on your newsroom's culture over time.

What if, despite your best, patient efforts, you find yourself in a job environment that's unethical or in some other way intolerable? According to Steele, you have three basic options. They are:

- *Survival.* A situation in which you've more or less given up, are just marking time, and are pretty much miserable.
- *Coping.* A step up from survival. You haven't totally given up and are still trying to have a positive influence, but you're pessimistic and unhappy.
- *Influence.* You refuse to give up and are determined to make a difference, through the tactics we've just discussed.

Of the three, Steele much prefers the third. But he acknowledges that some situations really are intolerable. "If you are convinced it is impossible to influence things for the better, then leaving and finding a better situation is a reasonable alternative."

Even in such cases, don't be in a hurry. As satisfying as it might be to tell your boss precisely what he or she can do with the job, you'll still be dealing with the consequences of your action long after the satisfaction has faded. Don't make career decisions in anger or haste. Unless you're the target of abuse or sexual harassment, even if you feel you "just can't take it another second," you probably can. Don't let an on-the-job crisis or setback push you into taking a rash action that you might regret. Think about it long and hard. As we've discussed, remember what got you into the business to begin with, reflect on your passions, and consider your viewers or listeners. Above all, be honest with yourself and make sure *you* aren't the problem. If that's the case, leaving isn't the solution. As the saying goes, "No matter where you go, there you are." Your personal problems always follow you. Deal with them first. Says Steele, "You don't want to leave a bad professional relationship only to have it re-created elsewhere."

That said, if after careful thought you decide that the current environment doesn't allow you to pursue the things you enjoy and doesn't allow you to serve your viewers or listeners, then it's time to vote with your feet. Do it on *your* terms. And while you're searching for a new job, continue to do your best in the one you have. Act ethically, serve your viewers and listeners, and give good value to your employer for the paycheck you're drawing. If you have a job in journalism, then regardless of what's happening between you and your employer you have an obligation to the public. Fulfill it. When it comes to your viewers and listeners, never say die, and never give up.

Conclusion

There are several sayings TV news professionals use to console themselves when their efforts go down the toilet. My personal favorite is, "No one ever died from bad TV." Probably the most common is, "Thank God it's not brain surgery." Indeed it's not. *It's more powerful and important than that.* Television news has the ability to build reputations or destroy them, to guide society to noble or ignoble action, to calm riots or start them, to start wars or end them, to make kings or dethrone them, to inspire the heart or depress the soul, to give hope or destroy it. The power we hold is incredible—so much so that people are always trying to take it away from us or limit it. The First Amendment to the U.S. Constitution was designed in part to protect Americans from such attacks, but it isn't always up to the challenge. Protection in other countries is even more uncertain. It's therefore incumbent upon us to wield this impressive power with sensitivity, responsibility, humility, a sense of ethics, and respect for the individual. Fewer and fewer news consumers believe we do that. Is that assessment justified? What do you think? And more important, what do you intend to do about it?

Television news is one of the few occupations available that allow you to have a wide impact on people's lives, for better or worse, while having more fun than the law allows. Do have fun. But never lose sight of the power in your hands.

Additional Readings

This chapter has been brief and introductory in nature. We hope your study of ethics won't stop here. Poynter Ethics director Bob Steele recommends the following additional reading:

Sissela Bok, *Lying: Moral Choice in Public and Private Life* (Vintage Books, 1999. ISBN: 0375705287).

Jack Fuller, *News Values: Ideas for an Information Age* (University of Chicago Press, 1997. ISBN: 0226268802).

Al Tompkins, *Aim for the Heart: Write for the Ear, Shoot for the Eyes: A Guide for TV Producers and Reporters* (Bonus Books, 2002. ISBN: 1566251761).

In addition, as of this writing two important codes of ethics can be found at the following Web sites:

Society of Professional Journalists Code of Ethics: *www.spj.org/ethics_code.asp*.

Radio and Television News Directors Association Code of Ethics: *www.rtnda.org/ethics/coe.shtml*.

Ethical DOs and DON'Ts

Do
- Plan now for how you'll deal with the next ethical challenge.
- Pay attention to your "gut feelings."
- Involve others in ethical discussions.
- Seek more information and identify alternatives.
- Be willing and able to publicly explain your decisions.
- Network with friends and colleagues to gain influence.
- Focus on what you enjoy about journalism.

Don't
- Forget that ethics isn't a set of virtues but rather a process for making decisions.
- Let your gut have the final word.
- Try to tackle tough ethical problems on your own.
- Let blind obedience to "the rules" make your decisions for you.
- Be timid about speaking up in editorial discussions.
- Forget that the first loyalty of journalism is to the public.
- Ever give up!

THE BRAVE NEW WORLD OF MULTIMEDIA CONVERGENCE

Convergence appears to be the media buzzword of the century. Whether it's one of fear, anger, enthusiasm, or just plain curiosity, the word seldom fails to elicit a reaction. Media enterprises are trying to figure out how to incorporate it into their business plans as they plot world domination. Employees wonder whether they'll soon be converged out of a job. Colleges and universities struggle with whether and how they must change to prepare students for this new world. Does the future really belong to the converged? If so, what will that future look like? Anyone who claims to know the certain answer to that question as of this writing is lying or delusional. But we are starting to get some pretty strong hints of where convergence might be taking us. In the pages ahead we'll examine one widely known convergence operation, with the

The News Center in Tampa houses the newsrooms of the *Tampa Tribune,* WFLA-TV, and TBO.com under one roof, in this building on the banks of the Hillsborough River.

goal of giving some idea of how journalists are coping with convergence now and how others might cope in the future. In keeping with the approach shown elsewhere in this book, there won't be a great deal of discussion about how things *should* be, but rather how they are.

Seven Levels of Convergence

In March of 2000 Media General made headlines in media trade magazines around the world when it moved its three Tampa media properties—the *Tampa Tribune,* TBO.com and WFLA-TV—into one building, which it named the News Center. Though there are other examples of cross-platform media operations, this was the first to combine a major daily circulation metropolitan newspaper, a major over-the-air broadcast television station, and an online news service into one building. Some scholars have stated that the News Center is about five years ahead of where the rest of the industry inevitably must go.

The News Center stands four stories high. Two TV studios and storage areas take up most of the first floor. The second floor is devoted to the television and TBO.com newsrooms. The newspaper newsroom fills the third floor. TV and Web administrative areas occupy the fourth. The central feature of the News Center is the atrium extending from the second floor to the fourth floor skylights. From the floor of the atrium rises the hallmark of the Tampa convergence model—the mul-

The News Center's Multimedia Desk, where television and print assignments editors, producers, and researchers work side by side.

timedia assignments desk, where newspaper staffers and TV assignments editors work together. The multimedia desk serves as a clearinghouse for information coming from scanner traffic, faxes, and phone calls from public information officers or from the public.

There are seven basic levels of daily convergence in the News Center.

Level One: Daily Tips and Information

The most common form of convergence cooperation also is the one least obvious to the News Center's readers, viewers, and *users*. Quite simply, the three News Center *platforms* do a lot of talking. Managers talk to managers. Beat reporters are encouraged to talk with their counterparts on the other platforms. Each platform holds several editorial meetings every day, including one specifically dedicated to convergence planning. This cross-platform sharing is the process whereby News Center journalists gang up on the competition, and deliver what they think is better service to the end users.

The day begins with WFLA-TV's 9:00 A.M. editorial meeting. *Tribune* Assistant Multimedia Editor Ken Knight attends that and most other editorial meetings in the News Center, working closely with the managers of all three platforms. At 10:15 A.M. the *Tribune* holds its first editorial meeting, devoting the first 15 minutes to the exchange of convergence coverage ideas. WFLA-TV Executive Producer Susan DeFraties usually represents the TV station there. The general idea is that by continually exchanging tips and information, each partner looks out for the other to ensure that no one misses any important story.

Not every story or tip that excites managers of one platform will play well on another. Sometimes a good newspaper story is just that, and not suitable for TV. The reverse is also true. The platforms cooperate best when coverage interests overlap. Such areas of overlap include investigative news, consumer news, spot or breaking news, medical reporting, weather, and so forth. If the platforms decide to cooperate or co-publish, this can take several forms, from the major to the minor. One "minor" form of convergence would be the presentation of a story on one platform credited as having originated on another. For example, on WFLA-TV's 11 P.M. news, you'll often see an anchor framed with a *Tribune* logo reading a story beginning with words such as, "The *Tampa Tribune* will report in the morning that. . . . " A major form of cooperation would be to carefully coordinate the co-publication of an enterprise story (more about that in a moment).

Level Two: Resources

From time to time the three platforms share resources, and by far the area in which this happens the most is photography. These days most of the WFLA-TV video photojournalists also carry digital still cameras. Many of the *Tampa Tribune* photographers carry small digital video cameras. The platforms often cover for one another, most often in cases in which their needs are simple. For instance, TV station managers might ask a newspaper photographer to grab b-roll of a ribbon-cutting ceremony, but wouldn't likely ask that photographer to shoot and edit a package. Less common is the trading of reporters on general assignment stories, but it does happen. If a verdict comes back unexpectedly in a trial the TV station is monitoring but not staffing with a reporter, it's not unheard of for a *Tampa Tribune* reporter to go live in the midday news with the verdict. Conversely, if a WFLA-TV reporter is present for a story the *Tribune* couldn't get to, that reporter might write a brief for the paper or website.

Level Three: Spot and Breaking News

Spot news is one area in which converged news coverage really shines in a way that's very obvious to the public. In a spot news crisis, the TV station often faces the task of going on the air immediately with live coverage—which of course means that the TV reporters have to find something to say. Television isn't known for letting a lack of facts stand in the way of continuing live news coverage. Fortunately, here convergence hits a home run. For example, when a multiple-alarm fire erupted in Tampa's Ybor City area, both the *Tribune* and WFLA-TV flooded the field with crews. *Tribune* and TBO.com reporters helped support WFLA-TV's live coverage with live reports by way of cell phone. *Tribune* business editor Dave Simanoff teamed up with the paper's archive and research desk to pull up information about the owners of the affected property. The burning area turned out to be a city block where a massive redevelopment project was underway. Because Ybor City is Tampa's prime entertainment district, the fire had profound implications for the area's economy. The TV station was able to get this information on the air almost immediately. Through convergence the News Center partners were able to provide immediate context, meaning, and perspective in a fashion not always typical of breaking television news coverage.

Level Four: Enterprise Reporting

The area in which convergence provides its most powerful journalism is **enterprise** reporting. In the News Center model, enterprise reporting expresses itself in two forms—planned and unplanned.

Planned Co-Publication

One very powerful way to showcase convergence partnerships is to select an important enterprise story and then time the release of that story so that it appears on each platform in a coordinated fashion. One reporter might write a story for each platform. Or, a print reporter might collaborate with a broadcaster, with the stories appearing under separate or even dual bylines. Both approaches work well.

A good example of converged enterprise reporting is an investigation WFLA-TV reporter Mark Douglas conducted into corrosion inside the Sunshine Skyway Bridge, where some of the central support cables were failing after only 10 years of service. *Tribune* editors asked Mark to write a print version. The *Tribune* graphics department generated artwork for both versions. By mutual agreement, the print version appeared first, with the byline, "Mark Douglas, of WFLA, News Channel 8." TBO.com also put a version of the story online. Yes—the TV managers had deliberately "blown" an exclusive by letting the paper break the story. What were they, nuts? To succeed in a converged environment journalists must put aside competitive instincts they've spent a lifetime learning. In this case, those traditional instincts were dead wrong. Admittedly, publication in the newspaper "cost" the TV station its exclusive; by 6 P.M. each television competitor had the story. But the front page presentation had stirred up market interest in the coverage, and people knew where to tune to find it. WFLA-TV's 6 P.M. ratings spiked by about 25 percent, giving the station a decisive victory in the time slot. The lesson here is that convergence can be a more powerful competitive advantage than is exclusivity alone. Further, unlike scoops—which can't be guaranteed every day—convergence is a *sustainable* competitive advantage.

The Breaking Enterprise Story

Somewhere between unscheduled spot news and carefully planned enterprise lies a more urgent form of unplanned original story one might call the "breaking enterprise story." Typically this happens when one platform digs up a "hot fact." For example, suppose the *Tribune* has confirmed that the suspect in a major murder case will cop a plea tomorrow. Should the *Tribune* give the story to WFLA-TV? The conference rooms and phone lines of the News Center frequently buzz with energetic discussions about questions like this. Two conflicting considerations guide such discussions. One is the concept of exclusivity, as outlined above. The other, frequently articulated by *Tribune* Managing Editor Donna Reed and Senior Vice President and Executive Editor Gil Thelen, is the idea that the story "belongs to the community, not to the journalists." This being the case, the first thought should be to get that story out to the community by way of what TBO.com General Manager Kirk Read likes to call "the first available printing press." When managers don't agree, the platform originating the story controls its release.

Here's an example of how this philosophy can work. Late one evening the *Tribune* confirmed a tip that two laptops had disappeared from a highly secure vault within Centcom at MacDill Air Force Base in Tampa—the very office coordinating the war in Afghanistan. The senior editor in charge released the story to WFLA-TV and gave approval for the station to break it on the 11 P.M. news. The TV newsroom did some digging and obtained independent confirmation. The station led its 11 P.M. news with the story—which credited the station's partnership with the *Tampa Tribune* more than half a dozen times. By releasing the story in this manner, the News Center had fulfilled its public promise of delivering the news when, where, and how the community wants it. The News Center partners continued to own the story as the week progressed. When investigators finally made an arrest, WFLA-TV reporter Diane Pertmer helped break the news—working with a producer at TBO.com.

Converged enterprise stories of this type transcend platform to become something else, a new and stronger form of journalism not seen before. Because such stories reach so many more people, they have the ability to achieve a far greater impact than any story appearing on a single medium. Greater reach and greater impact add up to greater effectiveness in one critically important role the media play, that of public watchdog. In an era of increasing audience fragmentation, the ability to command public attention and to direct that attention toward greater responsiveness on the part of government and business is, perhaps, the key strength and public benefit of convergence.

Level Five: Franchises

In TV terms, a **franchise** is a standing commitment to air particular content at regular times. WFLA-TV, TBO.com, and the *Tampa Tribune* cooperate on a number of such efforts. Examples:

- *Tampa Tribune* Religion Reporter Michelle Bearden appears on WFLA-TV once per week. Her television segment is coordinated with publication of her regular feature on the newspaper.
- WFLA-TV Consumer Reporter Vicki Lim writes a weekly column for the newspaper.
- A *Tampa Tribune* business reporter, usually Business Editor Steve Kaylor, presents a *Tribune*-branded business segment six days a week on WFLA-TV's morning newscast.
- WFLA-TV Meteorologist Steve Jerve contributes to the *Tribune* weather page.

Level Six: Events and Special Coverage

Major events such as the Super Bowl, Olympics, and elections provide excellent opportunities to showcase joint coverage. The three platforms will showcase their coverage with similar titles and push to one another's stories when appropriate. With such cooperative efforts, it's not necessary for reporters to cross platforms, but this does happen. In the 2002 Winter Olympics, *Tampa Tribune* reporter Bill Ward went live from Salt Lake City on WFLA-TV's Olympic segments, and TBO.com tied it all together with a set of Olympics pages. In the 10 days leading up to the first anniversary of the 9/11 attacks, the *Tribune,* WFLA-TV, and TBO.com co-published daily stories under the same coverage banner, "No Life Untouched." The joint showcasing was powerful even though no reporters crossed platforms.

Level Seven: Public Service

As media propose to become more powerful through convergence, arguably it's incumbent on them to hold themselves more accountable. In 1996 the SPJ added a section to its code of ethics exhorting journalists to hold themselves accountable to the public. Arguably few have acted on that challenge. Of 1,500 or so daily circulation newspapers, only about 40 have regular ombudsmen services whereby the public can get answers to questions about the newspaper's journalism. Only three or four local TV news stations have such a service. The first such *converged* service is the Citizens' Voice feature now in place at the News Center. Each week the three platforms solicit public feedback about their journalism. The *Tribune*'s Readers' Desk and an ombudsman on the TV side handle the calls. Once a week, the newspaper prints a column responding to selected comments. The TV station does the same with a once-weekly on-air segment. TBO.com wraps it all up with a Citizens' Voice page.

After the launch of Citizens' Voice, the platforms solicited the public's input for a statement of coverage principles. The resulting News Center Pledge (see *www.mhhe.com/tuggle*) is the first converged document of its kind. The partners pledge to provide ethical conduct; to approach privacy issues with sensitivity and compassion; to cover news of relevance and to present it accurately, fairly, and in context; to cover the full diversity of the community and give voice to the voiceless; to serve as a public watchdog and hold the powerful accountable; and, importantly, to hold themselves accountable to the public. With these steps the partners had stated what they stand for and had given the public a method by which to hold them to their promises.

Citizens' Voice and the News Center Pledge give the partners the opportunity to bond with the community by explaining their values in a way the public can understand and appreciate. For example, when some viewers complained that the television station had been too aggressive in questioning a local sheriff about a communications foul-up in the search for a missing child, the station explained in its Citizens' Voice segment that part of its mission is to ask tough questions and hold the powerful accountable. The following week viewers wrote in to congratulate the station for that very approach. Its act of self-accountability had led the station to forge an important bond with the public.

The partners also reach out to the public in other ways, such as community forums for election coverage, and a town hall meeting the *Tribune* and WFLA-TV co-sponsored about the quality of local news.

Cross-Promotions and Marketing

Cross-promotions—one partner "pushing" consumers to another partner by way of news content or marketing—are a prevalent feature of convergence cooperation. Some observers and critics believe that these pushes or "refers" (pronounced "reefers") are, in fact, the real reason behind convergence. To date there's no evidence that such pushes do any real good for ratings or circulation on a consistent basis, though there is evidence that many readers, viewers, and users sometimes find them annoying. It's not hard to see why the latter might be true. The "refer" practice runs counter to the stated goal of providing the news when, where, and how the public wants it. If someone is reading the newspaper, then by definition the newspaper is that person's platform of choice. The reader might not like being told to watch TV or go to the Web.

On the other hand, it would be a mistake to consider showcasing of convergence as futile. Research in the Tampa market shows that consumers do value convergence, understanding that when one platform works with others in the news-gathering process, it's likely to do a better job. It makes sense then to market converged stories as a product of those partnerships. This can build the image and reputation of each partner regardless of whether the consumer visits each available platform.

The News Center partners haven't abandoned refers. The challenge is to do them in such a fashion as to provide a valuable "menu" of what's available *without* making the viewer, user, or reader feel cheated of the story. For instance, a viewer is most likely to feel cheated if the story that the anchor "refers" could have been presented on television but wasn't. The viewer is less likely to feel cheated if the "referred" item is platform-specific, such as a page of Internet hyperlinks, a multimedia video report available for download, or an in-depth newspaper analysis. "Refers" that highlight the unique strengths of each platform's medium therefore will be the most valuable and least irritating.

Why the Shouting Starts: Common Convergence Misconceptions, Beliefs, and Questions

Misconceptions about convergence abound. Below is an examination of some common convergence misunderstandings and questions from the viewpoint of the managers who directly oversee the three news operations in the Tampa News Center—*Tampa Tribune* Managing Editor Donna Reed, TBO.com Senior Manager for Content Jim Riley, and the author, WFLA-TV News Director Forrest Carr.

Convergence Misconception: Tampa Bay's News Center Is a "Merged Newsroom"

At present, the newsrooms are converged, not merged. According to Riley, "It's a collaborative newsroom. It's a cooperative newsroom. It's really not merged in the sense that we have one news director for all three platforms." Each of the three News Center platforms maintains editorial independence. Will that ever change? Each platform operates a very different product line, requiring very different management approaches, techniques, and strategies. Merging these three product lines into one would be extremely difficult. It's impossible to know what the future holds, but it's a good bet the partners will continue to find new ways to cooperate. Indeed, as of this writing the partners are working on a proposal to merge or at least more closely converge their sports operations.

Convergence Misconception: The Converged Multimedia Desk Commands and Directs Operations for All Three Platforms

No, it doesn't. As Reed puts it, "The multimedia desk is a communications tool." It's a clearinghouse for incoming calls, viewer tips, beat checks, and police scanner traffic. Mid-level newspaper and TV decision makers sit side by side, sharing such information. They cooperate when it's appropriate, desirable, and possible to do so—voluntarily. "There's no centralized news direction," says Riley. "We still have the three voices, the three platforms."

Convergence Question: Must Reporters of the Future Be Equally Skilled in Print, TV, and Online?

When hiring a TV reporter, newsroom managers aren't looking for a Renaissance man or woman. They'll be most interested in that person's ability to succeed as a newscaster. Similar principles apply on the other platforms. New employees are expected to have some working knowledge of other media. But as Reed puts it, "I don't think any of us are looking for some 'Stepford Reporter,' where you crank 'em up and they go do television and then go write a story and then they go online. You're going to have a few of those. We have a few of those now. But they're in the minority." However, it's certainly true that employees with multiple skill sets are more valuable—whether you're a reporter, secretary, or janitor.

Convergence Question: How Must Journalism Schools Change to Prepare Students for the Future?

Although journalists of the future won't necessarily have to be equally skilled on every platform, it does seem obvious that J-schools must radically change their thinking. In some state university systems, if you want to study print journalism, you go to one city, but if you want to study broadcasting, you must go to a different campus—and heaven help you if you should want to study both. Students should still choose specialties but it no longer makes any sense to pretend that print journalists and electronic journalists are somehow in different professions—if, indeed, it ever did.

Convergence Belief: Convergence Has No Value Unless the Public Sees It, Accepts It, and Embraces It

The first and most immediate benefit from convergence doesn't depend on public perception. The collaborative process immediately strengthens each platform. According to Reed, "The main value of convergence is the quality of the journalism we deliver, and ultimately the public benefit if it's the most complete, if we get it first, if we get it right, if we put it into complete context." Reed says it's product satisfaction that counts most. But that's not to say the public's perception of convergence isn't important. Research shows the public values these partnerships. Therefore, showcasing convergence can build credibility for each platform. Convergence is a sustainable competitive advantage.

Convergence Question: Doesn't Convergence Diminish the Number of Voices in the Community?

In the Tampa model, this hasn't been the case. Reed is emphatic about this. "That was an interesting argument 20 years ago." With the Internet, cable, high-speed bandwidths, national and global news, and information systems we have in place today, Reed doesn't see any diminishment in voices. "It's people in the industry who are the critics. Our experience here is that the public is beginning to see the value of convergence, and that's what I really care about, the value it brings to the journalism."

Convergence can in fact create a *new* voice in the form of a new and stronger type of journalism not seen before. When one story is published at the same time on multiple platforms, especially if it's done in such a way as to capitalize on the unique strengths of each medium, the story has far more reach and potential impact than other types of stories do. If it's true that journalism is necessary to make democracy work well, then it follows that stronger journalism should make democracy work even better.

Convergence Question: Isn't This Really Just about Cutting Jobs?

This hasn't happened in Tampa. Convergence there hasn't been about trading two reporters for one who then has to do a half-baked job for two or more platforms. Says Riley, "The work's still gotta get done. I don't see it cutting jobs." Reed agrees. "Convergence is about using the combined resources of several media for the benefit of the television viewer, the online user, and the newspaper reader. It's to deliver better journalism, deeper journalism, strong enterprise, ahead of the pack, whenever readers want it, viewers want it, or online users want it."

Convergence Question: Is Cross-Ownership Necessary to Make Convergence Work?

Cross-ownership isn't utterly necessary, but it does remove some very powerful roadblocks. Cross-ownership makes it possible to drive convergence from the top down and to obtain the cooperation necessary to achieve convergence goals. Having each platform under common ownership also removes one of the biggest obstacles between potential convergence partners, the idea that each partner must always benefit equally from convergence.

Now that we've laid the groundwork for understanding the purpose and practice of convergence, we'll get down to the brass tacks of how to cope in a converged newsroom.

What Web Producers Want

What style of writing are Web producers looking for? In large measure, the answer is, "You name it, the Web uses it." The Web has the opportunity to showcase a wide variety of writing styles, and it does. Says Jim Riley, content manager of TBO.com, "Immediacy and depth are the other two buzzwords I throw at people. You've got to have it right away, but then you also have that chance to do depth on the Internet." In fact, one of the key strengths of the Internet is its ability to bring a broadcaster's sense of urgency and immediacy to a print reporter's in-depth, detailed approach. The new medium has the strengths of the two **"legacy" media,** with few of their drawbacks. So on TBO.com, during the approach of a hurricane you'll be able to get up-to-the-minute reports about the progress of the storm. You'll also be able to click through to find detailed background information about hurricanes, hurricane preparations, evacuation routes, and so on. You can even find "video explainers" about various hurricane-related topics from WFLA-TV chief meteorologist Steve Jerve. But the first and most important level will be the one providing immediacy. "The Steve Jerve video explainers are incredibly cool," Riley says. "But they're on the second level." So if Riley or one of his team leaders asks you to write something for their Web site today, chances are it will be an item of immediate interest, and will go on that "first level," known as the "TBO front."

Must You Be a Techie?

To get a full-time job at TBO.com, you'll need to know **HTML** language and also how to manipulate images through a program such as Photoshop. There was a time when TBO was willing to teach such skills to its new journalists, but that's not the case today. Says Riley, "It just takes too much time to have someone come in dead cold where I have to teach them how to make a little link blue, or how to move around in your directory tree in Windows." Nor will Riley hire a technician who wants to "move into journalism." He wants someone with basic technical skills who was trained as a journalist.

Technical skills aren't required if you're a print or broadcast journalist in the News Center and are contributing a story to TBO.com. All you need in that case are the basic reporting and writing skills you already have, combined with a little knowledge of what the Web producers are looking for. Television reporters accustomed to working with pictures and sound might find that writing without them for the Web or for newspapers is a whole new ballgame. The good news is that the style they'll need isn't difficult to learn.

The Inverted Pyramid

If you're a broadcast or print reporter in the News Center and you've been asked to write for TBO.com, chances are your story is one of immediate or breaking interest and it's destined for the TBO front. It will be relatively short, about the length of a VO or VOBITE. The style you'll be using, with one or two refinements, is **inverted pyramid.**

Newspaper reporters are very accustomed to the inverted pyramid style of writing. For broadcasters it will take a little getting used to. Basically, it requires you to present the most important facts at the top and then write your story in descending order of importance. Chronological order is less important. It's more of a recitation of straight facts than it is a "story." You won't make much use of narrative storytelling and you won't use the "diamond" approach we discussed earlier. Conversational writing isn't as important. Complex sentences with dependent clauses are more acceptable. There's a beginning and somewhat of a middle, but not always a clear ending. You'll just give the straight facts in a straightforward fashion, and then stop.

Here's an example. This story appeared as breaking news on the TBO front.

MACDILL AIR FORCE BASE—Two laptop computers that were reported missing from a vaultlike room at Gen. Tommy Franks' headquarters were found Friday and a member of the military was in custody, officials said. The suspect, whose name has not been released, confessed to stealing the laptops, which contained highly sensitive military data, said Maj. Mike Richmond, Public Affairs Officer with the Air Force Office of Special Investigations.

Although the military rank and job classification are also not being released, Richmond confirmed the suspect had official clearance to the room that contained the laptops.

A computer forensic expert must now determine what data, if any, was compromised or altered. Preliminary investigations indicate that there is no connection between the suspect and the ongoing leak investigation or espionage.

Once Richmond's team completes its investigation, the findings will be handed over to a commander who, in conjunction with a military judge, will decide the level of punishment for the suspect.

Forty-six agents assigned to interview military personnel will be returning to their posts shortly, Richmond said.

In writing this update, TBO.com producer Adrian Phillips updated a story that had appeared earlier on the Web site, using new information that WFLA-TV reporter Diane Pertmer provided to him. Notice that the style is very simple. It gives the salient fact right off the top—the news that the missing laptops had been recovered. The story ends with the least important fact, that the 46 agents assigned to the investigation can go home. The style was far different from the story that Diane put on the air that night for WFLA-TV.

Why do it this way? It's said that in the old days the pyramid style was necessary because reporters filing their reports by way of telegraph never knew when the line would go down. By cramming the most important information into the top of the transmission, they could be assured the story would get through even if the message were cut off at some point. In the modern Internet age, there's a similar concern, but in the 21st century the concern isn't that a telegraph line might falter, but rather than your reader's attention will. TBO Web producer Adrian Phillips puts it this way: "The reason they do inverse is because you capture their attention at the beginning and then the reader can sort of trail off—saying, you know, 'I got the idea.'" Web users are browsers. They tend to hit and run quickly. They don't like their time to be wasted. They're more likely to come back to your Web site if you respect that and if they know their time will be well spent with you. Inverted pyramid style makes that possible.

Story Elements

A typical TV story has three basic elements: the lead, usually read on-camera; the story body, typically containing video or graphics; and a tag line, often read on camera. Most print stories have two basic elements: a headline, followed by the story body. With TBO.com, we're up to as many as four elements: a headline, an **abstract,** related links, and the story body itself, usually accessed by a link.

The laptop story again serves as a good example. The day it broke, the story headline, abstract, and links appeared on the TBO front near the masthead in the "breaking news section" framed with a picture of General Tommy Franks. The copy read as follows:

BREAKING NEWS

Missing Laptops Found; Suspect Arrested

MACDILL AIR FORCE BASE—Two laptop computers that were reported missing from a vaultlike room at Gen. Tommy Franks' headquarters were found Friday and a member of the military was arrested, officials said. Tune into News Channel 8 for the latest.

- Full story
- Laptop probe draws 51 agents
- Experts fault government in losses
- MacDill Air Force Base insider

The headline for the story is similar to a headline that might appear in the newspaper, with one difference: headline writers aren't as limited as their print counterparts are in terms of space. The headline roughly corresponds to the lead line of a TV story. The abstract is one or two quick sentences summarizing what the story is about. There's no TV parallel. Some newspapers occasionally use abstracts but many don't. The "links" section doesn't really have a television or print parallel either. The Web producer uses it to guide the user to the main story and to related stories or multimedia "goodies." On this day, only the headline, abstract, and links related to the laptop story appeared on the TBO front. To get to the full body, users had to click on the "full story" link. The laptop update was one of a small handful of important stories given this kind of showcased treatment that day on the TBO front. Other stories appearing there were listed under a tab labeled "Tampa Bay News" as headlines only, which the user could click to see the full story.

If you're a TBO employee writing a story for the Web, you'd be expected to know HTML. You'd post the story yourself, write your own headline, write your own abstract, choose your own photograph or video still-frame and compose it into the layout, and choose and build your own links. But if you're "guest writing" a story for the TBO, you'll probably just write some quick copy and e-mail it to the producer. On some occasions reporters have been known to phone in their copy. The Web producer takes it from there.

Updates

One of the things Web producers really, really want is for the people who contribute to their pages to get used to the idea that the story doesn't have to be complete to be filed. This concept doesn't trouble broadcasters. A TV reporter might go live in the midday news having just arrived on the scene of an accident. She might know very little about what happened but won't hesitate to go live and tell viewers what she does know. Five hours later she'll update the story for the 5 P.M. news, giving more information. The Web approaches breaking news in the same way. Web producers don't care if you have the full story; they want you to file what you have. When you get more information, you can update the story then, an hour from now or 10 minutes from now. Peter Howard, who oversees the daily news operations for TBO, likens this process of continual updating to an old-style overhead projector, and the presenter using a series of transparencies to build layer upon layer of information. In the case of the Web, he says, "You're doing it as information becomes available, and you're doing it through a printing press that's always on." Howard says some reporters have a problem with this, particularly print reporters, who often want to wait for a contact to return that final phone call and provide the last nail for the story. Howard doesn't want to wait. "We don't need that final nail. Give us what you've got. And we can fill it in later."

Other Story Forms

A huge amount of TBO.com's content comes from the *Tampa Tribune* by way of automation every night. The content added during the business day consists mainly of special filings from newspaper reporters and some TV reporters, mainly in the form of briefs. However, the full range of story styles found in newspapers can also be found on the Web. Most often these longer forms will appear on that "second level" we mentioned earlier, often in special sections put together as part of a converged multimedia presentation. There's no "rule" for the type of story style used in these sections. Almost anything is possible. Reporters writing for such a section should talk with the section producer about how to proceed.

Web Summary

If you're a "guest" from another platform writing a brief for the Web, keep these simple guidelines in mind:

- Don't worry about the technical aspects. A producer will assist you.
- Write in inverted pyramid style, with the most important facts up top and presented in descending order.
- Write short. For TV reporters, think of about a **minute** of copy. For print reporters, you're writing a brief of 5 to 6 inches.
- Don't wait for that follow-up phone call. Give what you have when you have it. You can update the story later.

What Newspaper Editors Want

Writing for print presents special challenges to journalists not accustomed to the medium. We've already discussed the challenge broadcasters face in putting aside video and learning to tell a story in a more linear fashion. Newspapers also provide a wide variety of story forms, ranging from the quite simple to the very complex.

Story Measurement

The very first challenge a broadcaster who wants to write for a newspaper faces is learning how to measure story length. Broadcasters measure stories in seconds. Print journalists measure them in inches. In broadcasting, read rates vary from talent to talent but generally fall in the range of about 180 words per minute. In a newspaper, a **column inch** literally is a column of copy one inch in height. The number of words contained in such an inch might vary from paper to paper depending on the width of that newspaper's standard column, the size of font being used, line spacing, and so forth. In the *Tampa Tribune* a column inch averages about 32 words. A minute of copy works out to about $5\,^1/_2$ inches of newspaper space—about the size of a typical **brief.** Most newspaper stories run somewhat longer than that: 9 to 12 inches is about right for a medium-sized story, and it goes up from there depending on the type of the story.

Newspaper writers typically use specialized software that converts word count into inches. Broadcasters also use specialized software, but theirs converts word count into minutes and seconds. When a newspaper reporter gets an assignment, it usually comes with the number of column inches the newspaper editors have budgeted for the story. A newspaper assignment rundown, in fact, is referred to as the "budget." Broadcasters who receive an assignment to write for the paper can divide the space assigned by 5.5, and that will give a ballpark figure for the length of the desired copy in minutes. Done this way, a 14-inch assignment works out to about $2\,^1/_2$ minutes. If you prefer, you can also multiply the column-inch assignment by the number of words per column and then divide by 180, as follows:

14 column inches $\times$ 32 words per inch = 448 words

448 words $\div$ 180 words per minute = 2.5 minutes

The length of your assignment is critical to knowing how to approach it. An assignment of 5 to 6 inches is a brief. This is about the same as the Web update we discussed in the previous section, and the editor will probably expect you to write it the same way, in inverted pyramid style. If the assignment is longer, your story style might be different. In either case, you'll want to have a discussion with your editor regarding the story and any special needs such as photographs and graphics development.

Story Style

As discussed, the most basic story form in a typical newspaper will probably be the *brief*—5 to 6 inches, or possibly less, presented in inverted pyramid style, giving the story a very quick hit-and-run treatment. Story styles go up from there in complexity. Once upon a time virtually all stories in newspapers were presented in inverted pyramid style. Although inverted pyramid is still quite common, a wide variety of styles can be found in the typical newspaper. If you're writing a feature for the Sunday edition, you'll probably choose a narrative or analytical style. But if you're writing a hard-news daily assignment for the *Tampa Tribune,* the editor might ask you to employ a style that's sort of a cross between traditional narrative or anecdotal storytelling and the inverted pyramid.

Morris Kennedy is the *Tampa Tribune*'s editor for politics and government. He landed his first newspaper job in 1972, and in the past 30 years he's just about done it all—general assignments, police reporter, political writer, editorial writer, assignment editor, the works. He's had some experience in helping nonprint reporters write for the *Tribune.* Kennedy says, "Almost any story is better if it's not inverse pyramid, if you can pull it off." He describes a new style of reporting that's evolved to replace it, or at least supplement it. "What's developed beyond the inverse pyramid is the idea of hooking the reader at the beginning of the story then giving them a nut graph, that's basically the lead of the old inverse pyramid, about five graphs in, saying, 'Why should I read this?'" That "hook" at the top of the story can come in the form of an anecdote, but Kennedy says it doesn't have to. "It could be like just a real jazzy little two lines or one, like, 'Mr. Jones was hanging from his fingernails from the back of his car as it went off the bridge. And he thought about his cat.' Or whatever."

Once the writer has the reader's attention, about four or five paragraphs down the writer will present the **nut graf.** It's not a paragraph about nuts, but rather a passage or two that serves a function similar to TBO.com's story abstract. (In fact, when TBO runs a *Tampa Tribune* story, its producers often look for that print "nut graf" and pull it up as the abstract.) From there, the story can proceed in whatever manner the writer chooses. The writer can present it in narrative storytelling style, presenting the facts in chronological order. It can proceed "diamond style" as we discussed in our chapter about the television package form, beginning anecdotally with a typical "someone" who's affected by the issue, broadening to discuss the issue in general terms, and then returning to the person affected for a final thought. The writer can use an analytical style, presenting the issues along with quotes and observations from newsmakers and experts. Says Kennedy, "You might want to digress to some expert talking about whatever it might be. In a newspaper story a lot of it is not just what happened, but people commenting on what's going on." Comments from experts or observers can amplify the story, give greater depth, and provide context or perspective. After that, says Kennedy, "Then you go back to what happened. Or perhaps offer a dissenting view." Options are limitless.

Though you might decide not to write your story in inverted pyramid style, Kennedy suggests you start it that way with a quick summary. "For a television news reporter I would suggest just writing three paragraphs that say everything, and then build off of that." Those three paragraphs won't be your story, nor will they be *in* your story. But they will get you thinking of what the story is about, and how to develop it.

Working with Editors

When you write as a reporter for television or for the Web, you'll work with a line producer. The print equivalent of that is an assignment editor, also referred to as an assigning editor. Unlike television, in a print newsroom there's more than one assignment editor, each responsible for a different beat or coverage team. Kennedy says the very first thing you should do when you receive your assignment is to talk with that editor to find out what's expected and seek guidance about how to develop the story. The last thing you want to do, says Kennedy, is to just hand it in and hope for the best. "It's a lot better to work at the beginning and the middle and the end on these things. That's what editors are for."

When you submit your story draft, the assigning editor will check it in detail for grammar, spelling, style, and basic reporting. Among other things, he or she will want to know if you've left anything out. Are all of your facts verified? Have you treated all of the characters in your story fairly? Are all important viewpoints represented? Just as relationships between reporters and producers in television news-rooms can be challenging at times, so can the relationship between reporters and editors in a print newsroom. As with television, good editors work with the reporters to make needed changes, rather than make those changes unilaterally, but the closer the story is to deadline, the greater is the likelihood of changes being made without consulta-tion. Says Kennedy of editors, "If you don't like the whole opening five paragraphs or something, or you don't like the lead, or you've got questions that need reporting, then you mark the questions in the story and you put it back in the shared basket everybody works out of and you say, 'I've got some questions or I want you to rewrite the lead,' and they'll do that." Kennedy says editors will take it upon themselves to rewrite copy if it's late in the day and the reporter has gone home. But, he says, "If it's a really dramatic change, you would generally call them up and say, 'Here's what I did, what do you think?'"

When the assigning editor is happy with your copy, he or she will pass it up the line. A team leader, senior editor, or even the managing editor might also review it. If all goes well, eventually it will land in the hands of a copy editor. This person, according to Kennedy, will also double-check for such details as spelling, grammar, and style, but "is much less likely to make substantive changes." If the copy editor does have a major problem with the content of the story, then he or she will likely call the assigning editor to discuss it. Once the copy issues are fully resolved, the copy editor will write the headline and also add any computer coding necessary to format the story into the newspa-per's page production system.

Negotiating for Space: The Role of the Page Designer

Most television reporters assume that whenever a newspaper wants to report more news, it can just add in a few extra pages. This is theoret-ically possible, but it just doesn't happen very often, primarily because of the costs associated with producing extra pages. So just as a television producer has a set space to work with, so does a newspaper's content team. In fact, both platforms use the same term to describe the predetermined amount of space available for news each day: It's called the news hole. And it's not very flexible. So if you decide your story needs more space, you're asking a lot.

Still, it's possible to negotiate more space for a story. First you have to convince your assignment editor. If the editor agrees, he or she will have to go see the page designer. Just like a newscast producer, the **page designer** has many conflicting demands on the limited amount of space available. There's another parallel to television: The later you wait to ask for more time, the more difficult it will be to get it, and the more cross the page designer will be at you for asking. But Kennedy says such give-and-take happens all the time. "That's a constant conversation between one editor and another. And it's because you just can't, even though the people who lay out the pages would love it, you just cannot predict what the news is going to be that accurately." That explanation will certainly sound familiar to any television producer who's had to juggle the rundown at the last minute to accommodate breaking news or changing story lengths. When pressed, a page designer does what that newscast producer usually has to do: shorten someone else's story or kill it in order to make room for yours. So if you do want more space, ask for it, but make sure your request is reasonable and your case compelling.

Tips and Pitfalls

Read the Newspaper's Style Guide

Chances are the newspaper for which you're proposing to be a guest writer has a style guide. If so, get your hands on a copy. The guide will give you the newspaper's standardized way to handle job titles, place names, and other details in news stories. For example, a common mistake writers make is to refer incorrectly to the titles of members of Congress. If Jane Shoepound is serving in the Senate, her title in the *Tampa Tribune* will be "Sen. Jane Shoepound." If she's in the House of Representatives, then her title will be "U.S. Rep. Jane Shoepound." In neither case will it be "Cong. Jane Shoepound," which is a common mistake writers make in television as well. Says Kennedy, "The less time spent finding and fixing petty stuff like this means more time spent on the story's content and meaning. It's the reporter's responsibility to know these style rules and follow them."

Life without Video

The biggest change television broadcasters face in trying to write for the paper, of course, is doing without video. If you want to give your readers a picture, you have to paint it for them in words. Kennedy says this difference between the platforms is profound. With television, he says, "You can see the person cry, you can see the expression on their face, you can see the house they live in, you can see the blown up building or the wrecked car. You can see what the weather's like outside. But in a print story, you have to give them everything like that. You can't rely on the camera to convey anything. You've got to put it all in words." And those words must not only capture the pictures you might have shown in your television story, but also capture the nuances. "Details and subtleties of expression and tone of voice and whether someone's angry and yelling—you've got to say that in the story."

Be Specific   Television reporters sometimes gloss over the details. Newspapers fill them in. Be specific in your reporting. If you know the time something happened, give it. If the subject of your story is hospitalized, give the name of the hospital. Be very specific in your attributions, and be wary of referencing "officials," "authorities," and so on. Give their names.

Be Careful of First-Person Reporting   Kennedy recalls only one time when he asked for and received a complete rewrite. In that case, the TV reporter had written the newspaper story in the first person. Kennedy says newspaper reporters do that only rarely, and a first-person account wasn't a good choice for this particular story. "I had to get him out of the way so people could see what was happening to the people he was reporting on."

Use Multiple Sources   A television reporter or producer won't bat an eye at writing a story with only one quoted source—such is the precise nature of most VOBITES. But unless your print story is just a 5-inch brief, your assigning editor probably is going to want more than one source.

Give a Sense of Closure   Broadcast reporters also don't worry much about not having all the answers. As we discussed earlier, if you don't have the story nailed by noon, you'll catch up to it by 5 P.M. But newspaper managers do prefer that final stitch to sew up the story. Says Kennedy, "It's gotta sit there for 24 hours. And you certainly don't want people picking up the other paper and finding something that you don't have." Kennedy says newspapers, like any other medium, certainly have ongoing stories. Perhaps you can't end the novel, but do your best to at least close the current chapter before the presses roll.

Story Form Examples

As we mentioned earlier, newspaper story forms range from the very brief and simple to the very long and complex. In the Tampa News Center, it's not unheard of for a television reporter to write a long story, but the most common forms by far are much shorter. In the following section we'll look at a few examples and discuss the story styles employed in each. The goal won't be to make you an expert, but simply introduce you to some basic forms to help you get around on a print platform.

The Brief

Example 1: Narrative Brief

Deputy: Man Arrested after Fight, Boat Wreck

CLEARWATER—Two people were injured in a boating accident Saturday afternoon in Clearwater Pass.

Details were not available, but a deputy from the Pinellas County Sheriff's Office marine unit and witnesses at the scene said a husband and wife apparently began fighting aboard their boat as they throttled up to leave the busy beach on the north side of the pass.

The couple's boat broadsided another that was idling in the pass, and the passenger of the broadsided boat either jumped or was thrown from the vessel.

The victim was airlifted from the scene.

The sheriff's deputy said the husband was arrested on a domestic violence charge. His wife was transported to a hospital.

No names or formal charges had been released late Saturday.

This is a typical "hard news" brief. It appeared in a Sunday *Tampa Tribune* in the "Metro" section grouped with three other stories, under the banner "Law and Order." The story is 125 words long, not including the headline. Our rule of thumb of 32 words to the inch would predict a length of about 4 column inches, which is precisely what this brief measured without the headline. The style is very straightforward: just the facts to the extent that they're available. The way the story develops has parallels to a television VO. The first line is a summary providing an overview of the story. The story proceeds from there in more or less chronological order and concludes with a clear ending. This is a narrative style, which is very appropriate for a short spot news story of this nature. Unlike a television VO, every sentence including the lead is presented in past tense.

Example 2: Inverted Pyramid Brief

County Hoping to Reel in Big-Bucks Bass Tournaments

LAKE PLACID—Highlands County Commissioners considered a plan this week to develop a park on Lake Istokpoga in an effort to lure some big bass tournaments to the area.

Some of the events can last the better part of the week and provide a boost for the economy.

Officials have talked about the need for more access to Lake Istokpoga, but now the County Commission is faced with deciding whether Windy Point near Lake Placid is one of the spots where it would like to improve access for those big bass tournaments.

Commissioners took a first step recently when they voted 5–0 to authorize Parks and Recreation Director Vicki Pontius to apply for a $200,000 state grant to improve 38 acres adjacent to the county's boat ramp off Windy Point Road.

Bob Balgemann

This brief runs 132 words not counting headline and byline, which works out to about $4\,^1/_8$ column inches. The style is inverted pyramid. It begins with the most important fact, and then presents the remaining facts not in chronological order, but in more or less descending order of importance. This style is perfectly appropriate for briefs about the actions of governmental bodies or citizens' groups, which are often centered on meetings rather than incidents.

The common denominator in both of these examples is that both quickly presented "just the facts. "

Full-Length Stories   The newspaper equivalent of the TV reporter's **package** is a bylined report running a minimum of about 9 to 12 inches. Although much longer stories are certainly possible, if you're a "visiting" journalist and are asked to write a bylined story for a newspaper, chances are you'll wind up writing something of about the length and style of the example presented below. (The names and locations presented in this story and other examples below have been changed.)

Example 3: Hard News, Inverted-Pyramid Report

Deputy Cleared in Fatal Shooting of Bat-Wielding Suspect

By Bill Heery

An undercover deputy was in fear for his life and was justified when he fatally shot a Farthington man who came at him with a bat last month, the State Attorney's Office said today.

Michael Canton, 22, was no more than three feet from the deputy with the bat raised over his head when the officer fired a single shot from his .45-caliber pistol, Assistant State Attorney Carson Reagan wrote in a report released this morning. The deputy, who tried to retreat, was in imminent danger, Reagan said.

The deputy, whose name hasn't been released, was part of a team of officers who surrounded the home on Rose Road to serve a search warrant on the morning of July 26 when Canton, who lived in a converted shed, swung open the shed door suddenly with the bat over his head in a threatening manner, Reagan said. The deputy tried to retreat but Canton kept coming.

Powder burns showed that the suspect was within three feet of the officer when he fired, Reagan said.

The officers identified themselves as deputies before the fatal shooting, his report said.

Authorities said they seized about a half-pound of methamphetamine, 6 ounces of cocaine, two marijuana plants, and $900 cash from the house.

Deputies obtained a search warrant after a confidential informant twice bought methamphetamine there, Reagan said in his report.

The sheriff's office recently went to court seeking an injunction to prohibit The Bugle newspaper in Farthington from publishing the deputy's name. The department said making his name public would place him in danger.

A judge issued a temporary injunction last week, but on Tuesday another judge, Circuit Judge Bill Falcon, ruled that the newspaper was free to use the deputy's name. The Bugle hasn't said how the newspaper obtained the name and hasn't yet published it.

Bugle Executive Editor Louise Brackwater couldn't be immediately reached this morning for comment.

This story is 314 words long, not including the headline and byline. That's about $9\,3/4$ inches of copy. It's written with a traditional lead in inverted pyramid style. A television or Web reporter asked to write a newspaper story probably won't go wrong in choosing this style.

Though inverted pyramid is common, as Morris Kennedy showed us earlier, it's not the only tool in the box. Below are examples of other methods a writer might use to get into a story.

Example 4: "Quick Attention Grabber"

TAMPA—They Couldn't Run, and Ultimately, They Couldn't Hide.

The 2001 season proved a humbling experience for Tampa Bay's maligned offensive line. When fans began jeering, fingers were pointed and players retreated as the Buccaneers finished with the No. 30 ground game in a 31-team league.

(Ira Kaufman)

This example from a *Tampa Tribune* sports story shows the technique of using a "quick attention grabber" to get into the story.

Example 5: "Narrative Anecdotal Lead with Nut Graf"

TAMPA—Heat radiates from the vacant room as Bob Mills hides in the shadows behind a tattered window screen. On the street below, one man hands a small white rock to another, who stashes it into his jeans pocket and scurries away.

The radio in Tampa Police Sgt. Stephan Argent's unmarked car crackles to life as Patruski describes the buyer. . . . "On India right now. He bought rock cocaine." Argent revs the engine and whips the car north on Nebraska Avenue to Central Park Village. A left turn on India Street. There's the man.

Within seconds, backup detectives rush the buyer, handcuff him, and search him for drugs.

It's not quite 8 a.m. on a muggy Wednesday. The team known as the Quad Squad will make 12 more arrests by day's end; firehouse officers follow with an additional five. The group confiscated 15 grams of crack and five grams of marijuana.

[NUT GRAF:]

Quad Squad No. 85 formed in November 2001 as the city's fourth street-level drug unit. The team is dedicated to fighting drug traffic in communities east of Nebraska Avenue and south of Lake Avenue: Ybor City, East Tampa, and parts of downtown Tampa.

(Sherri Ackerman)

This is a very traditional "anecdotal" lead, jumping right into the story narrative and hooking the viewer with several paragraphs of fast-paced story action. The nut graf a few paragraphs down summarizes what this story is all about. (The full story ran about 30 inches.)

Example 6: "Teaser Anecdotal Lead with Nut Graf"

ST. PETERSBURG—Dog food and diapers. That's what Patricia McMinn had in mind while heading into the store.

Before she could grab a cart, she was asked to grasp this: Should voters get to decide whether to give constitutional protection to a resurrected statewide governing board for Florida's public universities?

Sure, McMinn decided, offering her signature and voter information to a paid petitioner.

Education is too influenced by politics, she said. And although she couldn't explain precisely how this new proposal would fix that, she could defend why stopping people cold outside a discount store is a fair way to get a sweeping higher education reform plan on the ballot in November.

"This is my only day off," said McMinn, 40. "Where else would I go, to City Hall to sign up for this? And how would I know there's a petition to sign? This makes it more convenient."

[Nut graf:]

Across Florida, roughly 520,000 people have given their approval to a university referendum only a sliver of them fully understand. Any day, supporters expect to wrap up months of collections with more than enough signatures to put their plan on the ballot.

(Ben Feller)

This example begins anecdotally, with an example or incident taken from real life for the purpose of illustrating the issue. The anecdote is short, a "teaser" designed to quickly hook the reader into the story. The author fully captures the issue a few lines down in the "nut graf."

Example 7: "Rhetorical Statement with Nut Graf"

TAMPA—Annexation isn't a word Hillsborough County likes to hear.

But Tampa City Council is expected to voice its desire today for the largest annexation of Mayor Dick Greco's era.

City officials expect K-Bar ranch, a high-end development on 2,280 acres stretching from New Tampa to the Pasco County line, will infuse its coffers with property, gas, and sales taxes.

Annexation is vital to Tampa's growth, said Ron Rotella, a consultant to Greco. He points to negative growth in population prior to previous annexations in the area around University of South Florida.

"That's not healthy for any city whether it's Tampa or a city in the Midwest," he said.

[Nut graf:]

But there is debate about whether annexing a large tract of rural land and providing city services as it develops is good economics. The city expands, but new homes require new roads, sewers, water, parks, fire and police protection, and other services.

(Kathy Steele)

This excerpt begins with a rhetorical statement, jumping right into the story. A few paragraphs down is the nut graf.

Example 8: "Rhetorical Question"

WASHINGTON—What do Florida's teachers, high-tech entrepreneurs, professional baseball teams, influential lobbyists, retired chief executives, most-feared trial lawyers, and thoroughbred race-horse breeders have in common?

All made six-figure contributions during the 2000 election to Florida's political parties, which raised more in unlimited "soft money" donations than the political parties in any other state, according to an analysis of state and federal records released Tuesday.

(Keith Epstein)

This example, from a 30-inch analysis piece, makes use of a question to hook the reader.

Print Summary   Newspapers and other print media present a wide array of story styles and lengths. If you're writing as a "guest" from another platform, you probably won't be expected to know all the nuances and ins and outs of the print world. Your editor will work with you to choose the story length and format that's right for you. Present the facts in a straightforward fashion. Closely attribute. Sweat the details. Keep it simple, especially when approaching print for the first time.

A Final Word about Convergence

As a model for journalism, convergence is in its infancy and has just begun to evolve. In an industry strongly bound by tradition, we're exploring new territory. University administrators wonder now how to prepare students for what's coming. Will journalists of today and those coming up behind them be able to survive in the converged workplaces of the future? It is, perhaps, the wrong question. The better question might be: Will the workplaces of today be able to attract and keep the converged journalists of the future? They're already here, and more are on the way. Adrian Phillips of TBO.com points out that today's journalism graduates want more. "They see the fact that you're getting video, you're getting audio, you're getting print . . . you're getting all the stuff that's just so exciting that they're now expecting out of their experience with the media. They're going to want to harness all of that stuff." And, he adds, "Employees are going to demand it from employers." In the world that's coming—and which is, in some measure, already here—it's not difficult to believe that the dominant news organizations will be those doing the best job of recruiting multimedia journalists using their skills to the fullest, for the benefit of the public.

DOs and DON'Ts in the Brave New World of Convergence

Do

- Know that the first benefit of convergence is cooperation.
- Understand that each platform has a unique copy style.
- Understand the basics of how to write for another platform.
- Know what editors expect from your story.
- Understand that utilizing another platform gives your story more reach and impact.

Don't

- Forget that the story belongs to the public.
- Try to use the same approach for stories on different platforms.
- Assume you have to be an expert to write for another platform.
- Start writing before discussing your story with your editor.
- Let your fears stop you from trying to cross over!

SO YOU WANT A JOB? THE ART OF THE RÉSUMÉ

The question I'm asked most often has nothing to do with any of the gems of wisdom thus far imparted in this book. It's simply this: "How do I land a job?" Or, in its indirect form, "What do you look for in a résumé tape?" This section will provide some answers to those questions and arm you with information that, we hope, will help you find, land, and keep a job. The information and advice herein are based on my own personal hiring preferences, on practices I've witnessed during my time in the industry, and on feedback from other news directors, some of whom are quoted here.

What Does a News Director Look For?

Of course, every news director is different. That's a good thing, or else few people would be able to land jobs! Tastes vary. What doesn't appeal to one news director might appeal to another. However, when a news director looks at a tape or résumé, some factors are of great or possibly even universal importance. Primarily these factors are talent, experience, qualifications, and references.

Talent

Plainly speaking, is the candidate any damned good? If the candidate is applying for an on-air position, the news director will judge talent— in most cases, rather quickly, I'm afraid—from the résumé tape. News directors will judge line producer, photographer, and editor candidates the same way. Assignments desk and off-line producing or writing candidates normally skip this step, and news directors make their preliminary judgments directly from the written résumé.

Experience

Has the applicant performed this job before, or done anything that might prepare him or her for the job? If the candidate currently holds a similar job, how long has he or she been doing it? Did he or she have any major successes, as judged by ratings, blockbuster stories, or professional awards?

Entry-level candidates with no professional experience aren't excused from this question. If the candidate is a recent graduate looking for an entry-level job, what kind of experience did he or she gain while in college? Internships or media-related extracurricular activities are important here. Woe betide the candidate who graduates from college and starts looking for that first job without having worked as an intern or at least gained experience some other way, such as by working at the campus newspaper, yearbook, or radio or TV station.

Minimum Qualifications

When posting a job many news directors will list the minimum qualifications required for the job—a college degree, perhaps of a specific type; thus-and-so years of experience; skills or experience with particular kinds of journalism; knowledge of particular software systems or equipment; and so forth. Candidates rightly perceive that there probably is some wiggle room in meeting these requirements, especially if the job advertisement uses the word "preferred" rather than "required" in listing the qualifications managers are seeking. But even if there is "wiggle room" you at least have to be close to the mark. Use some common sense. As News Director Christine Riser of WJHL-TV in Johnson City, Tennessee, puts it, "If I've written that I want someone with 4–5 years experience, it's a waste of my time and your postage for you to send me your materials if you graduated this past weekend and have never held a full-time reporting job."

References

What kinds of references does the candidate have? Here, what's important isn't the number of references, but the type and quality. It's usually a given that your cronies and friends will speak highly of you. What news directors really want to know is what your supervisors have to say about you. If a candidate doesn't list a single news manager as a reference, we distrusting, evil-minded news directors usually assume there's a reason why.

What if you don't want your supervisors to know you're looking for a job? Speaking personally, I've never worked for a television station that didn't respect and support the efforts of its employees to step up in the world. I once worked in a television newsroom in which the boss would even pick up the phone and help his employees find jobs elsewhere, if that's what they wanted to do. Not only were there no hard feelings, but this particular newsroom was known to hire some of those people back from time to time (in fact, I was one of them). Alas, not every television station is like that. But even if you must be discreet, you still should work hard to provide references who aren't just friends and cronies. For instance, producers and assignments editors, who are notoriously hard to please, make good references.

If you blew something up on the job and don't have any references, believe it or not, it's not necessarily the end. You can take some solace in the fact that not every news director checks references or, at least, checks them well. Even if a potential employer does learn of a problem on a previous job, history suggests many news directors might be willing to give you a second shot if you have the talent.

The Cover Letter and Résumé

How good should your résumé and cover letter be? In terms of spelling and grammar, they should be *absolutely perfect.* The cover letter and résumé speak volumes about the quality of the candidate. Presumably, landing a job is the single most important task on your personal agenda. If your résumé and cover letter aren't important enough for you to get right, then what will be? Is your potential employer to presume that if you exhibit sloppiness, illiteracy, or incompetence on the résumé and cover letter that you'll suddenly blossom into a quality performer *after* you get the job? Not. Your prospective employer will rightly assume that your cover letter and résumé represent your personal best, and will judge you accordingly.

An applicant for a writing job once sent me a cover letter that contained the following sentence (the locations have been changed to protect the guilty):

> I just currently moved down to Texas in June from Florida, where from time to time I worked for NBC, ABC, and ESPN from time to time in a freelance capacity from time to time.

Needless to say, the applicant didn't get the job. But I was so enamored of this particular line of prose that I framed it and hung it on the wall of my office.

Another common mistake applicants make is to address the letter to the wrong person, or to no person. If you're responding to a job ad, send your tape to the person and address the ad requests. If you're writing the news director directly, take a moment to figure out who the news director is. Do *not* address your letter to "News Director" and then begin with the salutation "To Whom It May Concern." It won't concern anyone. News Director Shane Moreland of WSLS in Roanoke, Virginia, puts it this way: "Right now I'm staring at 162 videotapes and résumés for one reporter position. And this is the 67th market! I can afford to be real choosy. If I get a cover letter that says "Dear Sir or Madam" or anything of the like, I toss it. When it comes to reporters, they'd better know how to dig. If they can't even discover my name, how will they ever break a story?" And by they way, when you're digging to find out who the news director is, do *not* rely on Internet reference sites, broadcasting yearbooks, and the like. Call the station directly and ask. It's the only way you can be assured of getting it right. Consider it your first demonstration of journalistic prowess. WJHL's Riser says she once disqualified an anchor candidate who flubbed this test. Her explanation to the infuriated candidate: ""First impressions are critical and yours was not an overly impressive one."

Although spelling and good grammar on your cover letter and résumé count, the news director is probably not looking for prose by Ernest Hemingway. Remember, you're proposing a business transaction here—your services in trade for a piece of the news director's hard-won and jealously guarded news budget. Your letter should state in plain terms what's in it for the employer. It should provide, in order of priority, the following information:

- What job it is you're seeking (you'd be absolutely amazed how many candidates don't say).
- Your qualifications for the job—and a brief statement as to why you believe you're the best candidate for it.
- Your salary requirements. Speaking personally, we aren't negotiating a final figure here, but I need to know if we're within shouting distance. I have a certain amount of money to

shop with, and if you're already making more than I can pay, then we're wasting each other's time. It's better to find that out sooner rather than later. Don't say "salary is negotiable" without naming a range, unless you really, really mean it—and as a test, if you aren't willing to accept a cut in pay, then you don't mean it.

- Whether you're under contract or any other legal encumbrances, how much notice you'd have to give your current employer, and how quickly you could relocate. Again, this is to avoid wasting each other's time. If you're under a contract that doesn't expire until six months from now, the news director needs to know this up front.

You don't need to provide any more information than that, unless you're responding to a job ad specifically asking for more information such as a detailed statement of news or management philosophy. As your prospective employer, I don't need to know how much you love the business; how much you'd like to live in my part of the country or in my specific city; the fact that your sister, brother, uncle, or mother-in-law lives here; or any of the other thousands of extraneous things candidates love to place on cover letters. In fact, this information could work to your detriment. For instance, if you convince a prospective employer that you really do want nothing more in life than to work for that station and live in that city, the station conceivably could offer you less money. After all, why pay a premium to entice someone who's already highly motivated to come?

For the résumé itself, keep it basic: name, objective, contact information, education, relevant experience, and employment history in the field of broadcast news, any relevant leadership or community service organizations or projects, and any awards you've won. In the contact section, if you have an e-mail address, be sure to include it. The ideal résumé is just one page long and should never run more than two.

When it comes to cover letters and packaging, take some advice: Don't get cute. Many applicants suffer from a strange and exotic mental condition known as *Resumus Tapus Sillyatus*—a thankfully still rare condition that forces candidates to take extraordinarily dramatic, sometimes outright goofy steps to call attention to their applications. I once received a tape contained in a plastic report case $8^1/_2$ inches wide, 11 inches long, and 4 inches deep. When I finally succeeded in prying my way into the case, I found a videotape recessed in a deep pocket on one side, and a three-ring binder enclosing a thick résumé packet including glossy photos and newspaper clippings on the other side. Very impressive—but the only impression I was looking for was what was on the tape, and it was only average. News Director Larché Hardy of WMBB-TV in Panama City, Florida, once received a huge box containing a videotape enclosed with a set of battery cables. According to Larché, the caption read, "Let me jump start your newscast." Larché says, "After all of that, I watched the first 10 seconds." He adds that the candidate wasn't that good. If you want to send me a bottle of salsa to emphasize that your reporting will add spice to my newscasts, I'll probably keep the salsa, but your tape will still have to speak for itself. Creative flair in résumé packaging might be appropriate if you're looking for a sales or marketing job, but for news jobs it's just a distraction.

Job Stability

Another factor many news directors look for is job stability. A certain amount of jumping from job to job is understandable, especially if you've started out in a small-market, low-paying job. But after a jump or two, one hopes you'd stop and catch your breath for a while. In addition to the rate at which you change jobs, news directors may also look at the *kinds* of moves you make. For instance, if you're a reporter and in the past 18 months you've moved from a job in the 90th market to one in the 95th market, and then to one in the 85th market, your prospective employer might reasonably wonder what's driving you, and whether you changed jobs voluntarily or were run off. On the other hand, if you've jumped upward several market sizes each time you've moved, this fits the profile of someone whose career is tracking upward.

Speaking personally, if you've changed jobs every six months for the past three years, I'm not going to be interested in you, period. I don't think I'm overly demanding, but for contracted jobs I'm going to want at least a two-year commitment. For noncontracted jobs, I usually request a one-year verbal commitment. These days, many news directors especially in the larger markets, ask for more than that. Your past track record will show whether you're inclined to make and keep such commitments.

The Interview Process

If you make it through the steps above, you'll be on a "short list" of finalists, from which the news director will choose one or two candidates for personal interviews. Some news directors hire by phone, but most will fly the candidate in for a face-to-face interview.

There's only one secret for success in getting through the interview: Be yourself! Don't try to be something you're not. In some (if not most) organizations, a person's personality is an important factor in the hiring process. News directors want to know not only that you'll be good at your job, but also that you'll fit well into that particular newsroom environment. The last thing you want to do is to present a false portrait of yourself and your personality. If you do and you land the job, then both you and your employer will be unhappy, if not miserable, in the long run.

It does help if you do a little homework to find out about the market and that particular newsroom's challenges. Again speaking personally, I'm almost always impressed with a candidate who knows something about my station's news philosophy and position in the market. Call ahead and speak with a few people in the newsroom. If you're feeling particularly industrious, you might even want to talk with some of the station's competitors. Doing so will allow you to talk with the news director much more intelligently about the job at hand.

During your visit, be prepared to demonstrate your skills. Many stations will give a writing test of one form or another, even for veteran candidates. Some have formal tests; others might simply throw wire copy at you and ask you to rewrite it. Some news directors have been known to take all reporting candidates for a "test-drive," asking them to actually go out into the field and turn a story. Some chief photographers do the same for photojournalist and editor candidates.

Remember that the interview process is as much for you as it is for the station. As much as it's checking *you* out, you must check *it* out. Ask tough questions. Talk with employees. Find out whether this particular company is one for which you'd like to work. It does go both ways, and keep in mind that there are a lot of really bad television stations out there! As the saying goes, look before you leap.

Negotiating

If all goes well, the news director will offer you a job. Now it's time to negotiate a salary, moving expenses, perks, and the like. Probably by this point you've named a salary range. The news director might attempt to lowball you (hey, nothing personal—it's just business). Make a counter offer. If neither you nor the news director is greedy (which is by no means a given), you should be able to reach a mutually acceptable figure without a great deal of pain and suffering.

Also keep in mind that not every news director plays this "you go high, I'll go low" game. Some will tell you flat-out that the job pays such and such a figure, nonnegotiable. Says WSLS's Moreland, "I really, really do offer the 'final' number up front. It takes the guess work out for both parties." If the news director is adamant that he or she has named the top dollar figure, saying "no" and walking away from the deal is certainly an option for you, but don't make the mistake of digging in your heels and being argumentative. Instead, you might want to see if there's anything else on the table to talk about. In the case of on-air people this could include, among other things, a clothing allowance, contract "outs" for certain markets or market sizes, and other considerations. For all employees, it could include such things as the shift to be worked, moving expenses, cell phone access, and so on.

When you think you're negotiating with the news director, actually you might be negotiating with the general manager. If the news director says to you, "Gee, I don't know if I can pay that much, I'll have to check with the GM," don't assume he or she is lying. In fact, in some stations the GM personally handles all negotiations with talent, although it's unusual for any GM to participate in direct negotiations with producers, photojournalists, and assignments editors.

Agents

One question I get asked a great deal is, "Do I need an agent?" Sometimes this question comes from a candidate with whom I'm negotiating. In that case, I consider it improper to give advice, mainly because if I say "no" and then the person doesn't get the money he wanted, he'll forever suspect that I misled him and that he could have gotten a better deal through an agent. But here, just between us, is the truth about agents. They can be very good at helping you find a job, especially if you aren't able to devote your full time and attention to a job search. If you're going into a new station, an agent will usually know what the job is worth and will help see that you get a fair offer. This service is valuable if you're negotiating with a big-market station or a network, but less valuable for most "normal" TV jobs in the medium to smaller markets. Agents would like you to believe they can browbeat a prospective employer into coughing up more cash and benefits. The reality is that in the smaller to medium markets, they're unlikely to be able to "squeeze" the employer enough to cover their commission.

If you're renewing a contract with an existing employer, the chances of your agent being able to extract enough additional money to cover his or her commission decreases dramatically. That's *not* to say, however, that the agent isn't useful or that you shouldn't hire one. A good agent will relieve you of the emotional burden of having to prove your worth and fight for cash. The agent slugs it out for you with the GM or news director. The battle rages around you but you're not part of it, leaving you to concentrate on other things—such as doing your job, for instance. Further, knowing that you have someone on your side who's an expert at employee contracts might give you much-needed confidence that the station is fairly compensating you and not taking advantage of you. Many people feel that peace of mind alone is worth the cost of the commission. Plus, if you suspect you might want to change jobs later, you might need to retain your agent for that reason. Bottom line: agents bring varying degrees of value, but they do cost. Whether you want to spend that money is up to you.

A final word about agents. After the contract is signed, be *very* careful about how you use the agent. Your agent is *not* a shop steward. Some employees like to ask their agents to intercede for them on the job. Many managers find this inappropriate—after all, the station employs you, not your agent. The station is *not* required, under any circumstances, to talk to your agent. This is true even during contract negotiations.

The Résumé Tape

As discussed above, for many positions the résumé tape is absolutely crucial. It's so important it merits a separate discussion.

Photojournalists

For photojournalists, the news director or chief photographer wants to see what you consider to be your best work. Don't load the tape with examples: four or five stories will do for starters. Show the range of your work: include one or two live shots, a good general assignment story, a franchise or series piece, a spot news story. The people hiring you want to see the range of your talents, including:

- How you shoot
- How you edit
- How you light
- Whether you capture and use natural sound
- Good pacing
- How you shoot live shots
- How you shoot stand-ups
- Whether you know when to use a tripod, and when not to
- Your creativity
- Your visual storytelling skills
- Your industriousness

Producers

WFLA-TV's assistant news director will typically ask producers to send "last night's newscast." Producers also usually want to send their best "four alarm fire" newscast. That's fine and we'll look at it, but first we want to see what you're able to do on a slow, "normal" news day. Many other stations hire by the same method.

In landing a job, producers face one hurdle not faced by most of their counterparts, and that's the fact that there are so many different "flavors" of newscast: conservative, middle-ground, tabloid, "big story," and so on *ad nauseam*. When we look for a producer at WFLA-TV, we hope to see a tape that reflects the following abilities and qualities, in descending order:

- Writing ability
- High production value (as reflected through aggressive use of graphics, maps, banners, and the like)
- Copy written to the pictures, and vice versa; no **wallpaper video**
- Live shots
- Team coverage (when appropriate)
- Appropriate story selection
- Stories about real people, not officials
- Good story flow
- Stories containing viewer benefit
- Teases that sell viewer benefit
- Good storytelling within packages (yes, I do hold the producer responsible for that, too)
- Stories showcasing context and perspective
- Anchor showcasing (through tags, 2shot transitions, and appropriate block-ender stories)
- Good pacing
- Stories that provide "breakouts" for the anchors to read (as opposed to having all the information contained within the packages)
- Newscasts that are comfortably timed (anchors aren't rushed or stretched)

The above list is unique to our station; not every news director looks for the same things. Some, for instance, don't care about breakouts. Some look for lots of anchor "happy talk"; others couldn't care less. Some place an extremely high premium on story count; others (us included) place more of an emphasis on stories that take enough time to provide the proper relevance, detail, context, and a human perspective. Most news directors and executive producers I've known place a high importance on the production quality of the newscast. Speaking personally, I place a greater emphasis on writing ability, on the grounds that I can easily teach the former, but not the latter. Bottom line: your tape can't possibly appeal equally to every news director, but basic talent as evidenced through good writing and high production value will stand out and have universal appeal.

If you're currently producing in a small market you might not have access to such goodies as quality graphics, artsy 2shot transitions, live shots, and the like. If so, explain this explicitly in your cover letter. Let the news director know what your limitations are, or else it might be held against you!

Reporters

If you're on the air or are seeking an on-air position, then you've entered a brutally competitive arena. Here's a sobering fact for you: When the news director pops your tape into the machine and presses play, you might have only about 10 seconds to get his or her attention. Most news directors have so many tapes to go through for any given position that they can't possibly view every minute of every tape. So, the tape goes in, the reporter appears, and the news director makes a very quick decision as to whether the candidate is a "keeper." Keeper tapes go into a "hold" box for further review. Many news directors quickly eject the other tapes and toss them into the recycle bin. It's highly subjective, it's brutal, it's unfair, and it's reality. Live with it. Ten seconds. Don't waste it.

Begin your tape with a montage of live and package stand-ups—four or five of the best ones. Follow this up with four or five of your best stories, including two or three examples of live shots. These can be the same stories from which you excerpted your stand-up montage. As mentioned, there's a chance the news director will hit the eject button during the montage and never get around to seeing your stories. Don't make the mistake of concluding that your reporting samples therefore aren't important. If your on-camera work makes the cut, then your stories will get a fair viewing. It's possible to have a decent stand-up montage and then blow your chances with poor packages! Take care to showcase your best work. News directors will want to see at least one example of how you handle spot news, and for most, enterprise reporting will be crucially important. Says WSLS's Moreland, "Anyone can put together a good 'major house fire' story. But I'm looking for reporters who can work their sources and break stories that no one else has."

In examining your résumé tape, news directors generally look for the following talents and qualities, in roughly descending order:

- Good physical appearance
- Good voice
- Good on-camera communication skills—no hesitation or "uhs" and "ahs," no "notes-diving"
- Stand-ups and live work in which the reporter interacts with his or her surroundings, pointing something out, demonstrating something, walking us through a scene, and so forth
- Good writing
- Stories presented in narrative storytelling style
- Stories centering on everyday people, not officials

- Copy written to the pictures, and vice versa; no wallpaper video
- Good use of maps, graphics, and artwork to support the stories
- Good pacing and use of natural sound within the stories
- Stories containing viewer benefit
- Stories containing details, context, and perspective

In your cover letter, make sure you explain the limitations under which your material was shot. If your station doesn't have a live unit, or if you have to shoot your own material, make sure you say so. Otherwise the news director will be looking for live and stand-up elements your tape can't deliver.

Anchors

These days, most anchors also report. Begin your tape with a quick montage showing yourself in different environments—in the studio reading a story, in the field doing live and or taped stand-ups, in the studio on a 2shot or 3shot, and so forth. Follow with some excerpts from some of your anchoring. Include some variety—examples of straight news reading, live shot introductions and tossbacks, reporter Q&A, and the like. Then edit on several examples of 2shot and 3shot teases, tosses, and chitchat. Finally, include three or four examples of your best reporting.

In viewing an anchor/reporter tape, the news director generally looks for all the skills mentioned above regarding reporters, *plus* some or all of the following:

- Good eye contact when reading
- Copy delivered without hemming, hawing, or stumbling
- Proper tone, inflection, and emoting
- Reading with comprehension
- Intelligent Q&A in live shots
- Tasteful and appropriate clothing
- Good posture and body language
- Good teamwork and intelligent interchanges with co-anchors on teases and tosses
- The right personality

"The right personality" can be one of the most important factors, and each news director might be looking for something different. What one news director finds appealing another might find distracting or even repulsive. It's an incredibly subjective business.

Other Issues and Questions

Which Tape Format Should I Use?

The days when $^3/_4$-inch U-matic was the universal professional broadcast video standard are long gone. But it's a poor news director indeed who doesn't have access to a VHS machine either at work or at home. Unless you're responding to a job advertisement that states otherwise, VHS is usually your best bet, and it also has the virtue of being the cheapest. (DVD will probably be next but we're not there yet.) Don't send exotic or computer-based formats unless specifically requested, and never assume the station you're targeting has access to whatever format your current station happens to be using.

The format of your tape might make a difference in your prospects of landing a job. For instance, I still get Beta tapes on occasion. Even when I *did* work in a Beta station, I didn't have a machine in my office (they're *quite* expensive). To view Beta tapes, I had to take them into an edit bay, and ours were almost always in use. So despite Beta being the standard in that newsroom, Beta résumé tapes were in fact the hardest for me to view. But I had a VHS machine in my office, so VHS tapes got first viewing. In my current station, it's even more difficult to play back Beta tapes. If I have a great number of tapes to slog through, the Beta tapes sometimes don't get seen at all.

Labeling and Packaging

You'll do news directors a great service if you label your tape with your name, address, phone number, and *the job you're seeking*. Also, remember that if your tape goes on a "keeper" shelf, the only thing showing will be the spine. Label that with your name and the job you're seeking.

Before mailing your tape make sure you protect it properly. Placing your tape in a hard plastic case is ideal. If you don't have access to one, make sure you at least use the cardboard box the tape came in and a padded envelope. The shutters on VHS tapes are particularly easy to break in transit, and they do.

Some applicants, for reasons that aren't readily apparent, lovingly cocoon their packages in several layers of tape as if they were wrapping a mummy or protecting the crown jewels. This isn't necessary. The tape isn't likely to break out and escape. I've never received a ruptured, empty envelope from a job hopeful. I have, however, been known to throw packages into the trash rather than go out and rent the acetylene torches and hacksaws necessary to get into them.

State Your Objective

Occasionally I receive résumés from applicants who state as a job objective that they're "seeking any job" that will make use of their "skills and abilities in the communications field." If you're willing to do anything, a reasonable assumption is that you're an expert at nothing. "Yes, we have an opening for you. And don't slam it on your way out."

By the time they graduate, serious students will have worked one or two internships in TV newsrooms and should have a good idea of what they'd like to do. Target a specialty and seek it aggressively. That's not to say you can't change your mind. For instance, if you spend six months seeking a reporter's job and come up dry, then you might want to begin again, targeting entry-level producing or copywriting jobs instead. But as former KGUN9-TV (Tucson, Arizona) Managing Editor Craig Smith puts it, "Before you can change your mind, you must first make a decision."

Should I Call?

If you're responding to a job ad that says "No calls," then do yourself a favor: Don't call. Many news directors disqualify people who disregard that admonition. Why? Because they can. If a news director, especially one in a large market, disqualifies you for breaking that rule, then he or she might be left with only 99 other tapes from which to choose. News directors do this not just because they're mean-spirited, cantankerous, antisocial grumps, but because they can't afford not to. Otherwise, they'll spend every waking moment talking to job hopefuls.

If the ad doesn't say "No calls," then the news director is fair game. It won't hurt to call and could help. Even if the news director is too busy to return your call, the message that you're still interested and still available will get through and could make a difference. But here again, do yourself a favor. Don't call with inane questions. Chief among them is, "Did you get my tape?" In my case, all tapes go into a set of drawers until I get the chance to go through them. I don't have the time or inclination to paw through dozens of tapes to find yours and verify its arrival. Believe it or not, FedEx, UPS, and even the postal service don't lose packages very often. Assume your tape has arrived.

News directors are busy people, and being the egomaniacs we are, we think we're even busier than we are. Again, speaking personally, if I get a tape from you, whether it's solicited or not, I'll look at it at some point. If I like it and it's going on the "keeper" shelf, I'll contact you— I promise. If it's not going on the "keeper" shelf but if I think you could benefit from some advice, I might send you some. If I don't like it and don't think there's much potential, you won't hear from me, but you might get a form letter at some point from our Human Resources office letting you know you didn't get the job. This isn't the way things should be, but it's the way things are; most news directors find there simply isn't enough time in the day to give personal service to every job hopeful, especially the unsolicited ones. So, if you haven't heard from the news director after a reasonable amount of time (three to four weeks), you can assume you're not the top candidate for the job.

So when *are* calls appropriate? If a news director calls you and asks you for a tape or informs you that you're on a short list of candidates, ask him or her at that time if it's OK for you to call for an update from time to time. Once a candidate is hired, many news directors will call or write their other "short list" candidates personally to inform them. Not all of them do this, however. Some Human Resources departments will get around to contacting all the candidates to inform them the position has been filled, but this process could take weeks and you can't count on it happening in every case or with every station. So a call to the news director might be the quickest way to find out if you're still in the running for a given job.

Don't abuse the privilege. If a news director doesn't return your call, this usually is a sign that he or she is very busy and you're not the highest priority item at the moment. Believe it or not, this doesn't necessarily mean you're out of the running. But one factor remains absolutely constant: If a news director is interested in you, you *will* get a call eventually.

One alternative to calling is to send e-mail. Some news directors are more likely to respond to a quick e-mail than go to the trouble of placing a phone call. Be sure to include your e-mail address on your cover letter and résumé.

Remember that on-air jobs usually aren't filled quickly. Again drawing on personal experience, once I get an opening, it takes two to three weeks to get approval to hire a replacement; about a week to 10 days to get the job posted on the Internet and in any trade magazines in which I might care to advertise; about three weeks to get in a good selection of tapes and résumés; then about three to four weeks to cull through the tapes, select a list of finalists, and negotiate a deal. This is the *fast* track. It can take much longer. If you've learned you're on a short list, don't despair just because the news director doesn't call you every week. If you're the number two or three candidate, you might not hear from the news director for weeks. Then the news director's negotiations with the top candidate fall through or go sour, and suddenly you find yourself with a job offer. This, too, is how the business works.

Should I Send a Tape Unsolicited?

If you have the time and money to send out unsolicited tapes, then you should do so. You never know when an unsolicited tape might strike a chord with a news director. Some agents make a very good living sending out loads of unsolicited tapes.

Do know that when you send out unsolicited tapes you're fighting an uphill battle. Don't expect instant results. To get a job, your tape must land on the desk of a news director who (1) has the time and inclination to look at it, (2) has an opening, or (3) will get an opening in the not-too-distant future. The odds of all these things coming together quickly at any given station aren't particularly good, but those odds are significantly greater than zero. If you send out a large number of unsolicited tapes, chances are some of them will wind up in the hands of interested news directors. Even if the news director doesn't have a current opening, if your tape goes into a "keeper" stack, then you'll get *first* crack at any openings that do arise. This technique does work, and it's a good choice for anyone who has an unlimited amount of time, energy, and money to devote to the effort of sending out tapes. I personally have hired candidates who sent unsolicited tapes at times when I didn't (yet) have an opening.

If you're not able to devote every waking moment to the job search, however, you'll find it's much more cost-effective to target stations that do have openings. Keep your eye on the trade magazines, scan the Internet, and, if necessary, cold-call stations (assignments editors usually are a good choice of people to call; they know everything).

Networking

The power of networking has been demonstrated again and again. It works. When you send out that first unsolicited tape, you've begun the process of networking. When you cold-call a TV station assignments desk to inquire whether there's an opening, you've opened a door to networking. When you ask a news director if you may call again and he or she says "yes," then you're networking.

A year and a half ago we had an opening for a management position here in the WFLA-TV newsroom. One of the candidates happened to be in town and asked if she could stop by to introduce herself. We hit it off, discovering that we had similar news philosophies. She was a strong candidate for the job and might have gotten it had we not lost the position because of cutbacks in the 2001 broadcast recession. But she kept in touch. When she changed jobs, she dropped me a line to let me know where she wound up. She's called or written a few times since just to chat. That's networking. Recently she called to ask me about an acquaintance of mine who she's thinking of hiring. I think the world of her candidate and said so. He's just been networked and doesn't even know it!

Landing a job where you don't know anyone is tough, though it can be done. Landing a job where you know someone is easiest. But the most *common* is to get a job where somebody knows somebody who knows you! One acquaintance of mine, who's now a major-market news director, uses this technique exclusively. He once told me, "When I want a job, I triangulate. It's a small business. I figure out who's doing the hiring, and then check to see if I know anyone who knows that person." Once he's identified a friend or acquaintance who knows the decision maker, he places a call—not to the decision maker, but to the acquaintance. If he's lucky, the acquaintance will then make a call to the decision maker on his behalf. That's how it works. And it *does* work. Here at WFLA-TV, we recently had an opening that attracted more than 125 applicants (and counting). There's just no way I had the time to return calls to everyone who inquired about the job. But guess which calls *did* get returned? Answer: calls from people offering references—in other words, the networkers. One candidate had three different people call me offering references on his work. By coincidence, that candidate later joined us in a freelance capacity.

If you're starting from scratch, you'll have an uphill climb. If you're a student, start with people you know—friends, instructors, faculty advisers, and so on. Get them to introduce you to their friends. Find out which professional organizations are available in your area and join them. If you can afford to go to conferences and conventions, do so. If you make those aforementioned cold-calls to TV assignments desks, take names and numbers. Ask if you can call again. Get to know people. Here's a hint, though: Don't waste time with people who clearly don't want to be bothered. There are plenty of warm and friendly people out there.

I've landed seven different jobs since leaving college. In six of those seven jobs, I either knew someone at the station, or knew someone who did. That's the power of networking.

Student Question: "What Are My Chances—Really?"

Students have often asked me to look at their tapes and tell them if they have what it takes to land a job in this business. I can examine a tape and tell a student what he or she needs to work on to do a better job, but I've gotten out of the business of trying to tell students what their prospects are for success. I've done this for two reasons. One, I've discovered that my tastes are strictly my own and might not apply to other news directors. Second, if there's any factor that's as important as raw talent, if not more important, it's persistence, and that doesn't show on a tape. I've seen students who I thought had little to no chance of landing an on-air position do just that—because they were persistent and believed in themselves. The converse is also true; I've seen students with an incredible amount of raw talent waste it through lack of ambition and effort.

Still, it's reasonable to ask how much time you should spend looking for that first job before you throw in the towel. My advice is this: Treat your job search the way an entrepreneur would approach a start-up business. If you go to a bank and try to take out a loan to start such a business, the lending officer is going to want to see a business plan. How much capital do you need? How are you going to become profitable? What will it take to get there, and by what timetable? Treat your job search the same way. You decide how much time, energy, and effort you'll be able to devote to searching for a job. Set a timetable. If you haven't begun to "turn a profit" by the end of that time through landing a job, then perhaps the marketplace is telling you something about your employability. You can decide at that time whether you want a specific job and are able to "reinvest" and keep looking, or whether you should change direction and try something else. If you're trying for an on-air position and don't land one, that doesn't mean you have to give up on television. The industry is just as hungry for good producers, assignments editors, and photographers as it is for on-air talent, and those jobs aren't quite so insanely competitive.

Final Points

- Some news directors get irritated at people who cold-call asking whether the station has any job openings—especially if the job hopeful then goes on to ask the mailing address of the station, to whom to address the letter, and the like. You're supposed to be a journalist. Show your journalistic prowess by finding out this information some other way than by calling the insanely busy news director.

- Don't bombard the news director with calls, even if you're on the short list of candidates. Making a pest of yourself isn't a good way to begin a working relationship. Call just enough to let the news director know you're interested and enthusiastic. As a general rule, once a week is fine.

- If you're a recent graduate applying for an entry-level job, you need to list on your résumé only those jobs that have prepared you for the field you're attempting to enter. News directors will assume that, like most students everywhere, you've held a series of part-time or full-time jobs as you worked your way through college. We really don't need to know that you worked as a server at the Bonanza steak house or flipped hamburgers at McDonald's, so there's no need to clutter up your résumé listing these types of positions. (You may, however, list supervisors from these jobs as references.)

If you held no media-related jobs, it's not a deal-breaker for entry-level positions. Instead, on your résumé treat your academic career as if *it* were a job. Explain how it's prepared you for the position you're seeking. List and emphasize any and all media-related extracurricular activities and internships.

- Don't put your life on hold waiting for a news director to make a decision! If you'd really like to go to Station A but Station B has made you a job offer, consider Station B's job offer on its own merits. If you're on the short list of candidates for Station A, then by all means give the news director a call and let him or her know you have another offer. But don't be surprised if Station A doesn't accelerate the selection process to accommodate your schedule. If they're not ready to make a decision, *you* might have to make one.

- If you have an aunt, uncle, or cousin who's a station manager or GM, don't ask him or her to pull strings to get you a job. Most news directors really, really hate this. If you can't succeed on your own merits, find something else to do in life.

- Don't send a résumé that says "references available on request." If you have them, give them.

- Don't make any errors of spelling or grammar on your cover letter or résumé—not any. Have friends and relatives proof it to be sure.

- If you're responding to an advertisement, make sure you tailor your résumé to the job at hand. This is another of Riser's pet peeves. "If I'm hiring a reporter, I don't care to see an entire tape of anchoring," she says. "I want to know the person can do live shots and can report from the field!"

- Never, ever send out an original, irreplaceable tape! Few news directors return tapes. If you want your tape returned, include a self-addressed envelope with the correct amount of postage—and even then, don't hold your breath.

- If you're having a tough time finding a job, don't give up easily. Television news is one of the most selective and competitive industries in the world. But like any industry, it needs good people. If you have the skills, the talent, and the desire, and you're willing to start small and go wherever the job takes you, then you'll make it eventually.

For a quick summary of the points made in this chapter, go to *www.mhhe.com/tuggle*. Good luck.

DOs and DON'Ts on the Résumé

Do

- Make sure your cover letter and résumé are absolutely perfect—zero defects.
- Clearly state the job you're seeking and outline your qualifications for it.
- Conduct some basic research about the station before interviewing.
- Make sure your résumé tape is brief and showcases a good cross-section of your best work.
- Closely follow any instructions in the job advertisement.
- Make a job-seeking plan with a timetable for success.

Don't

- Address your cover letter "To Whom It May Concern."
- Get cute with your packaging and presentation.
- Try to be something you're not in the interview.
- Forget that reporter and anchor tapes should begin with a montage of on-camera work.
- Call if the ad says "no calls."
- Give up too easily.

Word Usage and Grammar Guide

C. A. Tuggle

Many words in the English language are frequently misused. What follows is a list of some of the more common problem words and phrases for broadcasters. This guide or any other stylebook should be supplemented with a good, recently published dictionary, but it's important to note that dictionaries list all the ways that words are used, even in slang. Writers should stick to the definitions that are most accepted, usually the first two definitions listed. Going to the sixth or seventh definition of a word in the dictionary can cause broadcast writers problems in terms of the viewers or listeners being able to follow what's being said. We stress again, television and radio news writers should make sure that what they're writing is easily understood the first time it's heard.

Some Helpful Hints

In broadcasting, you can probably have a successful career without knowing the difference between a complex and a compound-complex sentence, or the difference between a gerund and a participle. But you do have to be able to recognize what the subject of the sentence is, whether verbs and pronouns agree with it, and so on. Here are three guidelines to help in troubling cases.

Using "I" or "Me"

These should be used in conjunction with other nouns and pronouns just the same as they're used when they're alone. For example, you wouldn't say "Bob went to the store with I." You also wouldn't say "Bob went to the store with Jill and I." The key is to remove the second person and the word "and" from the sentence, see if you should use *I* or *me*, and then reinsert the second person and the word "and." It would be "Bob went to the store with me," so it should be "Bob went to the store with Jill and me." Also, it would be "I went to the store," so it should be "Jill and I went to the store."

Identifying the Subject of the Sentence

This is sometimes a problem when the sentence includes a prepositional phrase. For example: "a group of students," "a herd of elephants" and "a coalition of English teachers" are all singular. The general rule is to remove the prepositional phrase, determine whether the subject is singular or plural, use an appropriate verb, then reinsert the prepositional phrase. So take out the phrases "of students," "of elephants," and "of English teachers," and you'll see that it would be "a group goes," so it should be "a group of students *goes*"; it would be "a herd charges," so it should be a "herd of elephants *charges*"; and it would be "a coalition votes," so it should be "a coalition of teachers *votes*."

There is one exception to this. If you're talking about something or someone who is one of many in a group, then the verb should agree with the group. So in situations when you're talking about one of many, don't apply the general rule of removing the prepositional phrase. For example: "She's one of the best teachers who *have* ever worked at City High." The reason you treat these differently is that if you removed the prepositional phrase, all you're left with is "She's one." One what?

Here's another way to think about it. If you lump someone or something into a group, the reference goes back to the group and is plural. However, if you pull that person or thing out of the group and consider the person or thing individually, then it's singular. For example:

"One of the boys is coming to the party."

"He's one of the boys who are coming to the party."

Subject/Verb Agreement

First, you have to determine what the subject is and whether it's singular or plural. How about "Two thousand dollars is/are enough to buy the stereo system"? That's singular, because you're talking about a quantity; so it should read "Two thousand dollars is enough. . . ." If you were referring to 2,000 individual bills, that would be plural, such as with "There were two thousand dollars stacked on top of one another." But with most quantities, the subject is singular. For example: 500 dollars, a million pounds, 2,500 square feet and so on. With most portions and proportions, the subject isn't the amount, but the noun itself. For example, "a third of our viewers," "27 percent of the respondents," and "half the supplies" are all plural.

Giving Human Characteristics to Nonhuman Things

Rescue boats can't pluck people out of the water, unless they're equipped with robotic arms. Plans can't intend to do anything, only planners can. Small craft can't exercise caution on the high seas, Mr. Weatherman, only boaters can. Storms don't *decide* to turn back out into the Atlantic, they just do it. When you write a sentence, make sure that subject is capable of the action (verb) you've assigned to it. Some

things can be done only by living organisms, and the more complicated the task (reasoning, for example) the higher the life form
required to do it.

Word Usage

a, the   Some writing texts advise not using "a" when referring to something that can be numbered because "a" sounds too much like "eight."
However, if we write and pronounce words as we do in conversation,
this isn't a problem. Pronounce the word "a" as "uh" and the word
"the" as "thuh." That's how we all talk, and it sounds very stiff to say "A
(long "a" sound) train derailed and spilled the (as in "thee") cargo."
Also, this allows us to say "a million dollars" and not "one million dollars." The latter sounds a bit stiff, and again, that's not how people talk.
    Also, don't use "the" in the first reference to something. For exam-
ple, don't say "police discovered the body" if the viewers don't know
which body we're talking about. Say "police discovered a body"; then
on subsequent references it's OK to say "the body" because we've
already established which body is the subject of the story.

about   Things happen about a certain time, not around a certain time.
See **on.**

abstinent   See **celibate.**

abuse, misuse   Both words mean to use wrongly or incorrectly, but
abuse often has the added connotation of physical injury or harm.

accept, except   Accept means to receive with approval; except means
to exclude. For example: The club voted to *accept* everyone *except* John.

across, around   Around means encircling; therefore, it's impossible
for things to be happening around a certain area. Instead, things happen across (from one side or end to the other) the state or nation. It
would be around the world, because as Columbus proved, the world
is round.

acute, chronic   Acute is something that's sharp, sudden, and of short
duration. Chronic is of long duration and might or might not also be
acute. So in most cases, acute pain is different than chronic pain.

administration   See **government.**

adopt, approve, enact, pass   Amendments, resolutions, and rules are
adopted or approved. Bills are passed; laws are enacted.

adopted, adoptive   Children are adopted, making their new parents
adoptive.

adversary, opponent   An opponent is anyone on the other side. An
adversary is openly hostile.

adverse, averse   Adverse means harmful or unfavorable, such as with adverse weather. Averse means not in favor of or disposed against.

advice, advise   Advice is a noun, and it's what you give. Some people seem to like to give it whether they're asked for it or not. Advise is a verb and means to give advice, to suggest a course of action.

affect, effect   These words create much confusion, but that doesn't have to be the case. Both can be used as verbs or nouns, but in the most common usage affect is a verb meaning to produce a change or to influence; effect is a noun meaning the change itself, the result. For example:

How will the vote *affect* the council's stance on the proposal?
The *effect* isn't likely to be seen for some time.

affluent, effluent   Affluent typically means wealthy; effluent means liquid waste.

afterward, backward, downward, forward, toward, upward   Not afterwards, backwards, downwards, forwards, towards, or upwards.

aggravate, irritate   Aggravate means to make something worse, as in "He aggravated an old football injury." Irritate means to annoy. You can't aggravate someone nor can you be aggravated about something.

agnostic, atheist   An agnostic believes there's not enough evidence to conclude that there's a God. An atheist believes there is no such thing as God.

allude, elude   To allude is to refer to something indirectly; to elude is to escape from or avoid, often by deceitful means.

although, while   Use although when you mean "in spite of the fact that" or "on the other hand." While means "at the same time as" or "during the time that." For example:

Although Sarah doesn't like sleeping on the floor, she agreed to do so *while* the relatives are visiting.

alumna, alumni, alumnus   A male graduate is an alumnus, a female graduate is an alumna, and more than one graduate are alumni.

among, between   Things take place among three or more people or objects, and between two parties or objects. However, even if there are three or more people or objects involved, if they interact two at a time, it's between.

amoral, immoral   Someone is amoral if that person has no morals, and is immoral if he or she breaks an existing moral code.

annual   An event isn't considered annual until it has taken place for three consecutive years. In its first year, call it the inaugural or the first. In its second year, call it the second.

anticipate, expect   Anticipate carries the added connotation of preparing for what's expected.

anxious, eager   If you're anxious about something, you're nervous, fearful, or apprehensive. If you're eager to do something, you're excitedly anticipating it.

anybody, anyone, everybody, everyone, nobody, no one, somebody, someone   All take singular verbs. For example:

Everybody *comes* to my house after Friday night football games.
Someone *knocks* on my door every Saturday morning at seven.
No one *jumps* when the tiny cannon is fired.
Anybody *has* the right to voice an opinion.

apparently, evidently   Both mean appearing to be so. However, apparently implies some doubt as to the truth of the statement. For example:

Apparently, Jane is sincere this time. (It seems that way, but you're not sure.)
Evidently, the burglar left some clues at the scene. (In this sense, you don't doubt that this is true.)

apprise, appraise   Apprise means to inform; appraise means to place a value on something. For example:

The jeweler *apprised* the couple that he had *appraised* the diamond necklace at two million dollars.

approve   See **adopt.**

arbitrate, mediate   After hearing the sides of an argument, an arbitrator comes to a decision that the parties must adhere to. A mediator helps the parties talk through and solve their differences.

around   See **across.**

as   See **like.**

assassin, killer, murderer   An assassin kills by secret assault and frequently for political reasons. Someone who kills with a motive of any kind is a killer. A murderer is someone who has been convicted of murder. However, be careful calling someone a murderer even if that person has been convicted of the crime. It's preferable to say he or she was convicted of murder, because we don't know the person did the crime unless we were there to witness it. However, we know that the person has been convicted. That's a matter of record.

assure, ensure, insure   Assure means to convince or make secure or stable. Ensure means to make certain that something happens. Use insure when referring to insurance. For example:

I want to *assure* you that I'll be there.
She *assured* him that everything would be OK.
I'll *ensure* that the package arrives on time.
Do you want to *insure* the package?

atheist   See **agnostic.**

athletics director   Not athletic director. The full title is Director of Athletics.

author   Use this word as a noun only. If you want to say someone wrote something, then say the person wrote it.

average   If you write about *the* average, it's singular. *An* average is plural. For example:

The average age of incoming students *has* risen in the past decade.
An average of 250 people *have* seen the play each night.

averse   See **adverse.**

backward   See **afterward.**

bad, badly, good, well   People feel bad or they feel good. If you say someone feels well or feels badly, it means that the person's sense of touch either is or isn't well developed. However, in terms of *doing* something, people either do well or do badly. If you say someone did good, the meaning is that he or she did a good deed such as feeding the hungry or working with Habitat for Humanity. The same is true of someone who does bad. So, on a test or project you do well or do badly. Don't be confused by the difference between how you feel and how you perform. However, if asked how you feel, it's appropriate to say "I'm well." The meaning is that you're not sick. But don't say "I *feel* well."

ban, bar   Ban means to forbid or prohibit; bar means to shut or exclude. People can be banned from doing something, and things can be banned. Only people can be barred from something. For example:

My father *banned* me from seeing Jill again.
Demonstrations are *banned* on the library lawn.
I was *barred* from entering the courthouse.

bear market, bull market   A bear market means declining stock prices; a bull market indicates rising stock prices.

because   See **since.**

because of   See **due to.**

benefactor, beneficiary   A benefactor does good; a beneficiary is the one who benefits from the doing of good.

between   See **among.**

biennial, biannual, semiannual   Something is biennial if it occurs every two years. It is biannual or semiannual if it occurs twice a year.

blatant, flagrant   Something is blatant if it's very noticeable, noisy, or offensive. It's flagrant if it's overtly outrageous, that is, not just a little harmful. Something can be blatant (there for everybody to see) and not be flagrant.

both, each   Both means two things collectively; each means two or more things considered individually.

boy, girl, man, woman, gentleman, lady   Only people in their teens or younger should be called boys or girls. Some suggest only those younger than 16 years of age should be called boys or girls. Man and woman are the preferred terms used to refer to physically mature individuals. Definitely *don't* refer to a group of males as men and a similarly aged group of females as girls. Use gentleman or lady only with titled people or in very specific circumstances when that's definitely what you're trying to say (as in First Lady, Lady Diana, everyone considered him a true gentleman, and so on). Don't use lady or gentleman in a generic sense as synonyms for woman or man, because most of the time you have no way of knowing if someone is a gentleman or is a lady. Also, don't use man as a replacement for human, human being, or person.

boycott, embargo   A boycott involves a group agreeing not to purchase goods or services from another group or business until certain conditions are met. An embargo is a legal restriction of trade and usually involves not allowing goods into or out of a country. For example:

Southern Baptists said they'll *boycott* Disney theme parks and products until the company quits producing R-rated movies.
The United States will continue its *embargo* of Cuba.

bring, take   You *bring* something toward the speaker or subject and *take* it away from the speaker or subject. For example:

Grandma wanted Red Riding Hood to *bring* her some cookies.
Red Riding Hood decided to *take* cookies to her grandma.

brothers-in-law, daughters-in-law, fathers-in-law, mothers-in-law, sisters-in-law, sons-in-law   Not brother-in-laws and so forth.

bug, tap   A bug is a concealed electronic listening device used to pick up sounds in a room. A tap is a device attached to a telephone line and is used to pick up phone conversations. Hence, offices are bugged and phone lines are tapped.

bull market   See **bear market.**

bullet   See **shell.**

burglarize   See **rob.**

but, however   Both of these words indicate that what follows contrasts with what's been said or written already, but many people use them to continue a thought. For example: "Bethany went to the store but came back with groceries." One would expect that she'd come back with groceries if she went to the store, so there's no contrast. That sentence should read: "Bethany went to the store and came back with some groceries." A sentence in which "but" would be appropriate is "Bethany went to the store, but she came back without anything." There's a contrast because what happened is different than what we'd expect. Likewise, "but" doesn't work in this sentence: "He only wanted to stop crime in his neighborhood but that might have cost a Miami man his life." There's no contrast here; it's a continuation of a thought. Either replace "but" with "and" or, better yet, make it two sentences. "He only wanted to stop crime in his neighborhood. That might have cost a Miami man his life."

can   See **may.**

celebrant, celebrator   A celebrant conducts a religious ceremony; a celebrator is someone having a good time. So, don't refer to celebrants on Bourbon Street on New Year's Eve. They're celebrators. Or, better yet, they're revelers or party-goers. Celebrators doesn't sound too conversational, does it?

celibate, chaste, abstinent   Celibate means unmarried, so priests who take vows of celibacy have agreed to remain unmarried. Chaste means abstaining from carnal love, and chastity often goes along with a vow of celibacy, but they're not the same thing. Practicing abstinence also means deciding not to do something, at least for a time, and is often used in reference to a decision not to engage in premarital sex.

cement, concrete   Cement is the powder that's mixed with water to make concrete. So houses are made of concrete blocks, not cement blocks. (And the Beverly Hillbillies didn't swim in a ce-ment pond.)

censor, censure   Censor (as a verb) means to delete as unsuitable, to find fault with. A censor (as a noun) is the person who does those things. Censure (as a verb) means to officially criticize or reprove. Censure (noun) is the criticism. Representatives and senators who run afoul of their colleagues are censured.

Centers for Disease Control   Considered one entity, so use singular verbs.

character, reputation   Your character is what kind of person you are; your reputation is what others think of you.

chaste   See **celibate.**

cheap, inexpensive   Both mean costing little, but cheap has the added connotation of poor quality.

childish, childlike   People who are childlike display the positive attributes of childhood, such as being innocent, trusting, loving, and the like. Childish is derogatory and means displaying negative and inappropriate traits often associated with children, such as stubbornness, selfishness, and so forth.

chronic   See **acute.**

citizen, resident   A citizen is a person who has acquired all the civil rights afforded by a nation through birth or naturalization. So, one can be a citizen of a country, but not of a state or city. Refer to Chicago residents rather that Chicago citizens. Some of the residents of any major city, we're sure, *aren't* citizens.

climatic, climactic   Climatic means having to do with the climate and is rarely used in broadcasting. Climactic pertains to a climax. So don't write about a *climatic* event unless you're talking about the weather, and be careful with *climactic*. It isn't very conversational, anyway.

coed   Out of date and considered sexist. Avoid it.

cohesive, coherent   Both mean sticking together, but cohesive is used in reference to people and objects, coherent in reference to ideas or other abstractions and has the added connotation of logical flow. For example:

The army platoon was a *cohesive* unit.
He made a *coherent* argument in favor of the bill.

collision, crash   For there to be a collision, both objects must be moving. A car can't collide with a utility pole, but it can crash into it.

comedian, comic   Use these for both males and females. Comedienne is considered out of date.

compare, contrast   When you compare you look at similarities and differences; when you contrast you look only at differences.

comprise, compose   Compose means to be the parts of; comprise means to include or contain. For example:

The 50 states *compose* the United States.
The United States *comprises* 50 states.

Make up or includes is preferred.

concrete   See **cement.**

constant, continuous, continual   Continuous means without ceasing; continual means repeatedly. If it were to rain continuously during an extended period of time, we'd all be looking for an ark in which to stay dry. It could rain continually for weeks without causing any major concern. Constant is a problem because it can mean either ceaseless or regularly recurring. Because constant is used in different ways and the viewers might not be able to figure out which way you're using the word, you're better off writing continuous or continual.

contagious, infectious   Something that's contagious can be spread only by physical contact. Something that's infectious is communicable by the spread of germs, with or without physical contact.

contemporary, modern   Something that's modern is recent or is happening now. Something is contemporary if it happens or happened at the same time as something else. So, something can be contemporary and not be modern.

convince, persuade   You convince someone *of* something; you persuade someone *to do* something.

could   See **may.**

couple   This word causes grammatical problems because it can take either singular or plural verbs. It depends on whether you're referring to the couple as a unit or as distinct individuals. For example:

The couple *has* standing dinner reservations at Bob's Steak House.
The couple *were* married at St. Vincent's Cathedral.
A couple of gang members *were* brought in for questioning.

Also, the "of" is needed. It's not a couple apples or a couple years; it's a couple of apples or a couple of years.

crash   See **collision.**

criteria, criterion   Criteria is plural; criterion is singular. For example:

The *criteria* for the contest have changed.
The primary *criterion* for membership in the club is a hefty bank account.

criticism, critique   Criticism carries the connotation of a negative evaluation; critique commonly means pointing out both the good and the bad.

cupfuls   Not cupsful.

currently, presently   Currently means now; presently means soon. Don't use presently to mean "at this time."

cynical, skeptical   Skeptical means inclined to doubt; cynical means contemptuous, quick to find fault. A good dose of skepticism is healthy in journalism. Cynicism can get you in trouble in a lot of ways.

data   Correctly used, data is a plural noun and takes plural verbs. Often when you use this word, you're doing a story involving scientists, economists, and the like, and they know the difference.

daughters-in-law   As written.

Daylight Saving Time   Not daylight *savings* time. When you're referring to a particular time zone, it's Central Daylight Time, for example.

defective, deficient   Defective means having a defect; deficient means lacking something. For example:

He sent the *defective* part back to the manufacturer.
He was *deficient* in the number of credit hours needed to graduate.

definite, definitive   Definite means exact or certain; definitive means conclusive or final. For example:

The incorporated area has *definite* boundaries.
The scientist's findings were *definitive.*

demolish, destroy   Both indicate doing away with something completely, so it's not possible to partially destroy something, and it's redundant to say something was completely demolished.

diagnosis, prognosis   A diagnosis tells us the state of something; a prognosis predicts the future developments related to that thing. For example:

The doctor's *diagnosis* was cancer and her *prognosis* wasn't good.

differ from, differ with   To differ from something is to be unlike it; to differ with someone is to disagree.

dilemma   A dilemma is worse than a problem or a concern. A person facing a dilemma has to choose between two unattractive alternatives.

disabled, handicapped   Disabled is preferred. However, neither should be used if the disability isn't germane to the story.

disinterested, uninterested   Disinterested means impartial; uninterested means having no interest in something. You can't be disinterested in a movie, unless you're rating it.

dispute   See **rebut.**

dissociate   Dissociate means to end a connection or association with. Note that the word does not contain an "a." It's not disassociate.

dived, dove   Dived is the past tense of dive. Dove is often used in this way (as in the boys dove into the water), but dived is more precise. Dove presents the additional problem that it might be pronounced as dove (a bird).

Down Syndrome   Not Down's Syndrome.

downward   See **afterward.**

due to, thanks to, because of   Because of is better. You certainly don't want to write a sentence like this, which we heard during one of the worst winter storms on record: "Power lines are down all across the area *thanks to* a severe ice storm." Why would anyone be thankful to be without electricity in subzero weather? The power lines were down *because of* the ice storm.

each, either, neither   Use either when referring to one or the other of two objects or people; use each when referring to both or all of two or more things or persons. However, *each* word takes singular verbs, unless either or neither is followed by both a singular and a plural noun or pronoun. Then the verb takes the form of the noun or pronoun closest to it. For example:

Each of us *needs* to make an effort to succeed.
Either of the two options *is* acceptable.
Either he or they *have* to show up.

Neither *is* suitable for the position.
Neither they nor he *wants* to leave the company.
Neither he nor they *want* to leave the company.

Also see **both.**

each other, one another   Two people look at *each other,* but more than two people look at *one another.*

eager   See **anxious.**

effect   See **affect.**

effective, efficient   Something that's effective gets the job done. Getting it done with a minimum of time and effort means you're efficient. So, something can be effective without being very efficient. You can skateboard from Chicago to St. Louis and you'd get there eventually, but you'd expend a lot of energy and use a lot of time doing so. It's an effective way to travel between the two cities, but it certainly isn't very efficient.

effluent   See **affluent.**

either   See **each.**

elicit   See **illicit.**

elude   See **allude.**

embargo   See **boycott.**

empathy, sympathy   Both words mean to share the feelings of another, but empathy goes a bit further than sympathy and means being able to imagine yourself in someone else's situation.

enact   See **adopt.**

enormity, enormousness   Enormity refers to something outrageously heinous or offensive; enormousness refers to massive size. For example:

The *enormity* of his crime was beyond belief.
The *enormousness* of the mountain was truly impressive.

ensure   See **assure.**

epigram, epigraph, epitaph, epithet   An epigram is a witty saying. Epigraphs and epitaphs are inscriptions on monuments or tombstones. An epithet is a word or phrase used to characterize a person or thing and often carries a negative connotation.

eternity, infinity   Eternity refers to endless time; infinity refers to anything that's infinite or endless.

everybody, every one   See **anybody.**

evidently   See **apparently.**

except   See **accept.**

excite, incite   Excite means to arouse the emotions of (normally taken to mean arousing positive emotions); incite means to influence someone to act.

expect   See **anticipate.**

explicit, implicit   Explicit means clearly stated; implicit means implied or suggested. Therefore, something that's implicit is open to interpretation. In broadcast writing, we should always clearly state what we mean.

famous, infamous   Famous means widely known and popular; infamous also means widely known, but carries a negative connotation. For example, at times in his career Mohammed Ali has been famous. At one point, however, he was infamous.

farther, further   Use farther to refer to physical distance and further for all other uses. For example:

Los Angeles is *farther* from New York than from Denver.
The board members voted to study the proposal *further.*
We have much *further* to go to come to an agreement.

fathers-in-law   As written.

fewer   See **less.**

figurative, literal   Figurative means symbolic, not literal. Literal means exact.

firm   A firm is a partnership, such as a law firm. The term shouldn't be used to refer to companies or corporations, both of which are incorporated business entities. Firms aren't incorporated.

flagrant   See **blatant.**

flail   The word means to whip or beat. Some dictionaries include "a wild waving of the arms" among the definitions.

flammable   See **inflammable.**

flaunt, flout   Flout means to show disdain for; flaunt means to make a showy display of something to draw attention.

flounder, founder   As verbs, flounder means to struggle helplessly and founder most commonly refers to ships and means to sink or run aground. Ships don't flounder because inanimate objects can't struggle.

forward   See **afterward.**

further   See **farther.**

gender, sex   Use gender when you're referring to the way a group of people is viewed by society; use sex when you're talking about the biological differences between men and women.

gentleman   See **boy.**

gibe, jibe, jive   Gibe means to taunt or sneer, jibe means to agree (or, in sailing, to shift direction) and jive means either swing music or talk meant to deceive or confuse. For example:

They *gibed* him about his lack of athletic ability.
The two suspects told stories that didn't *jibe.*
The senator's speech was nothing but *jive.*

girl   See **boy.**

good   See **bad.**

got   This is one of the most overused words in the English language. Got is the past tense of get. For example:

I got an "A" on the test. Got shouldn't be used to add emphasis to the words "has" or "have." For example, it's unnecessary to say: "You have got to see Joe's new car" or "The city council has got to make a decision soon." "You've got" means the same thing as "you have got" and shouldn't be used, nor should she's got, he's got, we've got, and so forth. A television station in central Florida uses the slogan: "We've got you covered." Perhaps the promotions people think that's catchy, but the news people should never put up with the use of such as that in the station's P.R. campaign. The line "I've got you babe" might be acceptable in a song by Sonny and Cher (we just admitted to having been around for a long time), but it's not acceptable when you're try-ing to write with precision.

government, junta, regime, administration   Governments and jun-tas are ruling groups. The only difference is that juntas are in power after a coup (an overthrow of the existing government). A regime is a political system, and an administration is the people who make up the executive branch of a government.

handicapped   See **disabled.**

hanged, hung   People are hanged (though not often anymore), and objects are hung. For example:

They *hanged* the horse thief at noon.
The stockings were *hung* by the chimney with care.

he, him, I, me, she, her   There's often a lot of confusion about which one of these pronouns to use when they're used in conjunction with a noun or another pronoun. The key is to remove the noun or the second pronoun and the word "and." In other words, consider the pronoun by itself. For example, look at this sentence: "Barbara went to the store with Veronica and I." It should be "with Veronica and me." Take the words "Veronica" and "and" out of the sentence. You wouldn't say Barbara went to the store with I; you'd say she went to the store with me. So, decide on the pronoun and then add the other words back into the sentence. Some other examples:

I watched the movie with Bob and *her.*

He and I are on the football team. (Here you have to use the singular verb with the singular pronoun "I" when you take "he and" out of the sentence. Considering the pronoun by itself the sentence would read: "I am on the football team." Don't be confused by the need to change from plural to singular verbs at times. The concept is the same.)

Lou's not as smart as *she*. (This type can be a little tricky. There are a couple of implied words at the end of this sentence. What we're really saying is "Lou's not as smart as she is smart." Turn the sentence around, and you'll see why it should be "she." If Lou isn't as smart as she, that means that she is smarter than Lou. You wouldn't say "Her is smarter than Lou.")

he, she   There's no gender-neutral singular pronoun in English. In the past, writers have used "he" when the sex of the subject was unknown, but this is now considered sexist. To say "he or she" sounds stiff, so in broadcast it's best to restate the sentence and use the plural pronoun "they." For example:

A student should do the best *he* can. (sexist—not all students are male)
A student should do the best *he or she* can. (grammatically correct, but sounds a bit awkward and nonconversational)
Students should do the best *they* can. (best choice)

historic, historical   Something is historic if it makes history or is significant in history. Anything that's part of history is historical. However, this distinction has virtually disappeared.

hopeful, hopefully   Use hopeful and hopefully to describe someone's feelings, not as a substitute for "I hope." For example:

I hope the professor will change my grade. (If you said "Hopefully, she will change my grade," you're saying she will change it and will be hopeful about something while she's doing it.)
Hopefully, I made my request for a grade change. (In other words, I was hopeful that my request would be honored.)
"Most Americans *hope* the tensions in the Middle East will end soon." (Rather than "Hopefully, the tensions will end soon." Tensions can't be hopeful.)

hung   See **hanged.**

I   See **he.**

illicit, elicit   Illicit means unlawful; elicit means to bring to mind. For example:

She was convicted of *illicit* use of campaign funds.
Seeing him at the reunion *elicited* memories of high school.

Note: These words are used frequently by reporters and writers trying to sound knowledgeable. Both sound somewhat nonconversational, don't they? In the first sentence "illegal" would work better, as would "brought back" in the second sentence.

immoral   See **amoral.**

impeach   Impeach means to accuse a public official of wrongdoing. It doesn't mean "to remove from office." Bill Clinton was impeached but not removed from office.

implicit   See **explicit.**

imply, infer   Imply means to suggest or indicate something without saying it directly; infer means to draw a conclusion from. For example:

The speaker *implied* that a new university president would be appointed. I *inferred* that there had been problems with the current university administration.

impromptu   Impromptu means without planning. Anything that involves an invitation or notice to attend can't be impromptu.

incite   See **excite.**

incredible, incredulous   Incredible means unbelievable; incredulous means skeptical. For example:

When he described the ride as *incredible,* she gave him an *incredulous* look.

indict   Indict means to bring legal charges against. Don't write that someone was indicted for murder because that sounds as though you think the person did it. Say the person was indicted on a charge of murder (or bribery, arson, and so on).

inexpensive   See **cheap.**

infamous   See **famous.**

infectious   See **contagious.**

infer   See **imply.**

infinity   See **eternity.**

inflammable, flammable   Both mean capable of burning, but inflammable sounds as though it means exactly the opposite. Use flammable if you mean capable of burning, and describe something that won't burn as nonflammable. (Hyphenate words like this to make them easier to read.)

insure   See **assure.**

inter, intra   The prefix inter means between two or more items in the same category; intra means within or between two parts of the same thing. For example:

interstate—goes from one state to others
intercollegiate athletics—contests between teams from different colleges or universities
intramural sports—students on teams within the same school play against each other

invaluable, valuable, valueless Invaluable means of immeasurably great value, and often carries the added connotation of irreplaceable. Valuable means of great value or price, but isn't as strong as invaluable. Valueless means without value.

irritate See **aggravate.**

issue An issue is a point in question or dispute. Therefore, all issues involve controversy; so there's no need to refer to a controversial issue, and there's no such thing as a noncontroversial issue.

itch, scratch Itch is a noun and scratch is a verb. To relieve the discomfort caused by an itch, you scratch. You can't itch something.

jail See **prison.**

jerry-built, jury-rigged Jerry-built means put together hastily and with flimsy materials. Jury-rigged means assembled quickly with materials on hand. So, something might have been jury-rigged without being jerry-built. Broadcast engineers have been known to jury-rig entire remote systems that are very sturdy and work beautifully.

jibe, jive See **gibe.**

junta See **government.**

jurist, juror A jurist is an expert at law; a juror is a member of a jury. A jurist might or might not be a judge.

ketchup Other spellings aren't correct and could lead to pronunciation problems (such as catsup or catchup).

killer See **assassin.**

kudos The word means credit or praise for an achievement and takes singular verbs. For example:

Kudos *is* in order for your graduation with honors.

lady See **boy.**

last, latest, past When one says last night, there's not much room for confusion about what's meant. Everyone knows the speaker is talking about the most recent period of darkness. The same is true of last week. But when you write "*the* last week," there *is* room for confusion, as in: "John wrecked his car twice in the last week." The question that arises is, In the last week of what? John's life on earth? Don't use "the last" unless there will be no more of whatever we're talking about. Therefore, the sentence we wrote earlier should read: "John wrecked his car twice in the *past* week." So, don't write something happened in the last month, or in last year, or in the last decade, or in the last millennium unless the world is about to end. Also, if you write something about John's last trip to the store, the implication is that John will never again go to the store. Write John's latest or most recent trip.

lay   See **lie.**

leave alone, let alone   Leave alone means to depart from or cause to be in solitude. Let alone means to allow to be undisturbed. If you ask someone to leave you alone, that means you want to be by yourself. If you want the person not to harass you, you would ask to be let alone.

lend, loan   Lend is a verb; loan is a noun. You lend something, such as your car or money. What you lend is a loan.

less, fewer   Use less when something can't be numbered and fewer when numbering is possible. For example:

There are *fewer* oranges on the trees this season.
There is *less* fruit on the trees this season.

You can number *pieces* of fruit or specific types of fruit, but you can't number fruit. Likewise, you can number hours or minutes, but you can't number time.
Note: Although it would be very time-consuming to count grains of sand, it is possible. However, although it's possible to number grains of sand, it's not possible to number sand itself. Think about it this way, using sand as an example: Can I say, "There's one grain of sand, and there's another?" Can I say, "There's one sand and there's another?" If the answer is yes, then use fewer (as in grains of sand, pieces of fruit, lumps of coal); if the answer is no, then use less (as in sand, fruit, or coal).

less than   See **over.**

libel, slander   Libel is defamation in writing or printing; slander is defamation by the spoken word. In the vast majority of modern legal cases, courts haven't distinguished between whether material was broadcast or printed, and most suits brought against media outlets are libel suits. Because of the reach and permanence of broadcast, material that defames is considered to have been "published."

lie, lay   Lie means to tell an untruth or to recline. Lay means to place something on something else. You *lie* down, but you *lay* something down. The problem comes with lie (recline) in the past tense, which is lay. For example:

He felt so bad he wanted to *lie* down and die.
He *lay* down and died.

Here's how to conjugate the verbs: *Lie (tell an untruth): lie, lied, lied*

I cannot tell a *lie.*
I *lied* to my mother.
I've *lied* in similar situations.

Lie (recline): lie, lay, lain

I will *lie* on the bed.
Yesterday, I *lay* on the couch until noon.
I've *lain* in bed all day when I've been sick.

Lay (place something) lay, laid, laid

I will *lay* my books on the table.
I *laid* my books on the table when I got home.
I've *laid* my books there before.

You can see that the two ways to use "lay" can create some problems. But you wouldn't want to say he lied down, because that leads to confusion. Initially, it sounds as though you're saying he told an untruth.

like, such as   Like means similar to. Use "like" when you're comparing two things and "such as" when mentioning something as an example of a broader category. For instance:

Joe is *like* Pete in many ways. (The two are similar.)
Mothers *such as* Betty Jones are in favor of the new grant for child-care facilities.
Betty Jones is among those mothers who favor the grant. If you write mothers *like* Betty Jones are in favor, what you're saying is that mothers similar to her are, but perhaps she herself isn't. Also, don't substitute like for "as" or "as if."
He studies, *as* he should. (He should study and he does.)
If you write he studies *like* he should, you're making a judgment about his particular study habits. Perhaps he studies with the CD player at full volume. Are you saying he should study in that way?

lion's share   This phrase means more than "the majority of." It means all or nearly all.

literal   See **figurative.**

loan   See **lend.**

majority, plurality   The majority is more than half the total, often referred to as 50 percent plus one. When there are more than two candidates for office, the candidate receiving more votes than any other has received the plurality of votes, but not 50 percent. This often means there must be a runoff between the top two vote-getters.

man, mankind   Other words are preferable, such as humans, people, or humanity for mankind, and a person or an individual for man. Also see **boy.**

masochism, sadism   Masochism means enjoyment of inflicting pain on yourself; sadism means enjoyment of inflicting pain on others. The pain doesn't necessarily have to be physical. People who fall into these categories are masochists or sadists.

Mass   Priests don't say Mass; Catholics celebrate Mass.

may, might, can, could   These are often used interchangeably. They shouldn't be. The key question, as with all words used in broadcast, is, Might the viewers take what you've written in a way that's different from how you intended it? For example, the following sentence could be interpreted two different ways.

Jane *may* go to the park.

Do you mean Jane might decide to go to the park, or that Jane has permission to go to the park? In instances when you mean that something might happen, use might and there will be less room for confusion. The same is true for "can." Use "can" when you mean "is able." For example:

Can Jane go to the park?

We don't know if you're asking if she has permission to (if you are, use may) or if she's physically able to. In that case, use "can." The word "could" should be used when there's a condition attached.

Jane *could* have ridden to the park if her bike wasn't broken.

me   See **he.**

media   The word media is plural and takes plural verbs. It means all forms of mass communication considered together. A single form of mass communication, such as television, is a medium. Mediums are palm readers.

mediate   See **arbitrate.**

medium   See **media.**

might   See **may.**

misuse   See **abuse.**

modern   See **contemporary.**

moral, morale   Moral deals with right and wrong; morale refers to one's confidence, self-esteem, and the like.

more than   See **over.**

mothers-in-law   As written.

Mr., Mrs., Miss, Ms.   All are courtesy titles. See Chapter 1.

murderer   See **assassin.**

neither   See **each.**

next of kin   This is brutally nonconversational. When's the last time you used that phrase in a chat with a friend? Use family or relatives, either of which would be used in a conversation rather than next of kin, which wouldn't.

nobody, no one   See **anybody.**

none   None means not one in most uses, and takes singular verbs. There are times when saying not one of something doesn't make sense, such as "not one clothes" or if you're referring to no amount of something. Read the sentence and substitute not one for none and see if it makes sense. If it does, use a singular verb. If it doesn't make sense, use a plural verb. For example:

None of the children *was* injured in the fire.

None of his clothes *are* worth much.

However, even if you know something is grammatically correct, it might sound wrong to you, and if it sounds wrong to you, it will probably sound wrong to some of the viewers or listeners. So in the first example, you wouldn't change the sentence to make it grammatically incorrect and you might not want to write it the way it's written because the word "none" is used incorrectly so often it sounds wrong when you use it the right way. So rewrite the sentence: "All of the children escaped injury in the fire."

notorious, notable   Notorious means widely but unfavorably known. Notable is a synonym for prominent or noteworthy. When one gains notoriety, he or she is *unfavorably* thought of.

number, total   "The number" or "the total" takes singular verbs; "a number" or "a total" takes plural verbs. See **average.**

obscene, pornographic   Anything that's highly offensive is obscene. Pornographic material is designed to stimulate sexual thoughts. Obscene material might or might not be pornographic.

observance, observation   An observance is the act of complying with a law or custom or of taking part in a ceremony. Observation is the act of noticing. So, to say that the couple celebrated the *observation* of their 50th anniversary would be incorrect.

occur, take place   Things that occur happen with no planning. Things that take place are planned.

olympics   This is a plural noun: "The Summer Olympics *are* held every four years." They are considered a collection of different sports events, not a single entity.

on, about   You give a speech on a stage, about a certain topic. You get and give information about things, not on them. Use on to mean "positioned upon."

one   The question of which possessive pronoun to use with "one" or "a person" creates some problems. To say, "one's home is one's castle" sounds very stiff, but so does "one's home is his or her castle." Also, you wouldn't want to use "is his castle" or "is her castle," nor would you say "is their castle," because you're talking about a single individual and "their" is plural. Try: "People's homes are their castles." The great majority of the time, when you use one you're referring to one at a time, and that's singular.

one another   See **each other.**

opponent   See **adversary.**

oral, verbal   Oral means of the mouth; verbal means using words, which can be written or spoken. You could say "she verbalized her feelings" or "they made verbal arguments" if you mean that someone spoke; but there's some room for confusion unless you explain that you specifically mean words were uttered. Of course, you wouldn't say "she oralized her feelings." Write: "She spoke about her feelings."

over, more than, under, less than Over and under are frequently misused. Use under and over when something is physically under or over something else. However, when you mean a greater or lesser amount or number of something, use more than or less than. For example:

The plane flew *over* the field.
The car cost *more than* 30 thousand dollars.
The car was *under* water.
The house sold for *less than* 100 thousand dollars.

Also, people don't argue *over* something; they argue *about* it. And "through the years" is preferable to "over the years."

overlook, oversee Overlook means to ignore or to fail to see. It also means to have a view of. Oversee means to supervise. For example:

I *overlooked* the small print in this contract.
I've decided to *overlook* your latest temper tantrum.
The house *overlooks* the canyon.
I'll *oversee* the construction project.

pardon, parole, probation A pardon results in the forgiveness of the charges against a person; he or she faces no further punishment. A pardon is granted by a chief of state. Parole means the person was let out of prison before the end of the sentence. It's granted by a parole board. A person on probation is convicted but doesn't actually serve time, if the person doesn't mess up again. A suspended sentence is the same as probation.

pass See **adopt.**

past See **last.**

persecute, prosecute Persecute means to harass; prosecute means to bring legal proceedings against. Members of the legal profession aren't supposed to persecute people, but some are supposed to prosecute those accused of wrongdoing.

person, people Use person when speaking about an individual and people when the reference is to more than one person. Avoid persons.

personal, personnel Personal means private or pertaining to an individual. Personnel means workforce or employees. There's a big difference between a manager making personal decisions and making personnel decisions.

persuade See **convince.**

phenomenon, phenomena Phenomenon is singular; phenomena is plural. You wouldn't write about *a* phenomena.

plurality   See **majority.**

pornographic   See **obscene.**

possible, probable   Something that's possible might happen; if it's probable, it's *likely* to happen.

precede, proceed   Precede means to come before; proceed means to move forward. For example:

Ninth grade *precedes* tenth grade.
Let's *proceed* to the next item on the agenda.

prescribe, proscribe   To prescribe is to suggest the use of something. To proscribe is to forbid or prohibit something. For example:

The doctor *prescribed* a powerful pain killer.
The judge *proscribed* him from having further contact with his ex-wife.

presently   See **currently.**

prison, jail   Generally, people serve time in prison for committing felonies. Jails are for minor offenders or those awaiting trial or sentencing on any charge. Penitentiaries and correctional facilities are prisons.

probable   See **possible.**

probation   See **pardon.**

proceed   See **precede.**

prognosis   See **diagnosis.**

proscribe   See **prescribe.**

prosecute   See **persecute.**

prostate, prostrate   The prostate is a gland; prostrate means lying down, in a prone position. Hence, no one suffers from *prostrate* cancer.

proved, proven   Proved is the past tense of prove; proven is an adjective describing something tested and shown to be effective. For example:

The lawyer had *proved* her case.
The program is a *proven* ratings winner.

ravage, ravish   Ravage means to inflict great damage or destroy; ravish means to rape or abduct and carry away. For example:

The storm *ravaged* the town.
The attacker *ravished* the sisters.

rebut, refute, dispute   To rebut or dispute is to argue to the contrary, to debate or quarrel; to refute is to prove something wrong or false. A television station in south Florida once ran a promotional spot that said its anchor was correct about something although other media in the area *refuted* him. If he was proved wrong, how could he have been right?

recur   Not reoccur.

regime   See **government.**

reluctant, reticent   Reluctant means unwilling to act; reticent means unwilling to speak.

reputation   See **character.**

resident   See **citizen.**

revert   Revert means to go back to a former place, position, or state of being. Revert back is redundant.

rifle, riffle   Rifle is to plunder or steal; riffle is to rapidly leaf through a book or paper. You can't rifle through someone's papers, but riffle is rarely used and might sound strange to some viewers. Use snooped or some other similar verb.

rob, burglarize, steal   Rob means to strip or deprive someone of something *by force.* Burglary is a crime of stealth usually involving breaking and entering. Therefore, people are robbed and places are burglarized. Anyone who takes something dishonestly has stolen.

runners-up   Not runner-ups.

sadism   See **masochism.**

sanction   This word has two different meanings. It can mean to approve or to punish. If you use this word, be sure your meaning is clear.

schizophrenia, split personality   These aren't the same. Schizophrenics can't distinguish fantasy from reality. Someone with a split personality has two or more distinct personalities, each with its own character traits.

scratch   See **itch.**

semiannual   See **biennial.** Semiannual is the correct spelling, but you might want to spell it semi-annual to make it easier to read.

sensual, sensuous   Both mean affecting the senses, and are often used with a sexual connotation. People are sensual and things are sensuous.

sex   See **gender.**

she   See **he.**

shell, bullet   Shotguns and some military weapons fire shells. Handguns and rifles fire bullets. The pellets from a shotgun shell are called shot.

since, because   In some instances, "since" can be used to indicate a causal relationship, but that's not the primary use of the word. It should be used to mean "from then until now." Sometimes since can mean "because," but because always means because. Why take a chance of using since incorrectly? Use because. For example:

Since she came to live here, she's been disagreeable.

Do you mean that she's been disagreeable because she came to live here, or that she's been disagreeable from the time she came to live here until now? "Since" leaves room for confusion as to your meaning. "Because" does away with the confusion.

sisters-in-law   As written.

skeptical   See **cynical.**

slander   See **libel.**

somebody, someone   See **anybody.**

sons-in-law   As written.

split personality   See **schizophrenia.**

steal   See **rob.**

such as   See **like.**

sympathy   See **empathy.**

take   See **bring.**

take place   See **occur.**

tamper, tinker   Tamper means to meddle harmfully; tinker means to fuss clumsily or to idly examine.

tap   See **bug.**

than, then   Than is used to introduce the second item of a comparison. Then means at that time or next in order. For example:

John is taller *than* Bill.
Then the board voted to give the mayor a raise.

thanks to   See **due to.**

that, who, which   Use "that" when you're referring to anything other than people or animals with names. In those cases, use "who." "Which" should only be used to introduce a nonessential clause or when "that" has already been used in the sentence. For example:

How to use "that" is the rule *that* is broken most often.
John is the student *who* breaks the rule most often.
Spike is the dog *who* accompanies John everywhere.
The rule, *which* is broken often, is the subject of much debate.
The professor said *that* it's the rule *which* is broken most often.

the   See **a.**

tinker   See **tamper.**

total   See **number.**

toward   See **afterward.**

under   See **over.**

uninterested   See **disinterested.**

unique   If something is unique, it's one of a kind. Things or people can't be quite unique or very unique or one of the most unique. They're either unique or they're not.

unknown, unnamed   Everyone has a name. Assailants, robbers, and the like are unknown, not unnamed. If the police know who the bad guy is but aren't saying, he still has a name. He's just unidentified.

upward   See **afterward.**

valuable, valueless   See **invaluable.**

verbal   See **oral.**

wait on, wait for   People in the service industry (servers in restaurants, for example) are the only people who wait on others. In all other contexts, use wait for.

watch, warning   In weather, a watch means that a hurricane might pose a threat to a specific area. A warning means that the hurricane is expected to hit a certain area within 24 hours. With tornadoes, a watch means that a tornado is possible; a warning means that a tornado exists or is suspected to have formed.

well   See **bad.**

well-known, widely known   People who are famous are widely known. (Note there is no hyphen in widely known.) A fact that is known by many people is well-known. For example:

Sylvester Stallone is *widely known.*
It's *well-known* that the sky is blue.

what, which   What should be used when the category is unknown, but which should be used when referring to a specific item in a category. For example: *What* do you want to do this weekend? I want to go to a movie. *Which* movie do you want to see? It would be incorrect to say, *What* movie do you want to see?

whereabouts   Takes singular verbs. For example: The whereabouts of the robber *is* unknown. However, whereabouts isn't very conversational. Use location or something similar.

while   See **although.**

who, which   See **that.**

woman   See **boy.**

wreck, wreak   Wreck means to destroy; wreak means to inflict.

GLOSSARY

abstract A quick one or two sentence summary of a story.

actuality Sound or sound bite in radio.

ambient sound The audio equivalent of b-roll natural sound in TV. Ambient sound enhances a radio story and figuratively puts the listener in the place where the story occurs.

anchor The person who hosts a television or radio newscast.

backtime A method of calculating the estimated "hit" time for a story within a newscast. This method calculates the hit time by subtracting the estimated running time for that story and of all remaining stories from the "end" time of the newscast. It's useful for learning whether the newscast is running long or short as the end time of the newscast approaches. See also **forward time.**

bite A short snippet of an interview chosen for on-air presentation.

block A segment of a television newscast, usually defined as the content between commercial breaks. The "A" block is all material up to the first commercial. The material that follows the first commercial is the "B" block. The B block ends at the second commercial, and so on.

brief A short newspaper or Web story, usually written without a byline, typically about 5 column inches long.

b-roll cover video

bullet points Two or three words of text summarizing a point, usually set off by an asterisk, circle, square, or some other form of demarcation at the beginning of the line.

chroma key (CK) Images are electronically inserted over a wall that's a solid color, usually blue or green. Typically, an anchor or weathercaster stands in front of the wall and refers to what the viewers are seeing.

column inch The space on a printed newspaper page one standard column wide and 1 inch long. At the *Tampa Tribune,* a copy inch averages 32 words.

consortium A groups of stations that share video and information, typically by way of a satellite connection.

convergence A communications industry movement wherein different forms of media, formerly in competition, cooperate and work together for mutual benefit.

copy minute The amount of copy necessary to fill up one minute of broadcast air time. This varies from reader to reader, but the average is about 180 words, or $5\,{}^1/_2$ column inches of copy.

cross-ownership An arrangement wherein a single parent company owns and operates different media platforms in the same media market.

cutaway A shot related to the main action, but which doesn't show the main action. An example is fans at a sporting event.

diamond style In a television package, telling a story about something that affects a large number of people by using a specific person or small group as an example.

donut A short television package preceded and/or followed by live reporter presence, either in the field, on-set, or in the newsroom. A donut typically doesn't include a taped stand-up or a sig-out.

editing script   The copy of a script given to a videotape editor. For a package, this usually doesn't include the anchor lead and tag or the technical directions.

entermation   When information takes a back seat to entertainment.

enterprise   A type of story requiring original reporting, digging, and research—as opposed to a story involving a news release, news conference, or accident, and so on.

forward time   A method of calculating the estimated "hit" time for a story within a newscast. This method is used to calculate the hit time by adding the running time of all of the preceding stories to the start time of the newscast. It's useful for estimating whether certain stories will fall within designated time periods, such as a satellite window. See also **backtime.**

franchise   A regularly appearing "titled" television news report. Often franchises will appear regularly in given newscasts on given days of the week.

full-screen   A television visual element that takes up the entire viewing screen.

full-screen graphic (FSG)   A graphic that fills the entire screen and contains statistics, bullet points, or other information relevant to the story.

gatekeeping   The act of deciding which stories are presented in a newscast and which ones aren't.

graphic   Used in a television context, the word "graphic" usually refers to a full-screen presentation used as a substitute for video, containing a combination of artwork and text over a color or textured background, used to help explain or illustrate a story. In a newspaper context, a graphic can be any combination of artwork and text laid out on the page, usually in support of a story.

HTML   "Hypertext Markup Language," the computer language Web producers use to create Web pages and Internet links.

IFB   An acronym derived from the phrase "interruptible feedback." It refers to a communications system by which an anchor or reporter can hear some or all of the television station's programming. True IFB implies that the producer is able to interrupt programming to speak to the talent, but the word is often used interchangeably with other forms of audio signals to the talent that aren't interruptible.

inch   See **column inch.**

incue   The first few words of a bite.

infotainment   Information presented in an entertaining way.

intro   Anchor- or reporter-read copy preceding a television news package.

inverted pyramid   A style of writing presenting the most important fact first, then proceeding with other facts in descending order of importance.

kicker   A nonserious story positioned at the end of a television news block or newscast.

lead   1. The first sentence of a story. In television, if the story is presented as a package, the lead is often called the anchor lead and includes an introduction of the reporter. All story leads should be written with the goal of attracting viewer attention. Within stories that include comments from news sources, writers lead to the comments, letting the viewers know who's speaking, why that person's comments are important to the story, and most important, "teeing up" the comment (bite) to let the viewers know what the comment will be about.

2. The first story in a newscast.

legacy media A term sometimes used to refer to traditional media such as newspapers and television that were in operation prior to the advent of the Internet.

lineup See **rundown.**

live shot A live camera remote, or live report from talent in the field utilizing a live camera signal, which typically is fed back to the television station by microwave, satellite, or fiber.

logging Scanning field tapes in order to pick sound bites, listen for and list specific snippets of natural sound, and provide a brief description of usable shots and where to find them on the tape.

Marti unit A portable radio transmitter.

minute See **copy minute.**

mix-minus Audio fed to an anchor or reporter via IFB containing some, but not all, of the program being fed to the station's transmitter. Typically the programming is mixed without audio from live remotes, in order to prevent the talent in the field from hearing a distracting delayed feedback of his or her own words.

Mom Rule Writing stories in the same way you'd tell the story to your mom.

Murphy's Law A mysterious but well-documented force that requires technical malfunctions or operational mishaps to occur if there's the least opportunity for them to happen, especially if there are no contingency plans to deal with the problem.

narrative style A style of storytelling presenting the facts in more or less chronological order with a clear beginning, middle, and end.

natural sound Any naturally occurring sound recorded in the field, other than interviews. Nat sound includes comments from people who aren't in a formal interview setting.

news hole In television: the portion of a newscast actually filled by news, minus sports, weather, commercials, bumps, teases, and other preproduced elements. In newspapers: the total amount of column inches available for news.

NPR National Public Radio.

nut graf A paragraph within a newspaper story that summarizes what the story is about. The nut graf usually is the fourth or fifth paragraph of the story.

open In television, this refers to the standard beginning of every newscast, typically consisting of a preproduced announcement over graphics and music.

OTS (over-the-shoulder graphic) Graphics information that appears in a box over the shoulder of an anchor.

outcue The final few words of a story element not being read by an anchor (bite, package, wrap, and so forth.)

over-the-shoulder graphic. See **OTS.**

package A television story filed by a reporter, which typically includes narration, a stand-up, bites, and accompanying video and natural sound. An anchor package (the anchor's voice is prerecorded, rather than that of a reporter) typically doesn't include a stand-up or sig-out. A nat sound package includes no recorded narration, just bites, natural sound, and perhaps music.

pad In a television story, a 10-second (or more) continuation of the final shot beyond the recorded track or the timed end of the copy. Used to avoid going to black on the air.

page designer The person responsible for the physical layout of newspaper pages.

PIO Public Information Officer. A spokesperson for agencies such as police and fire departments, the sheriff's office, and so forth.

platform A communications medium in a convergence environment. For example, if a company is operating a newspaper and a television station in a given market, the TV station might be referred to as the "broadcast platform" and the newspaper as the "print platform."

pod A group of related stories in a broadcast news block.

producer script The copy of the broadcast script that goes to the producer. For a package, this would include the anchor lead and tag and the technical instructions.

Q&A A live appearance in which the guest doesn't deliver written copy, but rather answers questions from an anchor or reporter.

reader A short television story read by an anchor with no accompanying video or full-screen graphic. Sometimes called a "tell" story. In radio, copy being read by an anchor.

reader/actuality (RA) A type of radio story in which the radio anchor reads the opening copy for the story, plays a cart or disk (which is the audio recording of the actuality or sound bite), and then reads the closing copy.

roll cue The final few words from a reporter doing a live introduction to a package. The roll cue lets the show director know when to roll the tape.

rundown The document that outlines the order of stories in a newscast and briefly notes how each story is to be presented. In some stations, the rundown is called the lineup.

shot Video taken from a live television camera. The term is used most often in conjunction with studio cameras aimed at talent, and is frequently used in combination with the numerals one through four to designate how many anchors or reporters will be framed within the shot.

sidebar A short story directly related to a longer story.

signal A live feed of video and audio. This can refer to a station's transmitter signal but more typically is used in conjunction with live feeds sent to the station from crews in the field for use within the newscast.

sig-out (signature outcue) The line all reporters at a given station use to end a standard package. A typical sig-out would include the location, the reporter's name, and the name of the news organization. For example, "In Waynesville, I'm Bob Strong, Newswatch 7."

skeleton time The time in a television newscast devoted to "standard" items appearing every night, typically including such items as sports, weather, teases, opens, closes, tosses, chitchat time, and pad time. The total news window minus the skeleton time yields the newshole.

slug Brief title assigned to a news story.

SOT (Sound-on-tape) Interview sound, recorded on tape or disk, to be used in a broadcast news story.

sound bite See **bite.**

spot news An unscheduled breaking news event involving a news "scene" or spot, such as a shoot-out, crash, or accident.

standard The word used on a package script to indicate to the technical staff that the package ends with a signature outcue.

stand-up A reporter appears on camera and delivers a line or two.

stinger A definitive ending to a cut of music at the end of a newscast.

super Graphics information superimposed over video. A typical identifier super contains a person's name and title.

SWAP Synchronized words and pictures. Results from writing from the video, letting the pictures dictate how the text is structured.

tag The anchor copy that follows a bite in a VO/SOT or follows a reporter package. The purpose of the tag is for the anchor to wrap up one story before the newscast moves on to the next story.

talent A term referring to anyone paid to appear on-camera or behind a microphone.

tease A short item appearing within a television newscast previewing other stories still ahead. Teases typically air just prior to commercial breaks.

track Recorded package narration.

upcut A technical or timing mistake in a television newscast that leads to one segment sliding over on top of the next segment, causing the viewer to miss part of the audio and/or video of the following segment.

user Short for "online user," someone who accesses an Internet Web site.

VO (voice-over) A short television story read by an anchor accompanied by video or a graphic presented full-screen.

VO/SOT (voice-over/sound-on-tape) A television story form in which an anchor reads the first part of the story accompanied by a video or a graphic presented full-screen. The anchor then pauses for a comment (bite) from a news source, before ending the story on-camera.

VO/SOT/VO Same as a VO/SOT except that the anchor concludes the story by reading the tag over more video rather than by reading on-camera.

wallpaper video Video having either an indirect match or no match to the copy. This "use of video for the sake of video" usually is inappropriate.

window A specific amount of time leased from a satellite broker for transmission of a news story.

wrap A type of radio story that includes the anchor lead and a voiced report from a reporter along with an actuality (sound bite); a "wrap" is the radio equivalent of a news package in television.

INDEX